ns.   *8 Trumpets.*

Henry Purcell, *c.* 1690. Godfrey Kneller

HENRY PURCELL
1659–1695

HIS LIFE AND TIMES

FRANKLIN B. ZIMMERMAN

MACMILLAN
London · Melbourne · Toronto

ST MARTIN'S PRESS
New York
1967

To Edward and Jill Croft-Murray

© Franklin B. Zimmerman 1967

MACMILLAN AND COMPANY LIMITED
Little Essex Street London WC 2
also Bombay Calcutta Madras Melbourne

THE MACMILLAN COMPANY OF CANADA LIMITED
70 Bond Street Toronto 2

ST MARTIN'S PRESS INC
175 Fifth Avenue New York NY 10010

Library of Congress catalog card no. 67–14079

PRINTED IN GREAT BRITAIN

CONTENTS

ILLUSTRATIONS   *page* vii

PREFACE   ix

ABBREVIATIONS   xvi

I   The Purcells of Westminster in the Early Years of the Restoration   1

II   Purcell's Boyhood   18

III   Years of Apprenticeship   34

IV   Purcell's Professional Début   48

V   Music on the Restoration Political Scene   58

VI   Purcell's Fantasia Year   76

VII   Purcell, Tory Composer   89

VIII   The London Musical Scene at the End of the Reign of Charles II   107

IX   London's Musical and Theatrical Life under a New Monarchy   123

X   Musical Life under the Most Catholic of the Stuarts   146

XI   Music and the Glorious Revolution   160

XII   Musical Life under William and Mary   177

XIII   A Royal Excursion Abroad   192

XIV   Catastrophe in the Microcosmos of London's *Theatrum Mundi*   216

XV   Purcell's Increasing Musical Activities in Church, Concert Hall, Court, and Theatre   229

XVI   A Time for Mourning   247

APPENDIXES

  1. Notes   270

  2. Documents   293

  3. Henry Purcell's Origins: A Genealogical Puzzle   374

  4. Bibliography   392

INDEX OF PURCELL'S MUSIC   409

GENERAL INDEX   415

ILLUSTRATIONS*

Trumpeters and kettle-drummer in the procession of the coronation of James II. *front end-paper*

Henry Purcell, *c.* 1690. Godfrey Kneller. *frontispiece*

1(a) 'A Ground-plot of part of the City of Westminster.' *page* 14

1(b) A view of Westminster Abbey, Westminster Hall, St. James's Palace, Pall Mall, and Conduit, *c.* 1660. Wenceslaus Hollar. 14

2(a) 'The Magnificent Form usually Observed in the Procession to the Coronations of the Kings and Queens of England . . .' 15

2(b) 'The Ground-plot of the Collegiate Church of St. Peter in Westminster . . . 23 April 1685.' 15

3(a) 'The Grand Procession of the Soveraigne and knights Champions. Anno 23 Caroli 2.' 1672. Wenceslaus Hollar. 30

3(b) Record of disbursement to Henry Purcell as 'Bishop's Boy' at St. Peter's College, Westminster, 1678. 30

4 'With Crowns of Peace and Love, kind Heavens on Katharin smile . . .' Frontispiece engraved by I. A. for *Complementum Fortunatarum Insularum*, 1662. 31

5 'The Cabal', *c.* 1675. J. B. Medina. 62

6 'Titus Tell-Troth: or, The Plot-Founder Confounded.' 63

7 Putative impaled coat-of-arms for Henry Purcell and Frances (?)Peters. 78

8(a) 'God bless Mr. Henry Purcell/1682 September the 10th.' MS. 88 (autograph) fly-leaf, Fitzwilliam Museum Library, Cambridge. 79

8(b) Sacrament certificate. 4 February 1682/3. 79

9 'The Inthronization of Their Majesties King James the Second and Queen Mary.' 126

10 'Gentlemen of the Chapel Royal, in number 32.' 127

* The end-papers and Plates 1(a), 2(a) and (b), 9, 10, 11, and 12(a) are from F. Sandford, *The History of the Coronation of . . . James II* (London: Thomas Newcomb, 1687).

11   'A Fife, 4 Drums, the Drum Major.'   127

12(a) 'The Proceeding to the Coronation of their Majesties
      King William and Queen Mary from Westminster Hall
      to Westminster Abbey, 11 April 1689.' Engraved by
      Samuel Moore.   142

12(b) 'A Perfect Description of the Firework in Covent Garden
      that was performed at the Charge of the Gentry and
      other inhabitants of that Parish for the joyful return of
      His Majesty from His Conquest in Ireland, 10 September
      1690.' Mezzotint by Bernard Lens. Bodleian, Gough
      Maps 45.f.48^R.   142

13   'The Protestants Joy; or, An Excellent New Song on the
      Glorious Coronation of King William and Queen Mary,
      which in much Triumph was celebrated at Westminster
      on the 11th of the instant April.' Bagford Collection,
      vol. II, p. 172.   143

14(a) Monument for William and Mary. Grinling Gibbons.   238

14(b) 'The Robin-Red-Breast Famous for singing every day on
      the Top of Queen Mary's Mausoleum Erected in West-
      minster Abbey, 1695.' F. Barlow, engraved by P. Tempest.
      Bodleian, Gough Maps 45.f.50.   238

15   Last Will and Testament of Henry Purcell, died 21
      November 1695. Public Record Office, London.   254

16(a) Colonel Edward Purcell. Miniature, presumed to be by
      Thomas Forster.   255

16(b) (?)Daniel Purcell, c. 1705. Presumed to be by Closterman.   255

'The Choir of Westminster in number 16; the Groom of the
      Vestry; the Organ Blower; Two Sackbuts, and a double
      Courtal' (rather, an alto cornetto).   back end-paper

PREFACE

HAVING attempted in compiling a thematic catalogue of Purcell's complete works a detailed survey of Henry Purcell's music and the manuscript and printed sources that originated during the century after his birth, I turn here to a study of his life and times. In a third volume, already in progress (under the provisional title *Henry Purcell, 1659–1695: Analytical Essays on His Musical Forms*), I plan to trace his technical and formal usages, hoping to clarify some aspects of his stylistic development, and to fill in partially, perhaps tentatively, the large gaps which now perplex the chronology of his works.

Hence the present work is addressed to the general public, as well as to those who are keenly interested in Purcell's musical legacy. Hence, also, musical examples and technical analysis are reserved for the third study, mentioned above. Here I have been content to discuss his major works for the light they shed on his life and times, with brief reference to lesser pieces where these relate to incidents or circumstances relevant to the biographical story. Because of discontinuity in the Purcellian chronology, and lacunae in sources of biographical data, indicated relationships between individual works and Purcell's life story sometimes are largely hypothetical. The hypotheses have been cantilevered beyond the foundation of solid fact only where circumstantial evidence is strong enough to provide inner reinforcement, and sufficiently specific to indicate new sources or types of information that may be sought after.

For these reasons I have delved somewhat farther into historical and sociological backgrounds than the biographical study of a musician might be thought to warrant, music being generally conceived as an art far above, or at least removed from, such material considerations. Here I have entered upon seeming digressions from a purely musical view, not to eke out an account otherwise too slender — new data *have* come to light — but rather on the conviction that music in Restoration London was both a function and an expression of seventeenth-century English life, and ought therefore to be studied in context. Such relationships cannot always be clearly delineated, but they can be shown to have existed. At any rate it is my hope that the view of Purcell against so broad a backdrop as that projected here will furnish perspectives as interesting and instructive to the reader as they have seemed to me.

We may never know fully the social and aesthetic processes that produced the 'British Orpheus' — significantly an appellation that Purcell earned in his lifetime. But this need not diminish our interest in the Purcell legend, which is so clearly and gloriously proclaimed by his music. In entrusting his trio-sonatas of 1683 to his contemporaries, and to a larger posterity than he can have reckoned on, Purcell expressed 'his hearty wishes that his book . . . fall into no other hands but theirs who carry musical souls about them'. This valedictory carried both admonition and challenge to his contemporary musicians and music-lovers, whom he led into a golden age of English music. That age knew no parallel in England until fairly recent times, when modern English composers, most of them inspired by his example, turned away from continental models to mine the riches of their own native traditions and language.

After nearly three centuries the challenge of Purcell's musical achievements has not lost its meaning in Purcell's own land. For other nations, and especially for those that have made the English language theirs, the challenge is also valid.

EXPLANATION

Sketching in backgrounds to Purcell's life and musical activities, I have depended heavily on quotations from contemporary documents and literary sources of various sorts. Not being interested in the character of each of these, either as archival artifacts or orthographic specimens, I have sought to make clear the purport and relevance of every quotation at the expense of all other considerations. Hence, while striving for accurate transcriptions, I have modernized all these without comment.

However, I have included the conventional symbol (...) for ellipsis and have enclosed editorial restorations of missing syllables or words within square brackets. To supplement these, and to place at the disposal of future researchers all the evidence I have found, I have included in Appendix Two relevant documentary information pertaining to each known member of the families of Thomas and the elder Henry Purcell — uncle and father, respectively, of the composer. This appendix also contains as complete an anthology of contemporary Purcellian poems (or sections of poems) as I have been able to discover.

Conventional abbreviations for references are listed on p. xvi, while those referred to by author only are marked with asterisks in the bibliography. Full bibliographical details for the latter, as for those referred to by author and short title only, are given in the bibliography, along with other works I have consulted in a general way.

Remaining appendixes are largely self-explanatory. My intention has been to restrict the notes in Appendix One to a minimum, including in the text all possible matter, and relegating to the back of the book only those comments or entries too long for inclusion at the bottom of the appropriate page, or too digressive to be worked into the discussion to which they pertain.

The essay on Purcell's genealogical background is offered as an interim report on a subject which has been fascinating, though refractory. The findings presented here speak for themselves up to a point, and I held reasonable hopes of carrying these much nearer to final solution when most of my research notes were burglarized. Items taken include an original indenture containing signatures and seals of Edward, Daniel, and Katherine Purcell, and all my genealogical files. When opportunity allows I shall research anew the sources from which these notes were made.

ACKNOWLEDGEMENTS

Since this second volume in the series of three which I hope to complete on Henry Purcell is based on the research and compilation which produced the first (*Henry Purcell, 1659–1695: An*

Analytical Catalogue of his Music, London, 1963), I might well
have repeated all the acknowledgements printed in that volume.
However, let this statement reaffirm those as I turn here to thank
individuals and institutions who have lent particular assistance to
this study. First of all, for the fellowship that facilitated the basic
research for this volume, and for a generous Grant-in-Aid later
on, I am grateful to the American Council of Learned Societies.
Similarly, I wish to express my thanks for timely aid from the
Dartmouth College Faculty Committee on Research.

Next, I must thank Mr. Edward Croft-Murray and his wife,
Jill, for their warm hospitality and enduring patience with a
troublesome guest. As Keeper of Prints and Drawings at the
British Museum, Mr. Croft-Murray lent valuable advice on all
the illustrations that appear in this book, and, with the Trustees of
the British Museum, graciously gave me permission to reproduce
the Kneller portrait, the two broadsides, 'Titus Tell-Troth' and
'The Protestants Joy', and the Monument for William and Mary.
Mr. Croft-Murray also informed me of the existence of 'The
Cabal', for the reproduction of which I am grateful to Nostell
Priory, Notts., for permission.

To Mr. Donovan Dawe, Assistant Archivist at the Guildhall
Library, I owe thanks for much expert assistance with parish
records and other documents housed there, as to the Trustees
of that institution for permission to quote from these documents.

To Professor Vincent Duckles, Music Librarian at the University of California at Berkeley, and to his assistant, Mrs. Harriet
Nicewonger, I owe thanks for placing at my disposal the rich
resources of their remarkable collection.

For permission to reproduce 'The Magnificent Form usually
Observed in the Procession to the Coronations of the Kings and
Queens of England', 'The Ground-plot of the Collegiate Church
of St. Peter in Westminster', 'The Grand Procession of the
Soveraigne and knights Champions', and the 'Proceeding to the
Coronation . . . of King William and Queen Mary' I am grateful
to Miss Mary Dunbar, former Assistant Archivist at Westminster
Public Library, Buckingham Palace Road, who also provided me

with valuable advice on Westminster rate books and residences in the latter half of the seventeenth century.

To Professor Theodore M. Finney, Chairman of the Department of Music at the University of Pittsburg, and to Professor Halsey Stevens, Chairman of the Department of Composition, University of Southern California, I am indebted for wise counsel in all these matters and, more especially, for their undertaking the heavy task of reading critically the whole typescript. Not charging them with responsibility for any imperfections that may have slipped through, I can best evaluate their help by pointing out that without it the book was scarcely publishable.

My thanks also are due to:

Dr. Nigel Fortune, Lecturer at Birmingham University, who told me of the reference to Purcell in the Ashtead Accounts, for which Mr. A. C. Lowther provided me with further information, and to the Trustees of the Guildford Museum and Muniment Room for permission to quote.

To Miss Phyllis M. Giles, Librarian, and to the Syndics of the Fitzwilliam Museum, Cambridge, for permission to reproduce Purcell's autograph inscription from MS. 88.

To Miss Barbara Gordon of New York for help in replacing a lost bibliography.

To the Curator of the Holburne of Menstrie Museum of Art in Bath for permission to reproduce the miniature of Colonel Edward Purcell.

To Lady Susi Jeans of Cleveland Lodge, Dorking, whose disinterested scholarly liberality and assistance with the records at Mickleham parish church and with many other matters have been most helpful.

To Dr. Neil Ker, Librarian, and Mr. T. S. R. Boase, President of Magdalen College, Oxford, as well as to Mrs. Rosamund McGuinness for assistance with the Magdalen College records.

To Macmillan & Co. Ltd., to Mr. Harry Cowdell, and particularly to Miss Phyllis Hartnoll, whose careful criticisms have much improved the book.

To the Trustees of the Bodleian Library, Oxford, for permission to reproduce 'The Inthronization of Their Majesties King James the Second and Queen Mary'; 'A Perfect Description of the Firework in Covent Garden that was performed at the Charge of the Gentry and other inhabitants of that Parish for the joyful return of His Majesty from his Conquest in Ireland, 10 September 1690'; and 'The Robin-Red-Breast Famous for singing every day on the Top of Queen Mary's Mausoleum Erected in Westminster Abbey'.

To Dean Lawrence Powell and his gracious staff at the William Andrews Clark Memorial Library in Los Angeles for permission to reproduce the illustrations from Sandford's *The History of the Coronation of . . . James II*, and for other kindnesses too numerous to list here.

To the Public Record Office, Chancery Lane, London, for permission to reproduce Purcell's Will and to quote various documents on the Purcell family.

To Mr. Harold Purcell, Managing Director of L.P.E. Television Ltd., London, for generous provision of unique genealogical data and for even more generous forbearance upon the loss of the original indenture belonging to him.

To the Royal Society of Musicians in London for permission to publish the putative portrait of Daniel Purcell.

To Mrs. Nera Smith of South Pasadena for generous and timely assistance with typing.

To the Rev. Professor H. F. D. Sparks, D.D., for assistance with the transcription of Edward Purcell's epitaph, and, for genealogical advice, to his wife, Margaret.

To Miss Alice Stanley of the Literary Department of the Probate Registry, Somerset House, London, for services beyond official requirements, and to that institution for permission to quote various testamentary documents and transcripts.

To Mr. Lawrence E. Tanner, C.V.O., F.S.A., Keeper of the Muniments and Library, Westminster Abbey, for permission to reproduce the Purcell coat-of-arms and to quote from the Treasurer's Accounts; and to him and to Mr. N. H. MacMichael, Assistant Librarian, for various aids, as well as to the Dean and Chapter of Westminster Abbey for permission to cite from the Westminster Abbey Precentor's Books.

To Mr. J. E. Thomas, F.L.A., City Librarian, Cardiff Libraries, who, through the good offices of Lady Susi Jeans, provided me with information on the Purcells of Cardiff.

To Dr. Virginia Tufte of Los Angeles for telling me of the frontispiece in P. de Cardonnel's *Complementum Fortunatarum Insularum*, and to the Henry E. Huntington Library, San Marino, California, for permission to reproduce it.

To Sir Anthony Wagner, K.C.V.O., D.Litt., Garter Principal King of Arms at the College of Arms, for permission to make use of his resources and for professional assistance.

To Sir Jack Westrup, who began it all.

To Mr. A. Vere Woodman for assistance with various genealogical problems bearing upon the Purcells of Buckinghamshire.

To my wife, Rachel Zimmerman, whose patience, persistent zeal, and perspicacity are perpetual cause for wonder.

To Mr. Arthur W. Woodman for assisting in the preparation of the index.

ABBREVIATIONS

Many of the references given in the footnotes have been abbreviated to the name of the author, and full details of these (marked with asterisks) can be found in the Bibliography. Other abbreviations used are:

Analytical Catalogue	F. B. Zimmerman, *Henry Purcell, 1659–1695: An Analytical Catalogue of his Music.*
Bodleian	Bodleian Library, Oxford.
Cal. S. P. Dom.	*Calendar of State Papers, Domestic Series.*
Cal. Tr. Books	*Calendar of Treasury Books.*
Cal. Tr. Papers	*Calendar of Treasury Papers.*
Cheque-book	E. F. Rimbault (ed.), *The Old Cheque-book, or Book of Remembrance, of the Chapel Royal, from 1651 to 1744.*
DNB	*Dictionary of National Biography.*
Grove's (5th ed.)	*Grove's Dictionary of Music and Musicians* (5th ed.).
Hist. MSS. Comm.	Historical Manuscripts Commission.
KM	H. C. de Lafontaine, *The King's Musick.*
LC	Lord Chamberlain's Department Records.
MGG	F. Blume (ed.), *Die Musik in Geschichte und Gegenwart.*
PCC	Prerogative Court of Canterbury.
PCW	Peculiar Court of Westminster.
PMA	*Proceedings of the Musical Association*
PRMA	*Proceedings of the Royal Musical Association.*
PRO	Public Record Office.
RMA	Royal Musical Academy.
Secret Services	J. Y. Akerman, *Moneys received and paid for Secret Services of Charles II and James II.*
SIMG	*Sammelbände der internationalen Musikgesellschaft.*

WAM	Westminster Abbey Muniments.
Westminster Abbey Registers	J. L. Chester, *The Marriage, Baptismal, and Burial Registers of the Collegiate Church or Abbey of St. Peter's, Westminster.*

CHAPTER I

THE PURCELLS OF WESTMINSTER
IN THE EARLY YEARS OF
THE RESTORATION

Too little is known of Henry Purcell's childhood to give substance to more than a bare, at times hypothetical, account of his early life. However, from various chronicles of events in London during the first decade of Charles II's restored monarchy something can be gleaned of the social and cultural environment that produced this Restoration musical genius, this 'Orpheus Britannicus', who in historical importance may be compared to such other famous Englishmen of his day as Dryden, Locke, Newton, and Wren. These were times which challenged greatness, and as a musician Purcell met their challenge. In the face of difficulties, which in the end proved insuperable, his achievements were such as to ensure for him renown as the greatest composer England could claim as her own for more than two centuries after his death.

Purcell's activities can be only surmised up until 1673, the year of the first extant record bearing his name. Conjecture, guided by inferences drawn from family backgrounds and from the cultural, political, and social history of the times will often be needed to formulate the story of his early years. For later periods information is only slightly less scant, although the general pattern of Purcell's life can sometimes be projected from the nature of his various musical responsibilities at Court.

Until recently even the identity of Purcell's father was open to doubt — doubt which has been allayed, however, by the discovery of several new documents. The most important of these is John

Hingeston's will, which definitely states that Purcell was the son
of Elizabeth Purcell, and therefore the son of Henry, and not of
Henry's brother Thomas.* The establishment of this relationship
fixes the City and Liberties of Westminster as the most probable
place of Purcell's birth. However, above the oft-quoted entry on
Henry Purcell from his manuscript notes on English musicians,†
Anthony à Wood has added the following: 'Born in London'.
Hence it cannot be determined whether London or Westminster
was actually his birthplace.

From 1659 onward the elder Henry's family lived in one of the
houses on the south side of the Great Almonry, a residential area
just south of Tothill Street and a few hundred yards west of
Westminster Abbey. It was there, very likely, that young Henry
Purcell was born. Cummings's statement placing this event in
St. Ann's Lane, Old Pye Street, has no factual basis. Although
Purcell did live there for a brief period after his marriage in 1680
or 1681, it is certain that he was not born in the house in St. Ann's
Lane so frequently pictured as his birthplace. Moreover, there is
absolutely no record showing that his parents ever lived there.
There *is* proof that the family lived in the Great Almonry, where
the elder Purcell's payment of 1*s.* 6*d.* for the poor-rates suggests
that he was in a lower income bracket than most of his neighbours, who were charged more.

The supposition that Purcell was born in Westminster is also
supported by one of the stipulations of the scholarship he was later
to enjoy as one of the 'Bishop's Boys' at St. Peter's College,
Westminster.‡ According to Bishop Williams's deed of 26 April
1624, holders of this scholarship had to come either from Wales
or from the diocese of Lincoln. If there were no acceptable
candidates from these places, scholars might be accepted from
one of the Liberties of Westminster, as is known from provisions
made (though never implemented, apparently) for four scholarships he founded at St. John's, Cambridge. These scholarships
were reserved for the 'Bishop's Boys' from St. Peter's, West-

---

* See App. Three, p. 389.
† Bodleian, MS. Wood D 19(4), fo. 104.
‡ See pp. 52–56 below, and Plate 3(*b*).

minster, and the letters of patent (drawn earlier than the above-mentioned deed, on 30 December 1623) make it clear that the scholars from St. Peter's might include Westminster boys, if sufficient Welsh or Lincolnshire applicants did not appear. Negative results of extensive searches of the records in Wales (by Mr. A. K. Holland and the present writer, both separately and together) and my own failure to find any evidence that Purcell hailed from anywhere near Lincoln suggest that Purcell probably qualified for the scholarship under the third provision.

This probability is further strengthened by positive evidence in favour of the supposition that the elder Henry Purcell was living in Westminster at about the time young Henry was born. Even though no birth or baptismal records have been found to prove the assumption, the absence of any record of birth or baptism elsewhere in Westminster endorses Mr. Jeffrey Pulver's suggestion that Purcell may have been christened within the Abbey itself. He definitely places the elder Henry Purcell's residence in Westminster in 1659,* and since records now available for the years 1661 to 1664 list him as dwelling in the house that had been occupied until 1658 either by William Crane or by Captain Hickes, it is fairly certain that Henry and Elizabeth had moved to that address with their three-year-old son, Edward, in 1659, the year in which, with scarcely a doubt, the younger Henry was born. There they lived on, next door to Mr. Babington — later Captain Babington — on one side and Henry Lawes on the other. (After Lawes's death in October 1662 this house was occupied by Mr. Swettenham.) Some time after August 1664, when the elder Purcell died, Christopher Gibbons moved into the building.[1]

The elder Henry, who had married one Elizabeth (surname unknown) some time before 1656 (when Edward Purcell was born), is named only once in any known pre-Restoration document.[2] In the dramatis personae for William D'Avenant's *Siege of Rhodes* (first published in 1656) he is mentioned as having taken the role of Mustapha alternately with Thomas Blagrave.†

---

* p. 387.
[1] Superior figures throughout refer to the notes forming Appendix One.
† See App. Two, XII, 1.

However, there is uncertainty as to the date of the actual first performance, and it is possible that it did not take place until 1658. Either way, the elder Henry would have been in London towards the end of the Commonwealth, professionally associated with a group of musicians living in Westminster, some of whom were later to be his neighbours.[3]

A precise date of birth for his third son,* Henry, is impossible to establish. Reinhold Sietz's guess that 10 September might have been his birthday is certainly worth considering.† But it is merely a guess, based on Purcell's enigmatic inscription on the fly-leaf of the Fitzwilliam Museum autograph, MS. 88, 'God bless Mr. Henry Purcell/1682 September the 10th'. It is possible that this cryptic inscription may have some other significance. For instance, the date coincides with the fifth anniversary of Purcell's appointment as composer-in-ordinary to the king. Perhaps Purcell was merely worried over possible discontinuance of his employment.

That he was born before 20 November may be safely inferred from the inscription on his memorial tablet in Westminster Abbey, which records that he died on 21 November 1695, in his thirty-seventh year. But the statement that he must have been born some time after June (also frequently found in biographical literature on Purcell) cannot be taken entirely at face value. It is based on the engraved frontispiece to the *Sonnata's of III. Parts* of 1683, where the reader is informed that Purcell was twenty-four at the time the engraving was made.

These sonatas were eventually published in June, but had been some time in preparation, as we know from notices published in the *London Gazette*, and from the explanation Purcell himself gave in the preface:

There has been neither care, nor industry wanting, as well in contriving, as revising the whole work; which had been abroad in the world much sooner,

* See Genealogical Table II, p. 383. About the supposed second son, Charles, very little is known. The one document that refers to him (PCC: 63 Lloyd) makes it clear that he cannot have been the Charles Purcell who died off Guinea in 1686.

† *Henry Purcell: Zeit, Leben, Werk*, p. 35.

but that he has now thought fit to cause the whole thorough bass to be engraven, which was a thing quite besides his first resolutions.*

The words 'has now thought fit' suggest that everything but the thorough-bass was done and that Purcell had even written most of the preface before coming to the decision to postpone. Furthermore, licensing, correcting, binding, and stitching must have taken some time. In the absence of any precise date for the completion of engraving and annotation, the evidence afforded by the portrait shows only that it was struck not later than June 1683, but possibly as much as a month or so earlier. Certainly May, or even April, cannot be entirely ruled out on evidence now available.

Anyway, Purcell was born a year, or slightly more, after Evelyn had recorded on 3 September 1658, 'Died that archrebel Oliver Cromwell...' Perhaps Purcell was born about the time the Protector's less forceful son, Richard Cromwell, retired from office. Absolutely nothing is known of Purcell's childhood, and only a few obvious inferences relating to it can be drawn from the records of his father's activities during the early years of the Restoration. These are strengthened by circumstantial evidence drawn from contemporary documents and accounts of major historical events, which do not yet provide for certainty. His distinguished musical neighbours living in or near the Great Almonry during this period were the elder John Banister (in King Street, West); Henry Lawes, who lived next door in the Great Almonry in 1661, but had moved into Dean's Yard before his death in 1662; Dr. Christopher Gibbons, who lived there also (as is known from later records); Captain Cooke, in Little Sanctuary; Thomas Farmer, in New Palace; Dr. John Wilson, in Dean's Yard; and, perhaps as important as any, young Purcell's future father-in-law, Captain John Peters, in New Palace.†

Dr. Richard Busby also lived in the neighbourhood, and must frequently have been visited by some of his famous pupils. Here,

---

* From the 'Violino primo' part-book, Purcell's *Sonnata's of III. Parts* (London: Playford and Carr, for the author, 1683) (British Museum, K.4.g.10).

† See Plates 1(a) and (b). Purcell's relationship to the Peters family cannot yet be proved, but the evidence for it is weighty, though circumstantial. (See below, pp. 81–82; 359.)

in the city where Chaucer once lived, Busby trained John Dryden, John Locke, Robert South, and no fewer than sixteen bishops.* Busby's name appears frequently among the donors of bene- volences in the Overseers' Accounts and the poor-rate books for St. Margaret's Parish, Westminster, for the years he was registered as an inhabitant of the parish, that is from 1628, when he received permission to 'proceed bachelor of arts',† until his death on 6 April 1695.‡

John Dryden, a graduate of Cambridge, was attracting universal attention at this time by his first three works (diametrically opposed to one another in the political loyalties that they variously reflected): *Heroic Stanzas* (1659, a tribute to the memory of Oliver Cromwell) and *Astraea Redux* (1660), followed by *Panegyric on the Restoration* (1661), the last two dedicated to a restored monarchy. Other literary inhabitants or frequenters of Westminster included Samuel Pepys, who had married Elizabeth Marchant de Saint Michel at St. Margaret's, Westminster, on 1 December 1655,§ and the ageing blind poet John Milton (married to Katherine Wood- cock at St. Margaret's in 1656‖), who had lived in Petty France at least until 1661. But if any of these men took any notice of the young Restoration genius, even after he had risen to fame, none troubled himself to record his views.

Pepys recorded a musical evening in which a Purcell took part, in the following oft-quoted entry of 21 February 1659/60. But whether this refers to Henry, or to Thomas, or to some other member of the family cannot be decided on the evidence at present available.

After dinner I went back to Westminster Hall with him [Mr. John Crew, M.P.] in his coach. Here I met with Mr. Lock and Pursell, masters of music, and with them to the Coffee House, into a room next the water, by ourselves, where we spent an hour or two till Captain Taylor came to us, who told us that the House had voted the gates of the City to be made up again, and the members of the City that are in prison to be set at liberty; and that Sir G. Booth's case be

* According to Rev. Canon Overton in *DNB.*
† J. E. Smith, *A Catalogue of Westminster Records* (London, 1900), p. 56.
‡ *DNB.*
§ St. Margaret's, Westminster: Parish Church Records, 'Weddings', 1645–81.
‖ Ibid.

brought into the House tomorrow. Here we had variety of brave Italian and Spanish songs, and a canon for eight voices, which Mr. Lock had lately made on these words: 'Domine salvum fac Regem', an admirable thing.

There may be some significance, however, in the reading of this passage given by Lord Braybrooke in his edition.* He renders the second sentence quoted above as follows: 'Here I met with Mr. Lock and Pursell, Master of Music . . .' Use of the title in the singular would argue that Pepys was referring to the elder Henry Purcell, for his name during this period or a little later was entered frequently as 'Master of the Choristers' in the Westminster Abbey records,† while Thomas held no such title until 1672 when he began to share with Pelham Humfrey the office 'Master of the King's Band'.

Both Henry and Thomas Purcell received official appointments soon after the Restoration. Thomas became a tenor in the Chapel Royal. Very soon after, he was appointed one of the musicians for 'lutes and voices, theorbos and virginals'.‡ Henry was made musician-in-ordinary for violins in place of Angelo Notari. He also shared an appointment as musician-in-ordinary for lutes and voices with Angelo Notari, as this retroactive warrant shows:

15 Nov. 1662
Warrant to admit Angelo Notari and Henry Purcell musicians-in-ordinary for the lutes and voices, with the yearly wages of £40, to commence from St. John Baptist 1660.

The terse official records give no reasons for the sharing of an appointment and indeed are not altogether in agreement as to whether there was only one appointment. But Notari, whom

* Memoirs of Samuel Pepys, vol. 1, p. 18.
† WAM 33695. At Michaelmas (29 Sept. 1661) Henry was retroactively paid £7. 10s. for three quarters as Master of the Choristers. His duties, therefore, were officially taken up in the previous January. Even earlier, Purcell's name, along with those of the choristers is recorded in various accounts of fees received for singing at funerals and other ceremonial occasions taking place in the Abbey.
‡ KM, p. 122; Cheque-book, p. 128. See also App. Two, XXII, 3.

Charles I had brought to England by 1625, was quite old by this time, and Court officials may have thought to shore up his responsibilities with the energies and resources of a younger man.[4]

Henry Purcell was also installed singing-man and Master of the Choristers at Westminster Abbey on 16 February 1661:

Mr. William Tucker, one of the Gentlemen of His Majesty's Chapel, and Mr. Jonas Caldecut were installed Petty canons: and with them Henry Purcell, Edward Bradock, William Hutton, Richard Adamson, and Thomas Hughes were installed singing-men, and the aforesaid Henry Purcell, Master of the Choristers also, by Philip Tynchare, Chanter. For whose installation the Chanter received of:

Mr. Will. Tucker	o	5	o
Mr. Jonas Caldecut	o	5	o
Mr. Ric. Adamson	o	5	o
Mr. Th. Hughes	o	5	o
Mr. Ed. Bradock	o	5	o
Mr. Hutton	o	5	o
Mr. Purcell, instead of money, this book.*			

The pages of the Westminster Abbey Precentor's Book and Treasurer's Accounts for 1660–4 are dotted with entries for various receipts, disbursements, and other transactions connected with the elder Purcell's official duties. These reveal that the Abbey musicians then lived precarious, hand-to-mouth existences, their small official stipends being frequently augmented by much-needed incidental payments for singing at burial services and official inaugurations, and by other institutional fees, such as those taken from visitors who paid to see the 'monuments', then, as now, housed in the Undercroft Museum. Here is the account of one such windfall, on 30 March 1661:

The Princess Royal, Mary, the King's eldest sister, mother of the Prince of Orange, was laid in a vault. And for the attendance of the choir was paid to the Chanter for the whole company of petty canons and singing-men (although many of them were not then installed, but allowed only to do service in the church because as yet the Chanter was elected only but not installed, for which cause also the Chanter's peculiar fee was left out of the bill) the sum of £6. 13s. 4d., which was thus divided:

* WAM 61228A (Precentor's Book, 1660–71), fo. 3.

To Mr. Tynchare Chanter	7	4
To Mr. Gibbons Organist	7	4
To Mr. Hooper	7	4
To Mr. Tucker	7	4
To Mr. Caldicot	7	4
To Mr. Hazard	7	4
To Mr. Harding	7	4
To Mr. Chapman	7	4
To Mr. Purcell	7	4
To Mr. Bradock	7	4
To Mr. Hutton	7	4
To Mr. Adamson	7	4
To Mr. Hughes	7	4
To Mr. Ambler	7	4
To Mr. Shorter	7	4
To Mr. Corney	7	4

To Mr. Finall and Mr. Dagnall   Mr. Dagnall paid 4*d*. Mr. Finall
paid 4*d*., due more 8*d*.

To Mr. Fisher for his attendance and then expecting a place
in the choir, but afterwards lost it   7   4*

The proceeds of such affairs were divided up according to a set
formula, more or less as the 'spoils' of the profession. From 1662
onward Henry Purcell, along with his fellow Gentlemen of the
Chapel Royal, found his economic plight eased somewhat by a
general increase in all salaries, from £40 to £70 per annum.†
Unfortunately this apparent gain was soon offset, if not nullified,
by arrears in salary, which began to be general about this time, as
is known from later complaints and retrospective settlements. The
Lord Chamberlain's accounts are filled with complaints and
demands having to do with overdue salary payments.‡ Small
wonder that pluralism was the order of the day, and that musicians
found life precarious even when they were supposedly enjoying
several stipends.

As the day for Charles II's coronation drew near — fittingly it
had been scheduled for St. George's Day, 23 April 1661 — the

---

* WAM 61228A (Precentor's Book, 1660–71), fo. 6.
† See Westrup, p. 7, n. 3, for a discussion of the probable effects of inflation
on the economic situation at Court.
‡ See *KM, passim.*

elder Purcell was extremely busy, as indeed were most musicians at Westminster Abbey and Whitehall at that time.* Not only did he have a great deal to do in preparing his choristers at the Abbey for festival services there, but he had recently taken on new duties as a singing-man in the Chapel Royal, being appointed shortly before the coronation, for which he was listed among the Gentlemen Singers.†

On the day before the coronation Ogilby's lavish and complicated 'Entertainment' brought out the citizens of London, who witnessed the processions of the nobility and the concert and pageants of an enormous complement of musicians and other entertainers. The elder Henry Purcell seems to have been one of a very few among well-known professional musicians who did not take an active part in the grand 'Entertainment' — a fact which is quite understandable in view of the elaborate ceremony that was to be performed at Westminster Abbey that same day as the culmination of the 'Entertainment'. In their diaries both Pepys and Evelyn described events almost ecstatically. To maintain the breathless excitement of Evelyn's vivid description I have deleted some details, naming only the more important personages who will figure prominently in the story of Purcell's life.

22   Was the splendid cavalcade of His Majesty from the Tower of London to Whitehall . . .

23   Was the coronation of His Majesty Charles the Second in the Abbey Church of Westminster . . . but indeed His Majesty went not till early this morning, and proceeded from thence to Westminster in this order: first went the Duke of York's Horse Guards, Messengers of the Chamber. 136 esquires to the Knights of the Bath, each [Knight] having two: most richly habited: . . . Clerk of the Parliament, Clerk of the Crown: chaplains-in-ordinary having dignities 10: . . . secretaries of the French and Latin tongue: gentlemen ushers; daily waiters; sewers, carvers, and cupbearers-in-ordinary, esquires of the body 4 . . . Chamberlain of the Exchequer, . . . Lord Chief Justice of England. Trumpets, Gentlemen of the Privy Chamber; Knights of the Bath 68 in crimson robes exceeding rich, and the noblest show of the whole cavalcade (His Majesty excepted) . . . trumpets, sergeant-trumpeter. . . . Lord Chancellor.

* Cf. *KM*, p. 131, where warrants are recorded for musicians' liveries; see also p. 136 noting remuneration to Captain Cooke for 'torches and lights for practising the music against His Majesty's coronation' was belatedly made on 16 Sept. 1661.   † *Cheque-book*, p. 128.

Lord High Steward of England; two persons representing the Dukes of Normandy and Aquitaine (viz. Sir R. Fanshaw and Sir Herbert Price) in fantastic habits of that time; gentlemen ushers garter; Lord Mayor of London; the Duke of York alone (the rest by twos); Lord High Constable of England; the Sword born by the Earl Marshal of England. Lastly the King in royal robes and equipage: afterwards followed equerries, footmen, gentlemen pensioners; Master of the Horse.... this magnificent train on horseback, as rich as embroidery, velvet, cloth of gold and silver, and jewels could make them and their prancing horses, proceeded through the streets strewed with flowers, houses hung with rich tapestry, windows and balconies full of ladies, the London Militia lining the ways, and the several companies with their banners and loud music ranked in their orders: the fountains running wine, bells ringing, with speeches made at the several triumphal arches: at that of the Temple Bar (near which I stood) the Lord Mayor was received by the Bailiff of Westminster who in a scarlet robe made a speech: thence with joyful acclamations His Majesty passed to Whitehall. (Bonfires at night)...*

Pepys's description of the cavalcade of the 22nd was similarly enthusiastic.

it is impossible to relate the glory of this day, expressed in the clothes of them that rid [sic], and their horses and horse-clothes ... Embroidery and diamonds were ordinary among them. The Knights of the Bath was [sic] a brave sight of itself; and their esquires ... Remarkable were the two men that represent the two Dukes of Normandy and Aquitaine.... My Lord Monk rode bare after the King, and led in his hand a spare horse, as being Master of the Horse. The King, in a most rich embroidered suit and cloak, looked most noble.... The streets all gravelled, and the houses hung with carpets before them, made brave show, and the ladies out of the windows, one of which over against us I took much notice of ... So glorious was the show with gold and silver, that we were not able to look at it, our eyes at last being so much overcome with it.†

The ceremonies Evelyn and Pepys witnessed and the music they heard were also described by Sir Richard Baker, who drew upon the accounts given by Elias Ashmole in his *Observations* and *Collection*.‡ The following five paragraphs give an abstract of the coronation day's ceremonial proceedings:

Very early in the morning of the 23rd the king went by barge

---

* Evelyn, 22 and 23 April 1661.   † Pepys, 22 April 1661.

‡ Baker, pp. 760–1. For other details of these ceremonies see John Ogilby's *The Entertainment of His Most Excellent Majesty Charles II, in his Passage through the City of London to his Coronation* and Eric Halfpenny, 'The Entertainment of Charles II', in *Music & Letters*, vol. XXXVIII, no. 1 (Jan. 1957), pp. 32–44. See also Plates 2(a) and (b).

along the Thames from Whitehall to Parliament Stairs, going to a room in the House of Lords to change, then on to Westminster Hall. At 9.30 a.m. the nobility took their places, rank by rank; then, after a short ceremony with music provided by the choirs of the Chapel Royal and Westminster Abbey, they departed through New Palace Yard Gate House, turning left along King Street to return through the churchyard into the Abbey, their whole way laid out for them on a carpet of brilliant blue. At last the procession arrived at the West door, proceeded along the nave and into the choir, where all the musicians remained on the north side, except for twelve men, four boys, and an organist, these occupying a raised gallery on the south side.

As the king entered, the Westminster choir (on the north side) sang an anthem, 'I was glad'. Then, after Charles II had been presented to the people as their king, the Chapel Royal choir sang 'Let thy hand be strengthened'. After the sermon both choirs sang the hymn 'Come, Holy Ghost', and for the anointing of the king with holy oils 'Zadok the Priest', composed especially for the occasion by Henry Lawes, another pre-Commonwealth composer who had returned to take up a post at the Restoration.

The choirs next sang 'The King shall rejoice in Thy strength' (possibly by William Child, another pre-Cromwellian composer who returned to Whitehall with the Restoration) and then the 'Te Deum' as the king sat in the chair of St. Edward. When Charles II had granted a general pardon and returned to his throne again, the Gentlemen of the Chapel Royal sang the anthem 'Behold, O Lord, our defender', which was sung in Gabrielian style 'cori spezzati' between the Gentlemen of the Chapel Royal in the south gallery and the 'violins and other instrumental music', who, in their scarlet mantles, were seated in a gallery on the north side. The work is anonymous, but may well represent the first anthem with Italianate instrumental ritornelli to be heard in England. (It was not the first with instrumental ritornelli of any kind, for both Byrd and Orlando Gibbons had already introduced these long since in their respective anthems 'Christ rising' and 'This is the record of John'.) This portion of the ceremonies closed with a brilliant flourish by trumpet and drums.

Both anonymous works (the 'Te Deum' and 'Behold, O Lord') may have been composed by Cooke himself, if a remark quoted by Baker (after Ashmole) may be taken at its face value. At any rate, more music in Venetian style was heard: the king then took off his crown, after which were heard the Epistle, the Gospel, the Nicene Creed (begun by the Bishop of London and sung by the Gentlemen of the Chapel to music by Captain Cooke, Master of the Children of the Chapel, and composer of the special music for this solemnity). Again the instruments played alternately.

The choirs next sang 'Let my prayer come up into Thy presence' — once more probably by Cooke* — after which the king was given the Mark of Gold, then the Blessed Sacraments, these actions being followed by another anthem, 'O harken unto the voice of my calling'. After communion everyone returned to Westminster Hall, where banqueting and musical entertainment continued far into the night.[5]

With such a beginning, small wonder that music at the Abbey and at the Chapel Royal remained the chief public attractions during the Restoration, as is shown by numerous references in the diaries and journals of the time. Pepys's frequent attendance at Westminster Abbey services was due largely to his enthusiasm for music — enthusiasm by no means dampened when, on 19 December 1661, he was allowed to sing in the choir.

Musical activities did not take place only at the Abbey and in the Chapel Royal however. Like his fellow musicians, both at the Abbey and at Court, the elder Henry Purcell practised his art before theatre audiences and managed also to keep in the public eye by supplying a few compositions for London's growing music-publishing trade. Before the Restoration, as we have seen, he had taken second billing as Mustapha in the first part of D'Avenant's *Siege of Rhodes*, although whether he also sang in performances of the second part of the 'opera' is not known.†️ But it may be assumed that he was often called upon, as were all Restoration musicians, to participate in various theatrical and 'operatic' musical affairs.

* Baker, p. 767.
† Reported upon by Pepys (15 Nov. 1661) and Evelyn (9 Jan. 1661/2).

Apart from such general influences, however, little is known of young Henry Purcell's life during these times. He was scarcely old enough to have been affected by the excitement attending the arrival of Catherine of Braganza on 13 May 1662, or to have shared in the gossip about Charles II's manifest disappointment upon finding his royal bride much plainer than her portraits had promised. Her physiognomy, perhaps more realistically portrayed in the interesting drawing published as a frontispiece to Philip de Cardonnel's *Complementum Fortunatarum Insularum,*[*] was not very prepossessing; even so the portrayal probably idealized the queen's actual appearance.

But Purcell may well have responded in one way or another to two other events which occurred that same year and influenced more directly the Purcell family fortunes. On 1 January Charles II had not only doubled his musical establishment, but nearly doubled his choirmen's salaries, raising them from £40 to £70 per annum. This was no doubt a very welcome augmentation of the family income, particularly after the second event: the arrival of a new baby early in March in the person of Katherine Purcell, baptized on 13 March.[†] (However, as pointed out earlier, there was little certainty that salaries would be paid on time, if at all; hence many benefits may have been more apparent than real.)

Nor would young Henry have been old enough to appreciate the new honours then bestowed upon Thomas Purcell, who at the very beginning of the Restoration period had been named as the first of ten musicians 'that do service in the Chapel Royal whose salaries are payable in the Treasury of His Majesty's Chamber'.[‡] On 8 August Thomas Purcell was also appointed composer-in-ordinary for the violins[§] — at first he shared the position with Pelham Humfrey, but then came into full enjoyment of the same in the place of Henry Lawes on 15 November 1662 — and on 10 November to the Private Music for lutes and voices.[||] His advancement was rapid, and before long he was to become one

---

[*] (?) London, 1662. See Plate 4.
[†] *Westminster Abbey Registers*, p. 67, quoted in App. Two, xix, 1.
[‡] *KM*, p. 121.   [§] *Grove's* (5th ed.), vol. vi, p. 997.
[||] *KM*, p. 151.

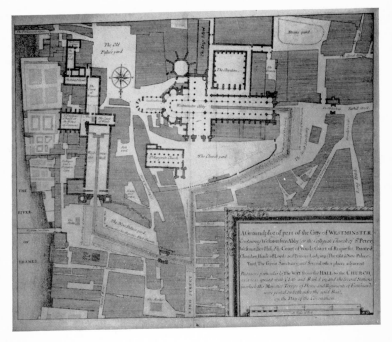

1a 'A Ground-plot of part of the City of Westminster'

1b A view of Westminster Abbey, Westminster Hall, St. James's Palace, Pall Mall, and Conduit, c. 1660. Wenceslaus Hollar

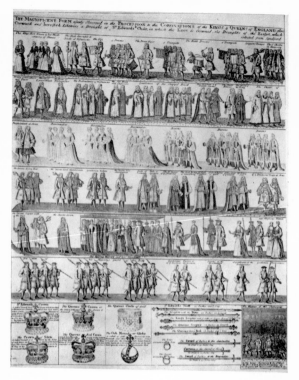

2a 'The Magnificent Form usually Observed in the Procession to the Coronations of the Kings and Queens of England . . .'

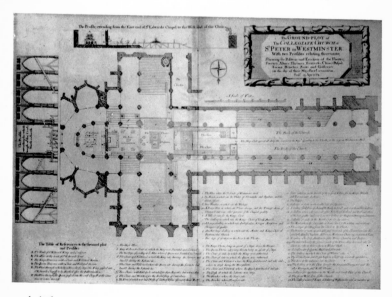

2b 'The Ground-plot of the Collegiate Church of St. Peter in Westminster . . . 23 April 1685'

of the most influential and affluent musicians of the early Restoration, an achievement not without significance in the life of his young nephew Henry, especially after the death of the latter's father in August 1664.

Although young Henry may have been old enough to be aware of the preferments at Court that his father[6] and uncle received, he was still young enough in 1663 to be dismayed at the arrival of another child in the household, if indeed the conventional but as yet undocumented assignment of Joseph Purcell's birthday to this year be correct.* This was also the year in which Hingeston's new official quarters were set up in Whitehall — quarters which young Henry was to know well a few years later when he took up his apprenticeship.† It was also the year of Thomas Baltzar's death (of the 'French pox and other distempers'). Baltzar was the musician whose violin playing had done more, according to Anthony à Wood,‡ to raise that instrument to respectability and popularity at the English Court than any other factor. Finally, and ominously, this was the year in which from Amsterdam came first word of the dreaded plague.[7]

During the course of his fifth year, 1664, young Henry may have gone along on occasion to the Abbey or to Whitehall with his father and his uncle Thomas, who was busier than ever while he bore the full responsibilities of the position at Court heretofore shared with Pelham Humfrey, now on the Continent absorbing the latest musical styles at Versailles, Venice, Paris, Rome, and other musical centres of Europe.§

But all other events and activities of this year would have been blotted out in young Purcell's mind by family tragedy. Henry the elder died — quite suddenly, it seems, since he is mentioned in the records right up to his death on 11 August[8] — and was buried

---

* *MGG*, vol. x, col. 1770. The death of Henry Purcell on 11 Aug. 1664 establishes April 1665 as the latest month in which Daniel (the youngest of the Purcell children) could have been born. Joseph was probably Daniel's elder brother — cf. App. Two and Genealogical Table II — but no records have been found to allow for worthwhile conjecture as to the date of his birth.

† *KM*, pp. 160, 162.

‡ *Life and Times*, vol. I, p. 94.

§ Westrup, p. 19.

at Westminster Abbey two days later, in the east cloister near Henry Lawes, interred there less than two years earlier.

Shortly after this time Elizabeth Purcell must have moved to Tothill Street South, for at this address her modest annual payment of four shillings for the poor-rates is entered in the St. Margaret's, Westminster, Overseers' Accounts[9] every year from 1665 until 1699 when she died within a few days of the anniversary of her husband's death★ and slightly less than four years after that of her illustrious son, Henry. There she lived, supporting her children on a slender widow's pension, eked out by various small sums granted her by the Westminster Abbey and Chapter officials,† and by income from lodgers, such as Frances Crump, recorded as follows in St. Margaret's Vestry Book no. 2416:‡

Wednesday, 5 July 1676
Mrs Purcell in Tothill Street made her application to the Vestry desiring some allowance may be made for her lodging of Frances Crump; it is ordered that that business be very well examined before any money be paid.[10]

Whatever her sources of income, it may be assumed, in the absence of any real evidence to the contrary, that Widow Purcell kept her family of six children — five sons (Edward, Charles, Henry, Joseph, and Daniel) and a daughter (Katherine)§ — under her own roof and provided for them as best she could until they were capable of fending for themselves. No doubt Thomas Purcell acted as foster-father and benefactor to the family. At least his income and influence would have enabled him to help a great deal. And no doubt, as traditionally supposed, he undertook to foster the growth of the musical talents of both young Henry and Daniel. But in proof of such help there is only meagre documentary evidence in the form of a letter supposedly written by

---

★ St. Margaret's, Westminster, Churchwardens' Accounts, vol. LXXX.

† See App. Two, VIII, *passim*, and various entries in WAM 61228A (Precentor's Book, 1660–71) (for instance, folios 56v, 57v, 58, 61). From the titles and benefits for 24 Dec. 1664 Widow Purcell received thirteen shillings as the regular share for a singing-man. After that date her name does not appear in the records of the sharings of occasional income.

‡ 1674–93, fo. 42.

§ See App. Two and App. Three for information on the children.

Thomas Purcell to John Gostling. The letter, however, was lost for years and has been brought to light only recently by Hugh McLean, who found it in the Nanki collection near Tokyo.*

Thus, after the administering of the elder Henry Purcell's estate on 5 October 1664, the year ended with sorrow for his friends, bereavement for his widow and orphans.

* See pp. 66–67 and n.

CHAPTER II

PURCELL'S BOYHOOD

The following year brought woes on a national scale. On 14 April 1665 the unpopular war against the Dutch was initiated,* and by the end of that same month the plague, no doubt carried from Amsterdam by ship, claimed the first of the more than 70,000 London inhabitants who were to be its victims. Pepys's entry for 30 April reflects the general feeling of horror that the news aroused:

Great fears of the sickness here in the City, it being said that two or three houses are already shut up. God preserve us all!

Although not so heavily 'visited' (the official euphemism for 'infected') as other parts of London, Westminster soon felt the disastrous effects of the plague. In fact the pestilence had first broken out at the end of the summer of 1664 in Westminster, according to Nathaniel Hodges. It is not therefore impossible that the elder Purcell may have been one of its first victims:

The plague, which we are now to give an account of, discovered the beginnings of its future cruelties about the close of the year 1664; for at that season two or three persons died suddenly in one family at Westminster, attended with like symptoms that manifestly declared their origin. Hereupon some timorous neighbours, under apprehensions of a contagion, removed into the City of London, who unfortunately carried along with them the pestilential taint; whereby that disease, which was before in its infancy, in a family or two, suddenly got strength, and spread abroad its fatal poisons. . . .†

The ecclesiastical and musical communities showed the devastating influence of the pestilence almost immediately. Less than a

* Pepys, 14 April 1665.

† Nathaniel Hodges, *Loimologia; or An Historical Account of the Plague in London in 1665*, pp. 1–2. See also J. W. Ebsworth (ed.), *The Bagford Ballads*, part I, p. 39, for a lugubrious broadside ballad on the plague.

month after his first entry on the plague Pepys, going to the Chapel Royal on 28 May, reported that he heard little music, presumably because everyone who could had withdrawn from London and its environs. It is even possible that Pelham Humfrey, John Blow, and John Blundeville had been released from active duty there on 17 May preceding,* not only because their voices had changed, but to get them away from Westminster as well.

By June 1665 the number of 'visited' had increased to 470 a week, a fact which 'put the gentry and principal citizens on the wings of safety'. (This is yet another reason for doubting the anecdote of the incredibly quick composition of the 'Club Anthem' by Humfrey, Blow, and Turner for the celebration of the Duke of York's victory over the Dutch at Lowestoft. No one, it seems, would have been very interested in mass public celebrations at such a time.†)

By July the Court had removed to comparative safety at Hampton Court, while a horror-striken populace watched the march of cross-daubed doors, their ominous red symbols spreading in all directions with the onslaught of the plague. On 12 July Pepys records that a solemn day of fasting had been ordained for 'this Wednesday and the first Wednesday of every month during the visitation'.‡ The wholesale death brought by the epidemic, and the universal horror it inspired, paralysed almost all community activities. By the end of the summer all London and its environs was caught up in a *danse macabre*, from which, it seemed, none could hope to escape:

In the months of August and September the contagion changed its former slow and languid pace, and having as it were got master of all, made a most terrible slaughter, so that three, four, or five thousand died in a week, and once eight thousand . . . In some houses carcases lay waiting for burial, and others, persons in their last agonies; in one room might be heard dying groans, in another the ravings of a delirium, and not far off relations bewailing both their loss and the dismal prospect of their own departure. Death was the sure midwife to all children, and infants passed immediately from the womb to the grave. Who would not burst with grief to see the stock for a future generation hang upon the breasts of a dead mother, or the marriage-bed changed the first night

---

* *KM*, pp. 178–9. † Westrup, p. 17.
‡ See Evelyn's entry for 2 Aug., also a Wednesday.

into a sepulchre, and the unhappy pair meet with death in their first embraces? Some of the infected run about staggering like drunken men, and fall and expire in the streets; while others lie half-dead and comatose, but never to be waked but by the last trumpet . . . the number of sextons were not sufficient to bury the dead; the bells seemed hoarse with continual tolling, until at last they quite ceased; the burying places would not hold the dead, but they were thrown into large pits dug into waste grounds, in heaps, thirty or forty together; and it often happened that those who attended the funerals of their friends one evening were carried the next to their own long home . . . in the course of [September] more than twelve thousand died in a week.*

The influence of all this upon the Church is reflected in the tenebrous scene described by an entry in the Westminster Abbey Precentor's Book:

In the year 1665 by reason of God's visitation by the plague of pestilence, no wax lights or tallow candles were used in the church, but the service was daily performed by daylight, by Mr. John Tynchare, one of the petty canons, and by him alone from the beginning of July to almost the end of December.†

Henry Purcell celebrated his sixth birthday during these benighted times. At so impressionable an age he undoubtedly was left with unforgettable memories of the Great Plague and its nightmarish reign of terror. The frequent spectacle of the 'visited' being carted off to the pest-houses by night and by day, the continual sound of the death knell and sextons' bells, the stench and the ugliness of death, indeed the whole frighteningly morbid experience must have remained as one of the strongest of all memories from his childhood. The renowned melancholy of Purcell's musical expression may well owe its origin to the overwhelmingly doleful experiences of this formative period of his life.

Portentous occurrences also marked the year 1666 throughout London and all England. Newton published his formulation of the law of gravitation and carried out his experiment with prisms and colours in light;‡ pestilence continued; the war with the Dutch went badly for the English; and during the night before 2 September dawned, the Great Fire broke out in Pudding Lane. Fanned by an unseasonable wind, in four days it reduced 450 acres

* Hodges, op. cit., pp. 16–17, 18, 19.
† WAM 61228A, fo. 138v.   ‡ DNB.

of London to ashes and charred remains. Altogether, 13,200 houses were destroyed by fire and by demolition gangs, and two-thirds of London's populace were left without roofs over their heads. Only famine was wanting to convince everyone that the Four Horsemen of the Apocalypse had been loosed.

If, as has been surmised, Purcell was born on 10 September, he would have celebrated his seventh birthday during the week of the Great Fire, which laid waste all the City about St. Paul's. Quite possibly he would have taken the short walk from West-minster along the Thames to the Tower just as Pepys had done on 2 September 1666, staring wide-eyed at the scene of conflagration and destruction to the north-west. This too would have remained as one of his most vivid childhood memories. The disaster had an immediate and direct influence upon the affairs of London musicians, as several contemporary documents reveal. The following is typical:

John Gamble, one of His Majesty's wind-instrument concert, pleaded for pay-ment of £221. 10s. 4½d., arrears of his salary over four and three-quarter years. All he possessed he had lost by the dreadful Fire, and he had contracted a debt of £120, for which one of his sureties had been sent prisoner to Newgate. Ruin awaited them and their families without this payment. Twenty-two musicians on the violin made similar plaint, having had houses and goods burnt in the Fire.*

By the end of the year these calamities had run their course, however, and London citizens held a feast day on 10 October for the end of the Great Fire, and on 20 November following observed a general thanksgiving for the end of the pestilence.† In his entry for the latter date, however, Pepys added:

but, Lord! how the town do say it is hastened before the plague is quite over, there dying some people still . . .

Such events, along with the thanksgiving for the victory over the Dutch at the mouth of the Thames (which had been celebrated at the Chapel Royal with Locke's anthem for the occasion, 'The King shall rejoice'), no doubt created a happier atmosphere for all Londoners and Englishmen in general during the latter half of

---

* W. G. Bell, *The Great Fire of London in 1666*, p. 229.
† Pepys, 10 Oct. and 20 Nov. 1666.

1666. As if by divine connivance the naval victory had occurred on 'St. James, his Day', 25 July, no doubt to the entire satisfaction of James, Duke of York, to whom it was credited.

Certainly the atmosphere at Court, with which young Purcell may by now have become officially acquainted as a Chapel Royal chorister, was gay enough. On 18 October Evelyn reported that Charles II had adopted the new 'unfrenchified' dress he called 'Persian', and penned a Jeremiad on the moral laxity encouraged by the introduction of women to the stage. For a special birthday treat for Queen Catherine on 15 November the king preferred her over his 'misses', according to Pepys:

I also to the ball, and with much ado got up to the loft, where with much trouble I could see very well. Anon the house grew full, and the candles light, and the King and Queen and all the ladies set: and it was, indeed, a glorious sight to see Mrs. Stewart in black and white lace, and her head and shoulders dressed with diamonds, and the like a great many ladies more, only the Queen none; and the King in his rich vest of some rich silk and silver trimming, as the Duke of York and all the dancers were, some of cloth of silver, and others of other sorts, exceeding rich. Presently, after the King was come in, he took the Queen, and about fourteen more couples there was, and begun the Bransles. As many of the men as I can remember presently, were, the King, Duke of York, Prince Rupert, Duke of Monmouth, Duke of Buckingham, Lord Douglas, Mr. [George] Hamilton, Colonel Russell, Mr. Griffith, Lord Ossory, Lord Rochester; and of the ladies, the Queen, Duchess of York, Mrs. Stewart, Duchess of Monmouth, Lady Essex Howard, Mrs. Temple, Swedes [sic] Embassadress, Lady Arlington, Lord George Barkeley's daughter, and many others I remember not; but all most excellently dressed in rich petticoats and gowns, and diamonds and pearls. After the Bransles, then to a Corant, and now and then a French dance; but that so rare that the Corants grew tiresome, that I wished it done. Only Mrs. Stewart danced mighty finely, and many French dances, specially one the King called the New Dance, which was very pretty; but upon the whole matter, the business of the dancing of itself was not extra-ordinary pleasing.

Pepys does not indicate why he found the dancing so bad. Perhaps the king's violins, having petitioned for arrears of salary without apparent success only the week before, were still glum and played accordingly:

Petition of the 22 musicians on the violin to the King for payment of part of their arrears out of the £15,000 ordered for payment of His Majesty's servants;

have attended His Majesty and the Queen in their progresses, besides daily attendance; are 4¾ years in arrear, and have had houses and goods burned in the late fire.*

Or perhaps the Queen's feelings towards 'la belle Stewart', however well concealed, lent a certain tenseness to the occasion. Certainly there was tenseness, occasioned by professional jealousy, in the orchestra. Only three days earlier Louis Grabu had been sworn in as Master of the English Chamber Music,† much to the chagrin and disappointment of John Banister, who must already have foreseen his own fall:

order that Mr. Banister and the 24 violins appointed to practise with him and all His Majesty's Private Music do from time to time obey the directions of Louis Grabu . . .

By 20 February the following year Pepys reported the latest Court gossip, writing:

Here they talk also how the King's violin, Bannister, is mad that the King hath a Frenchman come to be chief of some part of the King's Music, at which the Duke of York made great mirth.

By 14 March Banister's disgrace was completed by an order from the Lord Chamberlain which gave Grabu his position at the head of the select band of twelve violins. Grabu, it seems, before leaving France had learned a thing or two from Lully's machinations.

By the end of 1667 the French vogue had reached its zenith. Numerous favourable developments culminated in a splendid concert at Whitehall given on 1 October. It was attended and reported upon by the indefatigable Pepys, who was not pleased with the music itself, although impressed by the excellence of its performance:

to Whitehall, and there in the boarded-gallery did hear the music with which the King is presented this night by Monsieur Grebus, the Master of his Music; both instrumental — I think twenty-four violins — and vocal; an English song upon Peace. But, God forgive me! I never was so little pleased with a concert of music in my life. The manner of setting of words and repeating them out of

---

* *Cal. S. P. Dom.* 7 Nov. 1666 (see also entry for 2 June 1669).
† *Cal. S. P. Dom.* 12 Nov. 1666.

order, and that with a number of voices, makes me sick, the whole design of vocal music being lost by it. Here was a great press of people; but I did not see many pleased with it, only the instrumental music he had brought by practice to play very just.*

In 1667, when he was approaching his eighth birthday, Purcell may have taken part as a chorister in the gala ceremonies for the Order of the Garter held on 23 April, the anniversary of Charles II's coronation. Evelyn has left a vivid account of the colourful ceremony, in which music played no small part:

In the morning His Majesty went to chapel with the Knights all in their habits and robes, ushered by the heralds. After the first service they went in procession, the youngest first, the sovereign last, with the Prelate of the Order and Dean, who had about his neck the book of the statutes of the Order, and then the Chancellor of the Order (old Sir H. de Vic.), who wore the Purse about his: then heralds and Garter King-of-Arms [Clarenceux], Black Rod: but before the Prelate and Dean of Windsor, went the Gentlemen of [the] Chapel, Choristers, etc., singing as they marched, behind them two Doctors of Music in damask robes. This proceeding was about the courts of Whitehall, then returning to their stalls and seats in the chapel, placed under each Knight's coat armour and titles. Then began second service, then the King offered at the altar, an anthem sung, then the rest of the Knights offered [sic], and lastly proceeded to the Banqueting House to a great feast. The King sat on an elevated throne at the upper end, at a table alone. The Knights at a table on the right hand, reaching all the length of the room; over against them a cupboard of rich gilded plate, etc.: at [the] lower end the music; on the balusters above wind music, trumpets, and kettle-drums. The King was served by the lords and pensioners, who brought up the dishes: about the middle of dinner the Knights drank the King's health, then the King theirs. Then the trumpets, music, etc. played and sounded, the guns going off at the Tower. At the banquet came in the Queen and stood by the King's left hand, but did not sit. Then was the banqueting stuff flung about the room profusely. In truth the crowd was so great, that though I stayed all the supper the day before, I now stayed no longer than this sport began for fear of disorder. The cheer was extraordinary, each Knight having 40 dishes to his mess: piled up 5 or 6 high. The room hung with the richest tapestry in the world . . .†

The fact that it was one of the coldest Aprils on record‡ would

---

* Pepys, 1 Oct. 1667.   † Evelyn, 23 April 1667.
‡ Evelyn, 4 April 1667.

only have added zest to the ceremony. But the choristers were probably glad that the weather had warmed up when they made their annual procession round the parish on Ascension Day, a few weeks later.

Purcell may also have heard on 28 July the 'strange, bold sermon of Dr. Creeton ... before the King; how he preached against ... adultery, over and over instancing how for that single sin in David, the whole nation was undone; and of our negligence in having our castles without ammunition and powder when the Dutch come upon us. ...' Or even if he had not yet taken his place in the Chapel Royal he would have heard the talk which soon got round, as Pepys reported next day,* getting his information from Mr. Creed and his cousin Roger.

The comparison of Charles II to David was apt enough in other ways to be taken up later by Dryden in *Absalom and Achitophel* as a literary weapon against Charles II's enemies. Purcell also made use of this parallel in an anthem or two, as did other Restoration composers. But such puritanical admonitions had no noticeable effect on Charles II, who continued blithely to enjoy life as he saw fit. Perhaps the Church's position of moral and righteous indignation had been weakened by further gossip which came Pepys's way — again Cousin Roger was the source — telling it, 'as a thing certain', that the Archbishop of Canterbury 'do keep a wench, and that he is as very a wencher as can be'.† On this same day the king demonstrated his unrepentant attitude by the dissolution of both Houses of Parliament, and having dismissed all members with scant apology for having called them to London to no purpose, went back to being 'governed by his lust and women and rogues about him'.

In August 1667, just two months after the Dutch had blockaded the Thames and sailed up the Medway after burning the guard-ships there, all London was buzzing with news of the fall of Clarendon and the establishment of the Cabal, whose ministers (Clifford, Arlington, Buckingham, Ashley, and Lauderdale) wittingly or unwittingly did so much to further the cause of

* 29 July 1667.   † Pepys, 29 July 1667.

Catholicism in England during the next few years.* This, coupled
with the machinations of Charles and the Duke of York, led to
the secret Treaty of Dover (1670), based upon *quid pro quo*
measures to strengthen Catholicism in England and to bolster
Louis XIV's position all over Europe, and by indirection to the
Declaration of Indulgence of 1672, the second, very unpopular,
war with Holland, and eventually to the Test Act of 1673.

What the convictions of the Purcell family may have been
amidst all these actions and counteractions of the Catholic and
Protestant parties cannot be known. If later, however, the younger
Henry Purcell did entertain Catholic sympathies, as has been
suggested,† it is certain that these faced him with serious decisions.

When the French vogue in music declined, that of the Italian
musicians began to rise.‡ The decline was not slackened by
Grabu's own musical ineptitude (later to become painfully
apparent in a musical and political piece, *Albion and Albanius*,
upon which he collaborated with Dryden) or by the attitude of
young Pelham Humfrey, who returned from France in October
1667. According to him, Pelham's composition for the Sunday
service at Whitehall was a good anthem, but he could not call it
'anything but instrumental music with voice', nothing being made
of the words.§ Two weeks later (i.e. by 15 November 1667)
Pepys's distaste for the young 'monsieur' had grown to active
dislike, mainly because of the latter's complete lack of respect for
the Establishment, but particularly for his denigration of Grabu:

calling at my mercer's and tailor's, and there I find, as I expected, Mr. Caesar
and little Pelham Humphreys, lately returned from France, and is an absolute

---

* See Plate 5, 'The Cabal' by J. B. Medina. The entitlement of this conversation piece is probably fortuitous, but not therefore without interest in a
musician's biography. Of the figures shown, that on the far right is not unlike
Matthew Locke, and the central figure bears a more than passing likeness to
Henry Purcell. (See also Ebsworth's edition of *The Roxburghe Ballads*, vol. IV,
p. 582.)

† See pp. 100–2 below.

‡ See Pepys's entries for 12 Aug., 9 Sept., and 30 Dec. that same year for a
few straws in the wind.

§ Ibid. 1 Nov. 1667. According to the article in *Grove's* (5th ed.), vol. IV,
p. 404, Humfrey had been sworn in on 26 Oct. 1667 as a Gentleman of the
Chapel Royal.

monsieur, as full of form, and confidence, and vanity, and disparages everything, and everybody's skill but his own. The truth is, everybody says he is very able, but to hear how he laughs at all the King's Music here, as Blagrave and others, that they cannot keep time not tune, nor understand anything; and that Grebus, the Frenchman, the King's master of the Music, how he understands nothing, nor can play on any instrument, and so cannot compose: and that he will give him a lift out of his place; and that he and the King are mighty great! and that he hath already spoke to the King of Grebus would make a man piss.

Purcell's connection with Humfrey was not to begin for several years — perhaps not until 15 July 1672, when the latter was appointed Master of the Children after Henry Cooke's death. But Humfrey's presence at Court was undoubtedly important to the boy's musical development, if only because any affinity which Purcell had for French or Italian music would have been strengthened by Humfrey's display of the latest styles of composition and performance he had just learned at the Court of Louis XIV and elsewhere in Europe.

The following year, 1668, was uneventful for musicians at Charles II's Court. Nor, so far as the records show, did anything of importance occur within the Purcell family circle. Elizabeth continued to receive small sums from various officials at the Court and Abbey from time to time,[1] but these were scarcely sufficient to provide her large family even with bare necessities. Edward Purcell, now about twelve, was probably already a page at Court, since within a few years he was to emerge as a gentleman usher,* no doubt helped to that position by the good offices of his uncle Thomas Purcell, who was a groom of the robes. Cousin Edward also appears to have been employed at court, as a gentleman usher *daily waiter assistant*. The responsibilities with which Edward had been entrusted at least as early as 25 March 1673 were not those that would have been given one so young as Edward, son of Henry, who had not yet celebrated his seventeenth birthday:

Treasurer Latimer's subscription of a docket, dated 1673, Aug., of a warrant to the Treasurer of the Chamber to pay 100 marks per an. to Edward Purcell

* See the inscription from his memorial tablet in Wytham church in App. Two, IV, 13. There may have been two Edward Purcells at Court at about this time.

from Lady Day last; to be for preventing uncertain charges (by bills) which he shall be put to for His Majesty's service about making ready of standing houses and progress houses in the [King's] removes and other services as gentleman usher daily waiter assistant.*[2]

Of Henry's second brother, Charles Purcell, later Bursar of the English Royal Navy aboard H.M.S. *Tyger*, in Barbados, nothing is known for this early period.[3] Daniel Purcell was too young to augment the family income in any way, and probably did not begin as a chorister in the Chapel Royal for another three years;[4] Katherine was six, and perhaps helpful about the house.

On 3 June 1669 — in Purcell's tenth year — Cosimo III, Grand Duke of Tuscany, saw in London a comedy-ballet based on the score of *Psyche* when he attended a special performance at Drury Lane — a performance no doubt modelled after those being mounted about this time in France by Molière and by Lully, who already had an eye on the royal patent granted by Louis XIV to L'Abbé Perrin, Robert Cambert, and the Marquis de Sourdéac for the establishment of an Académie de Musique in France on the 28th of that same month.†

The year 1670, which saw the granting of a charter to the Hudson's Bay Company, seems again to have passed fairly uneventfully for Purcell, who by now must certainly have shown signs of the extraordinary musical promise that was soon to make him famous. However, the secret Treaty of Dover with Louis XIV, wherein on 22 April Charles II traded a few religious and political scruples for enough hard cash to gain some independence from Parliament, no doubt helped to ease the dire economic situation at Court. As a chorister Purcell had been directly affected by the impoverishment of Charles II's coffers, which had kept the boys in rags for some time. In or before June 1670 Captain Cooke had found it necessary to submit the following petition to the King:

Petition of Henry Cooke, Master of the Children of the Chapel Royal, to the King. The children are not receiving their liveries as usual, are reduced to so bad a condition that they are unfit to attend His Majesty, or walk in the streets. Begs an order for their liveries, the charge not being great, and His Majesty

---

* *Cal. Tr. Books*, 15 Sept. 1673.
† See *Grove's* (5th ed.) under 'Académie de Musique'.

having signified to the Bishop of Oxford that they should have their liberties continued.

On 30 June he received his answer:

Order on the above petition that the Children of the Chapel be for the future entertained and clothed as they were before the late retrenchments.

After some deliberation something at last was done, and the following orders were issued on 6 and 12 July:

Mr. Newport and Mr. Reymes called in with Captain Cooke about the clothes for the Children of the Chapel. [Ordered] that the King will have them made as formerly. The officers of the Wardrobe say they have no money. My Lords desire Captain Cooke to furnish the money by loan on the funds on which the Wardrobe has orders; which he promised.

Chapel boys; warrant for £214. 4s. 0d. to complete £300. They have had £85. 16s. To be employed and laid out for provision of liveries for the said children in full of the estimate dated 16 May last.[5]

During this same period Purcell, it has been supposed, wrote his first occasional work for Charles II: the 'Address of the Children of the Chapel Royal to the King, and their master, Captain Cooke, on His Majesty's birthday, A.D. 1670, composed by Master Purcell, one of the Children of the said Chapel'. The late Edward F. Rimbault, music fancier and antiquarian, claimed to own a copy of the work.[6] Alas! it is lost, and even though this manuscript, if it ever actually existed, may never come to light, it is tempting to speculate that such an address would have been in order, not only to wish the king 'many happy returns of the day', but to bring to his attention the disgraceful state of the boys' clothing and equipment.*

That autumn new preferment came to Thomas Purcell's family. In the Westminster Abbey Treasurer's Account for Michaelmas 1670 Charles Purcell's name is entered among the 'Bishop's Boys' who were recipients of the four scholarships founded by the Rev. John Williams, Dean of Westminster, in 1624:

Et in denariis solut. ad usum Scolasticor — xxv^{li} Decano Thesaur Ludomagist et Coll. xxvis 8d ex dono Johanis Williams nuper Episcopi Lincoln et Decan. Westm. In toto pro hoc Anno ... £26 – 6 – 8

* *Analytical Catalogue*, no. D120.

(And from the money devoted to scholastic use, £25 from the Dean's Treasurer and Master of the College, and 26s. 8d. from the gift of John Williams, former Bishop of Lincoln and Dean of Westminster. In all for this year ... £26. 6s. 8d.)*

Charles Purcell held this scholarship until 1678, when he was replaced by his more illustrious cousin, Henry, probably then attending St. Peter's College in a commoner's gown.†

The year 1671 saw the publication of Milton's *Paradise Regained* and also of his *Samson Agonistes*, a sombre view of the era by this Restoration Tiresias who had envisioned better times. It also saw the beginnings of theatrical developments that were to be of great importance to Purcell's career later on. On 9 November‡ the company of William D'Avenant, putatively the bastard son, certainly the godson, of William Shakespeare, opened the new theatre at Dorset Garden where so many of D'Avenant's supposed father's works were to be bastardized in the coming decade. Among these were *Macbeth*, *The Tempest*, and *Timon of Athens*, of which later productions were to be connected with Purcell's name.[7]

For Henry Cooke this theatrical outlet occasioned yet another drain on the slender stock of talent available in the choristers of the Chapel Royal. Above and beyond their duties in Chapel the boys were expected to participate in various stage performances requiring music, both at the Duke of York's Theatre in Dorset Garden and at the Theatre Royal in Drury Lane — this despite the express prohibition of such a practice in one of the original patents for 'taking up boys' granted to Nathaniel Giles in 1626:

Provided always, and we straitly charge and command that none of the said choristers or Children of the Chapel, so to be taken by force of this commission, shall be used or employed as comedians, or stage players, or to exercise or act any stage plays, interludes, comedies or tragedies; for it is not fit or decent that such as should sing the praises of God Almighty should be trained or employed in lascivious and profane exercises.§

---

* WAM 33703 (Treasurer's Account, 1670), fo. 4. For more detailed discussion of Henry Purcell's receiving one of Bishop Williams's scholarships, see pp. 52–55.

† See p. 52 below.

‡ See J. L. Hotson, *The Commonwealth and Restoration Stage*, p. 232. D'Avenant had died on 7 April 1668 (*DNB*).

§ *KM*, p. 485.

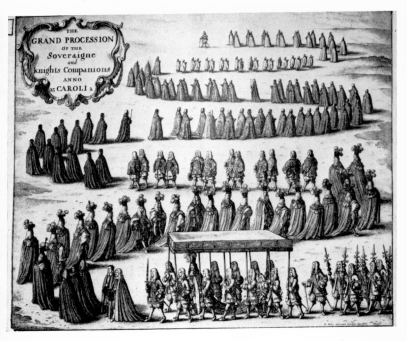

3a 'The Grand Procession of the Soveraigne and knights Champions. Anno 23 Caroli 2.' 1672. Wenceslaus Hollar

3b Record of disbursement to Henry Purcell as 'Bishop's Boy' at St. Peter's College, Westminster, 1678

With Crowns of Peace and Love kind Heavens on KATHARIN ſmile ❀ The jarring Elements to union do conſpire ❀

4 'With Crowns of Peace and Love, kind Heavens on Katharin smile …' Frontispiece engraved by I. A.

However, neither Cooke nor any succeeding Master of the Choristers could refuse to obey the frequent royal commands that called the choristers out to play in the theatre.*

It must have been a trying year for Cooke. Not only did he have to do his usual chores (teaching Latin, mending clothes, and travelling out to the provinces to look for new choir boys), but he had also to attend to several boys who had been ill:

23 May 1671.

The sum of £167. 17s. 4d. to be paid to Captain Cook, Master of the Children of His Majesty's Chapel Royal, for learning the children on the organ, on the lute and theorbo, for fire and strings in the music room in the Chapel, for doctors, nurses, and for looking to several of the children when they were sick; for going to Westchester, Lichfield, Canterbury, and Rochester to look for boys, and for other service for one year from Lady Day 1670 to Lady Day 1671.†

To top it all, the Chapel Royal was reduced to chaos during this time, while enlargements were made and new fittings hung:

21 March 1670/1.

Warrant to deliver to Captain Cooke, Master of the Children of His Majesty's Chapel Royal, three crimson damask curtains for the music-room in the Chapel, the music-room being enlarged.‡

At the end of May, however, he took all his charges to Windsor for a fortnight,§ remaining on with six of the boys until 25 July.[8] (Whether Henry Purcell remained the whole time is not known. Surely, though, he was among the twelve who travelled down for the first two weeks.) The following year, 1672, a leap year, was on the whole a very good year for the Purcell family. Already Thomas Purcell headed the list of musicians in the Chapel, as may be seen in a great number of the Lord Chamberlain's records for the period.‖ On 10 January he and Pelham Humfrey were appointed composers, as assistants to George Hudson (then aged and infirm, who died before the year was out) to come in ordinary

---

* See pp. 36–37 below; also *KM*, pp. 271, 318, *et al.*
† *KM*, p. 231.
‡ *KM*, p. 230. See also entries for 8 Feb., 13 March, and 23 March 1671.
§ *KM*, p. 235.   ‖ *KM*, p. 245 and *passim*.

with fee 'upon death or other avoidance'.* Shortly thereafter in
1673 he also assumed the responsibility for the annual payments
(involving the distribution of £400) to the king's musicians.†
After Humfrey's death at Windsor (on 14 July in the following
year) Thomas Purcell assumed chief responsibility and sole
authority. About that time, he was also appointed Marshal of the
Corporation of Musicians, replacing Henry Cooke, who had
'resigned office by reason of illness' and retired to Hampton
Court, where he died on 13 July.‡

After Cooke's death, Pelham Humfrey, his son-in-law, succeeded to his position on 15 July, Henry Purcell now being
directly under Humfrey's tutelage.§ Doubtless the close working-
relationship between Thomas Purcell and Humfrey had already
ensured that the new Master of the Choristers and the budding
Restoration genius would be well acquainted. But whether this
could be counted one of the fortunate occurrences of the year
from Purcell's point of view is problematical, in view of Pepys's
derogatory opinion of Humfrey. Presumably, though, this
'absolute monsieur' would have mellowed considerably in the
five years that had since elapsed.

Other members of the Purcell family also prospered. Daniel
Purcell took up his new appointment as a chorister in the Chapel
Royal; ‖ cousin Charles Purcell's stipend as a Bishop's Boy was
confirmed; and Edward Purcell (cousin to Henry and Daniel)
received the unusual (and secret) honour of being trusted with
100 marks per annum, for which he alone was responsible.¶

As the year ended, Henry Purcell must have been wondering
about his own fortunes. Now fourteen years of age and nearly
finished with his schooling, he must have realized that his days as a
chorister were numbered. His unusual talents as a singer and
instrumental performer had no doubt been recognized. But apart

---

* KM, p. 240; however, the date in the Cal. Tr. Books is given as 1673.

† Cal. Tr. Books: entries for 15 Sept. 1673; 17 Oct. 1673; 31 Dec. 1673;
30 Nov. 1674, etc.

‡ Grove's (5th ed.), vol. II, p. 420. See Plate 3(a) for record of a contemporary event.

§ KM, p. 247.   ‖ Grove's (5th ed.), vol. VI, p. 1019.

¶ Cal. Tr. Books, 15 Sept. 1673.

from the single composition written for Charles II's birthday in 1670 — even that being very uncertain — there is no evidence that Purcell had as yet given anyone the slightest inkling of his creative talent.

Nor, apparently, was anyone aware of the significance of the concert series that John Banister founded at the end of 1672, five years after his alleged peculations had brought about his fall from grace at Court. The first of his concerts — probably one of the first professional chamber music concerts supported by box-office collections in Europe — Pepys's earlier mention of the post office music-meeting notwithstanding* — was advertised as follows in the *London Gazette* for 26–30 December 1672:

These are to give notice that at Mr. John Banister's house now called the Music School, over against the George Tavern in Whitefriar's this present Monday [i.e. 30 December] will be music performed by excellent masters, beginning precisely at four of the clock in the afternoon, and every afternoon for the future precisely at that same hour.

Banister, motivated by the desire to repair his finances, as well as to recoup his sadly deteriorated prestige and musical fortunes, probably had no idea that he was setting a historical precedent. For many a Restoration musician, including Purcell himself, such concerts were to prove very useful, particularly during increasingly frequent seasons of economic distress at Court.

* Pepys, 10 Aug. and 5 Oct. 1664.

CHAPTER III

YEARS OF APPRENTICESHIP

Within the first few weeks of the new year Henry Purcell was given a taste of what lay in store for him. On 17 January 1673 came down from the Lord Chamberlain's office the royal warrant that accompanied the dismissal of Henry Hall, his schoolmate and fellow chorister in the Chapel Royal. Hall's voice had broken shortly before or perhaps during the previous Christmas season.* Thenceforward Pelham Humfrey was to receive £30 yearly for keeping and teaching young Hall — an arrangement reserved for the most talented choristers.

Evidently Purcell's voice remained firm and true throughout most of this year, for the warrant that ordered for him a similar arrangement was not recorded until 17 December, although it may have been a foregone conclusion much earlier. The stipend actually began at Michaelmas (29 September), by which time, presumably, his voice had broken or was about to do so:

17 Dec. 1673.

Warrant to provide outfit of clothing for Henry Purcell, late child of His Majesty's Chapel Royal, whose voice is changed and gone from the Chapel.

Warrant to pay to Henry Purcell, late one of the Children of His Majesty's Chapel Royal, whose voice is changed and is gone from the Chapel, the sum of £30 by the year, to commence Michaelmas 1673 last past.†

Purcell's 'perquisites' upon leaving were, no doubt, the same as Henry Hall's had been:

---

* KM, p. 251; see App. Two, XIII, 20, for Hall's eulogy to Purcell in a dedicatory poem to Orpheus Britannicus, 3rd ed. (1721).

† KM, p. 263; see App. Two, XIII, 4, for a warrant of this same date providing clothing for Purcell upon his leaving the Chapel.

two suits of plain cloth, two hats and hat-bands, four whole shirts, four half shirts, six bands, six pairs of cuffs, six handkerchiefs, four pair of stockings, four pair of shoes, and four pair of gloves.*

For Purcell then, no period of adjustment — awkward or welcome — intervened between the end of his chorister's duties and the beginning of his professional career. Six months before he left the Chapel Royal as a singer he had been assigned new duties there as an assistant to John Hingeston, who was charged with keeping the royal instruments in repair:

10 June 1673.

Warrant to admit Henry Purcell in the place of keeper, maker, mender, repairer, and tuner of regals, organs, virginals, flutes, and recorders and all other kind of wind instruments whatsoever, in ordinary, without fee, to His Majesty, and assistant to John Hingston, and upon his death or other avoidance of the latter, to come in ordinary with fee.†

While improving his fundamental knowledge of instrumental music in the most practical way, i.e. by taking apart, repairing, and reassembling and tuning all sorts of instruments, Purcell also learned from Pelham Humfrey other skills necessary to the successful practice of his profession. Unfortunately there is no record of the nature of the instruction. Humfrey had just been given an 'assistant instructor for viols and theorbos' in the person of John Lilly, and this perhaps may be construed to indicate the kind of instruction he particularly did not want to give.[1] Presumably he would have coached his talented striplings in the art of descant, or, as it would now be termed, composition and counterpoint, and emphasized those techniques and stylistic elements that he himself had so recently learned in France.

During the course of this year London's theatrical musical traditions had taken a new, indeed a modernistic, turn with the production in February of a 'transmogrified' version of Shakespeare's *Macbeth* with music by Locke. He also provided music for Settle's *Empress of Morocco* the following July, a month or so

---

* *KM*, p. 251; as if by an afterthought, Purcell's allotment was augmented by a supply of handkerchiefs shortly after the beginning of the new year (*KM*, 2 Feb. 1673/4).

† *KM*, p. 255.

after Charles D'Avenant had undertaken the management of the company in the new theatre in Dorset Garden long after his father's death more than a decade before.*

Early in 1674 Thomas Purcell added yet another position to an already impressive list. Shortly after 22 February, when John Wilson died,† full of years and honoured by all, Thomas Purcell succeeded him as musician-in-ordinary to His Majesty in the Private Music.‡ This brought to a total of six the number of paid positions he held at Court.[2] Small wonder that he was able to live in Pall Mall, the most fashionable residential area in the vicinity of the Court, and that he found it possible to leave his widow well off despite considerable arrears which the Court owed him at his death in 1682.

At the beginning of the year Londoners witnessed the arrival of Robert Cambert, newly ousted from an exalted position in the Parisian musical community by Lully's machinations at the Court of Louis XIV. His *Ariane, ou le mariage de Bacchus* (produced by the new Royal Academy of Music) was evidently successful, for it ran nearly a month after opening on 30 March 1674 at the newly restored Theatre Royal in Bridges Street.§ Grabu no doubt helped with the production and musical performance, witness the warrant of 27 March, which ordered the persons responsible to deliver

to Monsieur Grabu, or to such as he shall appoint, such of the scenes remaining in the theatre at Whitehall as shall be useful for the French opera at the theatre in Bridges Street, and the said Monsieur Grabu to return them again safely after 14 days' time, to the theatre in Whitehall.[3]

One good thing led to another, it seems, and on 4 July next twelve of the violins were ordered to report to Cambert at Whitehall at seven o'clock the following Wednesday morning (the 8th) for the royal entertainment to be performed at Windsor on Saturday, 11 July. ‖ The pieces performed included *Pomone* (the same work with which Cambert and Perrin had begun their

* DNB.

† *Grove's* (5th ed.), vol. IX, p. 312. Stephen Crespion, later a close friend, near neighbour and death-bed companion of Henry Purcell, signed Wilson's burial order on 27 Feb.

‡ KM, p. 268.   § MGG, vol. II, col. 695.   ‖ KM, p. 273.

unlucky enterprise in Paris three years earlier) and a *Ballet et musique pour le divertissement du roy de la Grand-Bretagne*. The libretto for the latter was printed by 'Thomas Nieucombe dans la Savoy' that same year.

Henry Purcell was not mentioned in the list of those who were to be on hand at Windsor,* but since everyone else was there, and since the whole musical establishment had been transferred to Windsor for the summer season, it is a reasonable conjecture that he heard the music. What he or any other Englishman thought of the work has not been recorded. But since no further entertainments by Cambert and Grabu were scheduled, it appears that the performance was not particularly successful.

In fact the disenchantment with French music mentioned previously now began in earnest. Perhaps the falling-off was not altogether due to musical misfortunes. It may also have been due partially to the fact that Charles could no longer afford openly to employ at his Court foreign musicians who were also prominent Catholics. As his impecunious condition placed him more and more at the mercy of his Protestant enemies in Parliament, he would have had to be increasingly careful. The failure of the 'Royal Academy of Music in Bridges Street, Covent Garden', which had undermined the joint venture of Cambert and Grabu, and the fall of the latter from grace that same year may have been due as much to political as to artistic shortcomings. Cambert was doubly *persona non grata* to anti-Catholic Parliamentarians. They disliked him equally for the enormous expenses his productions entailed, and for the fact that he was a very important person among Catholics, having been at the beginning of his career a close friend of the Papal Nuncio in Paris.†

Opportunities to hear other 'famed Italian masters' had been plentiful throughout the year. On 5 January Evelyn reported seeing 'an Italian opera in music, the first that had been in England',[4] and on 15 January G. B. Draghi's dances were performed in the production of Shadwell's adaptation of Shakes-

---

* *KM*, p. 280.

† *Grove's* (5th ed.), vol. III, p. 739 (Grabu), and vol. II, p. 25 (Cambert) respectively.

peare's *The Tempest*.* In May another performance of *The Tempest* included songs by Pietro Reggio,† which Purcell's former singing mates heard from behind the footlights, since on 16 May came down the order:

> It is His Majesty's pleasure that Mr. Turner and Mr. Hart or any other men or boys belonging to His Majesty's Chapel Royal that sing in *The Tempest* at His Royal Highness's Theatre do remain in town all the week (during His Majesty's absence from Whitehall) to perform that service, only Saturdays to repair to Windsor and to return to London on Mondays if there be occasion for them. And that [they] also perform the like service in the opera in the said theatre or any other thing in the like nature where their help may be desired upon notice given them thereof.‡

Nicola Matteis was a stellar figure in London's concert season that year, and remained on in England as a permanent, active, and very influential musician. At any rate, on 19 November, at the height of the season, John Evelyn reported in such enthusiastic vein as to suggest that no Londoner who was at all interested in music could have escaped hearing of him:

> I heard that stupendous Violin Signor Nicholao (with other rare musicians) whom certainly never mortal man exceeded on that instrument; he had a stroke so sweet, and made it speak like the voice of a man; and when he pleased, like a consort of several instruments ... nothing approached the violin in Nicholas hand: he seemed to be *spiritatoed*, and played such ravishing things on a ground as astonished us all.§

No documented account can be quoted to show that Purcell and Matteis actually did meet, as hinted by John Wilson in his book *Roger North on Music*, consequently no influence on Purcell during this early period can be proved conclusively. However, if Matteis did nothing more than create new respect and popularity for the violin among England's musical public, he accomplished enough in paving the way for Purcell and other young English composers.

* *Grove's* (5th ed.), vol. II, p. 760.
† Downes, p. 34.   ‡ *KM*, p. 271.
§ Evelyn, 19 Nov. 1674; see also North, *The Musicall Grammarian*, pp. 25, 34–37, and *Memoirs of Musick* (ed. E. F. Rimbault), pp. 122–3, for accounts, respectively, of his success as a teacher, of his intemperate arrogance upon first arrival, and of his later tractability.

Less than a fortnight after hearing Matteis, Evelyn reported on 2 December that he had

heard Signor Francisco on the harpsichord, esteemed one of the most excellent masters in Europe on that instrument: then came Nicholao with his violin and struck all mute, but Mrs Knight, who sung incomparably, and doubtless has the greatest reach of any English woman: she had lately been roaming in Italy, and was much improved in that quality.[5]

Matteis's spectacular rise and the new popularity enjoyed at the time by other Italian musicians in London preceded by only a few weeks the eclipse of Grabu's star early in 1675. On 29 January Nicholas Staggins replaced Grabu as Master of the King's Music. As an indication of Charles II's change of musical policy about this time the replacement is doubly significant. Staggins was an Englishman, and his appointment would have silenced, or at least rendered ineffective, the complaints of those Francophobes in and around the Court who, like Pelham Humfrey earlier, had little respect or love for the French composers and musicians whom Charles II had brought to Whitehall. Moreover, Staggins appears to have been an Italophile where music was concerned, and this also would have fitted in with the pattern of events that accompanied the rise of Italian music and the concomitant decline of French music at Court.

On 14 July Pelham Humfrey died (quite suddenly, it seems) of some unknown malady.[*] So, almost before he had got to know one teacher, Purcell found himself under the supervision of another, John Blow,[6] who was sworn into two of Humfrey's positions simultaneously,[†] a week after the latter was buried, on 17 July, in the cloisters of Westminster Abbey near the south-east door.[‡]

John Blow was, like Thomas Purcell, an expert and seasoned pluralist. He had been one of the organists at Westminster Abbey since 1668, a musician for the king's virginals since 1669, and a Gentleman of the Chapel Royal since 15 March 1674. On the death of Humfrey he acquired two new positions, as Master of the

---

[*] *Grove's* (5th ed.), vol. IV, p. 404; see also *KM*, p. 273.
[†] *KM*, p. 273.   [‡] *Grove's* (5th ed.), loc. cit.

Children of the Chapel Royal and composer in His Majesty's Private Music. Unquestionably, young Purcell had much to learn from his new master, even though there was but ten years' difference in their ages.[7]

A fellow pupil from about September 1674 was William Holder,[*] an ex-chorister and probably the son of the Canon of St. Paul's (later Sub-Dean of the Chapel Royal), who may well have been the composer of the service and the two anthems preserved in the Tudway manuscripts.[†] Henry Purcell may also have been composing about this time.

What Blow taught his young charges in the art of song composition need not be left entirely to conjecture, for he compiled two pedagogical methods, which undoubtedly reflect his principles of teaching music. One of these, 'Rules for playing of a Through Bass upon Organ and Harpsicon' [sic],[‡] represents the kind of training Purcell would have had in accompanying various songs and instrumental pieces; and the other, 'Rules for Composition', reveals some of the general principles and techniques of composition that he had learned.[§] For the most part his precepts are so simple, indeed so fundamental, as to give weight to Mr. Watkins Shaw's theory that he may have written them as a series of lessons for the young Henry Purcell.[||]

That Blow did teach Purcell is certain, from the commendatory verse in Blow's *Amphion Anglicus* (1700) by Henry Hall, who was also a pupil under Blow's instruction at this time and who had left the Chapel Royal only shortly before Purcell did:

> The Art of Descant, late our Albion's boast
> With that of staining glass, we thought was lost;
> Till in this work we all with wonder view

[*] *KM*, p. 288, recording a warrant for £30 to Blow for the maintenance of Holder, dated 1 April 1675, but made retrospective to 29 Sept. 1674.

[†] British Museum, Harleian MSS. 7338–42.

[‡] British Museum, Add. MS. 34072, folios 1–5. See also F. T. Arnold, *The Art of Accompaniment from a Thorough-Bass*, pp. 163–72. According to Arnold, the MS. is probably in Blow's handwriting.

[§] British Museum, Add. MS. 30933, folios 163–73*v*.

[||] *Grove's* (5th ed.), vol. II, p. 766; see also the *Musical Times* for Sept. 1936, p. 835.

Whatever art with order'd notes can do,
Corelli's heights, with great Bassani's too;
And Britain's Orpheus learned his art from you.

A warrant for a new felt hat arrived at Michaelmas 1674* to remind Henry Purcell of his days as a chorister. But by this autumn he may have begun, at least unofficially, his professional connection with Westminster Abbey, a connection that was to continue for the rest of his life. It was no doubt a matter of great pride to him to become a member of an establishment that could boast of the daily service of distinguished professional musicians such as, in addition to the men mentioned above, John Gostling, Thomas Blagrave, the hot-headed but very talented Michael Wise, William Turner.

But of his activities for the remainder of the year, nothing is known. Very likely he witnessed the elaborate preparations for Crowne's *Calisto*, for which Hall Theatre was gloriously refurbished. This was the last of a long tradition of self-contained English masques. Perhaps Purcell attended a rehearsal or two (as Evelyn must have done), even though he may have been unable to attend the performance or participate in it himself.† What he may have thought of this lavishly expensive production is a matter for conjecture. From a purely musical point of view, however, he would not have been much impressed by Nicholas Staggins's feeble music. If the few surviving songs are representative, the performance would have been a waste of time, however impressive the spectacle or entertaining the dances may have been.[8] His own masques, which were soon to be produced within operas, semi-operas,‡ and stage plays, would establish new musical standards for this form.

John Banister, who had had to step down for Grabu, played on as a lowly fiddler in the king's band, even though his reputation among London chamber music lovers had risen considerably by this time.[9] His views on the fall of his old rival and on Staggins's

* *KM*, p. 275.
† Evelyn, 15 Dec. 1674. See also Boswell, pp. 177 ff.; and A. Nicoll, *The Stuart Masques and the Renaissance Stage* (London, 1964), *passim*.
‡ Roger North coined this term; it appears in *Memoirs of Musick*, pp. 115–16.

new preferment have not been recorded. However, his reaction to this, as to other happenings at Court, may be imagined from the attitude he exhibited in making so bold as to sell his livery allotment (presumably in perpetuity) for £40.* No doubt he needed the money, as did others of his colleagues at this time. But he was less patient than they.

Whether or not Staggins's appointment had any effect on Thomas Purcell's connection with the king's violins cannot be discovered. It may be significant that he is not listed among the nine musicians who accompanied Charles II to Newmarket for nineteen days, from 9 to 27 March. Nor does the name Purcell appear in the warrant of 27 May 1675 for musicians employed by Staggins for the 'masque at Whitehall', although a very large and very interesting complement of performers was called for the event.† However, he continued to collect each year his five liveries and, presumably, attendant fees, in addition to his stipend as groom of the robes.

Meanwhile, Purcell was finding his way into his new job as apprentice to John Hingeston. During those first months his tasks as instrumental repairman and tuner for the Court establishment‡ must have been demanding and tedious, if at times challenging. These duties no doubt served Purcell in good stead in his later career as a composer. In those times close acquaintance with all instruments was considered an important qualification for a composer, as we know from Pelham Humfrey's statements concerning Grabu, who, he said, did not know how to play any instrument and therefore could not compose.§ He therefore no doubt profited much from his association with Hingeston, who not only repaired and tuned instruments, but was also a distinguished organist, violist, and composer. We may be sure that Purcell learned quickly, for in 1675 he was paid £2 for tuning the organ at Westminster Abbey, presumably on his own responsibility.[10]

About this time Purcell also received £5 for 'pricking out' some

* KM, p. 288; the agreement, with another musician, John Hill, was drawn up on 3 April 1675.
† KM, p. 290.   ‡ See p. 35 above.   § Pepys, 15 Nov. 1667.

organ parts. Westrup quite rightly challenges the notion that this payment had anything to do with an official appointment of Purcell as copyist. Regular copyists were paid far more than this paltry sum.[11] However, I think it is wrong to assume that this kind of work, like his slightly later work of copying Tudor anthems, was of small importance, either to the royal musical establishment or to Purcell himself. Sixteen years after the Restoration Purcell was indeed copying the anthems of Elizabethan and Tudor composers, and, as even slight acquaintance with his own anthems will prove, learned a great deal in the process.[12]

From 26 June until summer's end Charles II retired to Windsor,[*] accompanied by his musical retinue, as may be seen by a warrant for payment of £410. 8s., which Thomas Purcell distributed to eighteen Gentlemen of the Chapel Royal and an organist, John Blow.[†] Neither Hingeston nor his apprentice, young Purcell, is mentioned on the list, an omission which suggests that they did not go to Windsor until 15 August, although Staggins[‡] and, presumably, the rest of the musical entourage had been there all the summer. So for six weeks Purcell would not have had his regular instruction from Blow.

What his activities may have been during this period it is impossible to say for certain. He may have used this period of relative calm and quiet to finish his annual tuning of the organ in Westminster Abbey — a task for which he received £2 again the following Michaelmas. It is fairly safe to assume that he would have spent as much time as could be spared from his duties for Hingeston (and perhaps various odd musical jobs around the Abbey) to study and practise composition mainly on his own initiative, very likely through copying and studying 'old masters'.

On 24 October the main event on the day calendar at Westminster Abbey was the burial in the cloisters of Christopher Gibbons, who had died four days earlier.[§] His death severed another of the few remaining strands connecting pre-Cromwellian

---

* Bryant, p. 244. † KM, p. 294.
‡ KM, p. 292. § Westminster Abbey Registers, p. 189.

musical traditions with those of the Restoration. Gibbons, more famous as harpsichordist and organist than as composer, no doubt exerted an important influence on young Henry Purcell, whose main responsibilities as a practical musician were to be those he held as a keyboard artist. Christopher Gibbons had received his earliest training at the Chapel Royal while Orlando, his father, was organist there.* No doubt he was thoroughly grounded in the fundamentals of polyphonic music, both as regards actual composition and playing extempore. After his father's death on 5 June 1625 young Christopher, then just ten, is said to have been adopted by his uncle Edward (Orlando's elder brother), who was in charge of the musical establishment at Exeter Cathedral. There Christopher would have gained further training in traditional polyphonic style during his thirteen years of study and, presumably, apprenticeship under his uncle's guidance.[13]

His presence at Court and at Westminster Abbey thus established a definite link with the broad traditions of early Caroline and Jacobean music — a link which no doubt helped to provide Henry Purcell with the feeling for native English musical style which is so manifest in all his works, early and late. How important this influence may have been for Purcell's development as a keyboard artist must remain a moot point, since much of such influence would have been reflected in improvisatory techniques of which there are no contemporary descriptions or criticisms on record.

However, several pieces of circumstantial evidence suggest that Gibbons may have been intimately acquainted with Purcell and his family circle. In 1656 Gibbons was in the orchestra for the performance of D'Avenant's *Siege of Rhodes* in which, as noted earlier, Henry Purcell the elder had taken the part of Mustapha. From 1665 onwards the records show that Christopher Gibbons occupied the house in Great Almonry South in which the Purcells had lived up to the time of the death of Henry the elder in 1664. Furthermore, Orlando Gibbons's full anthems 'Hosanna to the son of David', 'Lift up your heads', and 'Almighty and everlasting God' are to be found as some of the few compositions

* Pulver, p. 198.

dating from before the Commonwealth which Purcell copied shortly after this time, presumably for his own study, since these full scores would not have been useful in other ways.[14]

The influence of the Gibbons family would also have reached Purcell at one remove through Matthew Locke, who had gone to Exeter as a chorister in 1638, the year in which Christopher Gibbons had taken up his appointment as organist at Winchester. Locke's influence upon Purcell has been made much of, on documentary evidence that is at best circumstantial and, at worst, hearsay. The best evidence is to be found in a comparison of Locke's and Purcell's musical styles. Various affinities between Locke's and Purcell's idioms do indicate greater rapport than can be explained by their sharing a common tradition or similar professional standing in English music. But there is scarcely anything more specific to go on in establishing a direct relationship.

The documentary evidence consists of the vague reference by Pepys mentioned earlier* and one letter. For the existence of the letter there is only the dubious testimony of E. F. Rimbault, as transmitted by Cummings, who wrote that he was 'indebted to the late Dr. Rimbault for a copy':

Dear Harry, — Some of the gentlemen of His Majesty's Musick will honour my poor lodgings with their company this evening, and I would have you come and join them. Bring with thee, Harry, thy last anthem, and also the canon we tried over together at our last meeting. Thine in all kindness,

M. Locke

Savoy, March 16

Despite the inaccessibility of this manuscript and the careless manner in which it was first published,† the information it presents is worth considering. It is at least interesting enough, I think, to warrant begging the question of authenticity until such time as further evidence comes to light. If only because documents of any kind are extremely scarce for this period, the letter ought

* See p. 6 above.
† Cummings, p. 27. For instance, it is unlikely that Locke would have used both polite and familiar form ('you' and 'thee') in addressing one and the same person.

not to be dismissed, even though in the past Rimbault and Cummings have not always proved the most reliable of authors.

The orthography and style of the letter seem authentic and the allusions to Locke's circumstances are credible enough, even though the notion of his 'trying over' an anthem in a private musical gathering (presumably held for enjoyment, as the tone of the invitation would suggest) seems unusual.[15] Locke's interest in an anthem — the most 'Anglican' of musical forms — would be hard to justify if Anthony à Wood's charge that he had 'turned Papist' shortly after becoming organist to Queen Catherine of Portugal were true.*

The date of the letter, unfortunately, cannot be precisely ascertained, since only month and day are given. However, various deductions make 1676 seem the most likely year. By 16 March 1676 Locke would have gained firm enough control over the Chapel Royal band (over which he officiated during Staggins's leave of absence for study in Italy)[16] for his invitation to 'some of the gentlemen of His Majesty's Music' to bear enough weight to bring them out.

Considering Locke's well-documented and long-standing relationship with the Purcell family,† the intimate relationship between himself and Henry the younger may well have existed. The extremely personal note struck in the text which Purcell set (and may have written) in memory of Locke's death further increases this possibility. It is unlikely, in view of suspicions about Matthew Locke's being a Papist, that he would have ventured into print with such an avowal as the following unless Locke had really been his friend: 'On the death of his worthy friend Matthew Locke, Music Composer-in-Ordinary to His Majesty, and Organist of Her Majesty's Chapel, who died in August 1677.'[17]

Perhaps the most important thing that Locke would have

* Bodleian Library, MS. Wood D.19(4), fo. 86v: 'Lock (Matthew) was bred a chorister in the Cathedral Church of Exeter (being, as I presume, a Devonian born) while William Wake was Master of the choristers there — Organist to Queen Catherine of Portugal — Afterwards turned Papist.'

† He composed the vocal music for the fourth entry in the *Siege of Rhodes* and was involved in the musical event recorded by Pepys for 21 Feb. 1659/60, as discussed above, p. 3.

passed on to Purcell, however, was a notion of the strength and nobility of the English musical tradition — from which Purcell had already imbibed much (from his work with Humfrey, and his duties as choir boy, copyist, organ novice, and so forth). However, it is also likely that Locke would have cultivated in young Purcell something of a taste for the vocal and instrumental styles of the great Italian schools, just then establishing undisputed pre-eminence in the musical world, what with the superior publications, performers, teachers, and composers these centres exported in such great quantities. English importation of all these in the latter half of the seventeenth century — a process paralleling the wholesale transplantation of the Italian madrigal in the first — was to become a significant factor in English musical life by the time Purcell came of age.

CHAPTER IV

PURCELL'S PROFESSIONAL DÉBUT

Upon Matthew Locke's death several new musical positions fell open at Court, as elsewhere in Westminster and London. He had held at least three appointments as composer (i.e. for the Private Music, for wind instruments, and for violin respectively) in addition to his duties as organist to Queen Catherine. Furthermore, he had had various musical commitments to London's theatrical life. Purcell, who succeeded him as composer-in-ordinary to the violins on 10 September 1677,* and who seems to have inherited some of his theatrical contacts as well, was the youngest of those who were advanced upon Locke's death.[1] The fact that he was appointed composer-in-ordinary, though but eighteen, adds further weight to the theory that Locke had been his mentor. Earlier, Purcell may well have earned the mantle that thus fell upon him by following the usual procedure of serving as musician extraordinary (that is to say, without regular pay) for a post that was to become his 'upon death or other avoidance' of the incumbent.

In these years Court finances had become so shaky that many must have wondered what difference it made to be registered in the accounts either as 'in-ordinary' or 'extraordinary' — i.e. with or without a regular salary. About this time the Gentlemen of the Chapel Royal banded together to petition for £877. 7s., owing to them since the summer of 1674, when they had travelled to Windsor. Despite the annotation 'Resolution hereon: let something be done', matters apparently were allowed to slide, for later the sum petitioned for grew to the alarming total of £1,422, and

---

* *KM*, p. 322; see also p. 282, where Purcell's name has been inserted for that of Matthew Locke as the recipient of livery fees of £16. 2s. 6d. per annum.

the Gentlemen now had the backing of a letter written by the Bishop of London himself.*

Another musician suffering from the Court's insolvency was Louis Grabu, now in very miserable state. Politically he had submitted to his 'grievous misfortune', even endured the king's 'willingness to receive another person into his place during pleasure'. But financial distress he could not face with such equanimity, and he submitted a series of abject petitions for aid.†

Charles II dodged the immediate issue by asking for an itemized account, which Grabu drew up for Arlington to submit a month later. Arlington, then Secretary of State, reported that Grabu was owed a total of £627. 9s. 6d., adding that he found his condition 'to be very poor and miserable'.[2] If the following letter, written by Henry Savile to the Earl of Rochester on 25 June 1678, may be credited at all, poor Grabu's situation must have seemed doubly hard, for Nicholas Staggins apparently lost no time in assuming full control:

From the rising of the sun to the setting thereof, I see nothing that pleases my eyes or hear nothing but what grates my ears; only I am promised a moment's titillation by Mr. Staggins, who is come over with great credit and many new airs. His Majesty has already constituted him lord paramount over all music. He may reign there like a Great Turk and cut whose cat's-guts he please if the harmony be not to his liking. With what moderation he will use his absolute power, I leave it to fate and the immortal gods to determine.‡

The French musical colony may have been dismayed by such maltreatment of a former chief, but their activities at Court about this time reflect no general despondency. For the celebration of King Charles's birthday on 29 May, the French complement turned out in full array to perform Paisible's music for Madame de la Roche-Guilhen's comedy-ballet, Rare-en-tout. In the wording of the order (passed through Nicholas Staggins, or, he being absent, through Matthew Locke) there is the suggestion that royal command was felt to be needed to curb recalcitrance:

* Cal. S. P. Dom. as quoted in Westrup, p. 42.
† KM, p. 317.
‡ Hist. MSS. Comm., Bath MSS. vol. II, fo. 165.

22 May 1677.

That all His Majesty's musicians do attend to practise in the theatre at Whitehall at such times as Madame Le Roch and Mr. Paisible shall appoint for the practising of such music as is to be in the French comedy to be acted before His Majesty on the 29 May instant.*

Purcell, who was shortly to become an official composer in his own right, no doubt absorbed the experience as part of his musical education. However, it may have been from affairs such as this that he gained the dislike for the 'levity and balladry of our neighbours' of which he wrote in his preface to the trio-sonatas of 1683.

In such quasi-bankrupt times for musicians Purcell no doubt was glad to receive on 13 February the benefits of a warrant for more clothing:

Warrant for payment for one and twenty ells, three quarters of holland, for four whole shirts, four half shirts, and for bands and cuffs for Henry Purcell, a child gone off from the Chapel.†

Within eight months, however, with his appointment as a musician-in-ordinary and an annual livery allowance of £16. 2s. 6d., he must have considered mere clothing warrants as part of his bygone boyhood career. Already he had enjoyed an official (though as yet apparently unpaid) position as assistant to John Hingeston for some five years; for at least three years he had been de facto, if not officially, organ-tuner and copyist at Westminster Abbey (where he was again paid £2 at Michaelmas 1677‡), and from 10 September he had begun to enjoy the high status of a regular appointment at the Chapel Royal. Furthermore, his reputation as a composer was considerably enhanced by the appearance in print of five songs and by the recognition accompanying the performance of an anthem and two chamber works which may with fair certainty be attributed to this year.[3]

On 13 September he finished writing the table of contents for a series of anthems which he had previously scored in fair copy,[4] presumably for his own use and study, since these scores would

---

* KM, p. 318. According to McGuinness, fo. 43, Blow's 'The Birth of Jove' was written for the same occasion.

† KM, p. 315.   ‡ WAM 33712 (Treasurer's Account, 1677), fo. 5.

have been of little use in practical performance. It can scarcely be attributed to coincidence that many of the anthems he copied were written by persons who had been his teachers and mentors. The list is short enough to be quoted in full:

Anon.	Instrumental movement à 4 in E minor		fo. 26*v*
Adrian Batten	Hear my prayer, O God	Full anthem	fo. 118 (rev.)
John Blow	Christ being risen	Verse anthem	fo. 93*v* (rev.)
	Cry aloud	Verse anthem	fo. 28*v*
	God is our hope	Full, with verse	fo. 141 (rev.)
	My God, my soul	Verse anthem	fo. 108 (rev.)
	O God, wherefore art Thou	Full, with verse	fo. 138 (rev.)
	O Lord God of my salvation	Verse anthem	fo. 99 (rev.)
	O Lord I have sinned (For General Monk's burial, 1668)	Verse anthem	fo. 142*v* (rev.)
	O sing unto the Lord	Verse anthem	fo. 9*v*
	Save me, O God	Verse anthem	fo. 134*v* (rev.)
	Sing we merrily	Verse anthem	fo. 14*v* (bef. 1674)
William Byrd	Bow Thine ear, O Lord	Full anthem	fo. 129 (rev.)
	O Lord, make Thy servant	Full anthem	fo. 125 (rev.)
	Prevent us, O Lord	Full anthem	fo. 126 (rev.)
William Child	Sing we merrily	Full anthem	fo. 114*v* (rev.)
Orlando Gibbons	Almighty and Everlasting God	Full anthem	fo. 112 (rev.)
	Hosanna to the son of David	Full anthem	fo. 136 (rev.)
	Lift up your heads	Full anthem	fo. 124 (rev.)
Nathaniel Giles	O give thanks	Full anthem	fo. 119*v* (rev.)
Pelham Humfrey	Lift up your heads	Verse anthem	fo. 23*v*
	Like as the hart	Verse anthem	fo. 7
	Lord, teach us to number	Verse anthem	fo. 21
	O Lord, my God	Verse anthem	fo. 4
	O praise the Lord	Verse anthem	fo. 1
Matthew Locke	I will hear what the Lord	Verse anthem	fo. 40*v*
	Lord, let me know mine end	Verse anthem	fo. 133*v* (rev.)
	Sing unto the Lord	Verse anthem	fo. 31
	The Lord hear thee	Verse anthem	fo. 38*v*
	Turn Thy face from my sins	Full, with verse	fo. 131 (rev.)
	When the son of man	Verse anthem	fo. 36*v*

William Mundy	O Lord, I bow the knee	Full anthem	fo. 122*v* (rev.)
Thomas Tallis	I call and cry	Full anthem	fo. 127*v* (rev.)
Thomas Tomkins	O Lord, I have loved	Full anthem	fo. 120*v* (rev.)

(All those pieces marked with reverse foliation appear to have been copied in a later hand, and may well be contemporary with or later than the date indicated in Purcell's autograph inscription on a fly-leaf: 'God bless Mr. Henry Purcell/1682 September the 10th'.)*

The wealth of evidence concerning his professional activity makes it all the more puzzling that the Westminster Abbey Treasurer's Account for 1678 should be the earliest extant records to provide any information on Purcell's schooling. Until this year Charles Purcell (Henry's cousin) had been studying as a 'Bishop's Boy' at St. Peter's College, Westminster, since 1670.[5] He was named (as 'Carolo Pursell', the documents being drawn up in Latin) in the same entry each year down to 1678. Apparently the accountant entered it again that year, then, discovering an error or perhaps making a last-minute change, scraped off the name Charles from the vellum, replacing it with 'Henrico' (later 'Henrici' and even 'Henri'), who continued to be named until 1680.†

In view of Purcell's age — by 1678 he was nineteen — and in consideration of the musical prominence he had already attained, this evidence of his having received a scholarship requires some explanation. Really there are only two possibilities. Either there was another Henry Purcell at Westminster at that time — a remote possibility — or the regulations concerning the age and required studies and activities of 'Bishop's Boys' were relaxed in Purcell's case.

If only because the presence at Westminster of another promising student named Henry Purcell seems scarcely possible in view of the lack of any contemporary mention of such a remarkable

* Fitzwilliam Museum Library, Cambridge, MS. 88. See Plate 8(*a*).

† The names of both Charles and Henry Purcell are listed in the Westminster School rolls for these years. See G. F. Russell Barker and Alan H. Stenning (eds.), *The Record of Old Westminsters* (London, 1928), vol. II, entries for Charles and Henry Purcell respectively. See Plate 3(*b*).

situation, the second of these two possibilities seems more plausible. Moreover, Dr. Richard Busby, the headmaster, was a friend of Purcell's, as is known from the fact that he left him a gold ring in his Will.* Faced with a sudden vacancy in the list of 'Bishop's Boys' (it is hard to think of any other satisfactory explanation for the clumsy erasure of Charles's and substitution of Henry's name which spoil the tidy, professional appearance of the page) and concerned for the welfare of an extremely talented young friend, who must have been working hard for little recompense, Busby may well have found it easy to temper any regulations that might have disqualified the young genius. Purcell, on the other hand, may have welcomed an opportunity to improve his education, which he still felt justified in depreciating publicly as late as 1683, when he wrote of himself in his preface to the trio-sonatas:

He is not ashamed to own his unskilfulness in the Italian language; but that's the unhappiness of his education, which cannot justly be accounted his fault....†

Finally, the shortage of cash at Court and the inordinate length of time Purcell had spent waiting for an opening may have given Busby, or perhaps other officials, reason to extend this encouragement to Purcell. Whatever the cause or explanation, it is fairly certain that Purcell spent at least the first part of 1678 as a 'Bishop's Boy'; for, as the following entry reveals:

Et in Denar. solut. ad Scholas Henrici. Purcell, Rogero Cooper, Edward Roberts et Sam. Langley xxv^{li} et Reverendis. Decano Thesaur ad Ludi magister xx^s ex dono Reverendis. Patris Johani Episcop Lincolnien. nup. Decan. Westmonastr. in toto hoc ano xxvi^{li}‡

(And for money for the use of the scholars Henry Purcell, Roger Cooper, Edward Roberts, and Samuel Langley, £25; and from the very Reverend Dean Treasurer to the Master of the School 20 shillings from the gift of the very Reverend Father, John Bishop of Lincoln, formerly Dean of Westminster. For the whole of this year, £26.)

---

* Cf. Frances Purcell's nuncupative Will, App. Two, IX, 3.

† Preface, 'To the ingenuous reader', from Purcell's Trio Sonatas of 1683, from the facsimile in the modern practical edition published by the Lyrebird Press, Paris, 1936.

‡ WAM 33713 (Treasurer's Account, 1678), fo. 5; see also 33714 and 33715.

And whether, with the increasing demands made on him as a professional musician, he was able to give the necessary time to his studies or not, it is a matter of record that he continued to receive the annual stipend up to and including Michaelmas 1680, at which time he may have been at last and totally disqualified by marriage.*

A 'Bishop's Boy' or 'Lord's Scholar' was one who held an exhibition under the benefaction of the Reverend John Williams, Bishop of Lincoln and later Archbishop of York before the Commonwealth, according to G. F. Russell Barker and Alan Stenning.† Elsewhere, these same authorities describe the founding of these scholarships and their administration as follows:

In 1623, while Dean of Westminster, [the Rev. John Williams] purchased two fee farm rents of £14 and £13 6s. 8d. issuing respectively out of manors of Sudbury and Great Stanmore in the county of Middlesex. By a deed dated April 26, 1624 he declared that the Dean and Chapter of Westminster should hold these rents in trust for four scholars of his own foundation, two of whom should be natives of Wales and two natives of the diocese of Lincoln, 'to be educated and maintained in the Grammar School of St. Peter's College in Westminster, and there to have their free education until they shall be from thence elected and transplanted into St. John's College, Cambridge'.

Amongst other provisions he ordered that each of the four scholars should be paid £5 annually 'towards their diet and maintenance' and 20s. should be allowed each scholar for a 'gown of cloth which shall be purple in colour'.

By letters patent dated Dec. 30, 1623, having previously given certain benefices and lands for their support, he founded two fellowships and four scholarships in St. John's College, Cambridge, and ordained that four scholars of the foundation should be chosen from the scholars of the foundation at Westminster, two to be natives of Wales and two of the diocese of Lincoln, or for want of boys so qualified boys born within the liberties of Westminster.

Adequate funds were not, however, provided to carry out the scheme, and though four boys, known first as Lord's Scholars and afterwards as Bishop's Boys, were annually elected at the School, but few of them were admitted to the scholarships at St. John's.‡

The bearing this may have had on the problem of ascertaining the place of Purcell's birth has already been discussed. But the additional light it sheds on Purcell's schooling remains to be

---

* See pp. 80–82 below.
  † *The Record of Old Westminsters*, vol. II, p. 66.
  ‡ Barker and Stenning, op. cit. vol. II, p. 1109.

explored. As a 'Bishop's Boy' Purcell would have come under the supervision of Dr. Richard Busby, the 'Flogging Head' of Westminster School, whom his charges had privately dubbed 'Sir Richard Birch-Hard'. Whatever his reputation in this respect, no seventeenth-century Englishman had greater fame for fostering intellectual development. Richard Steele, who lived long enough to assess Busby's teaching fairly by the mature accomplishments of his pupils, was only one of many who paid high tribute to him as the English Chiron of his age:

I must confess (and I have often reflected upon it) that I am of opinion that Busby's genius for education had as great an effect upon the age he lived in as that of any ancient philosopher, without excepting one, had upon his contemporaries. . . . He had a power of raising what the lad had in him to the utmost height. . . .*

Unfortunately there is at present no way of discovering what Purcell may have learned from this man who had taught John Dryden, John Locke, Christopher Wren, Henry Aldrich, along with a great many other leading intellects of the Restoration. But there is proof that Busby regarded the young composer with some esteem, in that he willed him money for a gold mourning ring. Purcell is not mentioned by name in the fifth (nuncupative) codicil to Busby's Will. But there is no doubt that he was the organist to whom the ring was bequeathed, for Frances Purcell specifically mentioned 'a mourning ring of Dr. Busby's' in her Will, made out on 7 February 1706.†

That Purcell was beyond the usual age for admission to St. Peter's College matters little. Busby was a rare pedagogue, with imagination enough to see beyond such petty regulations. Even before Purcell's time he had admitted Charles Sackville, later Lord Buckhurst, at nineteen. Nor is there reason to wonder that Purcell should have passed his twenty-first birthday and already become famous before giving up his scholarship. Samuel Johnson said that it was known 'to have been the practice of Dr. Busby to

---

* *The Lover*, 27 April 1714 (no. 27), as quoted in R. Blanchard (ed.), *Richard Steele's Periodic Journalism, 1714–16* (Oxford, 1959), p. 99.

† See App. Two, IX, 3.

detain those youths long at school of whom he had formed the highest expectations'.* It would be idle to speculate further on Purcell's actual schooling. But even without more precise evidence, it is safe to assume that Busby's influence was important to his development.

Whatever his activities in gaining a general education during those early years, Purcell's musical development was not neglected. Much of his practical training derived from the experiences he had had as Hingeston's apprentice, and as part-time copyist and organ-tuner at Westminster Abbey. Moreover, he must have had a great deal of time to practise playing the organ and to study composition, since he was so soon to qualify for two of England's highest posts in these two pursuits.

As a composer he had no doubt learned a great deal from Captain Cooke, Pelham Humfrey, Matthew Locke, and John Blow, not only by direct instruction, but by professional contact and close study of their music. He may also have learned a great deal from John Jenkins, who, apparently because of a final illness, was replaced at Court by John Moss on 14 October 1678.† At least, so the fantasias and other polyphonic chamber works that he was beginning to compose at about this time seem to show. Both Jenkins and Purcell belonged to the Norths' musical circle, and it is probable that the young Restoration genius and the grand old man of English instrumental polyphony became acquainted before the latter died, aged eighty-six, on 27 October 1678.‡

With Jenkins's death, yet another important connection between the Restoration and England's musical past was severed — but not before young Purcell had had time to absorb some of the musical tradition that the old composer had mastered. Indeed, Jenkins, whose fancies, along with those of his contemporaries, have too long lain under the obloquy of Burney's stern *obiter dicta*,§ created a great corpus of instrumental chamber works of all varieties, which undoubtedly provided both stylistic nurture

---

* As quoted in G. F. R. Barker, *Memoir of Richard Busby (1606–95)* (London, 1895), p. 122.
† *KM*, p. 337.   ‡ *Grove's* (5th ed.), vol. IV, p. 610.
§ Burney, vol. II, pp. 283–5.

and formal paradigms for young Purcell. In Jenkins's fantasias, particularly, were fulfilled those tendencies towards full dramatic and emotive expression, along with integrated thematic development, which had begun early in the century with Byrd, Orlando Gibbons, and their generation.*

The earliest masters of the fantasia had achieved technical emancipation from the rather rigid style of the motet, soon after dropping the text, by the obvious new freedom of melodic articulation and ornamentation. So far as its aesthetic spirit was concerned, it remained a part of the motet tradition until such time as music's own dramatic and emotive powers were discovered and developed.† Byrd and Gibbons founded the new style, which had a brief period of efflorescence among Jacobean consort composers, before being driven into private life by the Puritans. The effects of this seeming official suppression were not long lasting.‡ Jenkins, truly the 'mirror and wonder of his age', as Anthony à Wood styled him,§ wrote a great deal of music which now strikes the ear as 'Purcellian', perhaps because of the universal eponymic process which tends to unite every historic period around some monumental personality, even in music. In this instance both figures involved and their music are of such quality that the epithet can be taken as a tribute to both, whatever myth-making processes may have been at work.

* Cf. E. H. Meyer, *English Chamber Music* (London, 1946), pp. 217 ff.

† Cf. Robert A. Warner's 'The Fantasia in the Works of John Jenkins'. Warner revises and corrects E. H. Meyer's earlier, incomplete list, as given in *Die Mehrstimmige Spielmusik des 17. Jahrhunderts in Nord- und Mitteleuropa.*

‡ See Scholes, Pulver, Tilmouth.

§ *Life and Times*, vol. I, p. 209.

CHAPTER V

MUSIC ON THE RESTORATION POLITICAL SCENE

From 1678 to 1680 Charles II had trouble with other kinds of myth-making. On 12 August 1678, at the instigation of Titus Oates, a man with a history of trouble-making and opportunism, one Christopher Kirkby warned the king of a 'Popish Plot' to murder him and place his brother on the throne. On 27 and 28 September Oates and a fellow conspirator, Israel Tonge, were summoned to appear before the Privy Council, where Tonge produced a mysterious bundle of papers purporting to give details of this Jesuit plot. Then Oates was called in, and

as this strange creature — with neckless head and mouth set flat in the centre of the circle of his low brow and vast chin — told his story, the Council sat amazed. Gradually the wondrous tale unfolded: the Pope, the French King, the General of the Jesuits, the Provincials in England, Spain and Ireland, the Archbishops of Dublin and Tuam, and the Rectors of the Jesuit Colleges, linked together in a mighty plot to kill the King, set up the Duke of York, plunge Ireland in blood, impose Catholicism by the sword, and destroy English commerce; the four Irish ruffians who were to do the bloody work at Windsor, the Lancashire incendiaries to fire London, and the three thousand cut-throats to massacre the sleeping citizens; the poisoners in attendance, who included Wakeman, the Queen's Physician, and Coleman, the Duchess of York's Secretary. It was a horrible conception, and one well attuned to Protestant fears.*

After Oates had stirred Parliament on 21 October, and especially after the spectacular murder of Edmund Godfrey (who had heard Oates's depositions), the 'Popish Plot' was fairly launched. Whether the 'plot' was really a Whig and 'Phanatick' stratagem or not is still a matter for historians to decide.

* Bryant, p. 270.

Later, Purcell's music was drawn into the conflict, when scurrilous, anti-Whig broadsheets were circulated with new words adapted to some of his stage songs. Two of the popular tunes from *Theodosius* appear often in this context. (See Plate 6, where the tune of 'Hail to the myrtle shade' does service for 'Hail to the Knight of the Post', a diatribe against Titus Oates.)

In any case battle lines were clearly drawn, and Charles II at last saw his Whig and Puritan enemies out in the open. Their number and their political strength were such that he found it necessary to dissemble his own Catholic sympathies, even to the extent of agreeing to the exclusion of James, Duke of York, from his counsels and from public affairs, and of bringing out, on 7 December, 'an order from the King and Council prohibiting His Majesty's subjects to resort to the chapels of Her Majesty or foreign ministers where the Romish worship is celebrated, under severest of penalties'.* However, Charles held firm against Oates when he would have implicated the queen. The king may not have won many skirmishes at this stage of his lifelong cold war with the Whig faction, but he displayed infinite sagacity in evasive and delaying actions — such as the postponement of the Yorkshire Feast, which was to have been held on 12 November — while he marshalled his own political and propagandistic forces.†

For such purposes music was pressed into service, one of its chief vehicles being the catch, which had usurped the place of the madrigal as the popular 'social' form for amateur performance in England. From its beginnings (about 1609, when Ravenscroft's *Pammelia* was first published) the catch had had strong political associations; it is not surprising that Purcell carried on the tradition, firmly established in the interim. The 'Papist' or 'Jesuit' plot, for instance, is commemorated in one of his most successful political catches:

> Now England's great council['s] assembled
> To make laws for English-born freemen.
> Since 'tis dang'rous to prate of matters of state
> Let's handle our wine and women.

* Luttrell, vol. I, p. 5.
† *London Gazette*, 31 Oct.–4 Nov.

> Let's drink to the senate's best thoughts
> For the good of the King and the nation.
> May they dig on the spot as deep for the plot
> As the Jesuits have laid the foundation.
>
> A plague of all zealots and fools,
> And each silly Protestant hater;
> Better turn cat-in-pan and live like a man
> Than be hang'd and die like a traitor.

Traditionally this piece has been assigned to the year 1676 on the basis of a sub-title in *A Choice Compendium* published by one J. H. in 1681: 'A catch made in time of Parliament, 1676'.* However, the parliamentary session alluded to in this catch may well have been that which began on 15 January 1678. It is likely that the parliamentary meeting referred to was that held on 21 October 1678, when Oates and Tonge were summoned to appear and to substantiate the strange story they were busily spreading. Furthermore, it was about this time, according to Maitland,† that Charles II had informed Parliament, who 'unanimously addressed His Majesty for removing all popish recusants out of the cities of London and Westminster'.

In such times not even the anthem was considered too sacred to use for the strengthening of the royal political image. Under Charles II's open patronage it had regained its erstwhile pre-eminence as the chief of Anglican musical forms. To Evelyn's disgust‡ and to Pepys's general, though never uncritical, delight,§ the king had openly encouraged the production of anthems conceived in the style of the continental Counter-Reformation motet. Hence, from the beginning of the Restoration, Cooke, Pelham Humfrey, and others had reinforced the popular appeal of their anthems by the introduction of secular, even operatic, characteristics. The introduction of instrumental symphonies and ritornelli, the emphasis on soloists and solo vocal ensembles by way of contrast with 'full' and choral passages and, particularly, the recitative-like, affective styles of the latter, reminded some of the theatre.[1] All this, by increasing the anthem's popularity among

---

* *Analytical Catalogue*, no. 261.   † Vol. I, p. 462.
‡ Evelyn, 21 Sept. 1662.   § Pepys, 14 Sept. 1662.

a wide audience, ensured its effectiveness as a means for popularizing the Court position. Faced with solid antagonism, even hostility, in Parliament, and beleaguered by harsh budgetary policies, Charles's political situation was such that he could not afford to overlook any opportunity to improve his situation.

At any rate, under Charles II's open patronage the English anthem flourished, along with other kinds of liturgical Anglican music, as vigorously as in Elizabethan and Jacobean times. At first, while the ravages wrought by the Interregnum on England's musical institutions were yet to be repaired, Tudor and 'Jacobethan' anthems were called in to fill the breach. But very soon after the Restoration, men such as Christopher Gibbons, William Child, Henry Lawes, Matthew Locke, and, above all, Henry Cooke set to work in earnest to reconstruct England's musical culture, so sadly damaged by the military and political conflicts in which these same men had recently been engaged.

As in earlier times, the choice of texts was dictated by the Anglican liturgy, which provided for certain Psalms, hymns, and canticles for specific seasons. Within this 'proper' repertory there would have been scarcely any opportunity for topical allusion, except, perhaps, where coincidental correspondence between a 'proper' Psalm-text and a current event could be exploited. Where a Biblical passage would seem to reflect a given situation, it was even possible to invoke divine sanction for this or that political position.

But, as in its earlier periods, the Restoration anthem did not exist in a liturgical straitjacket. Rather, from its inception, it had also been used as a vehicle for hinting at State policy. At any rate, in anthems composed for important occasions (royal or otherwise) outside the divine service, there was larger scope for careful selection, or even editing, of texts. Sagacious politician that he was, Charles II did not neglect these opportunities to employ the anthem for a kind of communication that today might be called 'propagandistic'.

The Restoration anthem frequently represented the royal (i.e. Tory) position in musical dress. Hence texts were sometimes edited so as to reflect the bitter conflict between Whig and Tory that disturbed the calm of the last decades of the seventeenth century, with London as the main arena. It was for duty in this arena that the topical (read 'public relations') anthem was more often called into service. Those responsible within the Church were no doubt convinced that such means furthered the ends of a divinely ordained monarch, and suffered no religious scruples over possible tendentious programming of the Holy Scriptures.

Topical allusions in earlier anthems can be suspected in many cases and proved in at least a few. But, as in many another activity at his Court, Charles II, as a limited, not to say closely watched, monarch, found that he needed to outdo his predecessors in developing any technique that might bolster up the Court party's position. And if it was always anti-Whig in its drift, what of that? He who paid the fiddler — or at least who had promised to pay — had the right to call the tune.

Hence the Restoration anthem (if we are to understand its overall social significance) should be regarded as one of the most important musical expressions of Restoration society, at least until after the death of Charles II in 1685, when public concerts at last began to be self-sustaining, at times even profitable.* The importance to music-lovers of the musical part of the church service is shown by many entries in Pepys's *Diary*, such as the following:

To my Lord, and with him to Whitehall Chapel . . . After sermon, a brave anthem of Captain Cooke's, which he himself sung, and the King was well pleased with it!†

Like the Court ode, the anthem was part of King Charles's public relations paraphernalia. When it was an instrumentally accompanied anthem, there was really not much difference, musically speaking, between a large anthem, an ode, and even a masque for an opera or play. At first the Church's own cycle of annual events provided the occasions for which most anthems were written. As the anthem tradition developed, it became more and more the custom to find (or even edit) Psalm-texts to fit specific

---

* See pp. 223–8 below.
† 12 Aug. 1660; see also entries for 2 Sept., 7 Oct., *et al.*

5 'The Cabal', *c.* 1675. J. B. Medina

Titus Tell-Troth:

OR,

The PLOT-FOUNDER Confounded.

A Pleasant New S O N G. To the Tune of, *Hail to the Myrtle Shades.*

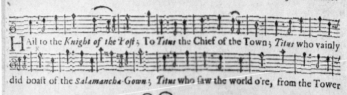

Hail to the *Knight of the Post*; To *Titus* the Chief of the Town; *Titus* who vainly did boast of the *Salamancha-Gown*; *Titus* who saw the world o're, from the Tower of *Valadolid*, Yet stood in the *White-horse* Door, and swore to it, like the *Creed.*

[2]
Titus at *Watton* in *May*,
  To *Titus* at *Islington*;
And *Titus* the self same day
  Both Here and There again.
Titus who ever swore *Truth*,
  His politick *Plots* to maintain,
And never yet bawk'd an *Oath*,
  When call'd to the *Test* again.

[3]
Then *Titus* was Meekest of all,
  When *Never a Peny in's Purse*,
And oft did on *Pickering* call,
  His Charity to Imburse.
But when He swore *Damnable Oaths*,
  And *Lying* esteemed no Sin,
Then *Titus* was *One* of those
  Whom the *Devil* had entred in.

[4]
Then *Titus* the Frown of Heav'n,
  And *Titus* a Plague upon Earth;
Titus who'l ne'r be *Forgiven*,
  Curs'd from his *Fatal Birth*;
Titus the *Curse* and the *Doom*
  Of the Rich and the Poor Man too;
Oh *Titus*, thou *Shred of a Loom*,
  What a plague dost thou mean to do?

[5]
Titus an *Orthodox Beast*,
  And *Titus* a *Presbyter Tall*;
Titus a *Popish Priest*,
  And *Titus* the shame of all;

Titus who ne'r had the skill
  The Wise with his *Plots* to deceive;
But *Titus* whose *Tongue* can kill;
  Whom Nature has made a Slave.

[6]
Titus the Light of the Town,
  Where *Zealots* and *Whigs* do resort;
Titus the Shame of the *Gown*,
  And *Titus* the Scorn of the *Court*;
Titus who Spew'd out the *Truth*,
  To Swallow the *Covenant*;
Yet never blush'd at an *Oath*,
  Whom *Lying* has made a *Saint.*

[7]
Yet *Titus* believed cou'd be
  Against any *Popish Lord*;
Whilst still against *S——y*
  The *Witness* and *Truth's* abhorr'd;
So *Titus* got Credit and Gold
  For *Lying*, nor thought it a Sin ;
But against *Dissenters* bold
  The *Truth* is not worth a pin.

[8]
Thus *Titus* Swore on apace,
  'Gainst those whom he never did see;
Yet *Titus* with brazen Face
  Wou'd our *Preserver* be.
But as *Titus* the foremost in Trust
  Discover'd this *Mystery*:
May *Titus* so be the *First*
  That leads to the *Triple-Tree.*

LONDON: Printed for *ALLEN BANKS*, 1682.

6 'Titus Tell-Troth: or, The Plot-Founder Confounded'

occasions of State, particularly when the sermon and anthem were part of a composite festive ceremony which began in a church and ended in a neighbouring banqueting hall, as did so many celebrations in those days.[2] Often the society responsible would be some guild or other business fraternity, the members of which saw no harm in mixing a little business with pleasure, throwing in a dash of religion as well.

As one of the most important musical genres of the Restoration the anthem[3] clearly reflected the conflict between the two main factions of society in seventeenth-century England: the royalists (or Tories), on the one hand, and the parliamentarians (or Whigs), on the other. Since Restoration anthem-composers drew almost exclusively upon the Book of Common Prayer[4] for texts, the opportunity for topical allusion would seem limited. However, then as now it was not only the devil who could quote Scripture to his own end, and many of the situations described in the Psalms (as elsewhere in the Old Testament) could be fitted to current events by a clever historiographer or Court poet. Rebellious Puritans or a monarch on a tottering throne could also quote these to their own ends, as is revealed in the following exchange between Charles I and the Scottish preacher who, having reproached the king for his misgovernment, ordered the following metrical Psalm to be sung: 'Why dost thou, tyrant, boast thyself, Thy wicked deeds to praise?'; whereupon the king stood up and called for 'Have mercy, Lord, on me, I pray, For men would me devour.' The congregation showed their sympathy for the king by singing the latter.* If an embattled monarch could thus so adroitly quote metrical Psalms to suit his political situation, what wonder that Charles II, with a whole covey of divines, Court poets, historiographers, and composers at his beck and call, would find means to use the anthem as a kind of sacred musical broadsheet to support his policies?

Whether or not Purcell wholeheartedly joined in the admonishment of too-ardent Parliamentarians, we have no way of knowing. At any rate, like many other Restoration composers, he set to music the third collect in the annual service of commemoration

* David Hume, *The History of England to 1688*, vol. VII, pp. 69–70.

F

of the martyrdom of Charles I. If the musical expression he forged
be any guide, Purcell may be considered a loyalist tried and true.
(Similar persuasion no doubt had prompted John Wilson to
publish in 1657 his *Psalterium Carolinum: The Devotions of His
Sacred Majesty in his Solitude and Sufferings*.) Purcell's music for
this text shows no trace of the perfunctoriness often found in
anthems for this occasion, but rather achieves a profound and
moving expression of poignant regret, suitable to the sentiments
expressed in the collect:

> Turn Thou us, O good Lord,
> and so shall we be turned,
> be favourable, O Lord, to Thy people
> which turn to Thee in weeping, fasting and praying,
> for Thou art a merciful God,
> full of compassion, long suff'ring
> and of great pity.
> Thou sparest when we deserve punishment,
> and in wrath thinkest upon mercy.
>
> Spare Thy people, good Lord,
> spare them and let not Thine heritage be brought to confusion.
> Hear us, O Lord, for Thy mercy is great,
> and after the multitude of Thy mercies look upon us.*

The text used is also that for the penultimate prayer in the
Commination Service in the Book of Common Prayer. This
association with official, organized penance no doubt had a special
point for those whose sympathies had been enlisted for the
martyred king.

Incidentally, Charles I still figured prominently in the topical
anthems of the Restoration. Naturally he was the chief figure in
the annual celebration of his martyrdom, observed on 30 January
in all parts of England throughout the Restoration. With all due
allowance for filial piety, Charles II's purpose in conjuring up his
father's ghost so frequently may have been partly founded upon
the desire to remind everyone of the horrors of 1649, and of the
perils inherent in unchecked Whig power.

Purcell composed his earliest anthem, 'Lord, who can tell'

* *Analytical Catalogue*, no. 62.

(Psalm xix, 12–14),* some time in the course of the year 1678. This Psalm is prescribed for Christmas Day, and also regularly to be read at Morning Prayer on the fourth day of each month. The meditative and melancholy mood of the verses used by Purcell makes it seem unlikely that the anthem would have been suitable for Christmas Day, even though the opening verses of the entire Psalm are quite appropriate. And since no one would have gone to the trouble and expense of commissioning and performing an anthem for an ordinary Sunday, it is at least a possible alternative that the text may have been chosen and edited for some special event. Of all the fourth days of the months of the year, none is so likely as 4 April, when, according to the *London Gazette* for that day, a general fast was proclaimed for 6 April.

About 1679–80 Purcell set another text, which would fit no other liturgical occasion prescribed by the Anglican calendar so well as that on which the martyrdom of Charles I was celebrated, as the following excerpts reveal:

> Who hath believed our report?
> And to whom is the arm of the Lord reveal'd? . . .
> He is despised and rejected of men,
> A man of sorrows and acquainted with griefs;
> and we hid as it were our faces from Him;
> He was despised, and we esteem'd Him not.
> Surely He hath borne our griefs and carried our sorrows;
> Yet did we esteem Him stricken and smitten of God, and afflicted.
> But He was wounded for our transgressions,
> He was bruised for our iniquities:
> The chastisement of our peace was upon Him,
> And with His stripes we are healed . . .
> He is brought as a lamb to the slaughter,
> And as a sheep before her shearers dumb,
> So op'neth He not His mouth.
> He was taken from prison to judgement:
> Who shall declare His generation:
> For He was cut off out of the land of the living:
> For the transgression of my people was He stricken.
> All we like sheep have gone astray;
> We have turned ev'ry one to his own way;
> And the Lord hath laid on Him the iniquity of us all.†

* *Analytical Catalogue*, no. 26.   † *Analytical Catalogue*, no. 64.

With the return of Charles II and the re-establishment of a resplendent, though qualified, Anglican monarchy, the anthem as a genre had also been 'restored', musically speaking, in entirely new guise. As everyone knows, its new musical characteristics were essentially secular in nature, a fact mainly, or at least initially, due to Charles II's recent exposure to similar musical styles during his travels on the Continent. However, his role in the development of this new anthem has surely been over-emphasized, since a king could only suggest, not instruct, in matters of musical taste. Who is to say that this effective, dramatic style would not have made its way without royal patronage? Certainly, there are a great many precedents for the adoption of similar styles, even within the religious sphere in England, long before the Restoration.

Anyway, a new kind of music found its way in England very quickly after the Restoration, and its quick rise was due not to the king's preference alone, but to its inherent appeal as well. The broadly popular styles originating in Italy at the beginning of the seventeenth century (in the works of major figures such as Giovanni Gabrieli and Claudio Monteverdi) had at long last found their way to England and to full acceptance by London society before the end of the century. Despite the scruples of men like Pepys and Evelyn, the new 'secular anthem', with its dramatic vocal line and theatrical ritornelli and accompaniments, had come to stay. As in Counter-Reformation centres, it was not that the secular spirit had invaded the Church, but rather that the Church had opened its doors to society, its customs and tastes, with premises something like those advanced by Ignatius Loyola more than a century earlier.

It is known that Purcell, early in 1679, had been busy composing sacred music for John Gostling, the celebrated bass, then chanter at Canterbury Cathedral, according to the following letter written by Thomas Purcell:

This for Mr. John Gostling, Chanter of the choir of Canterbury Cathedral. London the 8th of February 1678/9.

Sir, I have received the favour of yours of the 4th with the encloseds [sic] for my son Henry: I am sorry we are like to be without you so long as yours mentions: but 'tis very likely you may have a summons to appear among us sooner than you imagine: for my son is composing wherein you will be chiefly concerned. However, your occasions and ties where you are must be considered and your conveniences ever complied withall: in the meantime assure yourself I shall be careful of your concerns here by minding and refreshing our master's memory of his gracious promise when there is occasion. My wife returns thanks for the compliment with her service: and pray Sir, give both our respects and humble services to Dr. Belk and his Lady, and believe ever that I am, Sir, your affectionate and humble servant,

T. Purcell

Dr. Perce is in town but I have not seen him since. I have performed your compliments to Dr. Blow, Will Turner, etc.

F faut: and E lamy are preparing for you.[5]*

There are several points of interest in this letter besides that relating to Purcell's parentage, which has already been discussed. First of all, what could Purcell have been composing wherein Gostling could be chiefly concerned? Undoubtedly some sort of anthem for bass solo, for Gostling was unlikely to have been 'chiefly' concerned with anything else. The next sentence seems a response to some query from Gostling's prior letter — perhaps something to do with an appointment as soloist at Court. The letter gives no hint as to which of Purcell's compositions is referred to; but not many fit the situation. At any rate, Thomas Purcell's efforts to remind the king must have been efficacious. Before the month was out Gostling had become a regular member of Charles II's Chapel Royal.†

It is just possible that the piece in question may have been 'I will love Thee, O Lord',‡ a topical work, referring to Charles

---

* I quote the above letter from a transcript kindly supplied by Hugh J. McLean of the University of Vancouver, who recently copied it from the original in the Nanki Library, near Tokyo. The 'deed by F. Purcell, wife . . .' mentioned in the *Catalogue of the W. H. Cummings Collection in the Nanki Music Library* (Tokyo, 1925) turns out to be Thomas Purcell's deed of attorney in favour of his son, Matthew, which is reproduced on p. 94 below. It is worth pointing out that John Gostling's appointment was confirmed on 25 Feb. 1679, he having been called to replace William Tucker, who died on the 28th, three days later. (*Cheque-book*, pp. 16–17.)

† *Grove's* (5th ed.), vol. III, p. 722.

‡ *Analytical Catalogue*, no. N 67.

II's predicament in August 1679, when the party opposed to
Monmouth prevailed upon the king to bring James, Duke of
York, home from exile in Brussels, thus precipitating the first
of Monmouth's rashly conspiratorial actions. The situation was so
nearly parallel to that between King David and Absalom alluded
to in Psalm xviii that no editing beyond a little selecting of verses
was necessary to make it fit the occasion of Monmouth's disgrace
at the end of November that same year.[6] In fact, nothing was
changed in the text at all, editorial policy being apparent only in
the selection of verses 1–6 and 16–18 — a selection which, re-
vealingly, reinforces the picture of David as a lone, weak, and
weaponless mortal, surrounded by crafty, numerous, and vicious
enemies. To withstand these and to avoid the 'snares of death' laid
for him, the king had only the strength and wisdom of his merciful
God to fall back upon. Significantly, all the verses of the Psalm
that describe the terrible powers of a God of vengeance have been
omitted, leaving the stage clear for the figure of the lone king,
upheld not by awesome demonstrations of divine omnipotence,
but only by faith and righteousness. (See pp. 248–9 below for a
discussion of some of the omitted verses from this same Psalm,
which are used to represent a royal figure of a totally different
aspect. Similar editorial methods there produce a stern, warlike
hero, who contrasts strangely with the persecuted monarch
represented here.)

To make clear the political, yet dramatic, analogy in this piece,
see Dryden's anonymously released *Absalom and Achitophel*, where
the same parallel, extended to cover the whole of the political
situation in London, is developed at great length. The analogy is
clarified even more by copious marginal notes in the hand of
Narcissus Luttrell (Charles II's Royal Historiographer), which are
to be found in a copy of Dryden's political allegory at the
Huntington Library in San Marino, California. These identify all
the main protagonists in London's political arena, the personalia
exactly corresponding to that of Purcell's anthem. Charles II is
identified as David (who also had too many women about the
house, and too numerous and miscellaneous a progeny to be
certain that he was giving them all just consideration); Monmouth

as Absalom, Shaftesbury as Achitophel, the Duke of Buckingham as Zimri, Titus Oates as Corah, the Duchess of Portsmouth as Bathsheba, etc. Dryden's translation of the whole Biblical situation to the Court of Charles II is complete and apposite.

The above suggested interpretation of this Psalm is further strengthened by a contemporary paraphrase of Psalm iii, published about 1681.* Here are J. W. Ebsworth's introductory remarks and a few of the verses of the paraphrase:

We believe that this undated Paraphrase of 'A Psalm of David, when he fled from Absalom his son . . .' made its appearance before the excitement of Monmouth's rash attempt at insurrection, in the summer of 1685; certainly before Monmouth was butchered on the scaffold. The probable date seems to be between July, 1681, when Shaftesbury was a second time committed to the Tower, and the close of that year. Dryden's 'Absalom and Achitophel' appeared anonymously on the 17th November, and was republished in the following month. The whole subject of the rebellion of Absalom against David, even before Dryden's poem was written, was familiarly compared with the disaffection of Monmouth against his father and his father's brother; scripture names attached to other persons, Achitophel for Shaftesbury, Zimri for the Duke of Buckingham. Robert Bell remarked 'The characters assigned to the persons introduced, clung to them for the rest of their lives; the same scriptural titles were employed by hosts of poetasters and pamphleteers; and even the clergy volunteered to give increased notoriety to their application by bringing them into their discourses from the pulpit.' Again, 'The Characters hit home; the names passed glibly into the ballads, lampoons, and political tracts of the day; and Charles and David remained convertible terms to the end of the reign.' [viz. February 1684/5.]

> A Paraphrase on the Third Psalm, Entitled a Psalm
> of David, when he had fled from Absalom his son.
>
> Eternal Monarch, you who are
>   The shield of Injured Kings, and bear
>   For all Crown'd Heads more than a Common Care.
>
> Behold how they increase who join
>   To ruin me, how they combine
>   'Gainst Law Paternal, Regal and Divine
>   etc.†

* Reprinted as one of the *Bagford Ballads* in J. W. Ebsworth's edition, part 1, p. 95.
† *Bagford Ballads*, loc. cit.

The relevance of this text to the current political situation in England is further attested to by Purcell's own setting of the Latin version of the same Psalm about this time. This composition ('Jehova, quam multi sunt hostes'*) stands as one of the most dramatic works to flow from Purcell's pen — or indeed from anyone else's during the Restoration, whether written for church, theatre, or Court. This very dramatic quality itself lends further weight to the notion that it was part of the political struggle then beginning to disturb the whole of the English nation.

Ostensibly the controversy was political, since the royal succession was at stake; but, as with most other political controversies in seventeenth-century England, basically the issue was dynastic and religious, involving the question as to whether the Protestant or pro-Catholic party was to gain supremacy. On the economic plane the conflict appeared to be between landed aristocracy and the rising citizen shopkeepers, who were soon to take over the nation, their musical tastes being reflected in the new fashion for French and Italian styles, which had invaded even sacred music. Finally, in the social sphere the opposition manifested itself between conventional wisdom on the part of those with vested interests and innovations of the liberal-minded, to borrow an antithesis from Galbraith.† All these diametric oppositions are relevant to the topic in hand, for they not only influenced general musical styles in England, but are recorded in the texts of various other English anthems, as well as in the texts of birthday and welcome odes, in stage plays, in dynastic 'operas', and even in royal decorative paintings.‡

The winter season of 1678, which saw Oates and Tonge setting in motion across the nation a wave of fear of the Papists and their

* *Analytical Catalogue,* no. 135.

† John K. Galbraith, *The Affluent Society* (Boston, 1958), chap. i.

‡ Cf. E. Wind, 'Julian the Apostate at Hampton Court', *Journal of the Warburg and Courtauld Institutes,* vol. III (1939–40), pp. 127–37, where a similar propagandistic purpose is shown to have governed the choice of Verrio's subjects for the painting on the King's Staircase at Hampton Court. Here, however, the propaganda was directed against a Stuart (James II) who already had been satirized in a pamphlet as 'Julian the Apostate' as early as 1682. King William III figured as the hero (in various guises) in this instance.

alleged designs, also saw several important developments in the English public concert tradition. Banister, who had done so much to found the public concert in London six years earlier and who in the period immediately following his disgrace had had to take up private teaching to earn his living, mended his fortunes well enough to become one of the best-known, most influential London musicians of his day. The newspapers of the time and the pages of contemporary diaries and journals refer frequently to the various concerts and music-meetings for which he was responsible.[7]

On 18 November 1678 Banister moved his concerts to the Music School in Essex Buildings in the Strand. There he gave, on 22 November, what may have been a forerunner of the annual concert in honour of St. Cecilia, patron saint of music:

On Thursday next, the 22nd of this instant November, at the Music School in Essex Buildings, over against St. Clement's church in the Strand, will be continued a consort of vocal and instrumental music, beginning at five of the clock every evening. Composed by Mr. John Bannister.*

However, he did not live to repeat the celebration (if, indeed, such it was), for he died on 3 October 1679,† shortly after returning from a stay on the Continent for which he had been given a pass and six months' leave of absence on 23 May, probably to study foreign musical styles.‡

Historically his most significant achievement was that of establishing the public concert, where music was played and listened to as a noble and serious entertainment, free from courtly politics or ostentation, and from the subservience to religion or drama, which determined its functions in church and theatre. Thus the ideal of an absolute music for broad public consumption became attainable, though perhaps not immediately.

Already another weekly concert series had begun in July the previous year at the lodgings of Thomas Britton, the small-coals man who lived in Clerkenwell Street. In the thirty-six years this weekly concert was destined to continue, it became one of the

* London Gazette, 14–18 Nov. 1678.
† Westminster Abbey Registers, p. 197. (He was buried in the cloisters the following day.) ‡ KM, p. 340.

most famous of London's musical events, including among its distinguished auditors and participants the younger John Banister (son of the founder of the series discussed above), Roger L'Estrange, Dr. Pepusch, Handel, John Hughes, Ned Ward, and various members of the nobility.[8] Purcell also may have attended or taken part in some of these meetings; at least his music was no doubt heard there at one time or another, for many of his works are to be found in an autograph by Thomas Britton now in the British Museum.[9]

Although no evidence connecting Purcell with any of these public concerts has come to light, it would be odd indeed if he had not taken part in them in one way or another. He had by this time composed several small chamber works,* but it is not known whether these were written for public concerts or for use at Court, where he had succeeded to Matthew Locke's position as composer to the violins. Charles II's dislike of the fantasia may have meant that most of these pieces were composed for performance elsewhere than at Court.

Purcell himself was writing for concerts such as these a number of the songs which were published about this time. Indeed no fewer than four† of his light, amorous lyrics were brought out in Playford's second book of *Choice Ayres and Songs* of 1679. The collection also gave to the public Purcell's tribute to his 'worthy friend' Matthew Locke ('What hope for us remains'), and on its title-page alluded to Purcell's succession to his post, stating that all the songs were 'Composed by several Gentlemen of His Majesty's Music'. They were also 'Sung at Court and at the public theatres', and, as Playford's note 'to all lovers of music' advises, were 'the choicest new-mode songs that were composed . . . by several eminent masters of His Majesty's Music'. He had selected them from songs that had appeared since he had published his revised first book in 1676. Again no documentary evidence is available, but it is quite possible that Purcell's lighter songs would have been

---

* *Analytical Catalogue*, nos. 731–3, 745–52.

† 'Since the pox', 'Amintas to my grief', 'Scarce had the rising sun', and 'I resolve against cringing', *Analytical Catalogue*, nos. 471, 356, 469, and 386 respectively.

sung in the public theatres as well as at Court. At any rate Purcell's music for *Theodosius*,* printed in the following year, may not have been the very first of these theatrical ventures, as Downes claimed.†

As composer to the king's violins Purcell no doubt took notice of the 'Order directed to Mr. Nicholas Staggins, master of His Majesty's music, that His Majesty's four-and-twenty violins should attend His Majesty every night that a play is acted at Court', which came down from the Lord Chamberlain on 18 February 1679.[10] Again, however, no evidence beyond that discussed above in connection with Playford's *Choice Ayres and Songs* of 1679 is known. To establish firmly Purcell's connection with the theatre either as composer or performer before 1680, when he collaborated with Nathaniel Lee in *Theodosius*, such evidence is necessary.

Meanwhile Charles II's political difficulties continued. Indeed, by the beginning of 1679, the meddling of Louis XIV's agents, added to the proliferation of 'Popish plots' (now being revealed almost daily) and the steadily strengthening Whig opposition — all these together had produced such a web of schemes and stratagems that Charles II, playing his own double games both abroad and at home, at times must have had great difficulty telling friend from foe. In view of the situation he may have had a wry chuckle or two from the lines of the ode that Blow set to music for the celebration of New Year's Day 1679:

> While swell'd with Ambition and Boundless desires
> To Empire a turbulent Monarch aspires.
> His force like a deluge no border could find
> Till you to Restrain his fierce Torrent Inclin'd.
> But as soon as your mighty Resistance he found
> Tho' both potent and proud, he flew back to his bound.
> Thus your Lustre the Light of his Sun did outvie
> And gave his *Nec pluribus impar* [motto of Louis] the Lie ... ‡

Within a few weeks King Charles was driven to desperate remedies by Whig impeachments of the Catholic peers and by the

---

* *Analytical Catalogue*, no. 606.

† Downes, p. 38. See pp. 78–79 below and *Analytical Catalogue*, no. 606, for further discussion.

‡ As quoted in McGuinness, fo. 44.

trials and indictments of various members and servants of the
Court party. His coffers empty, he first applied to Louis XIV and,
being unsuccessful, dissolved Parliament on 24 January. Although
he was to lose the general elections in the following March, the
king had simplified the situation for the time being, had saved the
necks of a few of the peers then awaiting the mob's pleasure in the
Tower, and had rescued Danby, at least temporarily.*

Despite all these harrowing difficulties Charles II continued to
take care of his musicians. The best he could do for Grabu, it
seems, was to grant him a pass to France for himself, his wife, and
his three children.† For other Court musicians, salaries and other
emoluments were paid from time to time, though always belatedly. On 8 April 1679 the Gentlemen and Children of the
Chapel Royal, among them Daniel and Thomas Purcell, were
paid 'riding charges and other expenses in their attendance on his
Majesty at Windsor for 44 days, from 14 August to 26 September,
1678'.‡ From the lack of any mention of his name in the relevant
accounts, it seems that Henry Purcell had not gone that previous
summer either to Windsor or to Newmarket, but had stayed in
Westminster for one reason or another.

All the while the king's position worsened continually, as later
in April the new Parliament voted an Act of Attainder against
Danby, and on the 27th the House of Commons voted against
the Duke of York for 'recusancy', the latter having left England
on 4 March. Many a loyal musician in his Court must have found
himself in the position of one Melker Gold, who like Grabu saw
flight his only recourse, petitioning to the king for aid in view of
his service

as a trumpet in His Majesty's troop of Guards ever since His Majesty's happy
Restoration till last November, when he was dismissed for being a Roman
Catholic and, having had no allowance since November, is become so very
poor, he cannot go into Suabia [sic], his native country, without some relief;

---

* Bryant, pp. 278–80; see also Evelyn's entry for 25 Jan. 1678/9. Danby (Sir
Thomas Osborne) was Charles II's Lord High Treasurer until his impeachment,
after which he spent some five years in the Tower (DNB).

† Cal. S. P. Dom. 31 March 1679.

‡ KM, p. 339.

there is £75 due to him out of the fee-farm and rents, £60 upon the law bill, and half a year's salary out of the Treasury Chamber, being £30, and he prays His Majesty to allow him wherewith to carry him home. The petition is referred to the Duke of Monmouth, his just demands to be satisfied.*

Though defeat seemed inevitable, Charles II kept the helm until 26 May, when he found it expedient to prorogue both Houses.† During the hottest summer for many a year the Courtly position turned gradually for the better — indeed it scarcely could have grown worse — as Monmouth won a significant victory against the Scottish Covenanters at Boswell Bridge and the Whigs' impressive campaign of the previous spring began to lose motion. Towards the end of June Charles II apparently felt that the situation was well enough under control for him to order his musicians to Windsor on June 30th.‡ The wave of consternation that swept the country when his life was despaired of on 23 August (after a nearly fatal attack of 'ague')§ was as great a vote of popular confidence as he could have wished for.

* *KM*, p. 340.   † Bryant, p. 287.   ‡ *KM*, p. 346.   § Bryant, p. 292.

CHAPTER VI

PURCELL'S FANTASIA YEAR

Purcell's appointment in 1679 as organist at Westminster Abbey (about Michaelmas, or shortly after) brought his apprenticeship to an end, although he continued as Hingeston's assistant instrument-keeper and instrument-repairer until the latter's death in 1683. By means of this practical experience, along with his education as a chorister and the lessons given him by Humfrey, Blow, and perhaps Locke, Purcell had finished his formal musical training. His efforts to master all styles of music were to continue to the end of his life (as North so perceptively was to observe in discussing Purcell's importance in the history of English music),* but henceforth he was to be his own teacher.

Despite the remarkable perceptivity these statements show, North here seems to indicate that Purcell had failed, somehow, to master his art. But this intimation is the kind of nonsense often generated by 'progress theories' of aesthetic development, which always lead to the measurement of success in terms of outward show or 'extensive quantity'. Purcell did not succeed in establishing a viable English operatic tradition — in these terms, one that was both profitable and fashionable — and therefore was a failure, in much the same sense that Handel was to be spoken of as a failure in the operatic tradition several decades later. But the creative achievements of men like these cannot be so crudely measured. Nor do they have anything to do with theories of progress. Purcell's inspired fantasias of 1680† qualify as 'masterworks'

---

* 'Then followed the *Circe* and *King Arthur* by the *Orpheus Britannicus* Mr. H. Purcell, who unhappily began to show his great skill before the reform of music *al Italiana*, and while he was yet warm in the pursuit of it, died. But a greater musical genius England never had.' Roger North, *The Musicall Grammarian*, pp. 33–34.

† *Analytical Catalogue*, nos. 735–43.

equally with the better-publicized *Dido and Aeneas** and 'Hail, bright Cecilia'.† The essential differences between these works lie in their proportions and techniques — which *are* susceptible to development, comparative evaluation, and, in a sense, to 'progress'. The fire in Purcell's creative forge burned with as much heat in 1680 as in 1695, whatever accumulation of tools, methods, and workshop experience he had acquired in the meantime. These finely wrought fantasias reveal beyond argument that by 1680 he had long since left behind apprenticeship and journeymanship and had entered into the period of his masterworks.

Early in June Purcell found himself blessed with a large segment of free time — an occurrence all too rare in his harried, brief career — and was able to attack and solve a whole series of musical problems of considerable complexity within the twenty days that he took to produce the first seven of the four-part fantasias. There is at present no way of knowing where Purcell may have been for these twenty days, but it is likely that he found a quiet retreat at Windsor, where the Court had moved for the summer on 19 April.‡ In fact there may have been something of a respite for all Charles's summer retinue in June, for the king, heavily involved in Whig intrigues, publicly declared on 8 June that he had never married Lucy Walters (thus putting the royal seal upon Monmouth's bastardy). After Monmouth had sulked all summer at Hedge Lane, before going off to Wiltshire, Charles II departed on a three-day jaunt to Whitehall with James, Duke of York, to demonstrate Stuart family solidarity.§

Whatever the source of his creative freedom, Purcell made the most of it: witness the fantasias that poured out in such rapid succession during these few days. He celebrated Corpus Christi (Thursday, 10 June) by completing the first of the four-part fantasias, that in his favourite key, G minor. By the end of the following week he had finished five more fantasias and by the end of June yet another two or three. In August he wrote two more to end what must have been a busy summer indeed.

* *Analytical Catalogue*, no. 626.   † *Analytical Catalogue*, no. 328.
‡ Luttrell, vol. I, p. 41.
§ Luttrell, vol. I, pp. 46 and 53 respectively.

That Purcell had profited from his intense concentration on the fantasias in the summer of 1680 is immediately apparent in his first professional essay in a large vocal and instrumental form: the ode to welcome Charles back to Whitehall on 9 September, 'Welcome, Vicegerent'.* The stylistic disparity between his assured treatment of the instrumental sections and less confident mastery in the vocal portions also points up the value of his summer's occupation (of which the composition of this ode was also a product) in so far as the development of his own individual style was concerned. The vocal writing is by no means unskilful; but it does not reveal the sureness of touch shown in the instrumental passages.

Purcell's connection with the stage, heretofore only hinted at in the title-pages of various song collections, is definitely established for 1680, when he composed a masque scene and several act-songs for Nathaniel Lee's *Theodosius*. Here is vocal writing that does show the touch of a master. At any rate he must have been at work on these while he was composing 'Welcome, Vicegerent', perhaps even while he was composing the fantasias in the summer, for Lee's play was produced at Dorset Garden at least as early as October 1680 and published with Purcell's music within a short time afterwards.

Whatever the actual date of the first performance,[1] there can be no doubt that Purcell made his mark in this, his first big opportunity to show his talent as a theatrical composer. Downes explained this in no uncertain terms:

All the parts in't being perfectly performed with several entertainments of singing; composed by the famous master Mr. Henry Purcell (being the first he e'er composed for the stage) made it a living and gainful play to the company: the Court, especially the ladies, by their daily charming presence, gave it great encouragement.†

Three of the songs from *Theodosius* ('Now the fight's done', 'Hail to the myrtle shade' and 'Ah! cruel bloody fate') appeared in Playford's *Choice Ayres and Songs ... third book*, 1681 ... *sung at Court and at Public Theatres*, which was ready for publication on

---

* Luttrell, vol. I, p. 54. See *Analytical Catalogue*, no. 340.
† Downes, p. 38.

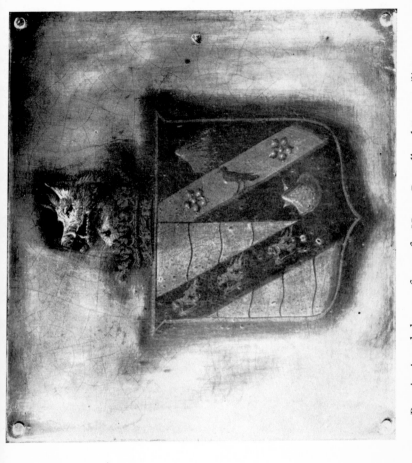

7 Putative impaled coat-of-arms for Henry Purcell and Frances (?) Peters

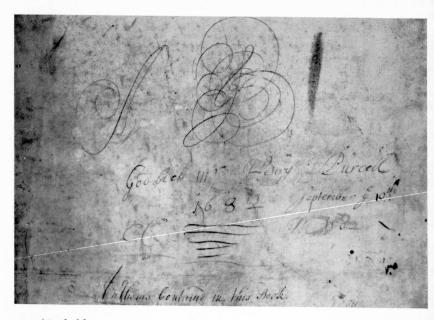

8a 'God bless Mr. Henry Purcell /1682 September the 10th.' MS. 88 (autograph) fly-leaf

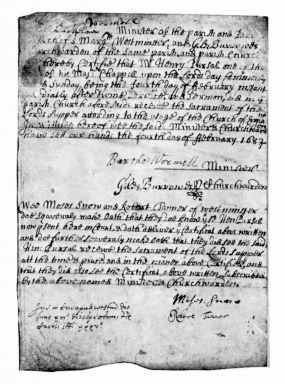

8b Sacrament certificate. 4 February 1682/3

2 November 1680, although not advertised in the *London Gazette* until 16 December 1680, and not published until early in the following year, as the epistle 'To all Lovers of Music' explains. For the interesting light it sheds on English song-composition at the outset of Purcell's career, this document is worth quoting *in extenso*:

GENTLEMEN, This third book or collection of new ayres and songs had come to your hands some months sooner, had I not been prevented by long sickness; however I hope it will not now be unwelcome. I need not here commend the excellency of their composition, the ingenious authors' names being printed with them, who are men that understand to make English words speak their true and genuine sense both in good humour and ayre; which can never be performed by either Italian or French, they not so well understanding the properties of our speech. I have seen lately published a large volume of English songs composed by an Italian master, who has lived here in England many years; I confess he is a very able master, but being not perfect in the true idiom of our language, you will find the air of his music so much after his country-mode, that it would suit far better with Italian than English words. But I shall forbear to censure his work, leaving it to the verdict of better musical judgements; only I think him very disingenious [*sic*] and much to blame, to endeavour to raise a reputation to himself and book, by disparaging and undervaluing most of the best English masters and professors of music. I am sorry it is (in this age) so much the vanity of some of our English gentry to admire that in a foreigner, which they either slight or take little notice of in one of their own nation; for I am sure that our English masters in music (either for vocal or instrumental music) are not in skill and judgement inferior to any foreigners whatsoever, the same rules in this science being generally used all over Europe. But I have too far digressed, and therefore beg your pardon. This book being bound up with the two others formerly published, will make a complete volume. To conclude, I desire you to think that I have herein as much studied your satisfaction as my own interest, and kindly to receive this collection, from GENTLEMEN, Your Hearty Servant, JOHN PLAYFORD. (From my house in Arundel-Street, near the Thames side, Novemb. 2 1680.)

Playford referred to the collection of *Songs set by Signior Pietro Reggio* advertised in the *London Gazette* for 11 March and again on 26 July and 9 December 1680. Reggio had dedicated these forty-six songs to the king, including among them a setting of 'Arise ye subterranean winds' for Shadwell's 'operatic' adaptation of Shakespeare's *The Tempest*, which he had contributed to

Shadwell's original production in April 1674.* Other texts Purcell also was later to set include 'She loves and she confesses too' and 'See where she sits',† both very dull compositions, worthy of neither the poet's nor the printer's arts shown to such good advantage and so lavishly in the collection. In fact it is not unlikely that Playford commissioned Purcell's settings of these same two texts at this juncture. Purcell's deliberate parodying of the two originals would seem to indicate that Playford had enjoined him to show Reggio how an English master would solve the problems he had set for himself in composing music for such fine poems as these by Cowley.

Playford touched upon a more serious problem, however, in his statements concerning the position of English masters *vis-à-vis* foreign competitors who flocked to London throughout the seventeenth century. In speaking of its being the 'vanity of some of our English gentry to admire that in a foreigner, which they either slight or take little notice of in one of their own nation', Playford was but adding his own arguments for preferment of the native art to those of such men as Henry Lawes, Matthew Locke, Pelham Humfrey, and John Banister. Already the strength of the new English Baroque idiom had been established — a strength for which, be it noted, England had drawn upon her own magnificent polyphonic traditions perhaps more directly and fully than any other musical nation had done. There wanted only a champion of Purcell's stature to demonstrate how essentially strong the English tradition actually was.

Meanwhile it appears that Purcell had married, or at least should have done so. Again, as at so many important junctures in Purcell's life, the lack of any solid documentary evidence beclouds the event. The baptismal registers of All Hallows the Less reveal that one Henry, son of Henry and Frances Purcell, was baptized there on 9 July 1681, to be buried in the churchyard of the same parish a little more than a week later, on 18 July.[2] First of all the identity of the parents must be established. Is it possible to make

---

* Nicoll, p. 430.
† *Analytical Catalogue*, nos. 413 and 508 respectively.

certain that the composer Henry Purcell was indeed the man named here? Unfortunately not. However, it is significant that of the four Henry Purcells whom the records show to have been living in London or its environs at this time[3] no other had a wife named Frances or seems to fit this particular situation in other ways. Hence it is quite probable that it is the composer who is named here. The probability, however, remains to be explored.

If Henry Purcell, musician, was the father of the child recorded, then his marriage must be moved back from the accepted date (1681)* by a year. Imperfect housing records do not help a great deal here, except in a negative way. For 1680–1 Purcell is not recorded as being a resident of St. Margaret's Parish, Westminster, where he apparently lived in 1682,[4] since John Baptista Purcell's birth is recorded in the Westminster Abbey accounts for that year.

Even the identification of Frances Peters as his wife is open to question. Arguing from evidence suggested by the Christian names of Purcell's second son, Westrup makes a good case for considering John Baptist Peters as Henry Purcell's father-in-law.† The case is further strengthened by the recent discovery of a photograph of an impaled coat-of-arms representing the Purcell and Peters family crests together.‡ The device suggests that the Purcell and Peters families were joined through the marriage of Henry and Frances. And indeed the photograph§ seems authentic. However, until the original from which this was made can be found, it cannot be accepted as conclusive proof of anything.

One further piece of evidence remains to be considered, even though it also is somewhat conjectural. If the infant Henry Purcell was the first-born child of Henry and Frances — a possibility even more likely when it is remembered that naming customs in Restoration England caused most first-born sons to be given their fathers' Christian names — then conventional reckoning back would make the wedding day about September 1680. This would provide yet another possible explanation for Purcell's

---

* Westrup, p. 262.   † P. 45.
‡ See F. B. Zimmerman, 'Purcell Iconography: Missing Items', in the *Musical Times*, June 1960, p. 369.
§ As shown in Plate 7.

cryptic entry in the Fitzwilliam Museum autograph, 'God bless Mr. Henry Purcell/1682 September the 10th'. It may have been written on his wedding anniversary.

If Mrs. Purcell was indeed Frances Peters before the wedding, and if 'Beati omnes'* was indeed a wedding anthem, the Latin text can now be explained on new grounds. The Peterses were a famous family of London Catholics, and nothing would have been more natural than for the text of a wedding piece to have been written in Latin. Furthermore, the slight musical value of the piece might well be explained by the fact that Purcell had dashed it off hastily just before a ceremony.[5]

Another composition occupying Purcell's attention about this time (as may be seen from its position in the same autograph†) may also have had topical associations. The sombre hymn 'Ah! few and full of sorrows'‡ has for its text George Sandys's paraphrase of Job xiv. 1, i.e. the funeral sentence 'Man that is born of a woman'. For mournful expressivity the composition bears comparison with Purcell's settings of the funeral sentences themselves.§

Although the work also survives only in fragmentary form, enough has been preserved to show that Purcell had conceived it as a composition of major importance — something, perhaps, designed as part of a memorial service for the death of some important person. If, as its position in the autograph suggests, it was written very late in 1680, no other event would have been then so much in the minds of those at Court as the funeral of William Howard, Viscount Stafford, which followed within three short weeks his unjust attainder in a trial that publicly mocked justice. Charles, prevented from rescuing Stafford by his own policy of non-interference with the Law, would have known no restraint in publicly mourning for him. And Purcell, a staunch friend of the Howard family, would have written music for the occasion, inspired by his own personal feelings, as well as by loyalty to the Court.

* *Analytical Catalogue*, no. 131.
† British Museum, Add. MS. 30930.
‡ *Analytical Catalogue*, no. 130.
§ *Analytical Catalogue*, nos. 17A, 17B, 27, etc.

Stafford's trial had another, less hypothetical, connection with Purcell's musical activity. On 11 December Nahum Tate's adaptation of Shakespeare's *Richard II*★ (with at least one song by Purcell, and perhaps some instrumental music) opened at the Theatre Royal, Drury Lane. Three days later, on the 14th, it was suppressed for political reasons — reasons undoubtedly connected with the trial of Stafford and with Shaftesbury's and Monmouth's truculent show of confidence and strength about town.† The year ended ignominiously for Charles II and his Court.

The king's parliamentary opponents under Shaftesbury's leadership now went from strength to strength. Charles II, however, was not one to back down before a show of force. The text of Blow's New Year's ode for 1681, 'Great Sir, the joy of all our hearts', showed the king's position in as favourable a light as possible, dwelling more particularly, it will be noticed, upon foreign than on domestic affairs:

> Then Long may he Live and Long may he Reign
> By whom we are blest with so happy a Chain.
> By whose prudent conduct and peaceable Care
> Our fortunate Isle thus flourishes
> While our Neighbours are Left to the fortune of War. . . .
>
> Your Friends unite, your Foes asunder Break;
> For now Commences under Charles the Great
> The Year of Wonder.
> Of this the Lucky Omen we
> Receiv'd from that most happy Tree. . . .‡

Despite the House of Commons's public resolution that whoever should advise a prorogation was a 'betrayer of the kingdom, a promoter of Popery and a pensioner of France'§ Charles II gave orders on 10 January 1681 for the prorogation of a 'fiery, eager and high-flying Parliament'‖ and had these carried out a

★ *Analytical Catalogue*, no. 581.
† Bryant, pp. 306–8.
‡ From the typescript of an article, 'Blow's Court Odes', fo. 6, lent to me by Rosamund McGuinness (as quoted). Similar sentiments were expressed in Blow's birthday ode for 29 May following, 'Up, shepherds, up'.
§ Bryant, p. 308.
‖ Wood, *Life and Times*, vol. II, p. 511.

week later, ordering it to reassemble at Oxford — still a Tory stronghold — on the 21st.* For professional musicians all this must have brought troubling reminders of 1641, when most of their predecessors had lost their livelihoods, especially when Charles II finally found it necessary to retrench by cutting down the salaries of those who served him at Court. Worse still, he had to urge strict economy upon members of the royal family,† which meant, of course, that he was having the worst of it in both worlds.

On 30 January the Court and the royal family, it may be stated with some certainty, turned their attention from all such pursuits, weighty or frivolous, to commemorate the martyrdom of the king's father. Falling as it did on a Sunday (Septuagesima), the occasion was no doubt celebrated with double solemnity. None of Purcell's works has been identified with the celebration, but both the text and the musical style of 'Who hath believed our report' make it suitable to the occasion, and it is just possible that the anthem may have been composed for this year, rather than earlier.‡

Meanwhile Purcell kept busy at the various tasks for which his several appointments made him responsible. Chief among these, we may be sure, despite complete absence of any kind of evidence, was that of developing as a composer. As to what kind of music he would have been composing, precise information again is lacking. However, in view of the fact that London concert life began really to flourish and to assume the character of a lasting institution about this time, it is a fair assumption that Purcell had taken notice of the new and potentially lucrative liaison between the composition, performance, and publication of chamber music. And since his twenty-two trio-sonatas (one a chaconne) were composed between 1680 and 1683, it is safe to assume that during the course of the year 1681 he devoted a fair amount of time to them. Indeed, comparing these to the fantasias in their stylistic and formal development, one sees that they represent an unbroken development from the latter.

* Wood, loc. cit.   † Luttrell, vol. 1, p. 68.
‡ As suggested above, on p. 65.

The thesis that Purcell would have had a great deal of spare time to devote to composition during the first seven or eight months of 1681 is supported by records revealing that Charles II and others at Court were preoccupied with political affairs throughout this period. So busy was the king, indeed, that his former frequent visits to the theatre appear to have been cut out altogether.*

During the Parliament which he had convened at Oxford in March, Charles had to face the effrontery of both Monmouth (who rode in over Magdalen Bridge on the morning of 21 March, when Parliament opened, his men armed with 'Protestant flails'†) and Shaftesbury, who tried to force the king to name Monmouth heir to the throne. Charles II's eventual reply was to dissolve Parliament once again, returning the same day (28 March) to Whitehall via Windsor.

April of 1681 saw the king busy with further negotiations with Louis XIV (and £400,000 richer afterwards);‡ with the affairs of the Navy; with preparations for Roger L'Estrange's first issue of the *Observator* (Charles's new propaganda weapon); and with arrangements for the departure of the royal family and their entourage for Hampton Court for the summer.

Among numerous propaganda pieces published about this time may be mentioned *The Deliquiam: or, The Grievances of the Nation Discovered in a Dream*, a pamphlet 'against those that appear against the Court'. (Here marginalia identify Almanzor as the Duke of York, Capriccio as Shaftesbury, Marcion as Monmouth, a Rogue as Dangerfield, a Son as Tonge, Towser as (Roger?) L'Estrange, and Hali as Halifax.§ The gist of another Tory tract may be gathered from the Whiggish reaction to it as shown in the following parody of it:

THE PROTESTANT DISSENTERS
Occasioned by a late Pamphlet called *The Royal Letany*

From Rome's tyrannizing o'er Kingdoms and Kings
From Religion that murder and massacre brings

---

* At least Nicoll (*passim*) records no royal visits for that part of the year.
† Whips loaded with lead weights (*OED*). Bryant, p. 312.
‡ Accompanied by the Catholic and already politically and musically discredited Grabu, of all people.
§ Huntington Library (San Marino, California), Bindley Pamphlets.

From TREASON styl'd merit and such dreadful things
Libera nos Domine.

From Plots and sham-plots good subjects to wrong
From those who to wade in our blood do think long
From Mass and from turning our Prayers to a song
Lib. etc.

From fashions of France and their murdering arms
From secret impoisonings and mischievous charms
From Roman locusts, with which England swarms
Lib. etc.

Printed for W.B. 1681*

May and June passed uneventfully, except for the business of
Fitzharris's arraignment and bloody execution for his part in the
'Irish plot' against the king, queen, and Duke of York.† Then
July brought the king unexpectedly back to London, where he
quickly examined Shaftesbury and committed him to the Tower.
For the rest of the month he was involved with the election of
London's sheriffs (also, by implication, that of the Lord Mayor)
and engaged in various negotiations with William, Prince of
Orange, against France and Spain. Charles was unsuccessful in
the City election and had to hold his peace while a Whig-packed
jury released Stephen College (author of the libellous anti-Tory
pamphlets The Raree-Show and The Protestant Tories). The
king's political fortunes still ran at low ebb, but were soon to
change for the better.

Purcell, whose musical activities during the period have been
conjectured above, meanwhile saw several events that affected the
fortunes of himself and his kinsmen. On 26 January one Richard
Robinson was appointed instrument-keeper in the place of Henry
Brockwell, who surrendered his position for unknown reasons.
The lack of any mention of Hingeston and Purcell prevents clear
knowledge of what this may have meant for these two, who
presumably still held joint duties under that same title.‡ On 11
February one Francis Purcell was admitted as groom-in-ordinary
to Charles II. The frankly nepotistic policy of the Court in such

---

* Ibid.   † Bryant, pp. 311 ff.   ‡ KM, p. 352.

appointments, and the fact that Thomas Purcell, in charge there as groom of the robes, may have been suffering serious illness, explains the preferment then given his son Francis, who was Henry Purcell's first cousin. Finding his son Court employment was indeed a wise precaution, as may be seen from Francis's promotion at Thomas's death.* Thomas, who made his Will on 4 June, may have been facing problems raised by his falling ill, and so would have been disposed to set up for the future as many of his kinsmen as possible.† Shortly afterwards, on 8 June, a Mr. Purcell received £37. 10s. from the secret service funds. Probably this was Edward, son of Thomas, who for some time now had held an important and responsible position at Court as a gentleman usher Daily Waiter.‡ Then on 9 July was baptized at All Hallows the Less the above-mentioned Henry Purcell, son of Henry and Frances Purcell, possibly the first of the composer's numerous but, for the most part, short-lived offspring.§

At the beginning of August, if no earlier, Purcell must have been busy with a major work, a welcome ode. (The indefatigable Luttrell records the return of the Court to Whitehall from Windsor, where Charles had evidently gone from Hampton Court during the course of the summer.) Purcell's next official responsibility was to compose the ode 'Swifter, Isis, flow'‖ for Charles II's homecoming.[6]

After the brutal execution two days later of Stephen College,¶ Charles was off at 5 a.m. to seek relaxation at Newmarket, 'for some time', as Luttrell observed in his entry for 8 September 1681. Again life at Court was relatively quiet, and Purcell very likely returned to projects for compositions that had absorbed his attentions earlier in the year. In addition to such works, however, he must also have been at work on the B flat major service and

---

* See p. 96 below for a notice of the promotion, and App. Two, XI, 9 for the text of the documents involved.

† See App. Two, XI, for information on Francis Purcell and XXII, 17, for a copy of Thomas Purcell's will.

‡ See App. Two, V.

§ See p. 80 above.

‖ *Analytical Catalogue*, no. 336.

¶ See Wood, *Life and Times*, vol. II, p. 552, for the ghastly details.

anthem,* for a payment of thirty shillings 'for writing Mr. Purcell's service and anthem' is recorded in the Michaelmas accounts of Westminster Abbey.[7] In fact the dimensions of the work make it probable that he had been working on the service for some time. Then, during August and September, Purcell must also have added to his musical responsibilities to the Church, Court, and chamber at least a few to the theatre. Before Michaelmas he had also provided a song for D'Urfey's *Sir Barnaby Whigg*,† a very topical piece, which was recorded in the Michaelmas Term Catalogue and probably produced early in October.‡

The year ended, as it had begun, with political strife. Shortly after Catherine of Braganza's birthday, which was lavishly celebrated with fireworks and a great ball at Court on 15 November,§ Whiggish factions rose. For the anniversary of Queen Elizabeth's accession on 17 November the Parliamentarians paraded London's streets all day, then at night held a great Protestant celebration, all by way of preparation for Shaftesbury's trial, which was held a week later. A packed jury returned 'Ignoramus' — a term soon beating about their ears in street ballads and scurrilous poetry — and Shaftesbury was acquitted. But, as Bryant has pointed out, he was set free with two cans tied to his tail, one by Charles II (the trial), the other by Dryden (*Absalom and Achitophel*). As numerous ballads of the time seemed to portend, Achitophel's days of political power were nearly over.

* *Analytical Catalogue*, nos. 230 and 35 respectively.
† *Analytical Catalogue*, no. 589.
‡ Laurie, fo. 167.
§ Luttrell, vol. I, p. 144.

CHAPTER VII

PURCELL, TORY COMPOSER

Political difficulties continued into the New Year, coming to a head with another of Monmouth's ambitious political progresses and his subsequent arrest. King Charles was beginning to see that Dryden's prophetic identifications in *Absalom and Achitophel* were not at all far-fetched, although he may have felt somewhat encouraged by the sentiments voiced by the anonymous poet who penned the words of Blow's New Year's ode for 1682, 'Arise, great monarch, arise':

> See how our troubles vanish.
> See how the Tumultuous Tribes agrow.
> Propitious winds bear all our Griefs away
> And peace clears up the troubled day.
> Not a wrinkle, not a scar
> Of faction or Dishonest war;
> But Pomps and Triumphs deck the noble Kalendar.*

Buckingham prudently had retired from Court and broken with the Whigs early that same month. After the Tories had celebrated their usual observance of the martyrdom of Charles I on 30 January 1682, the Whigs replied by offering 'an indignity' to the picture of the Duke of York at the Guildhall.[1] At Court, however, musicians were as yet little influenced by such events, being preoccupied with their own affairs. Evelyn comments on one of the most lavish celebrations in his description of the entertainment of the Ambassador of Morocco at 'the Duchess of Portsmouth's glorious apartment at Whitehall where was a great banquet of sweetmeats and music'.†

---

* As quoted in McGuinness, 'Blow's Court Odes', fo. 8.
† Evelyn, 24 Jan. 1681/2.

Meanwhile Purcell had moved into new quarters in Great St. Ann's Lane, his name being listed, with the annotation 'new arrival', twenty-fourth on the roster of names for that street in the St. Margaret's poor-rates for 1682. Among his more famous neighbours were John Dryden's brother Erasmus in Bell Alley; Mr. Stephen Crespion, Bowling Alley East; the publisher John Carr in Great St. Ann's Lane; John Hingeston in Absey and Bowling; Thomas Shadwell in Tothill Street; and Claudius Le Grange, John Blow, and John Wilson in King Street. John Banister and Robert Ramsey apparently had fallen on evil days, for both are listed among those who were 'in arrear to the assessment for relief of the poor of this parish'. Strangely enough, Widow Purcell's name does not appear in the lists for this year.* Perhaps she was staying with her son Henry, who now lived a very short distance from the back entry to the Dean's Yard, Westminster Abbey — a time-saving convenience which he was no doubt glad of a few months later, when he was appointed one of three organists of the Chapel Royal, as successor to Edmund Lowe, if only because his daily route to the organist's bench in Westminster Abbey was considerably shorter than it had been.[2]

On 17 May 1682 Purcell travelled to Windsor with sixteen other musicians. The complete list of musicians, with the sums paid to them, is given in the *Calendar of Treasury Books*:

to 17 of the King's music attending the King at Windsor, viz., John Twist £23. 5s. 10½d., John Banister £11. 12s. 8½d., John Lenthall £11. 12s. 8½d., James Banister £11. 13s. 2d., Thomas Finall £11. 12s. 8½d., Richard Tomlinson £11. 13s. 2d., Henry Brockwell £27. 16s. 8d., John Myer £11. 12s. 8½d., Gyles Stevens £11. 13s. 2d., Fred Steffkins £11. 12s. 8½d., John Hingston £15., Henry Gregory £11. 12s. 8½d., Dr. William Child £11. 12s. 8½d., Henry Purcell £11. 13s. 2d., Will. Hall £14. 0s. 7½d., Ed. Howton £27. 10s. 0d., Jeff. Banister £11. 13s. 2d. [Total] £247. 7s. 11½d.†

Purcell probably wrote 'What shall be done in behalf of the man'‡ (the third ode commissioned by the Court) to celebrate

---

* St. Margaret's, Westminster, Overseers' Accounts of poor-rates for 1681, *passim*. The names of Blow and John Wilson are to be found in the duplicate book, though missing in the rate-books.

† 17 May 1682.   ‡ *Analytical Catalogue*, no. 341.

the return of James, Duke of York, from Scotland on 27 May as well as for Charles's birthday on the 29th.

James indeed felt welcomed by the London 'mobile',* which had turned out to greet him.

> The glory of the British line
> Old Jimmy's come again.†

For his first line the anonymous poet made use of one of the burning questions of the day: 'What shall be done in behalf of the man?' (The Whigs, whose banquet for Monmouth had been suppressed a short time earlier, probably had a ready answer.) But the loyal poet — again probably Dryden — held to the party line, coming out strongly for James in the couplet:

> And now ev'ry tongue shall make open confession
> That York, royal York, is the next in succession.

Charles too was enjoying greater popularity than usual. The *True Protestant Mercury* (27–31 May) and the *Impartial Protestant Mercury* (26–30 May) recorded that the birthday was 'kept very solemnly by all true lovers of the King', and the recovery of the king from a minor indisposition had 'rendered the solemnity of this his birth- and Restoration-day much more glorious, the same having not for many years been celebrated with greater or more universal testimonies of duty and affection to so gracious a prince'.‡

For both of the brothers this was the first time in twenty years that the menace of a too-solid opposition appeared less fearsome. Even the Westminster bell-ringers, those perennial harbingers of happy occasions in English history, had reason to be pleased, since the king's journey to London gave them another day's profitable employ, witness the following entry from the Treasurer's Account:

More to them for ringing on six holidays, vizt. 5th of November, Queen Katherine's birthday, Queen Eliza.'s birthday, St George's Day, the 29th of May, and the 8th of April, being the day the King and Duke came from Windsor.   £2. 3s. 4d.[3]

---

* Etymological progenitor of the modern term 'mob' (*OED*).
† Bryant, p. 330.
‡ Quoted from McGuinness, fo. 47.

At any rate it was clear that the political pendulum had begun to swing back. Shaftesbury and Monmouth had already seen their followers dwindling the month before, when Charles II had found it easy to suppress a meeting scheduled by the Monmouth faction for the day already appointed to celebrate the king's escape from the toils of the 'Popish Plot'.* Now, it became obvious, a crucial test of strength between the two parties would be called for by the Parliamentarians. The first skirmish of this new political combat was not long in coming. On 19 June 1682 John Moore, Lord Mayor of London, confirmed his choice of candidates for the two offices of London sheriffs in the traditional

Ceremony of Drinking to one of his fellow-citizens; and accordingly, says my author (who at the very time published a true and impartial account of the Proceedings of the Common-Hall of the City of London at Guildhall, on the 24th of June 1682 for electing of Sheriffs) at the Bridge-House Feast, the 18th of May last his Lordship was pleased to pass the compliment of drinking to Dudley North, Esq.†

Since his candidates were staunch Tories and because control of London was essential to the control of England and Parliament, the Whigs had no option but to oppose, as forcefully as they could, Moore's nomination of Dudley North and Ralph Box in favour of their own candidates, Thomas Papillon and John Dubois. During the elections on Midsummer's Day (24 June), unruly demonstrations and grave irregularities aborted the issue. This, at least, was the Tories' claim when the election was said to fall upon Dubois and Papillon after a show of hands which gave them a majority of between 1,000 and 1,200 votes. A new poll was demanded; but in the ensuing process further irregularities called for another election. Then Charles II entered the lists and yet another election followed, in which his candidates were duly (or perhaps unduly, as some held) elected.

Charles II seemed to move from strength to strength as one by one he destroyed or weakened his enemies. Throughout the summer of 1682 the loyal party gradually gained the upper hand. Despite all Whig machinations, Tory sheriffs were finally placed in office by the end of the summer (not without a few of Charles II's deft touches) and the way was clear for the election of the Lord Mayor, in which election the Tory party was again successful with its candidate, Sir William Pritchard (once more with the aid of discreet royal intervention). A month later the new Mayor was inaugurated with more than the usual gala municipal ceremonies. This, however, was no mere 'City' affair, but rather one in which the interests of both parties and the welfare of the king were at stake.* This is not the place for a further account of the rigged elections, the riots, the false ballots, and the political conniving, all of which show the elections of 1682 to have been the bitterest of contests between Whig and Tory. Nor is it the moment to comment on the significance of the Court party's victory in these elections, which also boded well for their future, as it concerned the Shaftesbury trial, the 'Ignoramus' verdict, the quelling of the Scottish rebellions, and indeed the whole broad design of Charles II's strategy.

Charles's return from Newmarket on 21 October was celebrated by Purcell's setting of the ode 'The summer's absence unconcerned we bear'.† It is appropriate to point out that the text of Purcell's anthem 'Blow up the trumpet'‡ (Joel ii. 15–17) was that proper to the twentieth Sunday after Trinity, which in 1682 coincided with the Lord Mayor's celebrations on 29 October, and that the text of the first lesson for matins for that Sunday had obvious bearing on the current political situation. Charles II was no doubt most gratified to discover in this lesson allusions to 'elders', 'congregations', and 'a Northern army', and a battery of sentiments that might easily be construed as anti-Presbyterian, therefore anti-Whiggian. No more appropriate text could have been found to celebrate his hard-won victory over the Whigs or to publicize the fact that 'the King of England was King of London at last', as the newly appointed, but not yet infamously 'bloody', Chief Justice Jeffreys observed at the time. However

---

* Maitland, vol. I, pp. 473 ff.

† *Analytical Catalogue*, no. 337.

‡ *Analytical Catalogue*, no. 10. Though 'Biblical', the text is not from the Authorized Version.

much this victory may have accelerated Whig efforts, bringing the narrowly averted Rye House Plot* in its wake, and hastening the 'Glorious Revolution', it was the most significant political victory Charles had yet enjoyed.

Nor had the summer of 1682 been uneventful for the Purcell family. On 4 June Henry's cousin Charles Purcell had made his Will, apparently just prior to his sailing for the Gold Coast on His Majesty's sloop *Le George*.† At the beginning of the following month Henry Purcell found himself up for the above-mentioned preferment at Court, as is revealed by the entry in the *Cheque-book* for 11 July 1682:

> Mr. Edw[ard] Lowe, Organist of his Ma[jes]ty's Chapel Royal, departed this life at Oxford the 11th day of July 1682, in whose place was sworn Mr. Henry Purcell, the 16th of September 1682, but to take place according to the date of his warrant, which was the 14th of July 1682.‡

Then, at the end of that month, sadness fell upon the Purcell family. On 31 July died Thomas, who had been like a father to young Henry since the decease of the elder Henry in August 1664. Terse accounts in various records of the time mention no cause of death and give no particulars. However, Thomas had been ill for some while, if Rimbault's annotation be correct, and probably had succumbed to a very serious, but not suddenly fatal, illness. On 15 May 1681 a power of attorney was granted by Thomas Purcell of St. Martin's Parish, authorizing his son Matthew Purcell to receive his salary as Gentleman of the Chapel Royal:

> Know all men by these presents that I, Thomas Purcell, of the Parish of St. Martin's-in-the-Fields, in the County of Middlesex, one of the gentlemen of His Majesty's Chapel Royal, and servant to His Majesty, have assigned, ordained and made, by these presents do asign, ordain, and make my trusty and well beloved son, Matthew Purcell, my true and lawful attorney for me and in my name, and to my use to ask, take, and receive all such arrears and sums of

---

* Providentially undone by the Newmarket fire, its undoing calling for yet another celebration, for which Purcell composed the royal ode 'Fly, bold rebellion' (*Analytical Catalogue*, no. 324) in 1683.

† See App. Two, 1, 2.

‡ *Cheque-book*, p. 17. See also Westrup, p. 41, for a minute from the *Cheque-book* (19 Dec. 1663) describing the organist's duties and schedule.

money as are due, and hereafter will become due and payable to me the said Thomas Purcell out of His Majesty's Treasury, Chamber Exchequer, Coffery Office, or any other place or office whatsoever, giving, and by these presents granting unto my said attorney my whole power and authority in and about the premises, and upon receipt of any such sums of money aforesaid, acquittance, or other discharges for me and in my name to do and perform as fully and largely in every respect to all intents and purposes as I myself might or could do if I were there personally present, ratifying, confirming, and allowing all and whatsoever my said attorney shall lawfully do or cause to be done in and about the premises aforesaid by virtue of these presents. In witness whereof I have hereunto set my hand and seal this 15th day of May in the three-and-thirtieth year of King Charles the Second over England, etc. Annoq. Domini 1681.

T. PURCELL.

Sealed and delivered in the presence of
F. PURCELL.
Will (sic) WALLEY.*

By 4 June of that year it may have become apparent that Thomas's illness was very serious indeed, for it was at that time that he wrote his Will.† He died nearly six weeks later, on 31 July.[4]

The lateness of the date suggests that Thomas's last illness was a lingering one. Perhaps, as Westrup‡ and others have suggested, he fell victim to the scourge of tuberculosis, which may have proved fatal to other members of the family, including young Henry himself.

The extent of Thomas's influence at Court may be seen in the number of successors appointed to fill his various positions, this number also demonstrating his skill as a pluralist. On 6 August Josias Bouchier was appointed to fill his place as Gentleman of the Chapel Royal,§ and on 17 November John Goodwin succeeded him in the Private Music.‖ No record remains to reveal the disposition of his other musical positions, but the liveries listed

---

* Cummings, pp. 34–35, claimed that the 'original' was in his possession. F. Purcell may have been either Francis Purcell, son of Thomas, or Frances, wife of Henry. I have corrected the above against the transcript of the original document (in Nanki Library) sent me by Mr. Hugh McLean.

† See App. Two, XXII, 17.

‡ Cf. his discussion of the death of young Henry Purcell, 'Fact and Fiction about Purcell', in Proceedings of the Musical Association 1935–6.

§ Cheque-book, p. 17.   ‖ KM, p. 358. Cf. also N. French.

H

opposite his name in the 'Accounts for liveries for musicians' ending Michaelmas 1683,* indicates that there were still three to be disposed of. His son Francis replaced him as groom of the robes assuming full responsibilities at Somerset House.† It is not known who may have succeeded him as Marshal of the Corporation of Musicians, an office he held for a decade.

Exactly a week after Thomas was buried in the cloisters at Westminster Abbey (2 August), and only a short distance away, was baptized Henry's second son, John Baptista Purcell, whose initials would have been exactly the same as those of his maternal grandfather if, as Westrup holds, Frances Purcell was indeed the daughter of J. B. Peters.[5] At any rate, the new male heir must have been born within a few days of his great-uncle Thomas's death, only to join him in the community of cloister graves in Westminster Abbey after slightly more than two months.‡

The infant's death, or at least the illness that brought it about, offers yet another possible explanation for the origin of the oft-quoted inscription which Purcell wrote into a fly-leaf of the Fitzwilliam Museum autograph: 'God bless Mr. Henry Purcell/ 1682 September the 10th'.§ Other hypotheses are possible. Purcell may have been in some sort of difficulty with regard to his appointment as composer-in-ordinary, which had been made exactly five years earlier. (Interestingly enough, Blow's appointment as private musician-in-ordinary also began on 10 September 1685.‖) Or possibly there was some difficulty concerning his formal appointment as Edward Lowe's successor, to which position he was at last sworn in on 16 September.¶ Quite possibly this may have been the day of his birthday, as Reinhold Sietz suggests,** but so far as I know there was no established custom for this kind of inscription for birthdays in Restoration England.

---

* *KM*, p. 360.

† Not mentioned in Edward Chamberlayne, *Angliæ Notitia*, 15th ed. (1684), but see App. Two, XI, 2, where Francis's succession is documented, and XI, 3 and 4, for the position at Somerset House.

‡ *Westminster Abbey Registers*, p. 206.

§ MS. 88, fly-leaf verso. See Plate 8(a).

‖ *KM*, p. 372.   ¶ See p. 90 above.

** *Henry Purcell: Zeit, Leben, Werk*, p. 35.

At any rate the day after the king, the queen, their royal high-nesses, and all members of the Court returned from Windsor,* Purcell (who must just then have been finishing the new welcome song, 'The summer's absence') made this curious inscription, suggesting that he may have been at work on the autograph about this time.

At the end of the following month Purcell was involved, at least by authorship, if not by political sympathy, in the grand civic festival surrounding the inauguration of William Pritchard, Charles II's gratifyingly successful candidate for Lord Mayor of London that year.[6] However, it would be incorrect to assume, as some have, that Purcell actually wrote any songs for the occasion, whatever the truth may be concerning the anthem 'Blow up the trumpet' discussed above. For the secular festivities at the Guild-hall on 29 October a number of Purcell's song-tunes, which had been used in earlier skirmishes between Whig and Tory, were revived. For instance, Matt Taubman's doggerel on the dissolu-tion of Parliament, which had been sung to Purcell's 'Now, now the fight's done' (*Theodosius*) with the following text:

> Now, now the work's done and the Parliament set
> Are sent back again like fools as they met ... †

now gave way to the following words to the same tune:

> Now, now the time's come, noble Pritchard is chose,
> In spite of all people who would him oppose ... ‡

Thomas Jordan's account of *The Lord Mayor's Show: Being a Description of the Solemnity at the Inauguration of ... Sir William Pritchard, Kt.*§ also calls for tunes which may be Purcell's, includ-ing 'Let the traitors plot on' and 'Here's a health to the King'.||

---

* Luttrell, vol. I, p. 218. However, the *London Gazette* (7–11 Sept. 1682) gives 10 Sept. as the day of return.

† J. W. Ebsworth (ed.), *The Roxburghe Ballads*, vol. v, p. 22.

‡ Ibid. p. 166; a dozen such examples could easily be cited. See also pp. 234, 274, 279, *et al.*

§ (London, 1682), p. 4 (cf. *Analytical Catalogue*, no. 606/5). Although the title-page definitely refers to the Lord Mayor's inauguration, it is possible that Purcell may have written other songs for festivities the previous day.

|| Ibid. p. 6 (cf. *Analytical Catalogue*, no. D571/9).

In fact the several 'songs said to have been written for the inaugur-
tion of the Lord Mayor, Sir William Pritchard, on 29 October
1682'* may be reduced to one catch, which was introduced as
follows:

Or this new song, which is set to an excellent
tune by Mr. Pursell

Since the Duke is return'd we'll slight all the Whigs,
And let them be hang'd for politic prigs;
Both Presbyter Jack and all the old crew,
That lately design'd Forty One to renew:
Make room for the men that never denied.
To 'God save the King', 'and Duke' they replied;
Whose loyalty ever was fixt with that zeal
Of rooting out schism and proud common-weal:
Then bring up a bottle, each man in his place,
'Tis a health to the Duke; boy, give me my measure,
The fuller the glass is, the greater the pleasure.†

Since the text is virtually the same as that appearing in later
sources, it is quite likely that Purcell did compose the work for
this occasion, and that the catch can be dated as having been
first performed on 30 September 1682.

It is possible that more music than this may have been commissioned for the occasion, which was important not only in its
political implications, but also, as Chamberlayne pointed out in
Angliæ Notitia, because 'This great magistrate, upon the death of
the King, is said to be the prime person of England.'‡ The festival,
as Chamberlayne described it, was sufficiently lavish to call for all
sorts of music:

on the 29th of October [the Lord Mayor] goes to Westminster in his barge,
accompanied with all the aldermen, all his officers, all the several companies or
corporations, in their several stately barges, with their arms, colours, and
streamers; and having there in the Exchequer Chamber taken his solemn oath
to be true to the King, returns in like manner to Guildhall, that is, the great
common hall of guilds or incorporated confraternities, where is prepared for
him and his brethren a most sumptuous dinner, to which many of the great
lords and ladies, all the judges of the land, and oftentimes the lords of His

* *Grove's* (5th ed.), vol. VI, p. 998.
† See *Analytical Catalogue*, no. 271.
‡ 15th ed. (1684), part II, p. 202.

Majesty's most honourable Privy Council; also foreign ambassadors are invited; and of late years the King and Queen's Majesty; the Duke of York, and Prince Rupert have been pleased to honour that feast with their presence.*

Mindful of the value of his political victory, and, perhaps, of its narrowness, Charles II kept a tight rein on all activities that might have got out of hand. Thus he suppressed all bonfires, public fireworks, and festivals for Guy Fawkes (5 November) and for Queen Elizabeth's Accession Day (17 November). Both days were traditionally occasions for Protestant and Whig demonstrations, which Charles quite logically wanted none of at the time.

Hence it was quite appropriate that the anonymous poet of Blow's New Year's ode for 1683 should begin:

> Dread Sir, Father Janus, time's great overseer;
> Abhorring the factious designs of the past,
> With a loyal address is come in post haste,
> To present you the maidenhead of a new Year;
> Not debauched with trait'rous combinations ...

and end:

> The moving isle is fix'd and settled now,
> The basis of its empire rests on you;
> In Gordian knots you've tied the royal line;
> And made succession as your right divine.
> For all your suff'rings, all your cares
> Designing owes you the arrears
> Of steady joys and numerous years;
> And when you remove to be crown'd above
> Shall never want one to sit on your throne. . . . †

Throughout this period Purcell evidently had been busy composing other vocal works, for eight new songs appeared in the fourth book of *Choice Ayres and Songs to Sing to the Theorbo-lute or Bass-viol*.‡ The collection was entered in the Term Catalogue for February 1683, and must surely have been in the press for the usual six months or more. At any rate, except for 'Retir'd from any mortal's sight', which Purcell had set for the performance of

---

* Chamberlayne, *Angliæ Notitia*, 15th ed. (1684), part II, p. 202.
† As quoted in McGuinness, 'Blow's Court Odes', fo. 9.
‡ See *Analytical Catalogue*, nos. 195, 370, 390, 411, 413, 415, 435, and 581.

Nahum Tate's transmogrification of Shakespeare's *King Richard II*
on 14 December 1680, these pieces generally represent Purcell's
song style at this period. The most striking of these are the
beautiful 'Sleep, Adam, sleep', the 'mad-song' 'From silent
shades' ('Mad Bess'), and the lovely 'Song on a ground' on
Cowley's subtly erotic lyric, 'She loves and she confesses too'.*

By the beginning of February 1683 the political situation had
grown quiet enough for Monmouth to be released on bail, despite
his overt insubordination and complicity in various Whig
machinations. The event was celebrated immediately by the
usual publication of ballads in broadsheet form. As if for comic
relief, the little 'Battle of the Organs' between the Benchers of
the Inner Temple and those of the Middle Temple began about
this time. Both Bernard Smith and Renatus Harris had been asked
to build instruments so that the Benchers could choose the better
one for installation. It was a brilliant scheme for ensuring the
construction of a good instrument, which brought the societies
much publicity. But it brought difficulties also, and in the end
gave rise to a certain amount of skulduggery.†

In February also, Purcell had come to the notice of the authorities of Westminster Abbey. Perhaps it was because of his recent
appointment as Lowe's successor, or perhaps because of suspicions
of Catholic leanings on Purcell's part, or perhaps it arose out of
the general contention between Whig and Tory. Whatever the
reason, on 4 February, a Sunday, Purcell took the sacrament in
public according to the usage of the Church of England. And he
did this before witnesses, required by statute, in this case Moses
Snow,‡ a fellow musician (both vocal and instrumental) at
Court; Robert Tanner, occupation unknown; Bartholomew
Wormall, the minister; and Giles Borrowdell, a churchwarden:

[I,] Bartholomew Wormell, minister of the parish and pari[sh] church of
Margaret's, Westminster, and Giles Burrowde[ll] churchwarden of the same

---

* See p. 80 above.

† See pp. 113–16 below for the continuation of this battle, and p. 141 for
its conclusion. See also Westrup, pp. 51–53, and Edmund Macrory, *Notes on the
Temple Organ.*

‡ *KM*, pp. 393 and 436.

parish and parish church [do] hereby certify that Mr. Henry Pursal, one of the [Gentlemen] of His Majesty's Chapel, upon the Lord's Day commonly [called] Sunday, being the fourth day of February instant [imme]diately after divine service and sermon, did in the parish church aforesaid receive the sacrament of the Lord's Supper according to the usage of the Church of England. In witness hereof we the said minister and churchwarden have set our hands the fourth day of February 1682/3.

Bartho. Wormell, Minister
Giles Burrowdell, Churchwarden[7]

We Moses Snow and Robert Tanner of Westminster do severally make oath that they do know the said Hen. Pursal now present here in court, and doth deliver the certificate above written and do further severally make oath that they did see the said Henry Pursal receive the sacrament of the Lord's Supper at the time and place, and in the manner above certified, and that they did also see the certificate above written, subscribed by the above-named minister and churchwarden.

Iur in Cur apud Westm.   Moses Snow
die Lune & vi di Apr.   Robert Tanner
Anno Regni Regis Caroli Scdi
xxxv⁰

   [Sworn in court at Westminster Monday, 16 April, in the thirty-fifth year of the reign of our King Charles II.]*

The extraordinary amount of detail given in the document† indicates possible irregularities in Purcell's conduct. The suspicion that something may have been amiss is strengthened by an annotation at the bottom of the document recording that Moses Snow and Robert Tanner were called into court at Westminster Hall on Monday, 16 April 1683 to swear under oath that they had seen Purcell take the sacrament and the minister and church-warden sign the document. Such lengths seem to signify suspicion of something calling for investigation. Perhaps he had exhibited too much sympathy for John Dryden, or for the Peters family, or for the Howards, or for others who were suspect as Papists. Or perhaps Purcell did himself adhere secretly to the Roman Catholic faith.[8] Moreover, the breaking of the Rye House Plot about this time may have created a general attitude of wariness at Court. Certainly officials would have felt constrained to look more

   * Middlesex County Records: Sacrament Certificate 4/13.
   † The original of which is reproduced as Plate 8(b).

carefully into such matters after 23 March, when the plot was thwarted.[9]

On the other hand, this may have been merely one of the formalities that Purcell had to undergo as a result of his accession to Edward Lowe's position in the Chapel Royal in the previous autumn or because of his appointment as composer-in-ordinary to the 'King's Musicke',* or even because he was at last to succeed officially to two of John Hingeston's positions — positions for which he had long since been burdened with the chief responsibility. Although Purcell's appointments were not registered before the end of the year (when Hingeston died), it is a fairly safe assumption that he had taken over most of the work long beforehand.†

Then, in May, when all London was abuzz with political gossip about the trial of fourteen citizens (including the unlucky aspirants Dubois and Papillon) who had opposed Pritchard and his candidates in the riotous summer elections, Purcell advertised in the *London Gazette* for 24–28 May his first instrumental publication:

These are to give notice to all gentlemen that have subscribed to the proposals published by Mr. Henry Purcell for the printing his sonatas of three parts, for two violins and bass to the harpsichord or organ, that the said books are now completely finished, and shall be delivered to them upon the 11th of June next. And if any who have not yet subscribed shall before that time subscribe, according to the said proposals (which is ten shillings the whole set), which are at Mr. William Hall's house in Norfolk Street, or at Mr. Playford's and Mr. Carr's shops in the Temple; for the said books will not after that time be sold under 15s. the set.‡

Promptly on 11 June another notice appeared in the *Gazette*, advising subscribers 'to repair to his [Purcell's] house in St. Ann's Lane, beyond Westminster Abbey, or to send the proposal paper they received with the receipt to it when they subscribed ... and they shall receive their books paying the remaining part of the

* *Cheque-book*, p. 17.
† See *KM*, pp. 361–2 and pp. 105–6 below.
‡ Michael Tilmouth, 'A Calendar of References to Music in Newspapers published in London and the Provinces (1660–1719)', *RMA Research Chronicle*, no. 1 (1961), pp. 5–6, reproduces the same advertisement.

money'.* Apparently Purcell had not trusted Carr and Playford to collect and distribute for him, but had decided to do everything himself — perhaps to save money, or perhaps because he had found several errors and wanted to correct them himself before the books got into circulation.[10]

At any rate by midsummer — when he was busy composing the ode for the marriage of George, Prince of Denmark, and the future Queen Anne, which took place on 28 July† — he must have begun to reap the rewards of his labours. On 29 October that year he advertised in the London Gazette that 'Subscribers' requirements having been met, further copies of the "Sonatas of III Parts" by Henry Purcell are to be sold by J. Playford, J. Carr and H. Rogers'.[11] As for the Sonatas themselves, much, perhaps too much, has been written about their Italianate tendencies. Because Purcell himself claimed to have 'faithfully endeavoured a just imitation of the most famed Italian masters' there have been wild searches for borrowed themes, forms, or techniques, and all kinds of guesswork as to who these 'famed masters' might have been.

These putative Italian models, should they be discovered one day, were probably not very important. Purcell's trio-sonatas are so like some of his fantasias in style and expression that it is fairly safe to assume that here as elsewhere he had been for the most part his own instructor in studying English masterpieces of the immediate past. Furthermore, it was a very common thing to claim Italian provenance for all sorts of compositions. Such claims should be interpreted rather as a kind of window-dressing than as confessions of deliberate eclecticism on the part of the composer.

The implication that publication went hand in hand with public performance, and that profits from both were interchangeable, is most significant. One immediately wonders if Purcell may have followed a similar scheme to that discussed in connection with Kühnel's Sonatas.‡ If so, there is no known record at present, but it is likely that Purcell had his eye on concert performances in publishing as well as in composing these sonatas in the first place.

* Ibid.. p. 6.
† 'From hardy climes', Analytical Catalogue, no. 325.   ‡ See pp. 133–4 below.

Apparently he was quite willing to 'hawk his wares' in person, for Roger North reports that Francis North, Lord Chancellor until his death in 1685, had 'caused the divine Purcell to bring his Italian mannered compositions; and with him on the harpsichord, myself and another violin, we performed them more than once, of which Mr. Purcell was not a little proud, nor was it a common thing for one of his dignity to be so entertained'.[12]

While composing these sonatas and seeing them through the press no doubt occupied Purcell during the first half of the year, it is clear that he would have been kept very busy setting odes during the second half. For during this time he composed no less than four, possibly even five. The first of these was 'From hardy climes', written (by a poet whose name has not been recorded) for the marriage of Prince George of Denmark and the Lady Anne, one day to become Queen Anne. The Bishop of London presided over the ceremony on 28 July 1683, at St. James's, Piccadilly, and it is safe to assume that London's beau-monde turned out *tutti quanti* to witness the event and to hear Purcell's music.*

September was a happy month for those at Court, what with the frustration of the Rye House Plot being observed with the celebration of a special day of thanksgiving, which was probably the occasion for which Purcell wrote his ode 'Fly, bold Rebellion'. But October was a month of mourning for almost everyone. First of all, the Duchess of York miscarried of a male heir, thus dimming the hopes of the Court party so far as the strength of orderly succession was concerned.† Then, in October 1683, Dr. John Blow's wife died in childbirth, so that a good many of the musicians at Court would have been actually, if not officially, in mourning.‡ Finally, on 20 October, Charles II returned from Newmarket, at which time, as Luttrell observed:

His Majesty and the Court are gone into close mourning for the death of Alphonso 6th, King of Portugal, Her Majesty's brother.

The importance of the event is attested to by the fact that the

---

* *London Gazette*, 26–30 July, 1683.
† Luttrell, vol. 1, p. 284.
‡ *Grove's* (5th ed.), vol. 1, p. 769.

Westminster Abbey bell-ringers were paid a special stipend for their duties on this day.*

By 22 November Purcell had composed two, perhaps even three, odes to St. Cecilia. With two other odes to compose earlier in the year, and with the first book of trio-sonatas to see through the press, not to mention a large number of miscellaneous compositions, he must have been busy indeed. At any rate he had finished two of the works, 'Laudate Ceciliam' and 'Welcome to all the pleasures',† in time to rehearse them for the celebration on 22 November.

In addition to the odes and sonatas Purcell had also found time during the course of the year to compose a number of songs, both sacred and secular, and perhaps a few anthems as well. Several of the eight songs that Playford published in the fourth book of *Choice Ayres and Songs* were probably composed during the course of 1683, while all seven in the fifth book were surely composed in 1683 if not before, as Playford's 'Note to all lovers and understanders of music' clearly reveals:

Gentlemen, This fifth book of *New Songs and Ayres* had come sooner (by three months) to your hands, but the last dreadful frost put an embargo upon the press for more than ten weeks; and, to say the truth, there was an unwillingness in me to undertake the pains of publising any more collections of this nature. But at the request of friends, and especially Mr. Carr, who assisted me in procuring some of these songs from the authors, I was prevailed upon. Yet indeed the greatest motive was to prevent my friends and countrymen from being cheated with such false wares as is [sic] daily published by ignorant and mercenary persons, who put musical notes over their songs, but neither minding time nor right places, turn harmony into discord: such publications being a scandal and abuse to the science of music, and all ingenious artists and professors thereof.

As the year came thus to a close after one of the coldest Decembers in living memory,[13] Purcell came into yet another official position of responsibility at Court. Hingeston, who had willed him £5 as a godson's share of his material wealth, left him also the responsibilities connected with the acquisition, construction, and repair of instruments at Court. The first official notice came down from the Lord Chamberlain's office on 17 December, appointing 'Henry Purcell to be organ-maker and keeper etc., in the place of Mr. Hingeston, deceased'.[14]

This meant another livery for Purcell, that is, he would be paid each year £16. 2s. 6d. for clothing. As a regular annual stipend, he received another sum. The records do not show what this amounted to, but it would probably have been something more than the £30 Hingeston had received on 4 July 1663 and on other such occasions for attendance at Windsor in his official capacity as 'Keeper of the Organs'.* Possibly his salary was part of the £60 per annum Purcell was allotted on 16 February the following year. Certainly the two offices were lumped together in the entry for Hingeston as 'Tuner and Repairer of the Wind Instruments and Organs by patent under the Broad Seal, £60' recorded in the Treasury of the Chambers Office accounts for 1668.†

This account also records the interesting fact (which ought not to be overlooked) that Hingeston had a helper, one 'Mr. Brockwell, keeper of the King's instruments', who received £18. 5s. for his services. When young Henry Purcell was appointed as another assistant to Hingeston on 10 June 1673,‡ it must have been because there was too much for one person with only one helper to accomplish. Certainly the extant accounts, by no means complete, show Hingeston to have been a very busy man.

Purcell had been shouldering these responsibilities for so long that this official appointment probably altered his daily routine not at all, however much or little it may have improved his finances. Indeed, considering the various tasks to which he was committed, it is difficult to see how any further drain could have been made on his energy. The magnitude of his total responsibility during the next decade is astonishing. In fact the total burden of his labours suggests that he may actually have worked himself to death, whatever illness brought him at last to his death-bed.

* KM, p. 159. † KM, p. 207. ‡ KM, p. 255.

CHAPTER VIII

THE LONDON MUSICAL SCENE
AT THE END OF
THE REIGN OF CHARLES II

As the New Year of 1684 dawned on snowbound England Charles II found himself at last in a position to enjoy the fruits of his political victory. As a result social, cultural, and musical affairs at Court were more active than ever. The Court's new-found solidarity and strength were celebrated by the anonymous poet who provided the text for Blow's New Year's ode: 'My trembling song, awake, arise'.

Meanwhile Purcell was extremely busy, discharging his new responsibilities at Court more or less while he learned how to do so, and at the same time taking care of his former duties both there and at Westminster Abbey. Edward Chamberlayne's description of the Court hierarchy in general, and of Purcell's place in it, is worth quoting in full:

> Of the King's Court, The Ecclesiastical, Civil, and Military Government thereof, with a Catalogue of the King's Privy-Councillors, or the King's Judges, Servants, &c.
>
> The Court of the King of England is a monarchy within a monarchy, consisting of ecclesiastical, civil, and military persons and government.
> For the ecclesiastical government there is first a Dean of the King's Chapel, who is usually some grave, learned Prelate, chosen by the King, and who as Dean acknowledgeth no superior but the King ...
> By the Dean are chosen all other officers of the Chapel, viz. a Sub-Dean or Praecentor Capellae; thirty-two Gentlemen of the Chapel, whereof twelve are priests, and one of them is confessor to the King's household, whose office is to read prayers every morning to the family, to visit the sick, to examine and prepare communicants ...
> The other 20 gentlemen, commonly called the Clerks of the Chapel, are

with the aforesaid priests to perform in the Chapel the Office of Divine Service in praying, singing, etc. One of these being well skilled in music, is chosen Master of the Children, whereof there are twelve in ordinary, to instruct them in the rules and art of music, for the service of the Chapel. Three other of the said clerks are chosen to be organists, to whom are joined upon Sundays, Collar-days,* and other Holy-days, a consort of the King's music to make the Chapel music more full and complete . . .

In the King's Chapel thrice every day prayers are read, and God's service and worship performed with great decency, order, and devotion, and should be a pattern to all other churches and chapels of England.

The King hath also his private oratory, where some of his chaplains-in-ordinary read divine service to the King on working days every morning and every evening. . . .

There are belonging to the King's Chapel three organists, viz.

Dr. William Child.

Dr. John Blow, who is also Master of the Children of the Chapel.

Mr. Henry Purcel.

All eminent for their great compositions and skill in music. Mr. Thomas Blagrave is Clerk of the Check [*sic*]. The rest of the Gentlemen of the Chapel are great masters also in the Science of Music and most exquisite performers, as

Mr. William Turner.	Mr. Thomas Heywood.
Mr. James Hart.	Mr. Alphonso Marsh.
Mr. —— Goslin.	Mr. Stephen Crispins.
Mr. —— Abel.	Mr. Leonard Woodson.

Musicians-in-ordinary, sixty-two, which are ranked in these three degrees, viz.

Private Music,

Wind Music, and

twenty-four violins.

Of all which, as also of the instrumental music of the Chapel, Dr. Nicholas Staggins is Master.

Trumpeters-in-ordinary are sixteen and one kettle-drummer, of whom Gervas Pryce, Esq., is the sergeant-trumpeter. John Maugridge drum-major, and four other drummers and a fife.†

In addition to the tasks that his position as organist imposed on him, Purcell had also to bear the responsibility for those clearly set out in detail in the warrant for his appointment as 'Keeper of Musical Instruments', which came through at last on 16 February.

---

* The days on which knights wore the collars of their orders (*OED*).

† Edward Chamberlayne, *Angliæ Notitia*, 15th ed. (1684), part 1, pp. 142, 147, and 180.

These duties, which were above and beyond those he had inherited from Hingeston as 'organ-maker and keeper' on 13 December 1683, must have been onerous indeed. If he obeyed all his instructions, Purcell undoubtedly earned every penny of the £60 per annum his new appointment brought him:

16 February 1683/4.

Henry Purcell appointed 'keeper, maker, repairer and mender and tuner of all and every His Majesty's musical wind instruments; that is to say all regals, virginals, organs, flutes, recorders and all other kind of wind instruments whatsoever, in the place of John Hingeston, deceased.' Wages £60 per annum, together with the money necessary for the 'working, labouring, making and mending any of the instruments aforesaid'. 'And also licence and authority to the said Henry Purcell or his assigns to take up within the realm of England all such metals, wire, wainscot, and other wood and things as shall be necessary to be employed about the premises, agreeing, paying and allowing reasonable rates and prices for the same. And also in His Majesty's name and upon reasonable and lawful prices, wages and hire, to take up such workmen, artificers, labourers, work and store houses, land and water carriages, and all other needful things as the said Henry Purcell or his assigns shall think convenient to be used on the premises. And also power and authority to the said Henry Purcell or his assigns to take up all timber, strings, and feathers, necessary and convenient for the premises, agreeing, paying, and allowing reasonable rates and prices for the same, in as full and ample manner as the said John Hingston . . . formerly had.'*

Some notion of the kind of work Purcell was required to do may be gleaned from some of Hingeston's old accounts, such as the following:

3 November 1664.

Warrant to pay John Hingeston, keeper and repairer of His Majesty's organs, pedals, harpsichords, and other instruments £90. 19s. 8d. for repairing the organs, harpsichords, pedals, and other instruments from 29 September 1664; bill signed by Mr. Nicholas Lanier.

29 January 1667/8.

Warrant to pay John Hingeston, keeper and repairer of His Majesty's organs, the sum of £111. 4s. 6d. for mending the organs at Hampton Court, St. James's, and Whitehall, and for strings for the pedals, harpsichords, and virginals, and for other services done by him from 29 September 1664 to 29th September 1667.†

* *KM*, pp. 364–5.
† *KM*, pp. 173 and 200 respectively. See also pp. 214, 223, 231, 235, 253, 298, 346, *et al.*

Old accounts also give a general description of the workshop that was to be Purcell's. Probably this had not changed a great deal in the intervening decades:

20 August 1663.

Warrant to the Surveyor-General to make and erect a large organ-loft by His Majesty's Chapel at Whitehall, in the place where formerly the great double organ stood, and to rebuild the rooms over the bellows room, two storeys high, as it was formerly, the lower storey for the Sub-Dean of His Majesty's chapel, and the upper storey with two rooms, one of them for the organist in waiting and the other for the keeper and repairer of His Majesty's organs, harpsichords, virginals, and other instruments, each room to have a chimney, and boxes and shelves for keeping the materials belonging to the organ and the organ books.*

The mechanical pursuits this new responsibility called for apparently did not cause Purcell to slacken his more artistic musical activities. Early in 1684 he prepared for publication yet another composition with a preface written by himself, this to his 'Musical Entertainment', 'Welcome to all the Pleasures', performed in honour of St. Cecilia the previous November.†
As an indication of new social forces already at work upon English music and musicians, Purcell's choice of dedicatees, and the things he says to them, are significant:

To the Gentlemen of the Musical Society, and particularly the Stewards for the year ensuing, William Bridgman, Esq.; Nicholas Staggins, Doctor in Music; Gilbert Dolben, Esq.; and Mr. Francis Forcer.

Gentlemen, Your kind approbation and benign reception of the performance of these musical compositions on St. Cecilia's Day (by way of gratitude) claim this dedication; which likewise furnishes the author with the opportunity of letting the world know the obligations he lies under to you; and that he is to all lovers of music, a real friend and servant, HENRY PURCELL.‡

That Purcell had composed at least one other work for this occasion we know from an annotation in the largest of his auto-graph scores in fair copy, now housed in the British Museum as

---

* KM, p. 160.   † Analytical Catalogue, no. 339.
‡ Though advertised in the London Gazette for 12 May, the publication had no doubt been in preparation in the early part of the year. Purcell's reference to 'these compositions' may perhaps be taken as a sign that he had originally intended to publish more works for St. Cecilia than the one that appeared in print. The stewards named are those for 1684, not 1683.

Royal Music MS. 20.h.8. After the title of 'Laudate Ceciliam'* on folio 190 (rev.), Purcell added the description:

A Latin song made upon St. Cecilia, whose day is commerated [*sic*] yearly by all musicians, made in the year 1683.

Nothing in this entry indicates that the piece was performed on 21 or 22 November. That it was written in honour of St. Cecilia in 1683 is evidence enough to show that it was part of these celebrations. Purcell may have intended to publish this work together with 'Welcome to all the pleasures' — hence his use of the plural in the preface mentioned above. As for 'Raise the voice',† the third ode to St. Cecilia (which has been putatively assigned to this date on the basis of evidence in manuscripts now missing), nothing definite can be established, although the fact that it calls for the same instrumental complement as that required for 'Laudate Ceciliam' suggests that these two may have been performed on the same programme. That the Ritornello Minuet (section 6 in 'Raise the voice') appeared as a harpsichord transcription in the second part of *Musick's Hand-Maid* (1689), proves little, since it merely provides a *terminus ad quem* some six years later.

Meanwhile, the Court prepared for its annual summer stay at Windsor, leaving very early this year, according to Luttrell's entry for 5 April and to various notices in London newspapers.‡ Purcell undoubtedly went too. Although actual records are wanting to prove this, it is unlikely that he or any other important Court musician would have been excused from the ceremonies held on 8 April at Windsor to solemnize the installation of Prince George of Denmark as a 'Knight Companion of the Order of the Garter' to which he had been elected, along with the dukes of Somerset and Northumberland, at the beginning of the year.§

---

* *Analytical Catalogue*, no. 329.
† *Analytical Catalogue*, no. 334.
‡ See Luttrell, vol. I, p. 304; also *London Gazette*, 3–7 April and 15–19 Sept. 1684. (The latter records the return of the Court to Whitehall.)
§ Luttrell, entries for 1 Jan. and 8 April 1684 respectively (vol. I, pp. 294 and 304).

This Danish prince had also been involved in Betterton's plans, which failed, to set up French opera in England.*

The old player had gone to Paris with high ambitions, but had 'caught only the wretched Grabu', who published his equally wretched 'Pastoral in French' with Hudgebut and Carr towards the end of the following month. To palliate his 'frenchify'd' appetites Charles settled instead for the prince's players, who went straight to Windsor, baggage and all, immediately after their arrival in England with 'sixty-five trunks or packs of old clothes' on 26 May 1684.† However, these players could not possibly satisfy Betterton's operatic aspirations, and their influence even upon the English stage play must have been slight, since they departed the following 11 December after a very short theatrical season at Whitehall. The 'wretched Grabu' stayed on, of course, but his contributions to the establishment of French opera in London were worse than negligible.

Purcell also may have been concerned with the theatre about this time, it seems, for the next season saw a revival of Ravenscroft's *The English Lawyer*‡ (first produced in 1677 as an adaptation of a Latin comedy, *Ignoramus* (1614), by George Ruggle), for which Purcell provided the catch 'My wife has a tongue as good as e'er twang'd'.[1] This catch was probably introduced in the tavern scene just after one of the characters has said, referring to his wife: 'Come give us a flourish ... we'll sing her praises backwards.' The catch, for three voices entering at the interval of seven bars, certainly is not one of Purcell's most impressive specimens. The poetry is neither pointed nor witty, and the composition so short that there is no opportunity for the usual references or double meanings between the various voices. Perhaps the chief importance of the catch lies in its having been instrumental in starting the gossip concerning bad relations between Purcell and his wife. Apparently Hawkins had not much more to go on in spinning his tale about Purcell's having caught his death of a cold because he was locked out late one night, too late for Mrs. Purcell's liking.

---

* As Boswell (after Lawrence) points out, p. 126.
† Boswell, p. 126.   ‡ *Analytical Catalogue*, no. 594.

Another catch, 'Come, my hearts',* is both slighter and shorter, though polyphonically more interesting. Its topical allusions to Tory policy (that is, loyalty to the king and the Duke of York without benefit of the Test Act) probably represent its chief value, however:

> Come, my hearts,
> Play your parts
> With your quarts
> See none starts
> For the King's health is a drinking.
>
> They that shrink
> From their chink
> From their drink
> We will think
> That of treason they are thinking.
>
> Then to His Highness
> See here the wine is
> That has past the Test
> Above the rest
> For those healths deserve the best.

Towards the end of spring 1684 the battle of the organ-builders approached its decisive phase, as Renatus Harris asked the Benchers of the Inner Temple for permission to arrange a public hearing of his organ in the Temple Church. Presumably Bernard Smith got the same kind of permission about this time, if the reports made by Hawkins (after Tudway's letter to his son, now lost) and Burney be accurate.† By the summer both organists had their instruments ready for the contest, Harris's just south of the communion table, Smith's in the West-end gallery.

For some time Draghi (for Harris) and Purcell and Blow (for Smith) demonstrated the capabilities of the two instruments on alternate days. Then, as time wore on with no unanimous decision, all contestants played on the same day, presumably for

* *Analytical Catalogue*, no. 246.

† Hawkins, vol. II, p. 691; Burney, vol. II, p. 344. Burney's summary of the affair is as comprehensive and accurate (despite his confusing of J. B. Draghi with Lully) as any. Hence I have followed it, mainly, in this description.

ease of comparison. Even so, several years were to elapse before a decision was reached,* this being arbitrated at last in 1688 by Judge Jeffreys, who had by then achieved considerable renown as a man capable of making difficult judgements and decisions quickly. He bestowed the victor's laurels upon Smith, Blow, and Purcell, while Harris and Draghi had to be satisfied with a consolation award, their organ being sent partly to St. Andrew's, Holborn (where Purcell's son Edward was one day to play upon it), and partly to Christ Church, Dublin.

When finished, Smith's organ in the Temple Church was one of the most modern yet constructed in England, what with its separate keys for G♯ and A♭, D♯ and E♭, and its full and complex make-up. Here are the exact specifications of stops and pipes, along with a schedule submitted by Smith on 21 June 1688:

21 June 1688
Mr. Bernard Smyth's bargain and sale of the organ in the
Temple Church to both the societies of the Temples.

Know all men by these presents that I, Bernard Smyth, of London, Gent., for and in consideration of one thousand pounds of lawful money of England to me paid, [to wit] five hundred pounds, part thereof, by the Treasurer of the Society of the Middle Temple, London, and the other moiety by the Treasurer of the Society of the Inner Temple, London, for which I have given several former acquittances, and in consideration of twenty shillings now paid to me by the Honourable Roger North and Oliver Montague, Esq., Benchers, and William Powlett, Esq., now Treasurer of the said Society of the Middle Temple, and by Sir Robert Sawyer, Knight, now Treasurer, and Charles Holloway and Richard Edwards, esquires, Benchers of said Society of the Inner Temple, have granted, bargained, and sold, and do hereby fully and absolutely grant bargain and sell unto the said Roger North, Oliver Montague, and William Powlett, and the said Sir Robert Sawyer, Charles Holloway, and Richard Edwards, esquires, all that organ which is now set up and standing in the organ-loft in the Temple Church belonging to the said two societies; and all stops and pipes and other parts and appurtenances of the said organ, and particularly the stops and pipes in the schedule hereunder written mentioned, and also the curtain rods and curtains — and all other goods and chattels being in or belonging to the said organ and organ-loft — To hold to the said Roger North, Oliver Montague, and Willm Powlett, and the said Sir Robert Sawyer, Charles Holloway, and Richd Edwards, esquires, their executors and administrators, in trust for and to the use of both the said societies of the Middle and Inner

* *Grove's* (4th ed.), vol. III, p. 751.

Temples. In witness whereof I the said Bernard Smyth have to these presents (a duplicate whereof I am to seal to the said Treasurer and Benchers of the Society of the Inner Temple) have set my hand and seal this one and twentieth day of June one thousand six hundred and eighty-eight.

The Temple Organ

The Schedule

Great Organ

1 pipes Prestand of metal	61 pipes 12 foot tone
2 pipes Holflute of wood and metal . . .	61 pipes 12 foot tone
3 pipes Principal of metal	61 pipes 6 foot tone
4 pipes Quinta of metal	61 pipes 4 foot tone
5 pipes Super octavo	61 pipes 3 foot tone
6 pipes Cornet of metal	112 pipes 2 foot tone
7 pipes Sesquialtera of metal . . .	183 pipes 3 foot tone
8 pipes Gedackt of wainscot . . .	61 pipes 6 foot tone
9 pipes Mixture of metal	226 pipes 3 foot tone
10 pipes Trumpet of metal	61 pipes 12 foot tone
	948

Choir Organ

11 pipes Gedackt wainscot	61 pipes 12 foot tone
12 pipes Holflute of metal	61 pipes 06 foot tone
13 pipes A Sadt of metal	61 pipes 06 foot tone
14 pipes Spittsflute of metal . . .	61 pipes 03 foot tone
15 pipes A Viol and Violin of metal . .	61 pipes 12 foot tone
16 pipes Voice human of metal . . .	61 pipes 12 foot tone
	366

Echos

17 pipes Gedackt of wood	61 pipes 06 foot tone
18 pipes Sup. octavo of metal . . .	61 pipes 03 foot tone
19 pipes Gedackt of wood	29 pipes
20 pipes Flute of metal	29 pipes
21 pipes Cornet of metal	87 pipes
22 pipes Sesquialtera	105 pipes
23 pipes Trumpet	29 pipes
	401

With 3 full sets of keys and quarter notes.

BER. SMITH. (L.S.)

Sealed and delivered in the presence of
Geo. Miniett. Tho. Griffin. Richd. Cooke.[2]

Smith's organ was to become the pride of the church, with a range extending down to FFF, and the unusual tonal adaptability made possible by its 'quarter notes', which, as a contemporary chronicler boasted, were rarities 'no other organ in England hath; and can play any tune, as for instance the tune of the 119th Psalm (in E minor) and several other services set by excellent musicians; which no other organ will do'.*

The contest had been strenuous. North, who witnessed it, reported that the contestants had nearly ruined themselves with their extravagant competitiveness. And 'old Roseingrave', according to Burney, saw some ungenteel conduct on the part of Harris and his crew, who were reported to have cut the bellows on Smith's instrument one night before a crucial contest. Nevertheless, as we have seen, Smith won the day, possibly because he had built the more suitable organ, but partially, at least, because he had the sagacity to employ Blow and Purcell as his champions.

As the summer of 1684 drew to an end Purcell was busy with another welcome ode for Charles II's return from Windsor to begin the new season at Whitehall.[3] But before the celebration for which this was written, the king and the Duke of York set off on a small progress ('political fence-mending' a modern commentator would call it), touring from Winchester to London, where they arrived by 25 September to be greeted by Purcell's setting of Thomas Flatman's ode, 'From those serene and rapturous joys'.†

At the beginning of November Charles Purcell sailed for Guinea, as captain of the sloop Le George,‡ and began the strange series of adventures that later were to lead the family into such a tangle of legal difficulties. Otherwise the records provide no hint of Purcell's activities during the rest of the month. Undoubtedly he was involved somehow in the elaborate preparations for the queen's birthday, which had begun on 10 November,§ for Luttrell described it as one of the grandest affairs ever:

---

* *Grove's* (4th ed.), vol. III, p. 751.   † *Analytical Catalogue*, no. 326.
‡ See PRO Chancery Roll C5/64/74.
§ See the 'Warrant to make the theatre ready for dancing on the Queen's birthday', 10 Nov. 1684. Boswell, p. 238.

The 15th, being Her Majesty's birthday, was kept at Whitehall, and in the evening were very fine fireworks on the water before Whitehall, which lasted for about two hours; and at night was a great ball at Whitehall, where the Court appeared in much splendour and bravery.*

For such unwonted attention to the queen, Charles may have had ulterior motives. It can scarcely be coincidental that Monmouth slipped secretly back into England at this very time, or conceivable that his arrival in London was either unknown to or unforeseen by the king. What better camouflage than a gala affair at Court?†

In the week following the queen's celebration Purcell was very likely involved in the preparations for the St. Cecilia's Day celebrations for the evening of the 21st and the day of the 22nd. This time, however, Purcell's activities would have been completely behind the scenes — supervising the moving of instruments to and from the Stationers' Hall, perhaps doing last-minute repairs or tuning. By contrast with the St. Cecilia's Day celebrations of the previous year (in which Purcell had been the star composer of the show, with two, perhaps even three, of his own works to see into performance), the 1684 affair was dull indeed. Its dullness was due in no small degree to Blow's offering for the occasion, 'Begin the song'. This ode, after a rather promising overture (which Handel liked well enough to borrow lock, stock, and barrel for his oratorio *Susanna* in 1748‡), sinks from depth to depth in musical banality.

Meanwhile Purcell had not whiled away his time idly: witness the impressive number of his songs, dialogues, and catches that appeared about this time. In each of these genres several works reveal an impressive growth of Purcell's individual style and expression, and a marked increase in technical facility and control.§

The New Year of 1685 found Charles II and his Court happy, prosperous, and in even better political situation than the year

* Luttrell, vol. I, p. 320. See also Evelyn, *Memoirs*, vol. I, p. 540.

† Luttrell, vol. I, p. 320; Bryant, p. 354.

‡ See F. B. Zimmerman, 'Handel's Purcellian Borrowings in his later Operas and Oratorios', *Festschrift Otto Erich Deutsch*, p. 22.

§ See *Analytical Catalogue*, app. v, which lists twenty-three works in all for this period.

before. Having won the battle for London, and therefore the struggle for control of England as well, Charles could afford to treat his enemies with benevolence, forgetting old injuries and issues. For the first time during his reign his revenues seemed adequate, and there was relative tranquillity in domestic and foreign affairs. Somehow he had managed better than any other Stuart monarch to wield the powers of an extremely strong, if not absolute, monarchy without resort to over-violent means of control in keeping the peace. In short, he had won a victory in a long and arduous campaign, and was now in a position to enjoy its fruits.

Those of his more solemn subjects who, like Evelyn, censured the king for the loose company he kept and the fast life he led were seeing things too much in black and white. To be sure, he still enjoyed his lighter moments with his little circle of lady-loves. At the same time it must be recognized that his accomplishments were far greater than any profligate could have boasted of, reckoning political achievements alone. When cultural attainments also are measured, a true measure of his real stature begins to appear.

Although music and the arts had been virtually destroyed during the Interregnum, he had managed to re-create, against implacably fierce opposition an environment in which creative personalities could flourish. Within two decades all the arts, and particularly music, had attained such excellence as to command respect all over Europe.

For Purcell and others like him working conditions at Court must have seemed propitious, despite the fact that the 'wretched Grabu' had at last managed to get permission for a Court production of his opera *Albion and Albanius*, as it was later to be called — a production forestalled only by Charles II's death on 6 February 1685. On the first day of the year Edward Bedingfield had compromised his musical judgement as follows, in a letter to the Countess of Rutland:

We are in expectation of an opera composed by Mr. Dryden and set by Grabuche, and so well performed at the repetition that has been made before His Majesty at the Duchess of Portsmouth's, pleaseth mightily, but the rates proposed will not take so well, for they have set the boxes at a guinea a place and the pit at half. They advance £4,000 on the opera, and therefore must tax high to reimburse themselves.*

For the musicians the most important sign of the king's newly won solvency had been the unaccustomed promptness of payments of salaries and fees, for which they were duly grateful, their gratitude sharpening the grief which they shared with the whole Court when he died. He had indeed been a friend and an encouraging patron, and in the period just preceding his death had managed so to improve Court finances that current salaries, at least, could be kept up no matter how heavily arrears weighed upon the books. Purcell spoke for them all in his elegy for the king, 'If pray'rs and tears', which begins with a mournful, evocative C-minor recitative setting of the opening lines of these 'Sighs for our late sovereign King Charles the Second', as the anonymous poet subtitled his elegy:

> If pray'rs and tears
> The shields the Church of England only bears
> In some great exigence of State
> Could those have warded off the blows of Fate
> We had not fallen, we had not sunk so low
> Under the grievous heavy weight,
> The pressures of this day's sad overthrow
> Oh how the first amazing blow
> Bowed down each loyal head. . . .†

Meanwhile Purcell had moved from Great St. Ann's Lane to Bowling Alley East, as may be seen in entries in the St. Margaret's, Westminster, Churchwardens' Accounts for 1684‡ and 1685. Apparently the move implied no advance in social status or living standards, for the rate collected still stood at fourteen shillings per annum, a respectably high amount.§ Quite possibly he moved merely to be nearer to the Abbey, perhaps finding his

* Hist. MSS. Comm., vol. VII, Rutland MSS. II, p. 85.
† *Analytical Catalogue*, no. 380.
‡ Fo. 22 with 'Gone' written in marginally.
§ See Churchwardens' Accounts, E 197–8 (for the years 1684 and 1685 respectively).

house through the good offices of Stephen Crespion, Canon and Succentor in the Abbey, and one of Purcell's closest and staunchest friends.* That Purcell moved just before the last quarter of 1684 is shown by the fact that he paid only three-fourths of his yearly rate. That is to say, he paid 10s. 6d., leaving 3s. 6d. remaining in the 'arrears' column at the end of the book.

The move was no doubt accomplished under pressure. Apart from his regular duties he had recently become more and more involved in editorial tasks, a sign not only of his growing reputation as a composer, but also of the meticulousness that characterized every aspect of his musical endeavours. The first two books of the *Theatre of Music* (which must have been in the press by about this time) and the dedication of these to 'Dr. John Blow, Master of the Children, and one of the Organists of His Majesty's Chapel Royal and to Mr. Henry Purcell, Composer-in-Ordinary to His Sacred Majesty and one of the Organists of his Chapel Royal', reveal that Purcell had by this time attained first place among English composers, and that his achievements were recognized.

For New Year's Day 1685 the usual forces were assembled to perform the ode, 'How does the new-born infant year rejoice', again set by Blow.† Then, on 26 January, twelve of the king's musicians were rehearsing for a ball, which probably took place during the course of the next few days (though not on 30 January, when the martyrdom of Charles I would have been commemorated).‡ At any rate the month ended with much musical activity at Court, as well as in London and Westminster. Evelyn commented upon this, explaining that on 27 January he had dined at Lord Sunderland's, where he was

invited to hear that celebrated voice of Mr. Pordage, newly come from Rome. His singing was after the Venetian recitative, as masterly as could be, and with an excellent voice both treble and bass. Dr. Walgrave accompanied it with his theorbo lute, on which he performed beyond imagination, and is doubtless one of the greatest masters in Europe on that charming instrument. Pordage is a priest, as Mr. Bernard Howard told me in private.§

* See the account of the organ-loft incident, pp. 165–75 below. Crespion had lived at this address since 1678.

† McGuinness, fo. 50.   ‡ *KM*, p. 369.   § Evelyn, 27 Jan. 1684/5.

On the 28th he was invited to Lord Arundell's house, where he heard Pordage again, this time accompanied by 'Signor Jo. Baptist' (Draghi) on the harpsichord, and also his (Evelyn's) daughter Mary, who sang 'to the great satisfaction of both masters, and a world of people of quality present: as she also did at my Lord Rochester's the evening following, when we had the French boy so famed for his singing, and indeed he had a delicate voice and had been well taught'. Evelyn commented, too, on hearing the loud-voiced Mr. Packer and the 'stupendous' bass, Gostling.*

Then suddenly, on 2 February, a few days after Evelyn had heard the French boy again, 'singing love songs in that glorious gallery', Charles II was stricken with apoplexy (2 February, ironically, was also Nell Gwynn's birthday).† He died four days later, and the nation mourned. The event was announced in the *London Gazette* that came out the following Monday, 9 February, in the following laconic manner:

Whitehall. 6 February 1684/5.

On Monday last in the morning our late gracious sovereign King Charles the Second was siezed with a violent fit, by which his speech and senses were for some time taken from him, but upon the immediate application of fitting remedies he returned to such a condition as gave some hopes of his recovery till Wednesday night, at which time the disease returning upon him with greater violence, he expired this day about noon.

In the same journal Charles II's obsequies were described with very little reference to music and scarcely any of the pomp usually attached to such occasions. On the secular scene appeared numerous elegiac verses by the chief poets at Court.‡ For the most part these were neither worse nor better than the 'Sighs for our late sovereign King Charles the Second' mentioned earlier.

In the aftermath of the king's sudden death the gloom naturally attendant upon the death of so popular a figure seemed immeasurably deepened by contrast to the bright gaiety, not to say profligacy, that had reigned at Court a few days earlier. Evelyn's memento of the courtly scene of 25 January epitomizes the gaiety

---

* Evelyn, 28 Jan. 1684/5.   † *DNB.*
‡ See, especially, those by Tate and Thomas.

of Charles's love affairs, just as his entry for 6 February reveals the funeral woes that now weighed upon the king's erstwhile merry companions.

I can never forget the inexpressible luxury, and profaneness, gaming, and all dissoluteness, and as it were total forgetfulness of God (it being Sunday evening) which this day se'nnight, I was witness of; the King sitting and toying with his concubines Portsmouth, Cleaveland, and Mazarine, &c. a French boy singing love songs in that glorious gallery, whilst about 20 of the great courtiers and other dissolute persons were at basset round a large table, a bank of at least 2,000 in gold before them, upon which 2 gentlemen who were with me made reflexions with astonishment. Six days after was all in the dust!*

The contrast is mirrored, somehow, in two other songs by Purcell, written at this time, 'Love is now become a trade', and 'Farewell all joys, now he is gone'.†

* Evelyn, *Memoirs*, 6 Feb. 1684/5.
† *Analytical Catalogue*, nos. 393 and 368 respectively.

CHAPTER IX

LONDON'S MUSICAL AND THEATRICAL LIFE UNDER A NEW MONARCHY

Within a few short weeks preparations began for the coronation of the new monarch, who moved to St. James's Palace early in April. Scandalmongers, eager to capitalize upon rumours that Charles II had died by unnatural causes, repeated strange tales of a nocturnal apparition at White-hall. Perhaps the anti-Catholic party had had a hand in an attempt to conjure up a ghost story, their phantom, like that of Hamlet's father, unquiet because of a foul deed; but Luttrell discredited the story (as, indeed, he may have felt duty-bound to do, being the official historiographer at Court):

April 1685.
  There is a common report about town of some apparition that walks at Whitehall; and the King's removal to St. James's hath given many credulous persons the occasion to believe the same, tho' it was only for a little while, that the lodgings at Whitehall might be fitted up.*

For the credulous, and perhaps for wishful thinkers (or wishful believers), another omen occurred on the day of the coronation (23 April, St. George's Day), when the crown nearly toppled from James II's head; since it was indeed to do so within a few years, superstition for once upheld its followers. Otherwise the corona-tion was a splendid and happy ceremonial event, nothing being omitted but the Holy Sacrament to make it the equal of any pomp in Christendom. Luttrell, who made this observation, directed his readers to the 'public prints' for particulars, the most important of these being, of course, Francis Sandford's *The History of the*

* Luttrell, vol. I, p. 338.

Coronation of the Most High, Most Mighty and Most Excellent Monarch James II.

Sandford's account is too long and detailed to be reproduced or even summarized here. However, one or two quotations will be useful to lend vividness and verisimilitude to some of the scenes illustrated in the end-papers of this book and in plates 9, 10, and 11, and perhaps to identify some of the chief participants in the colourful ceremony. The first of the musicians to appear were a fifer, drummers, trumpeters, and a kettle-drummer:

A fife, in a livery coat of scarlet cloth, nicely laced with gold and silver lace, and lined with shalloon, and His Majesty's cipher and crown on the back and breast, with his fife and fife banners richly embroidered and trimmed with silver and gold fringe, viz.

Clement Newth.

Four drums, in the same livery as the fife, with His Majesty's arms depicted on the drums, with scarves of crimson taffeta fringed with silver, all in one rank, viz.

1. Jacob Langley	2. John Skyrme
3. Devorax Clothier	4. Tertullian Lewis.

The drum-major, in a fine scarlet cloth coat, richly laced with gold and silver, and a crimson taffeta scarf about his waist, richly fringed with gold, viz.

Mr. John Mawgridge.

Eight trumpeters, all in rich liveries of crimson velvet, laced with gold and silver, with silver trumpets, having banners of crimson damask fringed about with gold and silver, with strings suitable and richly embroidered . . . viz.

1. Henrick Davent	2. Michael Maer	3. Peter Mounset
4. Hugh Fisher	5. Jervais [Price]	6. Matthew Shore
7. William Bull	8. Benedict Ragway.	

The kettle-drums, with their banners of crimson damask richly fringed and embroidered with His Majesty's arms and supporters, and followed by the kettle-drummer in the same livery as the trumpeters, viz.

Robert Mawgridge.*

Then, after a number of other Court functionaries had marched by four abreast in equally colourful attire, the Children and

---

* *The History of the Coronation of . . . James II*, pp. 65 ff. These lists apparently identify the various musicians shown in the magnificent plates Sandford published. (See end-papers and Plates 9, 10, and 11.) The total number of musicians is considerably greater than the thirty-six musicians (among them Purcell) mentioned in the *Cal. Tr. Books* for 14 April 1685.

Gentlemen of the Chapel Royal came along, in their midst the Westminster Choir and 'two sackbuts and a double curtall'. Here, as above, Sandford's complete list provides a roster of the most important musicians employed in these organizations:

Children of the Choir of Westminster: (1) William Christian, (2) Thomas Price, (3) George Rogers, (4) William Morley, (5) John Bates, (6) John Walker, (7) John Howell, (8) William Williams ... The Children of His Majesty's Chapel Royal: (1) Charles Allison, (2) Jeremiah Clarke, (3) Thomas Richardson, (4) James Townsend, (5) Simon Corbet, (6) William Smith, (7) Jacob Wood, (8) George Rogers, (9) Richard Henman, (10) Charles Husbands, (11) Vaughan Richardson, (12) William Norris ... (Each had two yards of scarlet cloth as their fee.)* ... The Choir of Westminster in surplices, with music books in their hands: (1) Charles Green, Clerk, (2) Richard Cherington, Clerk, (3) Josias Boucher went as a Gentleman of the King's Chapel, (4) Robert Tanner, (5) Moses Snow, (6) Thomas Jennings, (7) Charles Taylor, (8) Morgan Harris went as a Gentleman of the King's Chapel, (9) Thomas Richardson went as a Gentleman of the King's Chapel, (10) Thomas Blagrave went as a Gentleman of the King's Chapel, (11) Thomas Finell, one of the King's musicians, (12) Edward Braddock went as a Gentleman of the King's Chapel, (13) John Charole, a Petty Canon, went as a Gentleman of the King's Chapel, (14) Thomas Linacre, Clerk, a Petty Canon, (15) John Tynshare (alias Littleton), Clerk, a Petty Canon, (16) Stephen Crespion, Clerk, a Petty Canon, went as a Gentleman of the King's Chapel. (Such of the Choir of Westminster as were Gentlemen of the King's Chapel, went in that qualification, and the places here were supplied [by direction of the Dean of Westminster] with other persons skilled in music.) ...

Gentlemen of His Majesty's Chapel Royal, in surplices, with mantles over them, four a-breast, viz.

Counter-Tenors

(1) Mr. Michael Wise, supplied by Edward Morton, (2) Mr. Thomas Heywood, supplied by Dr. Uvedal, (3) Mr. John Abel, supplied by Aug. Benford, (4) Mr. Josias Boucher, (5) Mr. William Turner, (6) Mr. Thomas Richardson, (7) Mr. John Goodgroom, (8) Mr. Nathaniel Watkins.

Tenors

(9) Mr. Morgan Harris, (10) Mr. Alphonso Marsh, (11) Mr. Henry Frost, (12) William Powell, Clerk, (13) Mr. James Cobb, (14) Mr. Edward Braddock, (15) Henry Smith, Clerk, supplied by George Hart, (16) John Sayer, Clerk.

* The Christian names Jacob and George appearing together here may be those mentioned in connection with *Timon of Athens*; see pp. 257–9 below.

Basses

(17) Richard Hart, (18) Samuel Bentham, Clerk, (19) Leon[ard] Woodeson, Clerk, (20) John Gostling, Clerk, (21) Henry Purcell, Organist of Westminster, (22) Nathaniel Vestment, (23) John Charole, Clerk, (24) Andrew Trebeck, Clerk, (25) George Bettenham, (26) James Hart, Clerk, (27) Blaze White, Clerk, (28) George Yardely, Clerk, (29) Thomas Blagrave, Clerk of the Check to the Gentlemen of the Chapel, (30) Nicholas Staggins, Dr. in music and Master of the King's Music, (31) John Blow, Dr. in music, Master of the Children of the Chapel and Organist, supplied by Francis Forcer, (32) William Child, Dr. in music, Eldest Gentleman of the Chapel.

(For Blow, the following marginal note: 'Dr. Blow had also five yards of fine scarlet cloth for his mantle as composer.')[1]

These musicians, followed by other Court and Abbey employees, all dignitaries of the City of London, and the entire English nobility, formed the brilliant procession, which moved 'from Westminster Hall, through the New Palace Yard into King Street, and so through the Great Sanctuary, unto the West door of the Collegiate Church of St. Peter, the passage being railed in on both sides ... and guarded by His Majesty's Horse and Footguards ...':

Two breadths of blue broad-cloth ... spread from ... the Hall ... to the Choir ... which cloth was strewed with nine baskets full of sweet herbs and flowers, by Mary Dowle, Strewer-of-Herbs-in-Ordinary to His Majesty ... The drums beat a march, the trumpets sounded several levets and the chorus sang all the way from the Hall to the church this anthem: ... 'O Lord, grant the King a long life'. [Marginal note: 'Composed heretofore by Dr. Child.']*

It would be tedious to recount all the details of the coronation ceremony. Suffice it to say that it followed in the main the procedure outlined for Charles II's coronation. However, the whole affair had grown much more complicated, probably because Mary of Modena was present also to be robed, anointed, crowned, and enthroned.

All told, nine anthems were sung, most of these being performed — as were other incidental instrumental and vocal pieces

---

* Sandford, *The History of the Coronation of ... James II*, p. 80. The wording may indicate that Child had composed this anthem for earlier coronations, but not for this one. Perhaps Purcell's setting was used for this occasion.

The INTHRONIZATION of their MAJESTIES King IAMES the Second and Queen MARY.

9 'The Inthronization of Their Majesties King James the Second and Queen Mary'

10 'Gentlemen of the Chapel Royal, in number 32'

11 'A Fife, 4 Drums, the Drum Major'

— in the 'cori spezzati' tradition which had been developing at San Marco's, Venice, for a century or more and, in England, at least since the coronation of Charles II.★ Sandford describes the performance of these anthems in detail,† beginning with the entrance of the king and queen into the Abbey, when the Westminster choir went before them, singing Purcell's full anthem 'I was glad when they said'.‡ As the queen entered the choir the King's Scholars of Westminster School sang 'Vivat regina Maria, vivat Jacobus Rex' from the gallery adjoining the organ loft, after which came the acclamations, followed by Blow's full anthem 'Let thy hand be strengthened', sung by all choirs as 'their majesties reposed themselves in their chairs of state'.

The Bishops of St. Asaph and Oxford then sang the litany, to which the choirs answered with the responses, this ceremony being followed by a sermon and the oath during which no music was heard. As a preface to the anointing, William Turner's setting of 'Veni creator' ('Come, Holy Ghost, our souls inspire') was sung, after which, just at half past two, the choirs sang Henry Lawes's anthem:

> Zadok the Priest, and Nathan the Prophet
> Anointed King Solomon, and all the people
> Rejoiced and said GOD SAVE THE KING
> Long live the King, May the King live for ever.

Before the investing Blow's short anthem 'Behold, O Lord our defender' was sung, and afterwards Turner's 'Deus in virtute' ('The King shall rejoice in thy strength'), followed by William Child's 'Te Deum', and then by Blow's 'God sometimes spake in visions'. After the coronation of the queen the ceremony ended, as it had begun, with a composition of Purcell's. This final piece was 'My heart is inditing of a good matter',§ 'performed by the whole consort of voices and instruments' — a splendid climax to the royal pageant.

★ For a view of the enthronization in Westminster Abbey, showing the positions of musicians, trumpeters, and drummers, as well as other persons participating, see Plate 9.
† Op. cit. pp. 82 ff.   ‡ Analytical Catalogue, no. 19.
§ Analytical Catalogue, no. 30.

K

If this last statement may be taken to mean exactly what it says, then the usual way of performing this anthem must provide us with only a pale approximation of the sounds produced in that original performance, which would have included not only those made by the quartet of strings and eight-part solo and choral ensembles, but also the brilliant sounds of hautboys, trumpets, drums, and other instruments (like those shown in Plate 12(*a*)). A further hint of what may have been involved here is to be gained from the following account, which could scarcely apply to any but the last and most glorious work heard at the coronation, Purcell's 'My heart is inditing':

9 November 1686.

These are to pray and require you to pay unto Dr. Nicholas Staggins, Master of His Majesty's Music, the sum of £19. 11s. 6d. for fair writing of a composition for His Majesty's coronation day from the original in score the 6 parts, for drawing the said composition into forty several parts for trumpets, hautboys, violins, tenors, basses, pricker's diet included, for ruled paper, pens, ink, and chamber rent, and disbursed in providing several musicians for the coronation day who were not His Majesty's servants.*

The day following the coronation brought further festivities, culminating that night 'with fireworks before Whitehall on the water' (in which, unluckily, three or four persons were injured) and a great ball afterwards.† No account of the music performed has survived, but it is certain that many of the king's musicians were on hand for the event. Two days later, as if to mark both an end to official mourning for Charles II and an auspicious beginning to the reign of James II, the theatres were reopened.

Early in June Purcell received compensation from the authorities for his expenses and services in setting up the second organ in Westminster Abbey for the coronation of James II and Mary of Modena. In view of the dilatoriness they had shown on similar occasions in the past, they were remarkably prompt this time. The documents mention other earlier services that Purcell had rendered without specifying what they were:

To Henry Purcell, for so much money by him disbursed and craved for providing and setting up an organ in the Abbey Church of Westminster for

* *KM*, p. 380.

† Luttrell, vol. 1, p. 339; see also Plate 12(*b*) for a later fireworks celebration.

the Solemnity of the Coronation, and for the removing the same, and other services performed in His said Majesty's Chapel since the 25th of March 1685 according to a bill signed by the Bishop of London . . .

$£34. 12s.$*

Also early in June, on the 3rd, Dryden's opera *Albion and Albanius* was at last performed, not at Whitehall as had been intended — Nicoll aptly described it as 'a vast piece of royal flattery' — but at Dorset Garden.† Originally Dryden and Grabu had intended thus to pay tribute to Charles alone, and had indeed even managed to get the production into rehearsal before the king's sudden death cancelled all plans. It was June before libretto and score could be revised to refer to James II (Albanius) as well as to his late brother (Albion). However, the run lasted for only six days, for on 9 June the sudden appearance of Argyll in Scotland and of Monmouth at Lyme Regis in Dorset sent scurrying off the boards all these fictive epic heroes and their symbolic representatives: Thamesis (Thames), Archon (Monk), and Zelota (Zealots). So Dryden and the 'wretched Grabu' had their hopes dashed again, while James II and his generals hurried off to make firm the foundations of the State, thus so arduously, if unprofitably, eulogized.

In little less than a month Monmouth's hopes ended ingloriously at Sedgemoor, he being taken prisoner at 7 a.m. on 8 July‡ and brought back to London to be beheaded hastily and unskilfully, though not unceremoniously, on 15 July. Purcell's interest in the affair is illustrated in his setting of D'Urfey's little allegory 'A grasshopper and a fly',§ which, though published in the following year, was surely composed as a topical piece for performance at Court about this time. The frankly double-edged satire in this dialogue was such, very likely, as to find little favour with King James II and Mary of Modena, who were not over-sympathetic towards English musicians in any case. To celebrate their victory, they apparently turned for music not to an English composer in the Chapel Royal, but to an Italian, G. B. Vitali, whose work the

* Bodleian, Rawl. MS. D872, fo. 99; *Secret Services*, p. 124.
† Nicoll, p. 158.
‡ *DNB.*   § *Analytical Catalogue*, no. 481.

queen had no doubt heard in her native Modena.* The great event was commemorated, probably in Italy, by his oratorio, *L'Ambizione debellata: ovvero, La Caduta di Monmouth*,† upon a libretto evidently produced rather quickly by the Venetian, G. A. Canal, since it was in print before the end of 1686.

This *azione drammatica* brought to the stage Ragione (Reason), Fede (Faith), and Innocenza (Innocence) to argue the royal cause against Ambizione (Ambition) and Tradimento (Treason), who represented Monmouth and his followers. The conclusion was foregone, having been announced in the title, and the libretto was therefore devoid of dramatic interest. The music itself, however, is often quite dramatic in its expression, and the overture and a few ritornelli and arias are quite worth hearing. Only the long and rather characterless recitative passages give any hint that Vitali also may have been working with some haste.

It was also about this time that Purcell wrote incidental music for his fifth play, Tate's *Cuckold's-Haven*, probably given at the Theatre Royal, as were the four previous plays for which he had written music. Here, however, the connection between Purcell's song, 'How great are the blessings of government grown',‡ and the play is even more tenuous than is usual for the Restoration stage. In fact, the duet was sung (between the second and third acts of the play) rather as a tribute to James II, who happened to be present, than as an integral part of the play. (Hence, the editor of vol. XXII of the Purcell Society Edition was not altogether wrong in including the duet among the songs rather than with the dramatic music.)§

Quite possibly this performance took place about the time of the public thanksgiving that James ordered for 28 July. Two more of Purcell's theatrical compositions have sometimes been assigned

---

* Just the year before, Vitali had dedicated to the queen his *Balli in stile francese* a cinque stromenti, consecrati alla Sacra Real Maestà di Maria Beatrice d'Este Stuarda, Regina della Gran Bretagna. . . . Opera duodecima... (Modena, 1685). Eleven years before, he had entered the service of Duke Francisco II, her brother.

† 'Ambition Brought Low; or, The Downfall of Monmouth'.

‡ *Analytical Catalogue*, no. 494.

§ Cf. Laurie, fo. 168.

to this year; however, neither can be dated for certain as belonging to 1685. The mad song in Lee's *Sophonisba** not only appears for the first time in print at a suspiciously late date,† but from a stylistic point of view appears to belong to Purcell's later period. The long fioriture for certain words and the echo are particularly uncharacteristic of this period in Purcell's stylistic development. Possibly he did write the song for a revival in 1691, or even in 1693.‡ His music for Charles D'Avenant's *Circe*§ also seems more advanced in style than are most works that may be assigned to 1685 with certainty. Again, the long melismas and echo effects argue for a later date. Purcell perhaps supplied the music for the performance on 7 November 1690, for which Mrs. Barry was paid '£25 for "Circe", acted by command'.‖ For all these reasons, I have considered it best to discuss these works in connection with his later years.

By the end of August James II and his Lord Chamberlain had at last returned to some of the administrative tasks involved in setting the Court's musical establishment in order. For although Staggins (on 25 March)¶ and a few others had had their positions confirmed, the official warrants had not been written. Thus it was probably with some relief that on 31 August thirty-four musicians (Purcell among them) found themselves at last being sworn in as His Majesty's musicians-in-ordinary. The lists of those named included twenty-three counter-tenors (the last two of whom, John Abell and William Turner, are listed inexplicably as 'The vocal part' in the Lord Chamberlain's warrant); five basses (including Gostling and Bowman); one flautist by the name of Monsieur Mario; a tenor, Thomas Heywood; and a bass violist, Coleman. Purcell was named as a harpsichordist, Blow as a composer, and Henry Brockwell as keeper of the instruments. During the two following months these appointments were all confirmed by

---

* *Analytical Catalogue*, no. 590.

† In *Orpheus Britannicus*, book II (1702), as Dr. Laurie points out in her dissertation, fo. 169.

‡ Again as Dr. Laurie has suggested.

§ *Analytical Catalogue*, no. 575.

‖ See *Analytical Catalogue*, no. 575, Commentary.

¶ *KM*, p. 369.

certificates,* which indicate that two other musicians had also been appointed, Solomon Eccles and Francis Mariens. Of these thirty-six musicians, less than half were on hand for Her Majesty's birthday on 25 September and the 'great rejoicings at Windsor and a ball at night, the court being there', which Luttrell recorded,† and which also is known from the warrant for riding charges paid out to Nicholas Staggins and fifteen other musicians who made the trip.

Purcell was not among these — probably because he would have been very busy preparing an ode to celebrate the king's birthday, which was proclaimed soon after the queen's birthday and observed on 14 October. It is strange that Purcell, officially a harpsichordist, was asked to compose for the occasion, although Blow was listed as official composer in the above-mentioned list. At any rate Purcell composed 'Why are all the muses mute'‡ for James II's fifty-second birthday, and Luttrell duly recorded the public demonstration of joy for the event.§ Evelyn, in his turn, somewhat boastfully dropped a royal name or two in his entry for the day following the occasion, 15 October. (The conversation he mentions appears to have taken place during the performance, a distraction which no doubt endeared him to the musicians.)

Being the King's birthday, there was a solemn ball at Court, and before it music of instruments and voices. At the music I happened by accident to stand the very next to the Queen and the King, who talked with me about the music.

The ode celebrated also the suppression of Monmouth's rebellion in the West, as is revealed by the lines describing the sending of the 'threatening monster Rebellion back down to Hell'. Monmouth's campaign, which had ended militarily at Sedgemoor on 5 July, politically on the executioner's block at Whitehall ten days later, was the real reason for the celebration for which Purcell provided the ode. (Hence 'Why are all the muses mute' may be considered in a way an English companion-piece to the

* *KM*, p. 372; see also Hist. MSS. Comm., vol. VIII, p. 12b.
† Vol. I, p. 358.
‡ *Analytical Catalogue*, no. 343.   § Vol. I, p. 359.

Italian oratorio *L'Ambizione debellata; ovvero, La Caduta di Monmouth* upon which G. B. Vitali and his librettist, Canal, were no doubt already at work at this time.)* Be this as it may, Purcell had had to compose the ode under the distressing, distracting circumstances of the aftermath of Jeffreys's 'Bloody Assizes', in which James II relentlessly pursued all enemies, either his or his Church's. Only the day before his birthday he had pushed the prosecution of one Henry Cornish, former Whig sheriff, who had persecuted Papist plotters in 1680, James being quite satisfied to see the poor man convicted, on the flimsiest of evidence, to be drawn and quartered ten days later.

The rest of the year 1685 passed rather uneventfully for musicians at Court. In fact the whole season must have seemed somewhat dull to the average Londoner. St. Cecilia's Day came and went without unusual stir. Nahum Tate and William Turner's ode for the occasion ('Tune the viol, touch the lute') sank even below the standard Blow had set the previous year with 'Begin the song'.† In fact the affair was such a fiasco from the musical point of view that no celebration was held the following year.‡

August Kühnel, a German musician who had come to England only shortly before, seems to have attracted a great deal more attention at this same time by his musical exploits, advertised in the following announcement in the *London Gazette* for 19–23 November, which incidentally confirms the direct connection between the music publisher's trade and concert life in London that was hinted at in the account of Purcell's sonata publications two years earlier:

Several sonatas, composed after the Italian way, for one and two bass viols, with a thorough-bass, being upon the request of several lovers of music (who have already subscribed) to be engraven upon copper plates, are to be performed on Thursday next, and every Thursday following, at six of the clock in the evening, at the Dancing School in Walbrook, next door to the Bell Inn, and on Saturday next, and every Saturday following, at the Dancing School in York Buildings. At which places will be also some performance upon the

* See pp. 129–30 above.
† See Jeffrey Pulver, 'The English St. Cecilia Celebrations of the Seventeenth Century', *Sackbut*, July 1927, p. 346.
‡ Husk, pp. 20–22.

baritone, by Mr. August Keenall [Kühnel], the author of this music. Such who
do not subscribe are to pay their half crown towards the discharge of performing it.*

On 3 December Grabu again returned from Paris, apparently
having recovered from the ill effects of the previous summer's
fiasco, almost to disappear from sight thereafter, although he
lingered about the Court for some time, and even managed to
mount a concert (as advertised in the London Gazette for 15
November 1694).† For 18 December Evelyn reported a magnificent entertainment given at Court for the Venetian ambassadors.
He was almost carried away by his own description:

> I dined at the great entertainment His Majesty gave the Venetian ambassadors
> Signors Zenno and Justiniani, accompanied with ten more noble Venetians of
> their most illustrious families, Cornaro, Maccenigo, etc., who came to con-
> gratulate their majesties coming to the crown, etc. The dinner was one of the
> most magnificent and plentiful that I have ever seen, at 4 several tables with
> music, trumpets, kettle-drums, etc., which sounded upon a whistle at every
> health. The banquet was 12 vast chargers piled up so high, as those who sat
> one against another could hardly see one another; of these sweetmeats, which
> doubtless were some days piling up in that exquisite manner, the ambassadors
> touched not, but leaving them to the spectators who came in curiosity to see
> the dinner, etc. were exceedingly pleased to see in what a moment of time, all
> that curious work was demolished and the comfitures etc. voided and table
> cleared. Thus His Majesty entertained them 3 days, which (for the table only)
> cost him 600 pounds as the Clerk of the Green-Cloth, Sir W. Boreman, assured
> me. . . .

London's musical life for the year ended on 31 December with
a concert, alluded to with annoying vagueness in a letter from
Peregrine Bertie to the Countess of Rutland:

> My cousins and the ladies have been in town. I had the good fortune to see
> them at a music-meeting for about three minutes . . . The last music-meeting
> but one, was sung the song of young Dorinda, which I suppose your ladyship
> has heard of. The last meeting was sung this enclosed song, I need not name the
> author, because I am sure when I say nothing of the author your ladyship may
> easily guess who it is.‡

* Tilmouth, RMA Research Chronicle, no. 1, p. 7.
† See Westrup, 'Foreign Musicians in Stuart England', Musical Quarterly,
Jan. 1941, p. 75, and Tilmouth, op. cit., p. 15.
‡ Hist. MSS. Comm., Rutland MSS., vol. II, p. 99.

Soon after the beginning of the new year (celebrated with a new ode by Blow, 'Hail, monarch, sprung of race divine')* the French opera company returned to London, this time to perform Lully's *Cadmus et Hermione*, possibly, as W. J. Lawrence has suggested, to make up for the dismal failure of Grabu's *Albion and Albanius*.†
Apparently the performance did not shape up as quickly as the producers had planned. At least Peregrine Bertie's references to the opera in three successive letters to the Countess of Rutland seem to indicate postponement and delay:

23 January 1685/6: Next week begins the French Opera.

28 January 1685/6: The French Opera will begin the week after next.

11 February 1685/6: Today was the French Opera. The King and Queen were there, the music was indeed very fine, but all the dresses the most wretched I ever saw; 'twas acted by none but French.‡

Whatever the feelings of the two mediocrities, Cambert and Grabu (thus pursued by Lully, their nemesis), Purcell may be supposed to have heard a performance and liked the music enough to borrow the melody from Lully's 'Entrée de l'Envie' for his own music for *The Tempest*§ nearly a decade later. No one has yet speculated upon the ten-year gap between the opportunity to hear and the alleged borrowing of this tune, || or upon the absence of a plagiarism in Purcell's hand. On the face of the matter it would seem strange that Purcell should borrow once, then never again, so far as is known — a consideration which lends additional weight to the argument of those who doubt if Purcell wrote all the music for *The Tempest* that has been ascribed to him. It is therefore quite logical, as well as pleasant, to suppose that such a plagiarism would have been uncharacteristic of Purcell, as is some of the instrumental music in *The Tempest*.

* McGuinness, fo. 51.

† W. J. Lawrence, 'The French Opera in London: A Riddle of 1686', *Times Literary Supplement*, 28 March 1936, p. 268.

‡ Hist. MSS. Comm., Rutland MSS. vol. II, pp. 102, 103, and 104 respectively.

§ *Analytical Catalogue*, no. 631/4.

|| *Cadmus et Hermione, Tragédie mise en musique par Monsieur de Lully....* Representée pour la première fois devant le Roy, à Saint-Germain-en-Laye, en l'Année 1674 (Paris, 1719). The 'Entrée de l'Envie', from which the melody only appears in *The Tempest* music attributed to Purcell, begins on p. 21 of this edition.

Meanwhile James II managed to clear up the arrears in salaries which must have kept Court musicians leading a precarious hand-to-mouth existence almost from the beginning of the Restoration. William Child, for instance, was given liveries for the years 1662, 1665–7, and 1679–84. Others received similar reimbursements, which amounted to £16. 2s. 6d. for each year in arrears, but Purcell's name is nowhere mentioned. Either his payments had been met regularly or he was not one of those so fortunate as to receive redress.

March passed uneventfully, although Matthew Purcell's application for administration of the Will of Charles Purcell may have caused some trouble in the family.* On the following 6 May the Will was at last proved. But Matthew and the rest of the Purcell family could scarcely have felt that the net results justified his efforts, since William Bayley's widow had by this time disposed of most of the estate.† April seems to have brought little work for musicians at Court, so far as extant records show. However, it is unlikely that St. George's Day (23 April) passed without some musical celebration, as it marked also the first anniversary of James II's coronation. Indeed, there might be some reason to suppose that the 'Pastoral Coronation Song' ('While Thyrsis, wrapt in downy sleep')‡ may have found a sequel in the delightful little river song, 'Whilst Cynthia sung',§ which appeared about this time in Henry Playford and Richard Carr's *Theatre of Music*, book III. Certainly, thematic resemblances in these two songs seem to indicate some such relationship, involving James and Mary in their own stylish circle of courtly love at Whitehall, which reflected, though palely, the more interesting circle that Charles II had kept revolving about himself.

About this time Purcell's purely instrumental pieces began to find their way into published collections, as they were to do henceforth with increasing frequency. He was not yet represented in John Playford's *The Dancing Master*, now in its seventh edition,

* See App. Two, I, 3.
† See App. Two, I, 4, for a full account of this matter.
‡ *Analytical Catalogue*, no. 437.
§ *Analytical Catalogue*, no. 438.

but the famous old publisher's new volume, *The Delightful Companion or Choice New Lessons for the Recorder or Flute*, did contain a purely instrumental piece 'Lilliburlero',* along with an instrumental transcription of the catch 'Here's that will challenge all the fair'.† However, 'Lilliburlero' is printed anonymously in the collection, and may have been associated with Purcell's name only two years later. At any rate it was in 1688 that the tune appeared with the anti-Jacobite text by Thomas Wharton, which tune, as he put it, was to help William III to 'whistle King James II out of three kingdoms'.‡ When Playford may have printed this collection is not certain; but it undoubtedly had appeared some time before 6 May, when Mrs. Ellen Playford announced the 'sale of the printing house of the late J. Playford in Little Britain'.§

The early summer weeks passed uneventfully, Purcell going along to Windsor, it may be assumed, when the Court moved there about 14 May. Then, some time before 3 August, he returned to Westminster Abbey to arrange for the burial of a son, Thomas, probably the third child he had buried in these five years. Westrup assumes that the boy died in infancy, perhaps only a few days after birth. But there is no evidence to show that he may not have been considerably older. Again records are lacking — but their absence proves nothing either way.

Whether or not Purcell made his way back to Windsor to rejoin the Court, he did not remain there until 1 October, when all the others returned, for he had business affairs to attend to in London:[2]

The organ being now finished, it is ordered that Mr. Joseph Cox do procure Mr. Purcell, Mr. Barkwell and Mr. Moses, masters in music, and Mr. White, organ-master, or such other competent judges in music as may be prevailed with to be at our church on Thursday next, the 30th of this instant September, at two of the clock in the afternoon to give their judgements upon the organ...‖

* *Analytical Catalogue*, no. 646.
† *Analytical Catalogue*, no. 253.
‡ Westrup, p. 65; see also pp. 161–2 below.
§ Tilmouth, *RMA Research Chronicle*, no. 1, p. 7.
‖ Vestry Minutes of St. Katherine Cree (now in London Guildhall Library, MS. 1196/1), also quoted in C. W. Pierce, *Old London City Churches, Their Organists and Musical Associations* (London: n.d.), p. 19.

A later paragraph from the same source, for 30 September, reads:

Doctor Blow, Mr. Purcell, Mr. Mosse, Mr. Fforcell this day appearing at our church, Mr. Purcell was desired to play and did play upon the organ, and after he had done playing they all reported to the Vestry that in their judgements the organ was a good organ, and was performed and completed according to contract.

Purcell then stayed on to hear the contestants for the organist's place, the procedure being carried on as follows:

Mr. Niccolls, Mr. Beach, Mr. Snow, and Mr. Heath this day appearing and according to an order of the last Vestry did severally play upon the organ in the audience of the above Dr. Blow, Mr. Purcell, Mr. Mosse, and Mr. Fforcell and several . . . parishioners of this parish. And the said Dr. Blow, Mr. Purcell, Mr. Mosse, and Mr. Fforcell after the said Mr. Niccolls, Mr. Beach, Mr. Snow, and Mr. Heath had done playing reported to the Vestry that the third person that played (which fell out to be Mr. Snow) did in their judgements play the best and most skilfully of them all, and that the first that played (which fell out to be Mr. Niccolls) played next best. And thereupon the Vestry proceeded to a choice of an organist, and the said Mr. Niccolls, Mr. Beach, Mr. Snow, and Mr. Heath being put in nomination for an organist, and every person of the Vestry then present giving this vote by scratch of pen or scrutiny, the choice by majority of hands fell upon Mr. Snowe, who had eight hands, and Mr. Beach but five hands, and Mr. Niccolls and Mr. Heath but one hand apiece. And the said Mr. Snowe being afterwards made acquainted with the said choice, gratefully accepted of the said place.*

Despite Purcell's finding that the organ was a good instrument some difficulty must have arisen, for Bernard Smith, who built it, did not receive the contractual payment of £250 until 28 May 1687. From the rest of the account given above it appears that Purcell and Smith were paid 14s. for their trouble and that Blow and Purcell received 5s. each for coach hire. Further sums laid out are recorded in the accounts audited for the same date:

Paid and spent at the Crown Tavern upon Dr. Blow and others when they approved of an organ and chose an organist   £008. 13s. 0d.
Paid Mr. Snow, organist, for one quarter salary due at Christmas   £005. 0s. 0d.
Paid Mr. Moses Snow for a quarter salary due at Lady Day   £005. 0s. 0d.†

* Ibid.   † Guildhall MS. 1198/1.

From all this it is evident that the proving of the organist and the hearing of the candidates was a serious affair; involving probably several days' sojourn in the area, apparently far enough from Westminster to warrant travel and accommodation expenses. But on these points, as usual, the records are silent, leaving basis for little but conjecture. The episode is rendered all the more interesting, however, by the fact that the minister at St. Katherine Cree at this time was Nicholas Brady,* who was to provide the 'Ode to St. Cecilia' ('Hail, bright Cecilia'), which Purcell set to music with such brilliant and successful results a few years later.

By 14 October Purcell had to prepare yet another birthday 'Ode for the King'. For this occasion he composed 'Ye tuneful muses, raise your heads',† in the text of which the anonymous poet took care to pay suitable and sufficient respect to the queen in the later stanzas of the ode. To add splendour to the day's events James ordered four troops of guards to assemble in Hyde Park and, as a finishing touch, brought his mistress, Mrs. Sedley, out of retirement in Ireland.‡ One wonders if Purcell may have introduced the raucous ballad tune 'Hey, then up go we' as the bass to the chorus 'Be lively then and gay' with tongue in cheek. About this time it had appeared in a broadside entitled 'The Popish Tory's Confession; or, An Answer to the Whig's Exaltation'.§

Meanwhile Purcell had been losing time over a petty but very annoying financial problem. His letter to the Dean of Exeter reveals the amount of time unnecessarily lost in an apparently vain attempt to collect a fee, and also brings to light news of the first of Purcell's recorded pupils. Very likely Purcell felt that his teaching time also had been largely wasted, since nothing came of Mr. Hodges's musical aspirations, so far as is known:

> Westminster, November the 2nd, 1686
> I have wrote several times to Mr. Webber concerning what was due to me on Hodg's account and received no answer, which has occasioned this presumption

* Husk, p. 29.   † *Analytical Catalogue*, no. 344.
‡ Luttrell, vol. I, p. 386.
§ William Chappel, *Old English Popular Music*, vol. I, p. 207. The text begins: 'Down with the Whigs, we'll now grow wise'.

in giving you the trouble of a few lines relating to the matter. It is ever since the beginning of June last that the money has been due: the sum is £27, *viz.* £20 for half a year's teaching and boarding, the other a bill of £7 for necessaries which I laid out for him, the bill Mr. Webber has. Compassion moves me to acquaint you of a great many debts Mr. Hodg contracted whilst in London and to some who are so poor 'twere an act of charity as well as justice to pay 'em. I hope you will be so kind to take it into your consideration and also pardon this boldness from

Sir, your most obliged
humble servant
Henry Purcell*

Again, the outcome is in doubt. But what with a slender stipend at Court and meagre resources otherwise, Purcell no doubt needed the money.

About mid-December the King 'permitted Cotterell, the Master of Ceremonies, to resign', as Luttrell put it, bringing his own natural son, Mr. Fitzjames, back from Germany to reign in his stead.† Cotterell, who, incidentally, had been a very close friend of Mrs. Katherine Philips ('the matchless Orinda'), and hence may have brought some of her works to the attention of young Purcell (who was later to set them so beautifully), was by now seventy-four years old, and no doubt happy to relinquish the responsibility of keeping the over-serious monarch and his rather petulant wife sufficiently entertained.

As if to recoup his ailing fortunes, Grabu advertised the forth-coming publication of his opera, *Albion and Albanius*, which was nearly ready, there remaining 'no more to be printed but ten sheets in folio'. It is significant that there was no mention of a performance or even of a request to Fitzjames that there be one.‡ Perhaps December was a bad month for theatrical productions, as John Dryden's *The Spanish Fryar* (for which Purcell was to compose a song several years later§) was suppressed by King James II, even though Charles II had let it be performed and published six years before.||

---

* Reproduced in facsimile, Westrup, opp. p. 236.
† Luttrell, vol. I, p. 390.
‡ *London Gazette* 20–23 Dec. 1686.
§ *Analytical Catalogue*, no. 610. || Nicoll, p. 10.

The year closed quietly, although Purcell may have been somewhat upset by the fact that the money for house-rent due to him
at Christmas was not paid on time, in fact did not come to him
until Michaelmas the following year. He may also have been
apprehensive for his friend and colleague, Bernard Smith, who was
no doubt put out by the handsome commission to build a new
organ at Whitehall, for which his arch-rival, Renatus Harris,
received £300 in advance on 31 December 1686, then another
£200, also in advance, on 18 October 1687, £137. 13s. on 3 April
1688, and a final and munificent £600 on 3 July 1688.*

The year of Newton's *Principia*, 1687,† saw Purcell engaged in a
major project, composing sacred songs for *Harmonia Sacra*, book 1,
upon which task, indeed, he may well have begun much earlier.
March passed without any notable occurrence except the death
of Lully on the 22nd in Paris. Then in April, as the Queen
Dowager came out of mourning, the atmosphere at Court
became more lively, especially after 7 April, when James published
the 'Declaration of Indulgence', which, though William III was
to countermand it, removed, at least temporarily, the necessity
for all oaths and tests.‡ Evelyn heard Siface sing again (as he had
done at the Chapel Royal on 27 January, a little less than three
months before). Some of his remarks no doubt reflected the
opinions of other Londoners:

I heard the famous singer Cifaccio, esteemed the best in Europe. Indeed his
holding out and delicateness in extending and loosing a note with that incomparable softness and sweetness was admirable; for the rest, I found him a mere
wanton, effeminate child, very coy and proudly conceited to my apprehension.
He touched the harpsichord to his voice rarely well. This was before a select
number of particular persons whom Mr. Pepys [Secretary to the Admiralty and
a great lover of music] invited to his house, where the meeting was, and this
was obtained by peculiar favour and much difficulty, the Signor much disdain-
ing to show his talent to any but princes.§

---

* *Secret Services*, pp. 144, 169, 180, and 196 respectively. In all, £1,237. 13s.
was spent on the organ.

† Duly ushered in by the usual New Year's celebration at Court, Blow's 'Is
it a dream' being performed (McGuinness, fo. 52.)

‡ Luttrell, vol. 1, p. 399.

§ *Memoirs*, 19 April 1687.

Siface, or Giovanni Francesco Grossi, as he was officially listed, had become acquainted with Queen Mary, it seems, during his tour of duty at Modena, or possibly at San Marcello's in Rome,* where his name had been one of the most prominent on the list of those retained to perform the almost weekly oratorios given there, during which time he was also, apparently, a member of the papal choir until 1679, when he entered the service of the Duke of Modena, there to find G. B. Vitali still serving as assistant chapel-master.† As Siface's fame as a performer continued to develop, he appeared also in the Neapolitan opera house, in Florence, Venice, indeed, in almost all the important Italian cities of the day, Queen Christina of Sweden being one of his greatest admirers at this time.‡

This international celebrity then it was whom Mary of Modena invited to join the Chapel Royal in London, where Siface appeared at the beginning of the year 1687. No doubt she and the king had him in mind for the new Chapel Royal musical establishment, which had been entrusted to James, Duke of Ormonde, by royal warrant:

Royal warrant to James, Duke of Ormonde, to pass, allow and pay the following establishment, which the King has thought fit to order for the Royal Chapel, which he has lately built in the Palace of Whitehall, viz. to a total of £2,042 per an. . . .

	[per an.] £
[payments include:]	
two sacristans at £50 each	100
two vergers at £50 each	100
six preachers at £60 each	360
four chaplains at £80 each	320
assistants	50
organist	100
assistant to the organist	20
seven chapel boys, for diet, washing, firing and servants' wages	300
to same, for clothes, linen, hats, shoes, stockings at £10 each .	70
for a master to teach them	30
for house rent for them	40§

---

* *MGG*, vol. v, col. 955.   † *Grove's* (5th ed.), vol. IX, p. 21.

‡ A. Liess, 'Materialien zur römischen Musikgeschichte des Seicento: Musikerlisten des Oratorio San Marcello 1664–1725', *Acta Musicologica*, vol. XXIX, fasc. IV, pp. 137–71.   § *Cal. Tr. Books* (26 April 1687).

12a 'The Proceeding to the Coronation of their Majesties King William and Queen Mary from Westminster Hall to Westminster Abbey, 11 April 1689.' Engraved by Samuel Moore

12b 'A Perfect Description of the Firework in Covent Garden that was performed at the Charge of the Gentry and other inhabitants of that Parish for the joyful return of His Majesty from His Conquest in Ireland, 10 September 1690.' Mezzotint by Bernard Lens

The PROTESTANTS Joy

O R,

An Excellent New Song on the Glorious *Coronation* of King *William* and Queen Ma
which in much Triumph was Celebrated at *Westminster* on the 11th. of this instant *April*.

Tune of, 𝔊𝔦𝔪 𝔎𝔦𝔫𝔤 𝔬𝔣 𝔱𝔥𝔢 𝔖𝔠𝔬𝔱𝔰: Or, 𝔥𝔞𝔦𝔩 𝔱𝔬 𝔱𝔥𝔢 𝔐𝔦𝔯𝔱𝔩𝔢 𝔖𝔥𝔞𝔡𝔢𝔰.   Licensed according to Order

LEt Protestants freely allow
　　their Spirits a happy good chear,
Th' Eleventh of April now,
　　has prov'd the best day in the year,
Brave Boys let us merrily Sing,
　　whilst smiling full Bumpers go round,
Here's joyful good Tydings I bring,
　　King William and Mary is Crown'd.

That power that blest the design,
　　afford them a prosperous Reign,
Wee'ne'r shall have cause to repine,
　　our Liberties they will maintain:

Some Villains that wou'd us destroy,
　　in strong Iron Fetters lies bound,
Whilst we are transported with Joy,
　　that William and Mary is Crown'd.

The Triumph all over the Land,
　　did rise from the East to the West,
At our great Monarchs command,
　　true Loyalty shall be exprest:
There's none shall our Freedom oppose
　　since we such a blest King have found,
For now in the spight of our Foes,
　　King William and Mary is Crown'd.

13 'The Protestants Joy; or, An Excellent New Song on the Glori
Coronation of King William and Queen Mary, which in much Triun
was celebrated at Westminster on the 11th of the instant April'

See also the entry in the same accounts for 5 July 1687, where the musicians are listed, along with their salaries:

Establishment for the music for the Chapel Royal:

					[per an.] £	
Seignr. Fede, Master	.	.	.	.	200	
Seignr. Grande	.	.	.	.	110	
Seignr. Sansoni	.	.	.	.	100	
Mr. Abell	.	.	.	.	60	
Mr. Pordage	.	.	.	.	60	
Mr. Analeau	.	.	.	.	60	
					—	£580

Gregorians

Master [organist]	.	.	.	.	50	
Mr. Nicholson	.	.	.	.	50	
Mr. Sherburne	.	.	.	.	50	
Mr. Reading	.	.	.	.	50	
Mr. Curkaw	.	.	.	.	50	
Mr. La Grange	.	.	.	.	50	
Mr. Desabaye	.	.	.	.	50	
Mr. Pawmester	.	.	.	.	50	
Mr. Arnould	.	.	.	.	50	
Seignr. Albricci	.	.	.	.	40	
					—	£490

Instruments

Mr. Hall	.	.	.	.	50	
Mr. Farmer	.	.	.	.	50	
Mr. Hooten	.	.	.	.	50	
Mr. Crouch	.	.	.	.	50	
Mr. Goodwyn	.	.	.	.	50	
Mr. Carr	.	.	.	.	50	
Mr. Peasable	.	.	.	.	50	
Mr. Finger	.	.	.	.	40	
Mr. Neydenhanger	.	.	.	.	40	
					—	£430
						£1,500*

How all this may have affected Purcell's life cannot be known. Apparently he had become acquainted with Siface, witness the

* *Cal. Tr. Books*, 5 July 1687. (Cf. p. 158 below, and *KM*, pp. 384, 389.)

L

little harpsichord piece (possibly satirical) that he wrote in the following year,* and through him may well have come to know of other 'famed Italian masters' with whom the famous castrato had worked in Italy.† Again, however, the records give us nothing concrete to go on, and at present only conjecture is possible. Nevertheless, it does seem that Purcell, along with other English musicians, found himself participating less and less in musical life at Court, as more and more foreigners were brought in.

On 9 June 1687 a new son, named Henry, was baptized.‡ No doubt the physical (and audible) presence of another member of the family reminded Purcell that he still had a large sum of money owing to him for his contributions of time, energy, and materials to the coronation the year before. At any rate, on the very next day he petitioned the king for payment of costs he had sustained in repairing musical instruments, asking not only for the £20. 10s. that he had already disbursed, but for an assurance of £60 per annum as well. The final outcome of all this is not known, but apparently this petition was at last graciously received by Edward Griffin (Treasurer of the Chamber), who reported

'that the petitioner's place of provider and repairer of organs and harpsichords for His Majesty's Chapel and Private Music for which he formerly had an allowance of £60 per an. is omitted in the establishment: and there being an absolute necessity for such a person and he hath hitherto supplied the same without any consideration, having disbursed £20. 10s. as by the bill annexed [missing] appears', therefore prays an order for payment thereof and that a provision be made for payment of what he shall disburse for the future.§

The fact that Purcell found it necessary even to submit such a petition, let alone wait for an answer, is sufficient commentary on the musical enlightenment of the new Court, and on the kind of understanding and co-operation he could expect there.

Perhaps those who controlled such matters at Court were too concerned with the general stir caused by James II's feud with

---

* Analytical Catalogue, no. 656.

† The list of those with whom he had worked included such notable figures as Carlo Caproli, Bernardo Pasquini, Ercole Bernabei, and, perhaps most significantly for Purcell's Italianate tendencies, Lelio Colista (cf. Liess, op. cit. passim).

‡ Westminster Abbey Registers, p. 219.   § Cal. Tr. Books, 10 June 1687.

Magdalen College, Oxford, to take notice of such small items of business.* Or it may have been the mourning imposed upon the whole Court by the death of the queen's mother in Rome,† or perhaps merely that customary procrastination was prolonged by the progresses undertaken by their majesties in August.‡ Whatever the cause, patience was Purcell's only recourse.

* Wood, *Life and Times*, vol. III, p. 217, and especially pp. 222 ff.
† Luttrell, vol. I, p. 410.   ‡ Luttrell, vol. I, p. 411.

CHAPTER X

MUSICAL LIFE UNDER THE MOST CATHOLIC OF THE STUARTS

B y mid-September 1687 Purcell's baby son Henry had succumbed to some illness, the exact nature of which is unknown.[1] Meanwhile life at Court went on its own merry way, and Purcell soon found himself very busy preparing another royal ode for James II's birthday, 14 October, the last such celebration, incidentally, that the king was to enjoy in England, although the anniversary was to come around once more before his final departure from Whitehall. For the occasion in 1687 Purcell set 'Sound the trumpet, beat the drum',* an anonymous, somewhat cliché-ridden, but musically suggestive poem, which he set to some of the best occasional music he had yet composed. In Purcell's creative development this ode stands as the first of its kind, representing his attainment of a new style, identifiable with that of many of his later works.

Meanwhile James II was having some difficulty keeping up the kind of musical establishment he wanted for his new Chapel at Whitehall. On 21 October an order issued from the Lord Chamberlain's office made it clear that more co-operation was required:

To Dr. Staggins, master of His Majesty's music.
Whereas you have neglected to give order to the violins to attend at the Chapel at Whitehall where Her Royal Highness the Princess Ann[e] of Denmark is present, these are therefore to give notice to them that they give their attendance there upon Sunday next and so to continue to do so as formerly they did.†

* *Analytical Catalogue*, no. 335.　　　　† *KM*, p. 383.

Musical development in James's and Mary's 'Papist' chapel was slow, perhaps because their Roman Catholic policies were beginning to arouse antagonism elsewhere. Evelyn voiced the general sentiments in his entry for 29 October that same year:

The King and Queen, and Dadi, the Pope's Nuncio, invited to feast at Guildhall. A strange turn of affairs, that those who scandalized the Church of England, as favourers of Popery, should publicly invite an emissary from Rome, one who represented the very person of their Antichrist! [*Memoirs*]

On 7 November Henry Playford's *Harmonia Sacra*, book 1 was at last advertised in the Term Catalogue. Viewed as a whole, the contents, both as to text and music, reveal a style that can best be described as very 'high church'. Had James II been sensitive enough to grasp the import of various straws in the wind, which revealed that his subjects were willing to go a long way towards achieving a ceremonial form and an outward show equal in dignity and pomp to that of the Roman Catholic Church, but that they would not convert to a foreign religion — had he realized all this, he might have averted the catastrophe that descended upon him in the following year. (Perhaps their majesties were not concerned with matters so subtle as these. They had had recourse to less debatable means for strengthening their hold on the monarchy, as we know from Luttrell's announcement,* which speaks of the queen's physicians having let blood on 27 November in order to prevent a miscarriage.)

Purcell had not only contributed a larger share than anyone else to *Harmonia Sacra*, book 1, but, as Henry Playford stated in a preface, 'To the Reader', had taken upon himself the responsibilities of music editor as well. For this information, for its commentary on the current theological and aesthetic speculations on music and its functions, and for the interesting insight into a Restoration 'Doctrine of the Affections' it affords, the passage merits quotation in full:

To THE READER. The approbation which has been given by those of the greatest skill in music, and the encouragement I have met with from a number of worthy subscribers do give me just reason to hope, that this collection of divine songs

* Vol. 1, p. 422.

(tho' the first of this nature extant) will find a kind reception with the best of men. The youthful and gay have already been entertained with variety of rare compositions, where the lighter sportings of wit have been tuned by the most artful hands, and made at once to gratify a delicate ear, and a wanton curiosity. I now therefore address to others, who are no less musical, though they are more devout. There are many pious persons, who are not only just admirers, but excellent judges too, both of music and wit; to these a singular regard is due, and, their exquisite relish of the former ought not to be palled by an unagreeable composition of the latter. Divine hymns are therefore the most proper entertainment for them, which, as they make the sweetest, and indeed the only, melody to a religious ear, so are they in themselves the very glory and perfection of music. For 'tis the meanest and most mechanical office of this noble science to play upon the ear, and strike the fancy with a superficial delight; but when holy and spiritual things are its subject, it proves of a more subtle and refined nature, whilst darting itself through the organs of sense, it warms and actuates all the powers of the soul, and fills the mind with the brightest and most ravishing contemplations. Music and poetry have in all ages been accounted divine and therefore they cannot be more naturally employed, than when they are conversant about heaven, that region of harmony, from whence they are derived.

Now as to this present collection, I need say no more than that the words were penned by such persons, as are, and have been very eminent both for learning and piety; and indeed, he that reads them as he ought, will soon find his affections warmed, as with a coal from the altar, and feel the breathings of divine love from every line. As for the musical part, it was composed by the most skilful masters of this age; and though some of them are now dead, yet their composures have been reviewed by Mr. Henry Purcell, whose tender regard for the reputation of those great men made him careful that nothing should be published, which, through the negligence of transcribers, might reflect upon their memory. Here therefore the musical and devout cannot want matter both to exercise their skill, and heighten their devotion; to which excellent purposes that this book may be truly effectual is the hearty desire of your humble servant, Henry Playford.[2]

Playford's last few sentences make it quite clear that Purcell had assumed responsibility for the musical correctness of the whole. Evidence of his skill as a proof-reader is to be seen in the emendations printed just after the preface.

Young Henry Playford did not yet have the reputation for being so skilful a publisher as old 'Honest John', but he was certainly deep enough as a thinker on music and its ultimate significance. Writing at a somewhat later date, Roger North remarked upon the same concept (that is, the affections), as it existed within the secular sphere:

My thoughts are first in general that music is a true pantomime or resemblance of humanity in all its states, actions, passions, and affections. And in every musical attempt reasonably designed, human nature is the subject, and so penetrant that thoughts, such as mankind occasionally have, and even speech itself, share in that resemblance; so that an hearer shall put himself into the like condition, as if the state represented were his own. It hath been observed that the terms upon which musical time depends are referred to men's active capacities. So the melody should be referred to their thoughts and affections. And an artist is to consider what manner of expression men would use on certain occasions, and let his melody, as near as may be, resemble that. And if it be said that it is impossible to produce speech out of inanimate sounds, or give an idea of thought, as speech doth, I answer that whenever a strong genius with due application hath attempted it, the success hath been wonderful; as when the great Corelli used to say *Non l'intendite parlare?*[*]

In the same vein, though somewhat lighter, a little poem from the *Gentleman's Journal* for April 1693 changes the simile, but not the thought:

> Man justly tuneful numbers may admire,
> His soul is music, and his breast a lyre;
> A lyre which, while its various notes agree,
> Enjoys the sweets of its own harmony.
> In us rough hatred with soft love is join'd,
> And sprightly hope with grovelling fear combin'd, ⎫
> To form the parts of our harmonious mind. ⎭
> Hence, since the soul to music is allied,
> Unmatch'd by force 'tis by consent decoy'd;
> Nor were the strings of the soft lute design'd
> As links to chain, but lines to guide the mind.
>   What ravishes the soul, what charms the ear,
> Is music, tho' a various dress it wear.
> Tho' none should lend an ear, tho' none a tongue,
> Yet music still shall live in Waller's song.
> Beauty is music too, tho' in disguise,
> Too fine to touch the ear, it strikes the eyes, ⎫
> And thro' 'em to the soul the silent stroke conveys. ⎭
> The music's heav'nly such as in a sphere
> We only can admire, but cannot hear.

[*] John Wilson (ed.), *Roger North on Music*, pp. 110–11.

Nor is the pow'r of numbers less below,
By them all humours yield, all passions bow,   ⎫
And stubborn crowds are chang'd, yet know not how. ⎬
Let other arts o'er senseless matter reign;   ⎭
Mimic in brass, or with mix'd juices stain:
Music the mighty artist man can rule
(As long as it has numbers, he a soul)
As much as man can those mean arts control.*

The slighter characteristics implied by this poem are reflected in a song collection which came out less than two weeks after it. On 18 November the *London Gazette* announced publication of the first volume in a new song-book series, *Comes Amoris: or, The Companion of Love*. This was brought out by John Carr and printed by Nathaniel Thompson, who had got together a 'choice collection of the newest scores now in use' in this rather nondescript song-book. Purcell shared pride of place with Samuel Akeroyde and 'Anonymous', there being five songs ascribed to each of these. (In fact one of Purcell's songs, 'When first Amintas sued for a kiss',† was printed anonymously here, indicating that Purcell probably did not have sufficient time for proof-reading as careful as that he had done for Henry Playford.) Other composers, including Thomas Shadwell,‡ Alexander Damascene, R. Courteville, Charles Green, William Turner, George Hart, Robert King, and Thomas Farmer, were represented by one, two, or three songs each. But they were definitely the lesser lights of the times, musically speaking, and so their songs show them to be.

Purcell's most prominent work in the collection is the 'Catch by way of epistle: To all lovers of music'§ (the usual publisher's announcement, set to music). Although of negligible musical value, it is of some slight historical significance, being, so far as I can discover, the first of that nauseous line of 'advertisement' lyrics that has proliferated so vastly in modern times.

A few days later the *London Gazette* for 21–24 November 1687

---

* *Gentleman's Journal*, April 1693, p. 167.

† *Analytical Catalogue*, no. 430.

‡ Not generally known as a composer, Shadwell is credited with the composition of five songs in Day and Murrie.

§ *Analytical Catalogue*, no. 282.

announced the appearance of another secular collection, in which Purcell figured conspicuously. This was the fourth book of *The Theatre of Music*, the last of a series, apparently published after Henry Playford and Richard Carr had parted company, not on the best of terms, as a pointed reference to 'new pretenders' who could be 'disparaging of this book' indicates. Playford's reference to his sometime partner seems particularly pointed in the remark: 'But I pass them over in charity with *Go on and prosper* not doubting but that (when it comes to the hands of judicious gentlemen and understanders of music) they will find the difference. . . .' Again, Purcell had a lion's share of the songs in the book:

To all lovers and understanders of music. gentlemen, this fourth and last book . . . will (I doubt not) be very acceptable to all the knowing gentlemen in the skill of music, for several reasons I here mention. First that most of these songs and dialogues were composed by the eminent Dr. John Blow and Mr. Henry Purcell, my ever kind friends, and several other able masters, from whom I received true copies, which were by them perused before they were put to the press.

Two days before publishing the fourth book of *The Theatre of Music* Playford had launched a new series patterned after that which it ended, as the following passage from the preface to *The Banquet of Music*★ reveals:

To the Reader. Having already published a collection of this nature, entitled, *The Theatre of Music*, containing many excellent songs, in four books, I am encouraged to proceed to this second volume, called, *The Banquet of Music*, whereof you are here presented with the first book; hoping that both this and the following will receive the same favourable reception with the former, which will further encourage the endeavours of Your humble servant, H. Playford.

In this collection Playford sought the advantages of extreme variety, including in it in the guise of songs, settings both sprightly and serious, catches, dialogues, and even a small pastoral cantata with recorder ritornelli and accompaniments, 'How pleasant is this flow'ry plain'.†
Among Purcell's contemporaries and elders, such as Samuel Akeroyde, Moses Snow, John Banister, and John Blow, his

---

★ Licensed 19 November 1687, according to a statement on the title page.
† *Analytical Catalogue*, no. 543.

brother Daniel seems to have been the youngest of the nine or ten composers who contributed to this collection. Two of Daniel's settings — 'By what I've seen' and ' 'Twas night and all the village' — are rather good songs. The musicianship they bespeak may be taken as evidence that his receiving the post of organist at Magdalen College, Oxford, that year was not due alone to his famous brother's influence.

This last publication almost coincided with the celebration of St. Cecilia's Day, being licensed on 19 November. The members of the London Society quite evidently had been marshalling their forces to regain ground lost in the fiasco of 1685, which apparently had undone any plans for 1686.* The society invited John Dryden to supply the poem for the celebration in 1687 (he complying with the unsurpassable lyrics of the ode 'From harmony, from heavenly harmony'), and turned to Giovanni Battista Draghi for the musical setting. Was Purcell too busy composing and editing pieces for the first book of *Harmonia Sacra* and other collections? Or was he, perhaps, out of favour under a Catholic monarch, whose 'Papist' policy at Court may have been reflected in the choice of these two prominent Catholics to provide the poetry and music for the celebration of 1687? For want of evidence, these questions cannot be answered. What is clear, though, is that Draghi's poetic sensibilities and musical powers were not such as to enable him to take full and imaginative advantage of the opportunity Dryden had provided. Now and then his setting strikes a happy grain of inspiration. But the full potential of the poem, which Purcell might have realized, was to remain more or less in limbo until Handel undertook to measure its musical capabilities more than half a century later, for the same annual celebration in 1739.

For the Purcell family the year ended with several perplexing distractions. Towards the end of November the miserable affair of Charles Purcell's estate had at last come into court, as Edward Purcell brought a suit against William Bayley's widow, Anne, who had made off with the goods of the late captain, apparently the only seafaring member of Purcell's immediate family. The

* Husk, pp. 20–21.

Chancery proceedings* were long and tedious, and produced nothing but exasperating procrastinations, so far as extant records show. On 20 December Anne Bayley brought forth no satisfactory answers, but only tiresome evasions, denying any knowledge of any 'goods and chattels', and questioning both Edward's authority as executor and Charles's former authority as captain. (In other words, she employed every delaying tactic she could think of.) It is difficult to imagine that the matter rested there, but beyond this the archives divulge nothing.

Another business matter was much nearer to Henry Purcell's own immediate interests, however much he may have been incensed by Anne Bayley's behaviour. On 12 December Henry Guy, Secretary to the Treasurer, wrote to the Bishop of Durham to report on the petition (now missing) in which Purcell had asked for payment of £20. 10s. for repairs to the king's organs and harpsichords. His additional request that funds be set aside to meet necessary expenses that might arise in the future indicates that he had in the past been forced to assume financial obligations he could not afford. As to whether or not his request was granted or even honoured with an answer, again extant records are silent.†

During or perhaps before the beginning of 1688 Purcell was busy with a new anthem, 'Blessed are they that fear the Lord',‡ which he was writing on royal commission for a thanksgiving ceremony for the queen's being with child, the child later to be the 'Old Pretender', Prince James Edward. The 'solemn and particular office', as Evelyn called it,§ was celebrated in his church and in all churches within ten miles round on 15 January, then two weeks later all over England. For this event, as well as for the actual birth some six months later, an anthem was called for in the document published before the event.

---

* Recorded for 28 Nov. 1687 in PRO Chancery Roll C5/90/90, addressed 'To the Right Honourable George Lord Jeffreys'. See App. Two, I, 4.

† *Cal. Tr. Books*, 12 Dec. 1687. Treasury warrant to the Bishop of Durham to report on the petition of Henry Purcell, praying payment of £20. 10s. appearing to be due him. See p. 144 above for record of the provision that was at least suggested.   ‡ *Analytical Catalogue*, no. 5.

§ 15 Jan. 1688. See also note 4 in E. S. de Beer's edition of the *Diary*, vol. IV, p. 567.

The text of this anthem can be construed as special pleading for the maintainance of the established monarchal house, just as the annual celebration of the martyrdom of Charles I, observed on the following day, can be interpreted as both a caveat on the dangers of Protestant revolution and a plea for loyalty to the House of Stuart. The scheduling of both celebrations on consecutive days was probably not coincidental. Altogether, it was a notable week for Stuart celebrations. On 4 February the first anniversary of Charles II's death was observed 'at the popish chapel, and two days later there was a festival for joy of the king's coming to the crown'.*

It was upon this composition that Burney wrote his absurd pronouncement that 'Purcell, who had so much distinguished himself in the former reign, does not appear, by the date or occasion of his exertions, to have produced any particular anthem, ode or drama, for the Church, Court, or stage, from the death of Charles II, his first royal master, till after the Revolution, except the anthem "Blessed are they that fear the Lord", which he composed by order of the Court in 1687, as a thanksgiving for the queen's pregnancy'.† Burney, perhaps misled by the old-style dating of the original document, not only got the date wrong, but, I am convinced, was wrong as well in his general statement.

In fact Purcell may already have been busy early in the same year with his incidental music for a revival of Fletcher's and Massinger's *The Double Marriage*,‡ which revival may also have been prompted by James II's feelings of political insecurity, as Luttrell's comment might be construed to show:

The 6th was observed as a festival for joy of the King's coming to the crown; there was music at the chapel, cannons discharged at the Tower, and at night was a play at Court.§

Both Nicoll‖ and Laurie,¶ as well as contemporary authorities Downes** and Langbaine,†† all name February 1688 as the most

* Luttrell, vol. I, pp. 430–1.
† Burney, vol. II, p. 379.   ‡ *Analytical Catalogue*, no. 593.
§ Luttrell, vol. I, p. 431.   ‖ P. 351.
¶ Folios 173–4.   ** P. 40.   †† 1699 ed.

likely date for the revival to which Purcell is supposed to have supplied incidental music. My own view, supported only by my reaction to the style of the works themselves, is that Purcell could not have been writing such awkward, unpolished stuff as late as 1688. A comparison of this piece with other Purcell compositions of 1688 suggests either that the music dates from a much earlier period or that it was not by Purcell at all.

Two weeks later, after putting up with nearly a year's bureaucratic temporizing, Purcell at last received notice that he was to be paid expenses and the instrument-keeper's stipend which he had petitioned for the previous season.* However, the royal warrant to the Board of the Greencloth (which produced, at last, the actual cash) was not entered in the accounts until early in the next month, by which time costs had mounted. The following stipulations were made:

And whereas it hath been represented unto us by the Bishop of Durham that £81 is due to Henry Purcell for repairing the organ and furnishing the harpsichords to Christmas last and that it is necessary for that service to allow the sum of £56 per an.; these are to require you that the same be passed, allowed and paid accordingly.†

Purcell must have felt quite well off for a change, so far as returns from his instrument-keeping responsibilities were concerned.

During the course of this same month he was probably also remunerated (though according to contemporary accounts not too handsomely) for the songs he wrote for Thomas D'Urfey's *A Fool's Preferment*,‡ a rehash of Fletcher's *Noble Gentleman* (first produced in 1626), except for one scene borrowed from an anonymous novel, *The Humours of Basset*. The play was licensed on 21 May,§ complete with Purcell's music, and most likely therefore was performed the previous month, as Nicoll, Laurie, and others have argued. That the play was received coldly, as Nicoll says,‖ cannot be attributed to any shortcomings so far as the incidental music is concerned. Nor is it logical to assume that this

---

* See pp. 144 and 153 above. † *Cal. Tr. Books*, 5 March 1687/8.
‡ *Analytical Catalogue*, no. 571. § Laurie, fo. 175.   ‖ P. 275.

would have been badly performed by William Mountfort, the ill-starred actor, singer, and playwright who took the part of Lyonel, and probably sang the upper part in the dialogue as well, according to Dr. Laurie's convincing arguments.[3] In fact, as she also points out, the anonymous author of the satire *Wit for Money*** makes one of his characters say that 'those scenes of Basset which gave offence to a very Great Lady, were the ruin of it'. Purcell's eight songs, in fact, are among the best that he had written up to that time, and represent a remarkably complete representation of all the various kinds of theatrical songs he undertook to compose throughout his career.

Two new collections of songs appeared also in May, as if to re-emphasize the fact that Purcell was now, by all odds, the foremost song-writer in England. The first of them to be announced in the *London Gazette* (for 7–10 May) was Henry Playford's second book of *The Banquet of Music*, in which he brought forth the 'newest and best songs sung at Court and at public theatres'. Apart from Purcell's four songs, the collection also contains an anonymous Italian song 'Dite, O ciele' (so spelt) and Blow's 'Eurydice my fair', a dialogue between Orpheus and Eurydice that reminds one of Monteverdi both in some of its musical characteristics and in its subject matter.

Purcell was also represented by four songs in John Carr's *Vinculum Societatis: or, The Tie of Good Company*, advertised in another May issue of the *London Gazette*, which appeared on the 24th. As the title suggests, the styles of both music and poetry in the collection were suited more to the common taste than those of *The Banquet of Music*, which aspired to the beau-monde. Carr's second book of *Comes Amoris: or, The Companion of Love* aimed at even lower, not to say lewder, tastes, so far as Purcell's contributions were concerned, there being four catches with the separate title-page *A Small Collection of the Newest Catches for 3 Voices.*†

---

* 1691, p. 26.

† *Analytical Catalogue*, nos. 260, 262, 275, and 277. Interestingly, in view of the anecdote referred to below (see p. 185), the collection also contains 'The last new Scotch song: Cold and raw'.

The rest of May seems to have passed uneventfully for Purcell, except perhaps for the occasion at Whitehall Chapel, which he may have witnessed, when one of the singing-men had to read James II's already much contested Declaration of Indulgence after morning lessons.* Few even among those already opposing the Declaration (such especially as Sancroft and Ken) realized what mischief the king had set in store for himself with this misguided attempt to lead at least two of his three kingdoms nearer to Catholicism. But all this, even if Purcell was present on that occasion, would have been erased from his mind by the birth of his daughter, Frances, on 30 May,† and the ceremony of her baptism at St. Margaret's, Westminster, on 1 June.

A week later, however, the Declaration would have been very much in Purcell's thoughts, as in those of most Englishmen at the time, as the famed Seven Bishops — Dr. Lloyd of St. Asaph, Dr. Ken of Bath and Wells, Dr. Turner of Ely, Dr. Lake of Chichester, Dr. White of Peterborough, Sir Jonathan Trelawney of Bristol, and Archbishop Sancroft of Canterbury — made of their opposition to the 'illegal' Declaration a national issue and were arrested and sent to the Tower. Purcell's own reactions to the affair are unknown, except as they might be guessed at from the lines of the jaunty little catch, 'True Englishmen drink a good health to the Mitre',‡ apparently written the following year, or at least published then in the comparative safety of the reign of William and Mary.

At any rate events developed rapidly, and on 30 June the seven bishops were acquitted, to the overt joy of the London populace, who danced in the streets round bonfires to the ringing of bells.

The general excitement generated by these happenings was so great that the sudden and premature birth of the young Prince James Edward on 10 June did not immediately arouse the disputes Evelyn lugubriously prophesied in his entry for that day, which, interestingly enough, was Trinity Sunday. As if dissatisfied that this great occasion had not brought forth the general applause he had been expecting, the king sought to call his subjects' attention

---

* Evelyn, 20 May 1688, and Hist. MSS. Comm., LeFleming MSS. p. 210.
† *Westminster Abbey Registers*, p. 74.   ‡ *Analytical Catalogue*, no. 284.

to the matter by ordering a day of thanksgiving on the 17th, ending with fireworks, and on the 18th a gala concert of water music, or, as Luttrell described it in his entry for the day, 'an exercise of music, vocal and instrumental, by the King's music'. The following week the royalist journal *Public Occurrences* came out on 26 June with a notice of the concert:

Mr. Abel, the celebrated musician, and one of the Royal Band, entertained the public, and demonstrated his loyalty on the evening of 18th June 1688 by the performance of an aquatic concert. The barge prepared for this purpose was richly decorated, and illuminated by numerous torches. The music was composed expressly for the occasion by Signor Fede, Master of the Chapel Royal, and the performers, vocal and instrumental, amounted to one hundred and thirty...

Great numbers of barges and boats were assembled, and each having flambeaux on board, the scene was extremely brilliant and pleasing. The music being ended, all the nobility and company . . . gave three shouts; and all the gentlemen of the music went to Mr. Abel's house, which was nobly illuminated ... The entertainment lasted till three of the clock the next morning, the music playing and the trumpets sounding all the while . . .[4]

The king, insensitive as ever to the mood of his subjects, could think of no better way to seek their support than to parade before them music and musicians, foreigners and 'Papists', all as if designed to give them greater cause for discontent. Court musicians may well have felt injured as well as insulted when they received on 19 August the order that

a number of His Majesty's musicians shall attend the Queen's Majesty's maids of honour to play whensoever they shall be sent to, at the homes of dancing, at such homes and such a number of them as they shall desire. And hereof the master of the music and the musicians are to take notice that they observe this order.★

The peremptory style of the order hints, between the lines, that there may have been reluctance on the part of some musicians to provide such lowly service to play music they thought beneath them.

So far as the records show, the remainder of the summer passed uneventfully for Purcell and other musicians at Court, most of

★ *KM*, p. 388.

whom attended the king at Windsor from 24 July until 20 September.[5] However, lack of mention of the two most prominent musicians in the records of the time lends substance to the various stories that would seem to indicate that James's and Mary's foreigners were not above, indeed were quite successful in intriguing against their more notable English colleagues. Relationships between English and foreign contingents, representing as they did the larger Protestant and Catholic factions that divided the country, must have been extremely unpleasant at times.

M

CHAPTER XI

MUSIC AND THE GLORIOUS REVOLUTION

Purcell was not commissioned to write any music for James II's fifty-fifth birthday, the last that unhappy monarch was to enjoy in England. When 14 October came round again, it was obvious to everyone that the Court's wisest policy would be to remain quiet. So uneasy were the times that even the salvo of guns from the Tower, usual for the occasion, was forbidden, as Evelyn remarked. He noted also that the sun had been eclipsed at its rising that morning, and that the day was 'signal for the victory of William the Conqueror against Harold . . .' These were ominous portents, which no doubt impressed the superstitious as they did Anthony à Wood, who also reported later that month of two suns seen rising at Winchester, of seeing a blazing star, and of hearing the story of two men fighting in the sky above Oxford about midnight.* Further auguries, and the events they foretold, were not long in appearing. Five days after the birthday of the bemused King James II, William of Orange sailed from Hellevoetsluis† for Tor Bay, under a red flag, while Father Petre and many of his Catholic companions hastily packed their belongings. Within a few weeks, on 4 November, William III celebrated the anniversary of his own birth just off the English coast. Next day — another omen, since it was Guy Fawkes' Day — he landed with his forces at Tor Bay. It must have seemed to everyone that the end of James II's reign was foreordained.

During this period, when few official duties would have been required of him at Court, and when no St. Cecilia ode or theatrical

* Wood, *Life and Times*, vol. III, pp. 280–1.
† Macaulay, *The History of England* (London, 1870), vol. II, p. 151.

commissions were forthcoming, Purcell evidently kept busy with various songs for publication, as we know from the fact that Henry Playford's third book of *The Banquet of Music* was licensed on 1 December 1688. Purcell furnished only two compositions for the collection, a catch, 'If all be true that I do think',[*] and an interesting duo, 'Were I to choose the greatest bliss'.[†] The latter was to achieve a certain popularity during the century after Purcell's death, appearing in no less than seventeen publications.

For musical life the time of the Glorious Revolution was a period of suspended animation. Apart from the 'music' of trumpets, drums, and other military instruments (which William had ordered to be sounded from the fleet before Dover to strike awe into the hearts of his prospective subjects, no doubt), and the little tune 'Lilliburlero'[‡] (for which the prominent Whig, Thomas Wharton, provided an anti-Jacobite text and Purcell a harmonization), the 'Revolutionaries' had little time or use for music. The original tune of 'Lilliburlero'[§] probably predates the Revolutionary period. As for the name of the tune, it may very well be associated with the harvest-song from south-east Ireland, which was sung when one of the maids fell behind in binding sheaves:

> Lully by lero
> Lully by lero
> Lully by lero
> Help her along.[||]

However, by Christmas James II was ruefully attending Mass in Paris, and affairs in England were returning to normal, though the normality was of a new kind. Charles Sedley spoke for himself when he said about this time that he 'wished to make the King's daughter a Queen in return for his Majesty's having made his daughter a Countess',[¶] but many in England had more sober reasons for welcoming William and Mary to the throne.

---

[*] *Analytical Catalogue*, no. 255.
[†] *Analytical Catalogue*, no. 517.   [‡] See Westrup, p. 65.
[§] For which, see Chappell's *Old English Popular Music*, vol. II, p. 58.
[||] *Notes and Queries*, 3rd series (July 1865), vol. VIII, p. 13.
[¶] Dalrymple, *Memoirs of Great Britain and Ireland*, p. 291.

Moreover, London music concerts had begun again, as is known from the Duke of Norfolk's notice that he had lost a muff at the music-meeting held in York Buildings on 30 December.* The undeclared suspension, which seemed to suppress other musical activities, persisted through January 1689 and early February, despite excellent opportunities for musical celebrations on 1 January, when a New Year's ode would ordinarily have been performed, on 31 January, when a 'Day of Thanksgiving was proclaimed for delivery of the nation from Popery and slavery',† and on 6 February, when both the Prince of Denmark's birthday and Parliament's declaration for William and Mary might have been observed with special (that is, musical) pomp.

Then, on 11 February 1689, a concert took place which Mr. Brattle and the American Puritan Judge Sewall went to Covent Garden to hear. This proved to be a harbinger of the very lively musical life that was to develop in London during the last decade of the seventeenth century and the first thirty or forty years of the eighteenth.‡ Two days later

the Lords and Commons assembled at Westminster, came both houses to the Banqueting House at Whitehall, and there presented the Prince and Princess of Orange with the instrument agreed on for declaring them King and Queen . . . and the night ended with bonfires, ringing of bells, and great acclamations of joy.§

Such an occasion must have called for music, even if only for that of William III's beloved trumpets and drums. But so far no record has been found to indicate anything of a serious nature written for the joyous event. (It is probably symptomatic of the general state of musical affairs at the time that documents usually containing musical allusions make no mention of any events more important than those discussed above for the period between Christmas 1688 and early March 1689.)

Then, throughout March, the Lord Chamberlain's offices were filled with bustling preparations for the forthcoming coronation,

* Tilmouth, fo. 23.
† Luttrell, vol. 1, p. 497. (See also McGuinness, fo. 52.)
‡ Scholes, p. 45. See portrait of Judge Sewall opp. p. 48.
§ Luttrell, vol. 1, p. 501.

with music again at the forefront of everyone's attention. Significantly, the king's first order towards renovating his musical establishment (apart from his authorizing a routine and belated warrant for winter clothes for Blow's Chapel Royal boys) had to do with equipment for the sergeant-trumpeter, sixteen trumpets, and a kettle-drummer, with 'the same for His Majesty's drum major, four drummers and a fife', three other kettle-drummers being added to the list by a later warrant of 28 March.*
Then on Lady Day (25 March) came down the list of His Majesty's thirty-nine musicians, all of whom had been provided with scarlet mantles — suitable dress for coronations — three days earlier. It is immediately apparent that the list had been pruned of the exotic foreign names that had ornamented James II's roster, and which, in all but one or two cases, had here been replaced by good English names. Again, the significance of the high salary and top billing given Mathias Shore, the new sergeant-trumpeter, ought not to be overlooked:

A list of such of the King's servants as receive their salaries in the Treasury of the Chamber's office, with an account of what was owing in arrears to each of them at Lady Day, 1689:

Mathias Shore, Sergeant-Trumpeter, £80
Dr. Staggins, Master of the Music, £100

Musicians £30 each

M. Farmer,	Edward Hooton,
Charles Powell,	Henry Heale,
Edmund Flower,	Theophilus Fitz,
James Paisible,	Charles Staggins,
Thomas Fashon,	John Lenton,
Edward Greeting,	John Abel,
Samuel Akeroyde,	William Turner,
Robert King,	John Gostling,
John Crouch,	John Bowman,
John Bannister,	Francis Mariens,
William Clayton,	Charles Coleman,
William Hall,	John Blow,
Robert Carr,	Balthazer Redding,
Nathaniel French,	Francis Le Rich,
Richard Tomlinson,	Richard Lewis,
John Goodwynn,	Solomon Eccles.†

* *KM*, pp. 390–1.   † *KM*, p. 391.

Equally noteworthy is the conspicuous absence of Henry Purcell's name. In fact no appointment seems to have been authorized for him until 22 July, when he was mentioned along with five rank-and-file musicians:

John Bannester [the younger], Robert Carr, Henry Heale, Charles Powell, Henry Purcell, musician composer, and Robert Strong, appointed musicians for the Private Music.*

Extant records support no hypothesis to the effect that Purcell may have been in disgrace during this time just before the coronation, as he most certainly was (unjustly, with scarcely a doubt) just after the great event.

Yet there appears no other cause for those in power at Court and in the Abbey to have mistreated their foremost musician, already universally acclaimed both at home and abroad. Like John Dryden, whose career also went into decline at this time, Purcell may have been a Catholic. (Certainly the absence of any official confirmation of an appointment to the Chapel Royal or the Abbey would suggest that any suspicion that may have been brewing would have had to do with religious matters.)

The evidence on Purcell's alleged Catholic persuasion is insufficient. It cannot be proved even that he held Catholic sympathies. So far as concerns reference to the subject in modern publications, Douglas Newton's discussions in *Catholic London* are typical, being based on hearsay and conjecture with some wishful thinking.† How carefully Newton argues his case may be seen in his statement that Purcell 'maintained his Catholic religion even in Elizabeth's Court'. Other conjectures, less demonstrably false, are perhaps vaguely entertainable, though undocumented. Apparently Purcell was allowed full scope for his 'Catholic talents':

St. James stands as he, James II, and his line left it, and as we go down St. James's Street and see its lovely red brick gateway, we look direct on one Catholic memory. Above that gateway, in a suite of apartments reached by a winding staircase, in a clock tower, lived Purcell, the glory of English music. It was his sanctuary from a world whose religion was not his. Dryden often went up those winding stairs to visit him. Purcell allowed him to make the rooms a hiding place, too, but from his debts.

* *KM*, p. 394.   † P. 74.

No mention of Mrs. Purcell and the children, who, presumably, as Newton would have it, were staying in Bowling Alley East, where Purcell continued to pay rates throughout the years until 1692, when he moved at last to Marsham Street.* But then this does not diminish the possibility that Purcell may have had a 'retreat' at St. James's. It would of course make it altogether unlikely that he later met his death from being locked out, as another unsubstantiated rumour would have it.

A thorough search of all accessible records having to do with a clock tower at St. James's, and a sifting of the literature on Dryden's later days, have been fruitless, producing no evidence to support Newton's bland assumption that Purcell was a Catholic. Purcell's constant association with other such prominent Catholics as Matthew Locke, the Howards, the Peters family (into which he married, it is thought), and a number of performing musicians, along with such evidence as that provided by his having to pass the Test Act in 1683 (long after his appointment, as if doubts as to his religious probity might just have arisen) all taken together perhaps leave the trace at least of a question as to whether or not he may have been a Catholic, secretly or openly.

On 11 April 1689 extensive preparations for the coronation, which had occupied everyone at Court and half the gentry of London, at last bore fruit. Purcell, of course, was involved heavily, even more heavily than usual, as we shall see. As for the 'Form and Order' observed in the coronation of William and Mary, there would be little point in describing them here in detail. Since the musical arrangements are not known, we can do little more than accept Luttrell's word for it that 'the coronation of their majesties was performed at Westminster, much in the manner the former was'.†

Few events in Purcell's life are so well documented as the altercation that he had with the Dean and Chapter of Westminster Abbey over funds collected from those who bought tickets to view the coronation of William and Mary from the organ-loft.

---

* 'Churchwardens' Accounts' (Poor Rate Ledger E. 307, p. 80).

† Luttrell, vol. 1, p. 520; however, see also Plates 12(a) and 13, the latter involving music by Purcell.

Besides various documents already quoted by several authorities on Purcell, new papers relating to the affair have come to light in the Westminster Abbey Muniments Room. There they have been virtually hidden through having been indexed with the accounts from the reign of Queen Anne, which were copied on the reverse sides. The information these papers afford does not entirely excuse Purcell's lack of promptness in attending to financial matters; it does, however, bring several mitigating factors into the reckoning and suggests other possible explanations of his conduct on this occasion.

From the very beginning of the Restoration period there seems to have been a great deal of confusion as to what the proper disposition of funds brought in by the sale of tickets to spectators at coronations really ought to be. This we know from one of the earliest of such documents, a petition for royal intervention in the 'business' of the coronation of Charles II on 30 May 1661:

The Verger's Petition May 30, for money at the coronation:
To the Right Wor[shipfu]l the Dean and Chapter of the Collegiate Church of St. Peter's of Westminster.

The humble petition of the Vergers, Sacrists, Bell-ringers and other the officers and the stewards to the same belonging.

Showeth:

That whereas your worships have been pleased upon some just and weighty consideration, to order, and declare in Chapter that all such sums of money that shall be taken, and received by Adam Osgood, Clerk of the Works of the said Church, for any galleries, seats, or other places upon the solemn day of His Majesty's most happy coronation, and the first day of this present parliament, should be brought in by the said Adam Osgood, and so distributed betwixt him and your petitioners, being all officers and servants to this church, after such manner and proportions as to your wisdom should seem meet.

Your petitioners therefore humbly pray that (in pursuance of the said order and declaration) your worships would be pleased to cause the said Adam Osgood to bring in all such monies as he retained, to hear what can be said betwixt him, and your petitioners as to the greatness of the same, and after to divide the same as to your worships shall seem most agreeable to the rules of equity.

And your pet[itioners] shall pray etc.
[unsigned][1]

This petition makes it appear that the handling of the ticket receipts for the coronation was ill-regulated from the start. Even without evidence as to the outcome of this controversy between Osgood and his colleagues, it is clear that official laxness had invited irregularities. From the very beginning the division of coronation fees had been a bone of contention. Long before Purcell appeared on the scene, as the above-quoted petition and the following entry from the Precentor's Book reveal, 'rules of equity' were so vaguely established as to call for royal arbitration:

In April 1661 a warrant was granted by the Rev. Dean to the Chanter and the rest of the Choir for the erecting of scaffolds in the Churchyard in respect of His Majesty's Coronation solemnized on St. George's Day. For which purpose agreement was made between the choir and the carpenter, that the profits thereof should be equally divided between them, the carpenter receiving the one half, he being at the whole charge of the scaffolds; excepting only that the choir paid for sail-cloths £0. 15s. 0d. and the carpenter but 5s. and that the choir pay [sic] also for watching and other expenses equally with the carpenter £0. 14s. 0d. and given by the choir to the poor of St. Margaret's Parish £0. 16s. 0d. The sum received by the choir was £17. 9s. 0d. out of which . . . there remains to be divided into 16 equal parts £15. 4s. 0d. which was to every part £0. 19s. 0d. But the Vergers who should have had a part being left out, they had between them £0. 19s. 0d. out of the money collected for the monuments. The organist being a good gainer by his organ loft and scaffolds being erected, had no share with the rest of the choir.*

Here the precedent for the organist's right to funds collected from visitors to the organ-loft is clearly established. Apparently the organist was given *carte blanche* to make his own terms with the carpenter, collect whatever entrance fees he could, and pocket them without further word to anyone, so long as he did not expect to have a share in the general income. Presumably this was the precedent Purcell later followed.

Any account of these matters that may have been kept among papers relating to the coronation of James II seems either to have been lost or to be too well hidden for easy discovery. However, two later documents refer to this coronation and shed at least some light on these proceedings, in which Purcell, as organist both for Westminster Abbey and for the Chapel Royal, must have taken part officially. One of these dates from the reign of George I, and is 'An account shewing in what parts of the Abbey

* WAM 61228A (Precentor's Book, 1660–71), fo. 15v.

the several scaffolds of the Dean and Chapter and their officers, etc. were erected at the coronations of King James, King William and Queen Mary, and Queen Anne':

At the coronations of King James, King William and Queen Mary, and Queen Anne the Dean and Chap[ter] of Westminster had scaffolds built for their families and friends on the south side of the Choir from the pulpit to the place where the trumpets and drums are seated.

The Chanter, minor Canons, Gentlemen of the Choir, and other officers of the same church by the Dean's leave did at those solemnities build scaffolds in all the aisles westward from the Choir and the South Cross of the Abbey till the coronation of Queen Anne. When some days after a scaffold was built in the South Cross one Mr. Negus took possession of that scaffold under pretence on an order from the Earl Marshall, tho' the same had been built in such manner as had been used at the cost and charges of the officers of the said church who were great losers thereby, being forced to compromise the matter not having time to apply for relief.

James La Freese, Sgt. to Brigdar Stwd.
Scaffolds for the D[ean] and Preb[endary] etc.*

This reveals not only that scaffolds were built for the coronation of James II, but that the lack of any firm and authoritative policy (which led Osgood, Purcell, and, evidently with more profit, Negus astray) still obtained as late as 1714. Another petition, apparently written just before the coronation of William and Mary, shows the Dean and Chapter of Westminster attempting to recover a 'concession' of which they had been deprived at the coronation of James II. He, no doubt, had other ends in view when it came to the enrichment of any clergy that may have been in attendance:

The Dean and Chapter's petition to the King and Queen for their fees due at their majesties' coronation. To the King and Queen their most excellent majesties. The humble petition of Thomas Bishop of Rochester, Dean of the Collegiate Church of St. Peter in Westminster and the Chapter of the same church
Showeth:
That your petitioners and their predecessors by right of their Charter and liber Regalia, have time out of mind at the coronation of the King and Queen of this realm, been used to claims and have (except at the coronation of King James the Second) several perquisites and advantages of very great value for

* WAM 51147 (Coronation Papers, 1714).

their service and attendance at the said coronations. And your petitioners having put in their claims before the Right Honourable the Lord Commissioners appointed by Your Majesty to judge and determine of matters of that nature in your Courts of Claims. The said Commissioners have allowed of your petitioners' claims and as to the fees due to your petitioners, they are deferred to Your Majesty's good will and pleasure.

Your petitioners do humbly pray Your Majesties, that you will be graciously pleased to allow unto them such compensation for their dues and services as in your princely wisdom shall serve. And your petitioners, as in duty bound, shall ever pray for the long continuance of Your Majesty's happy reign and government.*

A similar memorandum issued just prior to Purcell's troublesome embarrassment over coronation fees would have spared Purcell his chagrin had he known of its existence. Coming just after the above petition was submitted, the following order shows that the foregoing, or a similar request, was granted about three weeks before the ceremonial day:

25 March 1689.
It is ordered that all such money as shall be raised for seats at the Coronation within the church organ-loft or churchyard shall be paid into the hands of the Treasurer and distributed as the Dean of the Chapter shall think fit. And that all vacant places both in the church and churchyard which are not taken up and employed for the King's use be disposed of by the Dean and Chapter of Westminster as they shall think fit.†

Evidently Purcell and Crespion knew nothing of these arrangements, which seem clearly to have been aimed at the perquisites they were hoping to enjoy at the coronation of William and Mary. Following the precedent laid down at the coronation of Charles II, and possibly that of James II, they may well have fallen foul of the new regulations without knowing of their existence. It is hardly conceivable that they would have flouted royal will had they known it.

One can easily imagine the situation. Purcell, busy with his many other responsibilities at Westminster as well as at the Chapel Royal, would already have contracted with some local builder for scaffolding and other materials. By the time this

* WAM 51128 (Coronation Papers, 1689). In the original the last phrase has been struck out, as if its possible effect were called into doubt.
† WAM 51125 (Coronation Papers, 1689).

petition had been granted, just eighteen days before the coronation itself, he would already have begun to draw up a list of those who were to be admitted to the organ-loft, and perhaps might already have collected some money. In the midst of all the urgent preparations going on throughout the rest of the Abbey it would have been easy for someone who should have informed him of the new order to forget to do so. Or is it just possible, as Hawkins assumed, that 'ignorance or malice' had some part in the affair? Having quoted another version of the order to Purcell given below, in which Purcell was referred to as the 'organ-blower', he adds:

Upon which it may be observed that the penning of it is an evidence of great ignorance or malice, in that it describes him by the appellation of organ-blower who was organist of their own church, and in truth the most excellent musician of his time.*

Furthermore, Purcell may have had something more to go on than a mere precedent set in Charles II's reign, for Dr. Barton, describing the coronations of James II, William and Mary, and of later monarchs, sent the following details in a letter to Charles Low, Esq., in 1714:

The choir men had the rest of the Abbey given to them from the West door to the door of the choir. The gallery below the organ on the same side was left to the King's Scholars and Doctor Knipes's boarders. The organ-loft itself the organist had and what was above the organ eastward some great folks had.†

For whatever reasons, and by whatever means, Purcell certainly did wander into difficulties over the loft. Within a week of the coronation (which took place on 11 April) he was confronted with the following:

It was ordered that Mr. Purcell, the organist to the Dean and Chapter of Westminster, do pay to the hand of Mr. John Needham, Receiver of the College, all such money as was received by him for places in the organ-loft at the coronation of King William and Queen Mary by or before Saturday next, being the 20th day of this instant April. And in default thereof his place is declared to be null and void. And it is further ordered that his stipend or salary

* Vol. II, p. 744.
† WAM 51164 (Coronation Papers, 1714).

due at our Lady Day last past be detained in the hands of the Treasurer until further order.*

This was drastic treatment, indeed. But within a very few days — presumably within the prescribed time — Purcell turned over the money he had collected, keeping only the amount allowed by authority, as we know from another account in Needham's hand:

The account of the monies received at the coronation of King William and Queen Mary (and the payments thereof). The account of such monies as I have received from Mr. Crispyn and Mr. Purcell of the money received by them at the coronation.

	£	s.	d.
Of Mr. Crispyn	423	16	7
Of Mr. Purcell his poundage and other expenses being deducted	78	04	6
Total is	492	01	1 [N.B. £502. 1s. 1d.]

	£	s.	d.
Mr. Gregory's bill for erecting and pulling down the scaffolds for the use of the Dean and Chapter of Westminster	67	16	02
Paid to the woman for cleansing the effigies of King Charles the Second	10	00	00
Total is	77	16	02
There will remain in my hand the sum of	414	04	11
The money received by myself, all charges being deducted	064	09	6
	478	14	5†

In this context the accounts of Purcell's receipts could hardly have been made from any financial source other than that provided by spectators who paid to view the coronation proceedings from the organ-loft. The exact meaning of 'his poundage and other expenses' cannot be ascertained at present. 'Poundage', according to *OED* could have signified either 'a payment of so

* Westminster Abbey Chapter Minutes, 1683–1714, fo. 25 (18 April 1689). I have followed Sir Jack Westrup's transcription of Needham's almost illegible hand.

† WAM 51126 (Coronation Papers, 1689).

much per pound sterling upon the amount of any transaction in which money passes' or 'a percentage of the total earnings of any concern, paid as wages to those engaged in it, sometimes in addition to a fixed wage'. On the face of it the latter seems to fit the situation under discussion most closely, particularly in the light of other records which are to follow. As for 'other expenses', we can only suppose that these would have had to do with expenses incurred in setting up the seats in the organ-loft, tickets, and so forth. We have no way of judging Mr. Needham's probity in other matters, but it is certain that his arithmetic was not beyond criticism. The sum he arrived at is short of what it should have been by £10. What may have happened to the missing sum is anyone's guess, but it appears from this that no one watched the watchers. Moreover, the full bill for Mr. Gregory's services amounted to a larger sum, as the following receipt dated 17 May 1689 shows:

Rec'd of Mr. John Needham by order of the Dean and Chapter of Westminster the sum of one hundred and five pounds being in full for the scaffoldings and work done in and about the Church at Westminster with relation to the coronation either by order or by the order of the said Mr. Needham

(signed) By me, Tho. Gregory

The entry referring to the effigies, which might seem somewhat irrelevant in a statement of proceeds and expenditure, is quite in order. The showing of the effigies, or 'monuments' (as they are called in the Westminster Abbey Treasurer's Papers), provided another very profitable source of funds for the Abbey, these being divided up periodically among all interested parties. Although there seem to be no extant records after the reign of Charles II, the following account of May 1670 shows that the sums involved were not negligible: 'Collected for the sight of the monuments £138. 06s. 03d.'* For their part in the coronation of Charles II, it will be remembered, the vergers had had to be satisfied with nineteen shillings from the 'monuments money', their share having been overlooked when coronation proceeds were divided up.

* WAM 61228A (Precentor's Book, 1660–71), fo. 119v.

It has been supposed that this was the end of the matter, Purcell having kept his post, somewhat chastened by an official rebuke and seemingly poorer by nearly £80 than he had expected to be. Nevertheless he was in good standing at Westminster Abbey, as elsewhere in his plurality of posts. There is no way of knowing how his reputation fared. But financially he did not do so badly as the above account would suggest. Another disbursement record reveals that he was given back nearly half the money he had turned over:

All necessary charges being deducted out of the money which Mr. Crespion and Mr. Purcell paid to Mr. Nedham there remaining

	£414	4	11

Whereof he is to pay by gift of the Dean and Chapter to:			
To Mr. Crespion as chanter and petty canon	24	00	00
To Mr. Tynchare as sacrist and petty canon	24	00	00
To the three other petty canons at £18 each	54	00	00
To the six senior choirmen at £15 each	90	00	00
To the next choirmen at £10 each	40	00	00
To the next choirman	8	00	00
To the two that supply the 12th place in the choir at £5 each	10	00	00
To Mr. Baggs the sacrist	6	00	00
To the two vergers at £14 each	28	00	00
To Mr. Purcell	35	00	00
To the four bell-ringers at £5 each	20	00	00
To Mr. Hawkes as porter	3	00	00
To Mr. Lake	10	00	00
To the 12 almsmen at 30s. each	18	00	00
To the 8 choristers at 20s. each	8	00	00
To the college butler	2	00	00
To the gardener	2	00	00
To the three choir widows. *viz.* Mrs. Tucker, Mrs. Godfrey and Mrs. Kettlewell 10s. each	1	10	00
To the three sweepers 10s. each	1	10	00
To the cloister-porter	1	10	00

	£387	10	00

The remainder of the fabric £26 14 11
(signed) Tho. Rosten. Dec. Westmr*

On the reverse side of this page these names and amounts appear again, each payment being countersigned by its owner,

* WAM 51137 (Coronation Papers, 1689).

except for those to the sweeping-man, widows, almsmen, and choristers, some of whom may have been illiterate. For some obscure reason Mr. Needham's receipts were not subject to such wide distribution among the Abbey personnel:

Mr. Needham's money	£64	9	6
To Mr. Needham	20	0	0
To Mr. Knipe	20	0	0
To Moor, a librarian	5	0	0
The remainder to the fabric			
(signed) Tho. Rosten*			

Why were Needham and Knipe allowed to divide up their receipts between themselves (with a small allowance to Mr. Moor) when Purcell and Crespion had been called to book so peremptorily? And why were no sums or balances entered here? Surprise changes to suspicion with the discovery of another mistake in Mr. Needham's addition (again in his own favour) in his account of the funds set aside for 'fabric money':

Fabric Money:			
Out of Mr. Crispyn's and Mr. Purcell's	£26	14	11
Out of Mr. Needham's	13	9	6
The Churchwarden's	10	–	–
Tho. Rosten.†			

There should have been £19. 9s. 6d. for the 'remainder to the fabric' from Needham's account, not £13. 9s. 6d. as is entered here. What happened to the missing £6 is anyone's guess. Such laxity suggests peculation. Might Crespion and Purcell have argued that their attempt to retain their collections was justified both by past precedent and present corruption?

Incomplete accounts of this affair have been unnecessarily damaging to Purcell's reputation. At least there is room for the charitable supposition that he and Crespion thought in good conscience that they were merely abiding by tradition, not flouting authority. Furthermore, Purcell, like most English Court musicians of his time, found it extremely difficult to collect his salary and reimbursements on time. Even the injunction

* WAM 51132 (Coronation Papers, 1689).   † Ibid.

quoted above shows that Purcell's half-yearly stipend was already a month overdue at that time. How much longer he may have had to be patient is again a matter for conjecture. Certainly though, Court officials were not over-zealous in seeing that payments were met on time, or that the financial needs of their musicians were given very much thought. In fact overdue payments of stipends and salaries had long since become the rule rather than the exception, as may be seen from almost any page of the Lord Chamberlain's Treasury Papers.[2]

Just before this time, Purcell had found himself considerably out of pocket for repairing and keeping fit the organs and instruments of the Chapel Royal, and had had to wait for more than a year* to be reimbursed the £81 he had spent on materials. At the coronation of James II he had spent £34. 12s. on erecting an extra organ in the Abbey, and then had waited more than six months for payment.† History repeated itself at the coronation of William and Mary, except that his payment was delayed for more than a year.‡ Small wonder, then, if he should have adopted a catch-as-catch-can policy where financial matters were concerned. His self-interest was not only justified by earlier precedent; it was very probably demanded by his immediate economic situation.

During all these sordid incidents Purcell was busy composing music for Thomas Shadwell's 'Now does the glorious day appear' which he identified as 'An Ode on the Queen's birthday, sang [sic] before their majesties at Whitehall. . . .'§ Unlike his five other 'birthday songs' for Queen Mary, this one is undated. Since 1689 was the only year for which no ode is specified and Shadwell's poem was published in 1690,‖ it seems probable that 1689 was the year for which Purcell composed the piece. By this time, scarcely without a doubt, Purcell had begun work on *Dido and*

---

* Westrup, p. 57. Part of the bill had been owing for two years when he finally may have collected the money. See also pp. 144 and 153 above.

† Bodleian, Rawl. MS. D 872, fo. 99.

‡ Westrup, p. 62.

§ *Poems on Affairs of State*, vol. II (1697); see *Analytical Catalogue*, no. 332.

‖ A. S. Borgman, *Thomas Shadwell*, p. 81.

Aeneas, the first opera of the Glorious Revolution — indeed the first 'English Opera' truly worthy of the name. Like the foregoing ode, it was to be a magnificent musical tribute paid to his employers and countrymen, whatever the immediate, petty annoyances that may have beset him.

CHAPTER XII

MUSICAL LIFE UNDER WILLIAM
AND MARY

Meanwhile, two musical collections prominently bearing Purcell's name had appeared: the second part of *Musick's Hand-Maid* and *The Banquet of Music*, book III; both were advertised in the Term Catalogue for May 1689. The latter, licensed on 1 December 1688, belongs to Purcell's activities for the previous year. The first-named, however, dates from 1689. It links up with the first book, *Musick's Handmaid ... Lessons for Virginals or Harpsycon*, which 'Honest John' Playford had published in 1663. He re-edited it in 1678 along with the second part, and published both jointly with his son Henry. The latter brought out the second book in yet another edition in 1689, relying upon Purcell for musical editing, as well as for the majority of the compositions, as he had done in several other instances.

The Second Part of Musick's Handmaid: CONTAINING The newest Lessons, Grounds, Sarabands, Minuets, and Jigs, set for the virginals, harpsichord, and spinet. London, Printed on copper-plates, for Henry Playford ... 1689

The engraved illustration on the title-page of the second book shows that its basic purpose was the same as that of the first, despite the archaic dichotomy between *musica theorica* and *musica practica* that ostensibly divided them. The little pieces in these books were written for the instruction of amateur musicians, and hence were suitable for more or less talented daughters of rich or noble families who owned harpsichords and who could afford music masters.[1]

Purcell's connection with the educational world about this time led also to his setting of 'Celestial music',* a new ode

* *Analytical Catalogue*, no. 322.

performed 'at the house of Mr. Maidwell, a school master'.[2] This
house in Westminster later became Maidwell's school.[3] But
Purcell's reason for setting this text (by one of Maidwell's
students) has not as yet been discovered. (Cummings* was certainly wrong in stating that it was performed for the return of
the Prince of Denmark.)

Meanwhile, a much more significant school performance was
being prepared at Josiah Priest's Boarding School for Young
Ladies and Gentlewomen in Chelsea, where Purcell's *Dido and
Aeneas* was first performed. By 1689, according to an advertisement in the *London Gazette* for 22–25 November, Priest had been
nearly a decade in Chelsea, which at that time was separated
from London and Westminster by wide expanses of countryside:

Josiah Priest, dancing master, who kept a boarding school for gentlewomen in
Liecester Fields, is removed to the great School House at Chelsea, which was
Mr. Portman's ... there will continue the same masters, and others, to the
improvement of the said school.

As Michael Tilmouth has indicated,† Priest had been thinking
about the move some time earlier, having actually announced his
intention to move in the *London Gazette* for 25 November 1678.

Priest's venture had numerous precedents, as various accounts
of the time reveal, and under his predecessors' direction there had
been, in fact, an earlier musical stage work in 1676 at Chelsea
School itself, as the following title reveals:

Thomas Duffett: *Beauties Triumph*, a Masque. Presented by the Scholars of Mr.
Jeffrey Banister and Mr. James Hart. At their New Boarding-School for Young
Ladies and Gentlewomen, kept in that House which was formerly Sir Arthur
Gorges at Chelsea, Written by T. Duffet ... London: Printed in the year
MDCLXXVI.‡

Purcell was perhaps still somewhat in the shadow of official
disfavour at Court, where everyone was too preoccupied with
William's anti-Jacobite campaign in the Highlands and later in
Ireland to think about much else. (His Court appointment had
at last been recorded on 22 July.) At any rate the absence of any

* P. 50.   † *RMA Research Chronicle*, no. 1, p. 4.
‡ See William Barclay Squire, ' "Beauties Triumph" at Mr. Priest's School',
Musical Times, 1 April 1906, p. 250.

major events at Court throughout the summer freed him for other commissions, making it possible for him to write the ode for Mr. Maidwell's School, and to accept the much more important commission from Josiah Priest. Perhaps the impending arrival of a new son — Edward, who was to be baptized at Westminster on 6 September 1689* — caused him to receive gratefully any commission that paid well.

No later than October, and possibly as early as July 1689, Purcell's *Dido and Aeneas* was performed at Gorges House, Chelsea, the same house that Josiah Priest had taken over for his school for young gentlewomen. At least this is the approximate date usually agreed upon at present on the basis of evidence that seems solid, though much of it is circumstantial.† The only known copy of the libretto possibly was printed solely for the audience at the first production, since nothing beyond the following is given on the title-page: 'An opera perform'd at Mr. Josias Priest's Boarding-school at Chelsea by young Gentlewomen.'‡

As for the actual performance, this statement scarcely represents the whole truth, since it is unlikely that the school would have had sopranos capable of singing the parts of Dido and Belinda (not to mention Aeneas' tenor role, or the choral bass and tenor parts). Nor could a girls' school have provided the orchestral players and dancers required. Hence Priest very likely would have invited as many London professionals as needed, although his young gentlewomen may have done much of the dancing. Not knowing how, or when, or even actually where at Gorges House it was performed, we are also completely ignorant as to the reception *Dido and Aeneas* may have received. It seems improbable that such an important milestone in English music history would have gone unheeded at the time. But no source yet discovered mentions the original performance.§

---

* *Westminster Abbey Registers*, p. 74.
† Cf. Laurie, folios 51 ff. for a concise summary of the evidence.
‡ Music Library, Royal College of Music, London.
§ See, however, E. W. White, 'New Light on *Dido and Aeneas*', in *Henry Purcell, 1659–1695: Essays on his Music* (ed. I. Holst), pp. 14–34, and Laurie, folios 53 ff., for further discussion.

That the opera was written to commemorate some aspect of the Glorious Revolution is clear; but apart from certain general correspondences that the plot bears to the contemporary royal situation, notice has been taken only of the hint in the following passage from D'Urfey's Epilogue (spoken by Lady Dorothy Burk):

> Rome may allow strange tricks to please her sons,
> But we are Protestants and English nuns;
> Like nimble fawns, and birds that bless the Spring
> Unscarr'd by turning times we dance and sing.*

However, Tate's departures from Virgil's original story also suggest that he may have designed this little drama as a topical allegory relating to the ascendance of William III, Mary II, and the parliamentarian party. As Poet Laureate he would normally have been expected to supply such a 'dynastic' libretto for the reigning monarchs, just as Purcell, composer-in-ordinary, would have been expected to set it to music.

Certainly the parallels are there. Even in the Prologue to *Dido and Aeneas* one need not look too far beneath the surface to find topical reference. The allusion to William and Mary as 'Phoebus and Venus' is too obvious to call for further comment. Together with the reference to some special occasion (perhaps a royal birthday) in the line 'To celebrate this genial day' the following eulogy confirms that the opera was produced for some event of special significance in the lives of William and Mary:

> Nereid: Look down ye orbs and see
>   A new divinity
> Phoe: Whose lustre does outshine
>   Your fainter beams and half eclipses mine ...
> Phoe: Earth and skies address their duty
>   To the sovereign Queen of Beauty ...
> Cho: To Phoebus and Venus our homage we'll pay,
>   Her charms bless the night, as his beams bless the day.

This unequal tribute to the two monarchs correlates with the political situation at the time of their accession to the throne. In

---

* As reprinted in Thurston Dart and A. Margaret Laurie's edition of *Dido and Aeneas* (London, 1961), p. 106.

fact these lines sound as if written to ease reconciliation of the 'queen's party' to the terms of a joint sovereignty. And more explicit use of the same twin metaphor in Blow's ode for King William's birthday, 1692, substantiates this notion:

> Secured by Hyde's advice and Nassau's arm
> Our isle no threatening power can harm.
> Britain shall all attempts withstand
> Whilst these two live to shield the land.
>
> Whilst he abroad does like the sun display
> His active beams and gives to others day,
> She like the modest regent of the night
> Supplies his room but not with borrowed light . . .*

It is also possibly significant in this connection that Queen Mary went 'often in the evening to Chelsea reach in her barge' and was 'diverted there with a consort of music'.† Very likely it was her delight in music that accounts for the more refined aspects of the affair taking place at Court on Sunday, 20 October, when 'their majesties dined the first time publicly at Whitehall, with music, heralds . . . etc. as their predecessors did'.‡

D'Urfey, who had written the epilogue to *Dido and Aeneas*, was also responsible for the ode celebrating William III's birthday (on 4 November), 'Cloudy Saturnia drives her steeds apace'.§ But if its three movements (that is, stanzas) and chorus were ever set, no trace of the music remains. There was, however, a ball at the theatre for the king's birthday, 'with scenes and lights'.|| Apparently this affair, which fell on Thursday evening, pre-empted the services of a number of musicians who would otherwise have been playing at the weekly York Buildings concerts, resumed the previous April after disturbances attending the

---

* As quoted in McGuinness, folios 57 and 116. The similarity suggests that Nahum Tate may have written the birthday ode ('Welcome, welcome genial day') hitherto anonymous. (Note also the correspondence with the line 'To celebrate this genial day' quoted above.)

† Luttrell, vol. II, p. 57 (June 1690).

‡ Luttrell, vol. I, p. 595.

§ Thomas D'Urfey, *Pills to Purge Melancholy* (New York, 1959), vol. II, p. 289.

|| Boswell, p. 238.

Glorious Revolution had subsided. At any rate, on 28 October the *London Gazette* appeared with an announcement that

The Bow Street Consort defer their performance in York Buildings until November 11th on account of the King's birthday. Thereafter to be given weekly.

Then, on the day of this concert, a Monday, the same journal reported the merger of the Bow Street and York Buildings series, and the resumption of the regular season on Thursday the 14th — an indication that London musicians had had a busy fortnight, what with all the rehearsals and performances that had been required. Something of the popularity of this sort of concert and of a certain eagerness on the part of some members of the audiences that attended is reflected in the special licence granted on 25 December 1689 to Robert King for the Vendu concerts:

Whereas we do well approve of the abilities in music of Robert King, one of our musicians, and he having besought us to have our authority to set up a consort of music, and to have the sole government thereof, and that none force their way in without paying such prices as shall be set down. Our will and pleasure therefore is, and we do hereby license and authorize the said Robert King to set up a consort of music to be performed by such as he shall appoint and as often as he shall think fit, and we require and command all persons to forbear rudely or by force to enter in or abide there during the time of performing the said music without observing such rules and paying such prices as shall be by him set down. And all our officers civil and military are required to be aiding and assisting herein. Given at our Court at Whitehall the 25th day of December 1689 in the first year of our reign.

By His Majesty's command
SHREWSBURY*

The times had been too unsettled for the preparation of a concert celebrating St. Cecilia's Day,† but the musical activity at the Vendu and at York Buildings show that London concert life had already regained its former vigour.

For New Year's Day Luttrell‡ recorded that the

King and Queen came to Whitehall, where many of the nobility and gentry came to wish them a happy New Year; and there was a great consort of music,

---

* *Cal. S. P. Dom.* 1689, as quoted in R. Elkin, *The Old Concert Rooms of London,* pp. 38–39.

† Husk, p. 25.   ‡ Vol. II, p. 1; see also McGuinness, fo. 53.

vocal and instrumental, and a song composed by the poet laureate. The mayor, aldermen, and sheriffs waited on their majesties also to compliment them . . .

Shadwell's song, 'With cheerful hearts let all appear', as set by Blow, could scarcely have furnished all the music performed for the occasion, but nothing else appears to have been recorded.

During the last weeks of 1689 Purcell must already have been occupied in composing his first work to celebrate the Glorious Revolution. Although the ode 'Of old when heroes thought it base'* was not actually performed until later, the Society of Yorkshiremen in London had commissioned it for 14 February 1690. Supposedly Purcell would have had the work nearly completed when an announcement in the *London Gazette* for 7 February 1690 put off the performance until the 27th of the following month, after the parliamentary elections. These brought into power not the Whigs, who had placed William III on his throne, but the Tories. The new monarch demonstrated his political sagacity by promptly joining forces with the latter.†

Because of this postponement, or perhaps by Tory design, the first performance of Purcell's 'Yorkshire Feast Song' very nearly coincided with the first anniversary of the beginning of the reign of William and Mary, whose monarchy had been recognized a year and a day before, even though their coronation had not been celebrated until later, on 11 April. For such an occcasion the ode seems to have been lavish enough, as we know from the descriptive title given it by the poet, D'Urfey:

An ode on the assembly of the nobility and gentry of the City and County of York, at the anniversary feast, March 27th, 1690. Set to music by Mr. Henry Purcell. One of the finest compositions he ever made, and cost £100 the performing.‡

D'Urfey's enthusiastic description of this ceremonial composition is confirmed by an advertisement in the *London Gazette* for 14 March 1690:

The Annual Yorkshire Feast will be held the 27th instant at the Merchant Taylors' Hall in Threadneedle Street, where will be a very splendid entertainment of all sorts of vocal and instrumental music.

* *Analytical Catalogue*, no. 333.
† J. Dalrymple, *Memoirs of Great Britain and Ireland*, p. 463.
‡ D'Urfey's *Songs Compleat, Pleasant and Divertive* (1719), vol. I, pp. 114–16.

William's Whig supporters were no doubt resentful of all this Tory splendour, particularly since they had just been deserted. On the other hand, they must have joined their opponents in applauding these rousing lines in the final chorus, which might have served as the battle song of the Glorious Revolution, had such been needed:

> Sound trumpets, sound, beat every drum,
> Till it be known through Christendom;
> This is the knell of falling Rome . . .

D'Urfey's rhymes and metre are by no means impeccable. But his grasp of the nation's mood could not be improved upon.

Those Whigs of quasi-Puritanical persuasion must have been pleased with William and Mary's austere moral code, which regulated manners as well as morals at Court and elsewhere. They not only proscribed 'prophane swearing and cursing, prophaning the Lord's day, drunkenness, and such immoralities',* but instituted a general fast

to be kept . . . the third Wednesday in every month successively during the present war, for supplicating God for pardon of our sins, imploring his blessing and protection in the preservation of His Majesty's person and prosperity of his arms in Ireland . . .†

As in Puritanical times, this proscriptive attitude evidently extended to certain musical practices, which were forbidden on fast-days:

Mr. Comptroller has complained to the Green Cloth against Mr. Story for keeping music and revelling in his house on the fast-day; and 'tis believed he will be turned out.‡

Apparently William's attitude towards any but martial music when not apathetic was negative. As Purcell and his fellow musicians were soon to learn, the Court could no longer be looked upon as the centre and home of English musical culture. Nevertheless Purcell was commissioned to produce more music

---

* Luttrell, vol. II, p. 263.   † Luttrell, vol. II, p. 16 (2 Feb. 1689/90),
‡ Luttrell, vol. III, p. 489 (25 June 1695). Mr. Story may have been either George Walter Story, author of *An Impartial History of the War in Ireland* (1691), or his brother, Thomas Story, friend of William Penn (*DNB*).

for their majesties a little more than a month after the original performance of the 'Yorkshire Feast Song'. The occasion was again Queen Mary's birthday, and the poet again Thomas D'Urfey, who evidently provided two poems for the same event: 'Arise, my muse'* and 'High on a throne of glitt'ring ore'.†

The first of these, which was no worse than D'Urfey's usual stuff in quality, apparently was too much for Purcell in quantity. At any rate, he did not take the trouble to set D'Urfey's last two choruses,‡ with the result that the ode ends proclaiming King William's brave deeds, rather than extolling Queen Mary's virtues, as the poet intended. The queen cannot have been pleased, for the piece ends comically, with the chorus exhorting William to 'Go on, go on, illustrious man' (*ad infinitum*), just after she has been portrayed entreating him to stay at home. If indeed Queen Mary was nettled by Purcell's setting of her birthday ode, her displeasure might well account for her deliberate slighting of Purcell's music in favour of the Scottish tune 'Cold and Raw', as Hawkins recounted in his gossipy little anecdote, granted, of course, that the anecdote be true.§

Whether or not it was written for the same occasion as the foregoing, Purcell's sprightly setting of D'Urfey's 'High on a throne of glitt'ring ore' occupies a special place in the very happily conceived series that he composed for the queen. Since the text appeared in D'Urfey's *New Poems* of 1690, definitely labelled 'An Ode to the Queen especially set to music by Mr. H. Purcell', and since the text referred to her having sat on the throne, the piece could only have been written for either 1689 or 1690, the latter year being the more likely.

Purcell provided for another event that was to have been part of the celebrations for Queen Mary's twenty-eighth birthday this same year in his songs and instrumental music for Dryden's *Amphitryon*. Boswell|| lists a warrant to prepare the theatre for a

---

* *Analytical Catalogue*, no. 320.   † *Analytical Catalogue*, no. 465.

‡ As published in D'Urfey's *Songs Compleat, Pleasant and Divertive* (1719), p. 62. Purcell also disregarded D'Urfey's formal divisions and instructions for choral performances in that portion of the poem he did set.

§ See p. 210 below. || P. 238.

play on Wednesday, 30 April, being the queen's birthday. Nicoll★ also records an entry in the Lord Chamberlain's accounts which posted a box for the queen, and another for the maids of honour for this same performance. However, the entry was cancelled, without explanatory note, and another made for 21 October for a performance that the queen evidently did attend with her maids of honour, since a payment of £15 is recorded opposite that date.

Purcell's music for *Amphitryon* (including a full set: tripartite overture, act-tunes, and three songs) no doubt contributed a great deal to the general popularity of the play, which was to have fairly frequent revivals during the next decade. Dryden, whose musical sensibilities had been so underdeveloped that he had found it possible to bear Grabu's dull music for his first opera *Albion and Albanius*, at last had seen the light. After allowing credit in the dedication to Plautus and Molière and the players for any excellence the play might have, Dryden continued, with further false modesty:

But what has been wanting on my part has been abundantly supplied by the excellent composition of Mr. Purcell, in whose person we have at length found an Englishman equal with the best abroad. At least my opinion of him has been such since his happy and judicious performances in the late opera... To all which, and particularly to the composition of the Pastoral Dialogue, the numerous choir of fair ladies gave so just an applause on the third day. I am only sorry, for my own sake, that there was one star wanting, as beautiful as any in our hemisphere; that young Berenice, who is mis-employing all her charms on stupid country souls, that can never know the value of them; and losing the triumphs, which are ready prepared for her in this Court and town.

(Here Dryden alluded to Berenice, wife of Ptolemy III, who had dedicated a lock of her hair as a votive offering for her husband's return from an invasion into Syria. The parallel to Queen Mary's situation in the spring and summer of 1690 is too clear to need further explanation, in view of William's successful summer campaign in Ireland.)

The musical establishment at Court had been growing, but in about May it suddenly received a serious set-back with the king's

★ P. 352.

order 'that the musicians be presently reduced to 24 and an instrument keeper, and that though there is provision made only for that number by the establishment, yet care will be taken for paying the rest for the time they have served...'* The list for 25 March 1689 included thirty-four musicians (at an aggregate salary of £1,140 per annum plus liveries, which would have amounted to an additional £548. 5s.). To these sums were to be added the stipends of the instrument-keeper, the salaries of twenty gentlemen of the Chapel Royal and of the Master and Boys of the Chapel, and stipends for sixteen trumpeters and kettle-drummers, who apparently occupied a place very near to William's heart. Significantly, in the account for the following St. Andrew's Day only twenty-six 'musicians to the King and Queen' were named.† All this reveals how profoundly the musical situation at Court had changed since the seventies and eighties. Charles II had rather found ways to protect his musicians from similar orders, not enforce them, and the change in royal attitude after the Glorious Revolution is reflected in the reduction of the number of musicians in the king's employ, before and after the retrenchment. Here perhaps lies one explanation for the great rise of concert life in London about this time. Musicians were unemployed.

The relative infrequency of Purcell's name in official lists is significant, and probably explains his having turned increasingly to the theatre both for income and for a musical outlet. His increased involvement with theatre music, possibly originating from adverse financial conditions at Court, very likely explains the sudden upsurge of his popularity in theatrical circles about 1690, for which he had prepared the way with his earlier works for the stage. The above-mentioned retrenchment would have found him hard at work on music for Betterton's revision, 'with alterations and additions after the manner of an opera', of Beaumont and Massinger's *The Prophetess: or, The History of Dioclesian*.‡ The new production, which marked Purcell's pro-

* *Cal. Tr. Books*, 2 May 1690; William Jephson to the Lord Chamberlain.
† I.e. one more than allowed for in the retrenchment discussed above; see *KM*, p. 397.
‡ *Analytical Catalogue*, no. 627.

fessional début on the operatic stage, was announced in the
London Gazette for 16 June 1690. It is fairly certain that it was
mounted at the Theatre Royal, Drury Lane, soon after the notice
had appeared, for Carr and Playford were advertising for subscriptions for the printing of Purcell's music in the same journal
for the following 7 July.

The plot of the opera is quite simple, and its topicality trans-
parent, what with William III's having departed for Ireland just
twelve days before the advertisement had appeared. Delphia had
prophesied to Diocles (later the Emperor Dioclesian) that upon
killing a certain mighty boar he would become emperor. By
happy coincidence the murderer of the previous emperor was
named Aper ('boar'), so that when Diocles had slain him (with
the complicity of Niger, an honest Roman; Charinus, current
Roman Emperor; and Aurelia, who had provided added incentive
by offering herself in marriage to the slayer of 'the boar') he was
acclaimed first as hero, then as emperor. (Though nothing is said
here about Emperor Charinus, history reveals that he actually was
quite complacent about sharing the emperorship not only with
Dioclesian, but with Maximilian as well.) Topically as well as
musically the work was well suited to the temper of the times, and
was most successful. As Downes pointed out:

being set out with costly scenes, machines and clothes: the vocal and instrumental music done by Mr. Purcell, and dances by Mr. Priest, it gratified the
expectation of Court and City; and got the author great reputation.[*]

An anonymous 'Epistle to the Rt. Hon. Charles, Earl of Dorset and
Middlesex'[†] confirms the case for such topical uses of music and
the operatic stage by conjectures as to what would happen if
France had had a William III:

> Their plays, their songs, would dwell upon this wound,
> And operas repeat no other sound;
> Boyne would for ages be their painters' theme.

Purcell's star as a theatrical composer was rising rapidly. As if
Dryden's public recognition of the worth of his music for

[*] Downes, p. 42.
[†] *The Vocal and Instrumental Music of the Prophetess, or the History of Dioclesian*,
London, 1691. (See also pp. 337–9 below for a direct allusion.)

Dioclesian* had unleashed new forces in his favour, suddenly he found himself in continual demand, both at Drury Lane and at Dorset Garden. During the last few months of 1690 his music was being performed in four, or perhaps even five or six, London productions, including Dryden's *Amphitryon* (as mentioned above) and Elkanah Settle's *Distress'd Innocence†* in October; 'A New Play' mentioned for 'Why, my Daphne', which was published in the fifth book of *The Banquet of Music* — licensed on 2 December 1690;‡ *The Gordian Knot Unty'd*, possibly as early as December 1690;§ *Sir Anthony Love,*‖ and (just possibly) *The Knight of Malta.*¶ All told, these had required thirty-five separate compositions, including the eleven (or twelve) that Purcell had probably finished in the previous spring. A regular theatre-goer would have found it quite difficult *not* to hear Purcell's music in play after play that season, such was his popularity.

Something of a mystery surrounds the play *The Gordian Knot Unty'd*, written by an anonymous Francophile, as P. A. Motteux explained at the time:

You have often asked me who was the author of that [play] called *The Gordian Knot Unty'd* and wondered with many more why it was never printed. I hear that gentleman who writ lately a most ingenious dialogue concerning women, now translated into French, is the author of that witty play, and it is almost a sin in him to keep it and his name from the world.**

The author alluded to was almost without a doubt the same person who wrote *A Dialogue concerning Women, Being a Defence of the Fair Sex Written to Eugenia*, also an anonymous work, although it has a preface signed by John Dryden.†† The French version was also printed, under the title '*Défense du Beau Sexe . . .* Écrit en

---

* Cf. Dryden's preface to *Amphitryon*, quoted on p. 186.

† *Analytical Catalogue*, no. 577.

‡ *Analytical Catalogue*, no. 525, and Laurie, fo. 181. Laurie points out that this dialogue may have been intended for *The Gordian Knot Unty'd*.

§ *Analytical Catalogue*, no. 597, and Laurie, fo. 180. However, see arguments below regarding the probable date.

‖ *Analytical Catalogue*, no. 588.

¶ *Analytical Catalogue*, no. 599.

** *Gentleman's Journal*, Jan. 1690/1, p. 33.   †† London, 1691.

anglais par une personne de qualité, et traduit en français par une Dame anglaise', the preface signed by 'Jean Dryden'.*

Denis Arundell has identified one William Walsh as the author of the play, which he traced to Molière's *Monsieur de Porceaugnac*† (for which Lully had supplied music in France twenty years earlier). A reference in the 1691 edition of John Bancroft's *King Edward III* seems to indicate that *The Gordian Knot* was performed in 1690, some time before December.‡ However, the fact that Motteux speaks of the play as contemporary to the *Dialogue concerning Women*, published in 1691, makes the latter date equally probable.

On the political scene, September had brought William III back to England as the hero of the Boyne — very little was made then of Limerick — just as the musical season was getting under way in London. As usual there is no record of what music, if any, was performed for his arrival in London on the 10th after a four-day progress. Very likely he would have been more than content with fireworks and a flourish of trumpets and drums for this occasion as well as for the general thanksgiving proclaimed on the 14th in the City of London. The king's disregard for music may account for the existence of two odes for his fortieth birth-day — Shadwell's 'Welcome, thrice welcome' and Matthew Prior's 'As though Britannia's raging sea' — with no known musical setting for either.§ Nor was the St. Cecilia celebration for 1690 an affair grand enough to excite either great interest or commentary worth recording. Perhaps the lack of any organized public performance for the years 1688 and 1689‖ put extra-ordinary difficulties in the way of the organizers of the celebration for 1690. If so, these cannot have been alleviated, but only aggravated by the selection of the inept Shadwell as the poet for the occasion and the slight song-writer Robert King as composer.

* Londres, 1691.

† '*The Gordian Knot Unty'd*', *Times Literary Supplement*, 4 June 1925, p. 384. Dr. Laurie (fo. 181) finds flaws in his reasoning.

‡ Laurie, fo. 181.

§ McGuinness, fo. 54. See Plate 12(*b*) for a depiction of the 'Firework', by Bernard Lens.

‖ Husk, pp. 24–25.

Apparently little care was taken to see the music preserved, for it cannot now be found — a fact that may be taken in lieu of any contemporary commentary on the composition.*

The tune 'Lilliburlero', with its Purcellian associations, was again heard in the streets, as a new broadside ballad to this tune appeared about the time William III returned to share his victory with loyal Englishmen: 'The Courageous Soldiers of the West; or The undaunted Countrymen's Resolution in taking up Arms in the defence of King William and Queen Mary, together with the Protestant Religion.'† We have no way of knowing what William's reaction may have been to the pointed lack of reference to his own heroic exploits on the occasion, or the even more pointed reference to:

Marlborough both true and loyal now with the rest did add to the train.‡

* Husk, p. 25.   † Ebsworth, *Bagford Ballads*, part II, p. 365.

‡ See Ebsworth's ed., part II, pp. 369, 373, and 426 respectively, for other military victories for which Purcell's tune was called into service.

CHAPTER XIII

A ROYAL EXCURSION ABROAD

William insisted on more impressive musical forces for a long postponed return to his native land, for which he crossed the channel in January 1691. The king's first journey back to Holland since he had embarked there at the end of 1688, leading a successful expedition to topple James II from his throne, was not just a nostalgic voyage. On the contrary, he had been 'earnestly entreated by the States of Holland, and the confederate Princes in Germany, etc., to meet at a general Congress at The Hague, in order to concert military and economic forces for the next campaign'.[*] He acquiesced, of course, having cherished a life-long ambition to diminish the strength of the French empire.

The accounts of this splendid affair, though indicating glories reminiscent of the Field of the Cloth of Gold, are disappointing in so far as descriptions of musical events are concerned. Contemporary chroniclers seem to have interested themselves only in graphic scenes, admittedly splendid, and said nothing of the music. There is one exception, however, since Govard Bidloo included a description of a musical event:

Na eenige reijen en drommen van Staatelijke Perzoonagiën in lange praal-kleederen en Hof-en Gerechtsbedienden, koomen de Pypers, Bazuin en Klaaroenblaazers, Reukwerkdragers, Bomme-en Tromslagers, Dryhoeken Harpspeelders, Zangers, Danszers ... [†]

[After several groups of state officials and bailiffs in long ceremonial dress, come the fifers, trumpeters, sackbut players, incense-bearers, drummers, three cornered-harp players, singers and dancers ...]

William III did appreciate the importance of impressive music for good foreign policy, though he slighted it domestically, for he

[*] An Exact Relation of the Entertainment of His Most Sacred Majesty, William III ... at The Hague.
[†] Komste van ... Willem III. Koning van Groot Britanje, enz. in Holland, p. 76.

took along to Holland with him no fewer than forty-three musicians. Nothing is known of the music they may have played, but the following list leaves no room for doubt that the English king had transferred most of his musical staff (Purcell among them) to Holland for the occasion:

These are to certify the Right Honourable Lord Chamberlain of their majesties' Household, that the persons hereafter named did attend His Majesty into Holland, who do humbly crave your Lordship's favourable assistance towards the attaining the money that is ordered them in the Treasury Chamber, which cannot be received till your Lordship does declare your pleasure therein:

	Nico. Staggins, Master	
	John Goodwin	
	Edward Hooton	
	Hene Heale	
	Robt. Carr	
	George Bingham	
	Morgain Harriss	
	Hene Eaccles	The part that
	Soll. Eaccles	attended His Majesty
Band of	Fred. Stofkins	into Holland.
violins	Christn. Stofkins	
	John Lenton	
	Charles Powell	
	Richard Thomlinson — deceased	
	Richard Lewiss	
	Franciss Cruse	
	Edmond Flower	

—

Robt. King	
John Banister	
Wm. Clayton	
Theopy. Fittz	The remaining part
Wm. Hall	that attended the
Daniell Short	Queen in England.
Robt. Strong	
Alixander De-lature	
Charles Coleman	

—

John Mosley: Instrument-keeper

—

| 'Hooboys' that were in Holland: only for that voyage | George Sutton Franciss Lari —— Brazong —— Baptist —— Granvell | These are to be paid for their journey into Holland and no longer. |

John Blow: Composer
Hene Purcell: Harpsicall

| Vocal concort to be added voices | Wm. Turner —— Gozlin —— Bowman —— Damazen —— Robert Lenard Woodson —— Richardson Alfanso March Joseph Boucher Moses Snow[1] | These to be continued. |

Although their repertoire is not known, it is certain that the musicians were properly rehearsed, since they had gone to Holland some weeks before William himself made the trip. Many if not all of the musical band seem to have spent three and a half months in Holland, as can be seen from the records of their riding charges:

Warrant to pay Dr. Nicholas Staggins, Master of His Majesty's music, Edward Hooton, John Goodwin, Robert Carr, Henry Heale, Henry Eagles, George Bingham, Morgan Harris, Christian Stephkins, Solomon Eagles, Francis Cruys, John Lenton, and Charles Powell, musicians-in-ordinary to His Majesty; La Rush, George Sutton, Greenville, Baptist and one more hautboy, the several sums following viz:

To Dr. Staggins 5s. by the day for the space of 103 days, from 1 January 1690 to 13 April 1691 for his riding charges and other expenses in attending His Majesty unto Holland, amounting to £24. 15s., and to each of the said musicians and hautboys 3s. by the day for the said time, amounting to the sum of £15. 9s. each.*

No records have come to light to show when or where the English musicians performed. Certainly they took part in the pageantry of William's public entry into The Hague on 26

---

* KM, p. 404; frequent other references (Cal. Tr. Books, vol. IX, part III, pp. 902, 912, 916 — 3 new silver trumpets — 935, 940, 967, 978, et al.) show how extensive and expensive were the preparations for the trip.

January, the triumphal arch surmounted by Fame sounding her golden trumpet reminding Purcell and his colleagues of the by now well-known song heard in *Dioclesian* the year before.

Frequent public audiences, such as that granted to the Elector of Brandenburg on 16 February or to the Governor of the Spanish Netherlands, the Marquis de Gastanaga, on 18 February, also provided opportunities for music. Indeed, for the public audience granted to the Count of Winditzgratze on 24 February the Master of Ceremonies managed the whole affair. On the following day a public demonstration called for even more elaborate ceremony. Then, suddenly, the besieging of Mons by the French armies put an end to the festival. William III immediately assumed a soldier's role and marshalled forces to save Mons. But he was too late, and the city capitulated on 9 April, three days after William had set out with his army to lift the siege.

With some forty of the royal musicians away the records for January and February 1691 naturally reveal little important musical activity in London, and yield no direct references to Purcell, who had gone on the expedition as an official composer. Perhaps the hard frost which Luttrell recorded in his entry for 8 January had reduced musical activities somewhat. Nevertheless the lull in London concert life came to an end about 20 February 1691, as the following announcements from the *London Gazette* on 19 and 26 February 1690/1 reveal:

19 February 1690/1.
The consort of music lately in Bow Street is removed next Bedford Gate in Charles Street, Covent Garden (where a room is newly built for that purpose), and by command, is to begin on Friday next the 20th instant, where it is afterwards to be continued every Thursday, beginning between 7 and 8 in the evening.

26 February 1690/1.
The new consort of music which began on Friday the 20th instant ... will be performed at the aforesaid place this present Thursday the 26th instant, and so continue every Thursday, beginning between 7 and 8 in the evening.

Just a month later — still some two or three weeks before the royal musicians returned — Frank and Robert King advertised in the *London Gazette* the resumption of their royally approved concerts at the Two Golden Balls, inaugurated at the beginning of the previous season on 9 October.*

Then, in the *London Gazette* for 26 February to 2 March 1690/1, appeared good evidence that Purcell had not been idle, though absent. The music for *Dioclesian* (as *The Prophetess* was now called) was ready for publication, and it seems that he had had no little trouble in preparing it:

The book, containing all the vocal and instrumental music in *The Prophetess, or The History of Dioclesian* (composed by Mr. Henry Purcell) is now finished; and will be delivered to the subscribers by John Carr at his shop near the Middle Temple Gate, upon receipt of the remaining part of the subscription money.

A note, or 'advertisement' inserted in the printed edition explains how it was that a work actually 'in the press' nearly a year before should only at this late date be ready for sale:

In order to the speedier publication of this book, I employed two several printers; but one of them falling into some trouble, and the volume swelling to a bulk beyond my expectation, have been the occasions of this delay.

It has been objected that some of the songs are already common; but I presume that the subscribers, upon perusal of the work, will easily be convinced that they are not the essential parts of it. [Here Purcell no doubt referred to several of Thomas Cross's engraved single-sheet songs, such as 'Sound Fame' and 'Tell me why', which had appeared in 1691.]

I have, according to my promise in the proposals, been very careful in the examination of every sheet and hope that the whole will appear as correct as any yet extant.

My desire to make it as cheap as possible [*sic*] I could to the subscribers, prevailed with me so far above the consideration of my own interest that I find, too late, the subscription money will scarcely amount to the expense of completing this edition.

The whole document is interesting, as much for explanations left out as for those given. How was it possible for Purcell's songs to have got into print before this time? What was his arrangement with the publishers, whereby he could lose money even before the book had gone on sale to the public? Did he have no royalties? The plaintive tone Purcell adopts in the last paragraph seems to indicate that he had little hope of adequate recompense, but could not really afford any loss. Straitened financial circumstances, as

* *London Gazette*, 9 Oct. 1690.

here intimated, however, were to be his lot during his last five years, as were the overwork and over-worry that this sort of débâcle always brings on.

For the next few weeks Purcell was preparing a new ode for Queen Mary's birthday. For the celebration of this, the twenty-ninth festival of its kind, Purcell found himself burdened with the delightful verses of an anonymous ode, 'Welcome, glorious morn'. Even while composing this, Purcell must also have been engaged upon the task of supplying music for Dryden's *King Arthur*,* his second major semi-opera for the London stage. Dryden had written the libretto first to celebrate the wisdom and sagacity of Charles II, altered it to eulogize James II, and modified it again to entertain William III. Poor Dryden! In his *magnum opus* for the musical stage not only did he find it necessary to make changes dictated by the rise and fall of monarchs; he had also to submit to Purcell's demands for certain alterations, as the following lines from his preface reveal:

But the numbers of poetry and vocal music are sometimes so contrary that in many places I have been obliged to cramp my verses, and make them rugged to the reader, that they may be harmonious to the hearer.

Whatever the difficulties, or the damage to Dryden's ego, this collaboration with Purcell produced a work unique in English music history, indeed without parallel anywhere. Though it is primarily an entertainment, it remains a unified work, unlike *The Fairy Queen*, and a truly poetic stage piece, unlike *Dioclesian*. In describing its essentially English character despite the taste for foreign styles displayed by both author and composer, Sir Jack Westrup got to the heart of the matter:

However Dryden might attempt to imitate the accents of the Italian tongue, he could not avoid the flavour of his native English. That flavour is to be found, too, in Purcell's melodies.†

As Nicoll points out,‡ the first production took place at Dorset Garden in 1691, possibly as early as May, a date which indicates that Purcell must have been at work on *King Arthur* even before

* *Analytical Catalogue*, no. 628.
† *Listener*, 29 April 1943.   ‡ P. 407.

composing the queen's birthday ode. Indeed, he had probably spent a great deal of time on this opera during the period of hectic activity discussed above. As a matter of fact at least two pieces for the opera were written even earlier. Purcell wrote the first chaconne for the ode for King James of 1687, 'Sound the trumpet',* while he had already used the first overture to introduce a birthday ode he had written for Queen Mary in 1690, 'Arise my muse'.† One of the most famous pieces may have had previous existence outside Purcell's music. Captain Walter Scot, in his *True History of Several Honourable Families of the Right Honourable Name of Scot* (1688),‡ describing preparations for a battle wrote, 'Meantime the trumpets sounded "Come if you dare".' § Purcell therefore may have borrowed this trumpet challenge from actual military practice.

As intimated above, Dryden had written his opera in 1683 or 1684, to be performed with some of the stage machinery used in the 1685 production of his *Albion and Albanius*.‖ Indeed the latter had grown out of the sung prologue that Dryden had conceived for *King Arthur*.¶ He must have had a great deal of revision to do in resurrecting *King Arthur* (now subtitled *The British Worthy*) after seven years, for an opera written to eulogize Charles II now had to be transformed into a fitting tribute to William III and all his military prowess — particularly that which he had just proved in the bogs and on the battlefields of Ireland. As Robert Moore has pointed out,** Dryden's direct reference to William in the final chorus is unmistakable, although what he hoped to gain by such left-handed compliments is hard to say. Being completely out of favour at Court, perhaps he did not care very much:

> Our natives not alone appear
> To court his martial prize;
> But foreign kings adopted here,
> Their crowns at home despise.††

---

* *Analytical Catalogue*, no. 335/7.   † See *Analytical Catalogue*, no. 320/1ab.
‡ J. C. Winning (ed.) (London, 1894), p. 20.
§ As quoted by Bucinator in *Musical Antiquary* for January 1911, p. 124.
‖ Nicoll, p. 47.
¶ Dryden , *King Arthur* (London, 1735) 'Epistle Dedicatory', sig. Q3.
** Moore, p. 72.   †† Dryden, *King Arthur*, p. 419.

The opera was very successful at its first performance and quite probably lived up to Dryden's conditional prognostication in the 'Epistle Dedicatory':

In the meantime . . . I humbly offer you this trifle, which if it succeed upon the stage, is like to be the chiefest entertainment of our ladies and gentlemen this summer.*

Downes, writing much later, after it had proved itself, described *King Arthur* in glowing terms, remarking that

it was excellently adorned with scenes and machines. The musical part set by famous Mr. Henry Purcell; and dances made by Mr. Jo. Priest. The play and the music pleased the Court and City, and being well performed, 'twas very gainful to the company.†

The work was successful enough to be revived and performed several times, probably about December or January, as is known from Motteux's remarks in his advance notice of *The Fairy Queen* in the *Gentleman's Journal* for January 1692.‡

Even before he had seen these signs of success, Dryden demonstrated that his musical tastes had improved considerably since 1685, when he had written in the preface to *Albion and Albanius*:

When any of our countrymen excell him [Grabu], I shall be glad to confess my error; in the meantime let virtue be recommended though in the person of a stranger.

Dryden's remarks in the preface to *King Arthur*, as revised for the 1691 production, although not an explicit confession, do reveal that he had seen the error of his old ways and had recognized the excellent musical countryman he had prophesied, though in a negative way, six years earlier:

There is nothing better than what I intended but the music; which has since arrived to a greater perfection in England than ever formerly, especially passing through the artful hands of Mr. Purcell, who has composed it with so great a genius that he has nothing to fear but an ignorant, ill-judging audience.§

---

* Ibid. sig. Q5.   † Downes, p. 42.
‡ See p. 204 below. Luttrell (vol. II, p. 31) records a performance attended by the queen and dowager queen on 7 Jan. 1691/2.
§ Dryden, *King Arthur*, sig. Q5.

This was high praise indeed, and it no doubt crowned for Purcell this his most successful season to date, giving him a foretaste of the universal acclaim that was to be his in full measure, if ever so briefly, before he died.

Meanwhile, Purcell was preoccupied with another matter that arose that same month. On 18 June his sister, Katherine Purcell, married suddenly, to the surprise of her family, who no doubt had given her up to spinsterhood long since. The marriage licence in the Vicar-General's office — which gave the lowest age warrantable for spinsterhood — improved upon the matter by mentioning her mother's consent:

20 June 1691.

William Sale of Sheldwich, Kent, Clerk, Bach., abt 33 and Mrs Catherine Purcell, of St. Margaret's Westminster, aged 22, with consent of her mother; at St. Mary Magdalen, Old Fish Street, London.

Although he gives 18 June as the date, the entry is verified by W. H. Challen's typescript of marriages in the Guildhall Library, London. And that this was indeed Henry Purcell's sister — who was baptized 13th March, 1662* and therefore was twenty-nine not twenty-two — is attested by an entry in PCW Admon. for 7 September 1699, which shows that the estate of Purcell's mother, Elizabeth, was administered by 'Katherine Purcell, wife of William Sale'.†

The following week the Lord Chamberlain's office issued a warrant authorizing payment to Nicholas Staggins and his musicians for 'riding charges and other expenses in attending His Majesty unto Holland' as we have seen.‡ Neither Purcell's nor Blow's name appears on this list, nor in that accompanied by another such warrant issued on 10 July following. Perhaps they did not stay for the whole period of one hundred and three days cited in these documents. Whether they were back in England or merely were paid separately we cannot know. Again, the records are mute.

---

* *Westminster Abbey Registers*, p. 67.

† See the Genealogical Tables and explanatory matter in App. Three for further details.

‡ *KM*, p. 404.

The summer of 1691 found Purcell concerned with nothing of great moment, except, perhaps, his need for rest, and preparations for various commissions for the following year. However, he wrote two catches celebrating historical events and perhaps even a third, of a more domestic nature, during this period. The two historical ones, 'Let us drink to the blades'* and 'The surrender of Limerick',† celebrated respectively the siege and eventual surrender of Limerick. Thus, even though they were not published until some time later, the two works may be dated fairly accurately. The text of the first referred to the situation at Limerick some time before General Ginkel approached the city on 25 August, and the second to William's capture of it on 3 October.

On the 26th that same October Ginkel returned victoriously to London to bask in the grateful admiration of the populace, the nobility, and the royal family. That evening, already marked in the calendar as the beginning of the Charles Street concerts,‡ the king, who had just arrived from Holland, and Ginkel met the Lord Mayor at a splendid dinner at the Merchant Taylors' Hall, both heroes being duly fêted and acclaimed. The following week, while the joyful acclamations of the populace were still ringing in everyone's ears,§ came another, two-day celebration, for William's forty-first birthday (4 November) and the regular annual celebration of Guy Fawkes' day on the 5th, given special and official significance this year. Additional zest accrued, at least in loyal Tory circles, from the fact that 5 November was also the fourteenth anniversary of the marriage of William and Mary, and the third anniversary of William's landing at Tor Bay. Luttrell, who called attention to this fact,‖ described with obvious enthusiasm the resplendent scene at Court:

the Court was all in their splendour, the Queen very rich in jewels; and all the great officers attended: the Archbishop of York preached before the House of Lords, Mr. Fleetwood before the House of Commons, and the Bishop of Salisbury before their majesties: after which their majesties dined publicly. The night concluded with a great ball and dancing at Court, bonfires and illuminations throughout the city, with ringing of bells, etc.

* *Analytical Catalogue*, no. 259.   † *Analytical Catalogue*, no. 278.
‡ *London Gazette*, 26–29 Oct. 1691.   § Maitland, vol. I, p. 495.
‖ Vol. II, p. 302.

No specific musical compositions are recorded for any of these events.

For the St. Cecilia celebration this year (which was held on 23 November, since the 22nd fell on Sunday in 1691)* John Blow and Thomas D'Urfey pooled their talents for the ode, 'The glorious day is come'. D'Urfey's handiwork is recorded for all to see,† but Blow's music has been lost except for 'Couch'd by the pleasant Heliconian spring' and 'Ah heav'n! What is't I hear', two duets preserved in his *Amphion Anglicus*.‡ Neither of these fragments kindles sufficient interest to cause regret for the loss of the remaining portions of the ode, although the first part of 'Ah heav'n!', a duet on a ground, resembles Purcell's 'In vain the am'rous flute' from the St. Cecilia ode for the following year, and the second sounds as if taken directly from 'If so, your goodness may your pow'r' in *The Indian Queen.*§

Motteux was evidently interested enough in the 1691 celebration not only to comment on the music and poetry, but also to describe something of the workings of the organization in his issue for January 1691/2:

...St. Cecilia's day is observed through all Europe by the lovers of music. In Italy, Germany, France, and other countries, prizes are distributed on that day in some of the most considerable towns, to such as make the best anthem in her praise.... On that day, or the next when it falls on a Sunday, as it did last time, most of the lovers of music, whereof many are persons of the first rank, meet at Stationers' Hall in London, not through a principle of superstition, but to propagate the advancement of that divine science. A splendid entertainment is provided, and before it is always a performance of music by the best voices and hands in town, the words, which are always in the patroness's praise are set by some of the greatest masters in town. This year Dr. John Blow, that famous musician, composed the music, and Mr. D'Urfey, whose skill in things of that nature is well enough known, made the words, 6 stewards are chosen for each ensuing year, four of which are either persons of quality or gentlemen of note, and the two last either Gentlemen of their majesties' music, or some of the chief masters in town: Those for the last year were, the Honourable James Saunderson, Esq.; Sir Francis Head, Baronet; Sir Thomas Samwel, Baronet; Charles Blunt, Esq.; Mr. John Goodwin; and Mr. Robert Carr. And those chosen for the next:

* Husk, p. 27.   † Husk, p. 159.

‡ (London, 1700), pp. 86 and 79 respectively. The first occurs in the first stanza, while the second is to be found in the fourth (Husk, p. 159).

§ Cf. *Analytical Catalogue*, nos. 328/10 and 630/4h respectively.

Sir Thomas Travel, Bart.; Josias Ent, Esq.; Sir Charles Carteret, Bart.; John Jeffrys, Esq.; Henry Hazard, Esq.; and Mr. Barkhurst. This feast is one of the genteelest in the world; there are no formalities nor gatherings like as at others, and the appearance there is always very splendid. Whilst the company is at table, the hautbois and trumpets play successively. Mr. Showers hath taught the latter of late years to sound with all the softness imaginable, they played us some flat tunes, made by Mr. Finger, with a general applause, it being a thing formerly thought impossible upon an instrument designed for a sharp key.*

Besides providing a catch for the revival of Beaumont and Fletcher's *The Knight of Malta*† (which can be assigned to this year only tentatively), Purcell also wrote one rather longer song for a current revival of Dryden's *The Indian Emperor*, 'I looked and saw within the book of Fate'.‡ The song is known in the Gresham autograph manuscript,§ and also in a single-sheet edition which identifies the singer as Mr. Pate,|| who played the part of 'Kalib' in the shape of a woman.

Close on the heels of this production came that of Southerne's new comedy, *The Wives' Excuse*,¶ which apparently was too frankly satirical to go down well. Of the five songs mentioned in or associated with the play, Purcell set four, two written for specific singers — Mrs. Butler and William Mountfort respectively.

As for publicity among the denizens of London's beau-monde, 1692 began very pleasantly for Purcell, since Peter Motteux published in the January issue of the *Gentleman's Journal* a very flattering essay on his successful fusion of French and Italian musical styles, citing *Dioclesian* and *King Arthur* as evidence of Purcell's mastery not only of these two foreign manners, but also of his successful attempts to capture an English public with the 'semi-opera', or 'ambigue', which their own stage traditions caused them to prefer:

* *Gentleman's Journal*, pp. 4–5.
† *Oxford Companion to English Literature*, 3rd ed., Oxford, 1953 ('Fletcher').
‡ *Analytical Catalogue*, no. 598.
§ London, Gresham College Library, MS. VI.5.6.
|| Laurie, fo. 185.
¶ *Analytical Catalogue*, no. 612; Motteux in the *Gentleman's Journal* for January 1691/2, p. 33, pointed out that Southerne's play had been given the month before.

Now I speak of music, I must tell you that we shall have speedily a new opera, wherein something very surprising is promised us: Mr. Purcell, who joins to the delicacy and beauty of the Italian way the graces and gaiety of the French, composes the music as he hath done for *The Prophetess*, and the last opera called *King Arthur*, which hath been played several times the last month.

Even Bedford, in *The Great Abuse of Musick*,* had to admit that operatic music seemed most attractive, really second only to sacred music:

The operas are a musical entertainment upon the stage, for the diversion of such gentlemen and ladies, who are lovers of this science consisting of acts and scenes, like a comedy or tragedy. The design thereof is not only to divert the hearer with such as amusement; but also to advance the science of music to the utmost perfection: and indeed, that which is divine being only excepted, this method seems most likely to accomplish the same.

Roger North, however, probably held the more sensible and balanced view when he wrote, in his *Memoirs of Musick*:†

[These semi-operas] were followed at first, but by an error of mixing two capital entertainments, could not stand long. For some that would come to the play hated the music, and others that were very desirous of the music would not bear the interruption that so much rehearsal gave; so that it is best to have either by itself entire.

Motteux, however, had already explored this problem in much greater detail, going into some of the reasons for the English predilection for 'semi-operas':

Other nations bestow the name of opera only on such plays whereof every word is sung. But experience hath taught us that our English genius will not relish that perpetual singing. I dare not accuse the language for being over-charged with consonants, which may take off the beauties of the recitative part, though in several other countries I have seen their operas still crowded every time, though long and almost all recitative. It is true that their trios, choruses, lively songs, and recits with accompaniments of instruments, symphonies, machines, and excellent dances make the rest be born with, and the one sets off the other: But our English gentlemen, when their ears are satisfied, are desirous to have their mind pleased, and music and dancing industriously intermixed with comedy or tragedy. I have often observed that the audience is no less attentive to some extraordinary scenes of passion or mirth, than to what they call *Beaux endroits*, or the most ravishing part of the musical performance. But had those

* P. 104.   † P. 117.

scenes, though never so well wrought up, been sung, they would have lost most of their beauty. All this, however, doth not lessen the power of music, for its charms command our attention when used in their place, and the admirable consorts we have in Charles Street and York Buildings are an undeniable proof of it. But this shows that what is unnatural, as are plays altogether sung, will soon make one uneasy, which comedy or tragedy can never do unless they be bad.*

As he had seen the old year out, Purcell saw the new year in with more music for the theatre, writing a song or two for *The Marriage-Hater Match'd*† by D'Urfey, who had just provided the text for Blow's New Year's ode, 'Behold how all the stars give way'.‡ Motteux, writing of the play as a recent event in the *Gentleman's Journal*,§ said it had a fairly successful run of six days, despite a bad start caused by poor preparation on the part of the actors.

There is, however, some question as to how much music Purcell did write for D'Urfey's comedy. The duet 'As soon as the chaos' is certainly his, for it appeared in *Orpheus Britannicus*, book I. As for the little soprano solo 'How vile are the sordid intrigues of the town', justifiable doubt lingers as to Purcell's authorship because of conflicting contemporary ascriptions to both Purcell, in *Joyful Cuckoldom* (1693), and to D'Urfey, in *Comes Amoris*, book IV (1693).||

Had Purcell lived long enough to develop and unify the expressive means of the 'semi-opera', he might have forged an English style, founded a native English form that could have invoked the blessings of all three national muses: Italian *Euterpe*, French *Terpsichore*, and English *Thalia*. At any rate Purcell's major work for 1692, *The Fairy Queen*, a musical setting for Elkanah Settle's revision of Shakespeare's *A Midsummer Night's Dream*, reveals that he had made great progress towards the fusion and successful realization of all three genres.

Although no contemporary document has been found to prove such an hypothesis, circumstantial evidence strongly indicates that

---

* *Gentleman's Journal*, Jan. 1691/2, p. 5.
† *Analytical Catalogue*, no. 602.
§ February 1691/2, p. 26.
‡ McGuinness, fo. 55.
|| See p. 222 below.

The Fairy Queen, like its model, was conceived as a tribute to the reigning feminine monarch of its time. References to Queen Mary as Gloriana were quite common in the lyric poetry of the Restoration period. The parallel was obvious and intentional, since this was also the term by which Elizabeth's poets had referred to her. This fact becomes particularly significant in view of the fact that Queen Mary was the first truly popular queen since Elizabeth's reign.

The timing of *The Fairy Queen* also supports the notion that it may have been intended as a congratulatory piece to the queen. It was first announced in the *Gentleman's Journal* for March 1691/2, when she had taken up the reins of government, as Luttrell recorded:

On Sunday last the Queen assumed the government, on notice of the King's being sailed off at Harwich; the sword was carried before her to the Chapel in the morning by the Lord Westmoreland, and in the afternoon by the Lord Grand.*

However, Luttrell did not record the actual performance of *The Fairy Queen* until two days before the queen's birthday (30 April), when he stated that it was to be acted on the following Monday (2 May), the 'clothes, scenes and music' costing £3,000. The performance may well have coincided with the annual celebrations for the queen's birthday. Evidence that the play was performed at this time is found in the *Gentleman's Journal* for May 1692:

The opera of which I have spoken to you in my former hath at last appeared, and continues to be represented daily; it is called *The Fairy Queen*. The drama is originally Shakespeare's, the music and decorations are extraordinary. I have heard the dances commended, and without doubt the whole is very entertaining.

This evidence is further supported by the announcement of the publication of the first edition of the opera in the *London Gazette* for 5–9 May 1692:

The Fairy Queen: a new opera. Represented at the Queen's Theatre by their majesties' servants. Printed for Jacob Tonson, at the Judge's Head in Chancery Lane. Where complete sets of Mr. Dryden's works in 4 volumes are to be sold. The plays being put in the order they were written.

* Vol. II, p. 378, referring to Sunday, 6 March.

The anonymous adapter's share in this first edition was quite large, and Shakespeare's portion small indeed. Hence, the first production must have seemed a Restoration piece throughout. That these were not good times for Shakespeare is shown by the further diminishing of his representation in the second edition, which appeared the year after the first. Here the 'opera' moved even farther from the original pattern provided by *A Midsummer Night's Dream*, approaching masque and entertainment in style, as if the producer had withdrawn those Shakespearean elements that had not pleased his audiences.

The bustle of affairs at the Queen's Theatre must have stepped up to a feverish pace about this time. One can imagine Purcell, Settle (or whoever the anonymous adapter may have been), and Josiah Priest doing all their errands and rehearsing one day, then rushing home to burn up several candles for the next. In spite of all hasty preparations the opening performance was a real success. The pecuniary hopes expressed in the last couplet of the Prologue[*] were evidently disappointed, but this was not due to a poor reception by the public. On the contrary, the production was successful from every point of view excepting the financial, and, as Downes recorded,

in ornaments was superior to the other two; especially in clothes for all the singers and dancers, scenes, machines, and decorations, all most profusely set-off; and excellently performed, chiefly the instrumental and vocal part composed by the said Mr. Purcel, and dances by Mr. Priest. The Court and the town were wonderfully satisfied with it; but the expenses in setting it out being so great, the company got very little by it.[†]

By mid-June Purcell also had written a song, and perhaps a drinking catch[‡] for John Crowne's *Regulus*, a tragedy performed at Drury Lane 'before the long vacation', as Motteux predicted in the May issue of the *Gentleman's Journal*, reporting in that for the following month that the play had been produced on 17 June.

[*] And all that we expect, is but to find
Equal to our expense the audience kind.

[†] Downes, pp. 42–43. The 'other two' operas were *King Arthur* and *Dioclesian*, in both of which the score also was composed by Purcell, the choreography by Priest.

[‡] Laurie, fo. 189.

P

In the August issue he published the song, 'Ah me, to many deaths decreed',* describing it as 'set by Mr. Purcell the Italian way' and paying both the song and the songstress who first performed it pretty compliments:

had you heard it sung by Mrs. Ayliff, you would have owned that there is no pleasure like that which good notes, when so divinely sung, can create.

This 'Italianate style', in which no contemporary Italian composer was capable of writing with such mastery, characterizes most of Purcell's vocal works from this period, however frequently he may have cast his musical thoughts in the triadic, 'tonic-and-dominant' style, which had become popular after the accession of William III. Certainly the 'Italianate style' figures very prominently in most of Purcell's florid theatrical songs written about this time. Upon closer examination, however, the style turns out not to be Italian at all, but rather Purcellian. The artful melodic sequences, the adroit fitting of fioriture and rhythmic figures to English prosody, and especially the graphic illustration of the word and affective demonstration of the phrase are all characteristics for which Purcell could have found no worthy Italian model. He had by now demonstrated that he had no superior and few equals as a composer of music for the stage. Despite the lack of any solid foundation for opera in England, he had created in *Dido and Aeneas* a work that no continental composer could surpass, however favourable the milieu in which he worked. Here as in other works for the theatre he demonstrated so keen an ear for the language of the stage, whether for accents of tragedy or comedy, that he had no reason to model his style after that of any composer or nation.

But the Court and the town had not devoted their musical attention solely to staged works in the first half of 1692. On the contrary, the year had begun with a great visitation of the nobility at Court for which Luttrell recorded the observance of a 'Happy New Year' followed on 6 January by a great ball at Kensington, during which, however, the dour Dutchman 'His Majesty spent the evening in the Treasury'.† It would be pleasant

* *Analytical Catalogue*, no. 586.   † Luttrell, vol. II, pp. 327 and 331.

to suppose that his musical and poetic sensibilities were too refined for the coarse concoctions of Blow and D'Urfey (who had written music and poetry for the New Year's ode, 'Behold how all the stars give way'). But it is more likely that he was planning finances to sustain the campaign in the Low Countries, upon which he was to embark again in slightly more than two months' time.* On the evening of the 7th, as Luttrell reports, 'The Queen and the Queen dowager went . . . to the play of Mr. Dryden's opera' — presumably *King Arthur*.

The atmosphere of ceremonial gaiety continued through January and February with the annual Twelfth Night gaming (which this year made King William £200 poorer, his porters that much richer); with another great ball at Kensington for Princess Anne's twenty-seventh birthday, celebrated two days late, on 8 February, so that it might not coincide with the anniversary of King Charles II's death on the 6th;† and with a splendid entertainment mounted by the Lord Mayor on 27 February.‡

March, on the other hand, was a month of royal leave-takings, some more genuinely sorrowful than others, it may be suspected, since the queen bade good-bye first to her husband on 3 March, and then, at the end of the month, to the Dowager Queen Catherine of Braganza. Both wept at the parting, which took place finally on 31 March, after several postponements,§ even though they had not been on the best of terms during the preceding year. March saw also the announcement in the *Gentleman's Journal*‖ of the long-postponed tragedy by Dryden and Southerne, *Cleomenes, the Spartan Hero*.¶ Then, in the April issue** Motteux had to announce that it had been suppressed by Queen Mary,

---

* Luttrell, vol. II, p. 374, records his departure for Flanders on 4 March 'without leave of prince or princess'.
† Luttrell, vol. II, p. 355.
‡ Luttrell, vol. II, p. 369.
§ See Luttrell, vol. II, pp. 352 ff., 374, 375, 379, 382 for various postponements, and 403 for leave-taking, at last, with weeping.
‖ P. 9.
¶ *Analytical Catalogue*, no. 576.
** See also Luttrell, vol. II, p. 413, who makes clear that the play was politically offensive.

perhaps for political reasons; mentioning it again in the May issue as follows:*

since that time the innocence and merit of the play have raised it several eminent advocates who have prevailed to have it acted and you need not doubt but it has been with great applause.

Luttrell† on 16 April reports however that offensive passages had been expunged before the first performance, for which Purcell provided a song, 'No, no, poor suff'ring heart'. Then, at the end of the month, came the celebration of Queen Mary's birthday, which had become one of the chief musical events of the year. Again Purcell was chosen to compose the ode, a setting of Sir Charles Sedley's 'Love's goddess sure'. If Hawkins's story concerning Purcell's use of the old Scottish melody 'Cold and raw'‡ can be accepted as true, Purcell must have been performing chamber music for some time before the Queen, who perhaps had not forgotten his unpolitic treatment of D'Urfey's poem for her birthday ode in 1690.§

As if all these musical duties had not been enough to occupy his time during the first few months of the year, Purcell had also taken the trouble to move his family to new quarters before Lady Day (25 March), when the parish overseers came around with the poor-rate assessment books. On page 80 of the St. Margaret's Parish Accounts for this year occurs the marginal annotation 'Gone' opposite Purcell's name, still among those of the residents of Bowling Alley East. Next to this is written 'Ann Peters — 2 houses'. Ann Peters, possibly a member of his wife's family, apparently was the new resident. But this does not tell the whole story.

Another entry, in the St. Margaret's Vestry Book for 1692,|| reveals that Purcell did not relinquish ownership in the house in Bowling Alley East, but merely sublet it. At least the record in question still refers to the house as 'Mr. Purcell's', then goes on to list four other female dwellers (not including Ann Peters):

* P. 17.   † Vol. II, p. 422.
‡ Quoted by Westrup, pp. 74–75.
§ See p. 185 above.
|| Now in Westminster Public Library, no. E 2415, fo. 19v.

28 April 1692.

At Mr. Purcell's in Bowling Alley, Mrs. Ann Davis, Mrs. Lucy Davis, Rebecca Davis, Letitia Davis to be summoned to appear to show cause why they should not be assessed £1 per quarter.

And a little farther down the same page, a fifth (or, if Ann Peters lived there, a sixth) woman is named:

Madame Carhile at Mr. Purcell's to be summoned.

The book from which these entries came is entitled:

A true Duplicate of Schedule of the Assessment of the Several Wards and Divisions within the Parish of St. Margaret's, Westminster, in the County of Middlesex. Made by virtue of an Act of Parliament for raising money by a Poll payable quarterly for one year for carrying on Vigorous War against France.

The collectors, some of whose names are familiar from the poor-rate book (e.g. Erasmus Dryden, William Read, William Carning, Francis Ayres), managed to collect a sum total 'after all appeals determined' of £919 15s., all from St. Margaret's Parish and signed, sealed, and delivered on May Day 1692 for the glory of England and William III. Appeals came mainly from those who had been advised that they might be let off if they could prove either that they were worth less than £300 or that they were 'married women'.

What dispositions were made in the cases of the five or more women living at Mr. Purcell's, or what basis their appeal may have had, are moot points. (Certainly, considering the various Restoration usages of the term 'Mrs.', that title alone would not have sufficed to prove that they were 'married women' at all.) As must so often be said, here again the records tell us nothing more.

Whatever the situation in Bowling Alley East, Purcell apparently had found a more attractive dwelling-place in Marsham Street, not far away. At any rate, his name appears in the Overseers' Accounts two years later as the tenant of a house inhabited until 1692 by one Ann Law.* Or perhaps during the two years in which he paid rates neither in Bowling Alley East nor in Marsham Street, he may have taken up lodgings in the Dean's

---

* Cf. St. Margaret's Westminster, Overseers' Accounts, E 307, p. 118.

Yard (or elsewhere in Westminster Abbey precincts), where no secular records would have been kept.

The money collected upon this occasion evidently served its purpose well. Before the end of May England had great occasion to rejoice when, aided by a second 'True Protestant Wind', the Netherlands fleet sailed from the Dutch coast in time to join the English fleet and soundly trounce the forces of Tourville and the French, thus drowning James II's hopes for a victorious return to England in these 'fatal Ides of May'.* Purcell must have been proud of the fact that his tune 'Let the soldiers rejoice'† (from *Dioclesian*) was chosen to celebrate the occasion, announced in a broadside brought out almost before the smoke of battle had cleared as:

The Royal Triumph Or, The Unspeakable Joy of the three Kingdoms, for the glorious Victory of the FRENCH, by the English and Dutch Fleets; to the Joy and Comfort of all True Subjects. Tune is, Let the Soldiers Rejoice ...

> Valiant protestant boys
> Here's millions of joys
> And triumph now bro . . . ught from the ocean;
> etc.

As earlier discussions have revealed, Purcell's activities at Court and in the theatre had kept him extremely busy during the early months of 1692. As Church musician and composer, however, he appears to have had an easy time. No anthems appeared during this period, or any services, or other liturgical music. Chamberlayne‡ records a rise in salary for Purcell in 1692, and a new position as well. Whereas before Purcell had received only £70, as did other musicians, now he was paid the same as the other two organists, as the following extract shows:

> The Organists Three
> 1. Dr. William Child   £100 per annum
> 2. Dr. John Blow   £100
> 3. Mr. Henry Purcell, Master of the Twelve
>   Children   £100

Presumably the annotation 'Master of the Twelve Children' was a

---

* Cf. J. W. Ebsworth's edition of *The Bagford Ballads*, part II, pp. 292–9, for more detailed commentary upon which the foregoing is based, and for the text of the poem following.

† *Analytical Catalogue*, no. 627/9b.   ‡ 17th ed. (1692), p. 172.

slip, for Blow is given this title in both the fifteenth and eighteenth editions of *Angliæ Notitia*. It scarcely seems possible that Purcell would have replaced him for the short period intervening. If Purcell did have this new responsibility, he would have been busy indeed. But if the entry is erroneous, his responsibilities as one of three organists would have been fairly light.

By the summer of 1692 he must already have been at work composing and collecting together the sacred songs and dialogues that were to appear in the second book of Henry Playford's *Harmonia Sacra* the following year. Each of these illustrated something new and original. 'In guilty night',* or 'Saul and the Witch of Endor' (as it is subtitled in this collection, and on many a programme), is a dramatic little *scena*, which defies accurate classification solely as a cantata, oratorio, or sacred song. It partakes of the styles and techniques of all three and, indeed, reveals that Purcell's sacred compositions were not shut off from the large amount of experience in writing music for the stage that he had had over the five years which separated this collection from *Harmonia Sacra*, book i.

In selecting the eighth to twentieth verses the anonymous paraphraser had chosen the very passage from i Samuel xxviii that would have come nearest to paralleling the circumstances of English monarchs, past and present, just after the Glorious Revolution. Saul, who had lost Jehovah's favour through royal misconduct, was in a situation very much like that of James II in Ireland. The parable is particularly close in the part of the story just before these chosen passages, where David had Saul in his power momentarily (xxviii. 7–17), but refused to 'stretch forth his hand against the Lord's anointed'. So William, at the Battle of the Boyne, refused Schomberg's very sound tactical suggestion to seal off James II's avenue of escape, presumably to avoid having the ex-king's blood on his hands. William was James II's son-in-law, as David was Saul's, which strengthens the parallel.†

---

* *Analytical Catalogue*, no. 134. Purcell may have been at work on this dramatic *scena* at the end of 1690, as its topical reference suggests.

† Cf. H. D. Traill, *William the Third*, pp. 84–90, especially p. 87.

After the Battle of the Boyne on 1 July 1690 James must have realized that his cause was lost, just as Saul had had his very accurate premonitions before the Battle of Gilboa. Certainly William III knew, for he had returned to London to enjoy a general thanksgiving on 14 September. After addressing Parliament on 2 October the king issued a public proclamation for another general thanksgiving to be held on Sunday the 19th that same month. Possibly Purcell had composed 'In guilty night' for a performance at the Chapel Royal. But it is perhaps more likely that it was intended for Westminster Abbey, since no ensemble instrumental movements or passages are required.

The 'Italianate style' discussed above is very much in evidence here, as it is also in the next major work upon which he had no doubt begun work during the summer and autumn of 1692, attempting the most ambitious musical project for St. Cecilia's Day yet undertaken by anyone in England. With 'Hail, bright Cecilia'* he not only laid bare the grey mediocrity of all the music written for celebrations between 1683 (when he had entertained the Society with 'Welcome to all the pleasures') and 1692, but revealed the enormous progress he had made in mastering old and evolving new techniques of composition during the course of these nine years. In every movement from the five-part overture which opens the ode to the majestic choral *da capo* which ends it, Purcell showed his genius in the richly inventive polyphonic style, the delightfully imaginative turn of musical metaphor, the subtly skilful clothing of the English language in musical dress, indeed all the best attributes of his stylistic maturity. His consummate skill and astonishing variety are shown in the magnificent hymns of praise to St. Cecilia (movements 2 and 13); the compositions dedicated 'to music', of which art she was patron saint (movements 3, 4, 5, 6, and 12), and to its instruments (movements 7, 8, 9, 10, and 11).

Purcell also demonstrated on this occasion musical skill other than that normally expected of a composer, if Motteux's account may be believed:

* *Analytical Catalogue*, no. 328.

The following ode ['Hail, bright Cecilia'] was admirably set to music by Mr. Henry Purcell and performed twice with universal applause, particularly the second stanza [beginning ''Tis Nature's voice'], which was sung with incredible graces by Mr. Henry Purcell himself.*

The strength of the immediate success the work achieved may be judged not only from the double performance given at its first hearing, but by frequent revivals given during the course of several ensuing decades.†

Small wonder, in view of the strain this celebration must have placed on the musical resources at Court, that William III's birthday had come and gone with scarcely a stir at the beginning of that same November. Blow may have composed 'Welcome genial day' to commemorate the king's celebration, and 'Whilst he abroad does like the sun display'‡ to compliment Queen Mary. But neither work, if indeed either or both were performed this year, attracted enough attention at Court for Luttrell to consider them worth recording. At any rate, in his entry for 5 November he records the celebration of the king's birthday, but mentions no ode.

* *Gentleman's Journal*, Nov. 1692, p. 18.
† Cf. *London Gazette*, 22–25 Jan. 1693/4 and Husk, pp. 29 ff.
‡ McGuinness, fo. 55.

CATASTROPHE IN THE MICROCOSMOS OF LONDON'S *THEATRUM MUNDI*

Within less than a month all London's attention was drawn to the theatrical world by two tragic deaths which brought to a sudden end the careers of Anthony Leigh, the comedian and William Mountfort, the playwright, musician, and, as Cibber called him, 'affecting lover in tragedy'.* William Mountfort's violent death — some called it murder — came as the climax of a series of events which his skill in portraying an 'affecting lover' may have set in motion. Among regular theatre-goers at that time were two friends, Charles, fourth Lord Mohun of Oke-hampton, about fifteen years old, and Captain Richard Hill, about twenty, just home from campaigns in Flanders and Ireland. Hill had conceived a strong passion for the beautiful but, according to contemporary report, unusually virtuous actress-singer, Mrs. Bracegirdle. Because she repulsed his advances (he thought, mis-takenly, because of a clandestine affair with Mountfort), Hill decided to abduct her. On 9 December, as she was leaving Gawen Page's house on Princes Street, he appeared with a hired coach and several ruffians to kidnap her. However, his plan was foiled by Page's courageous and adroit defence. Armed only with a walking stick he managed to spoil the attempt. Frustrated and enraged, Hill wandered through the streets, naked sword in hand (having lost his scabbard, or thrown it away in the scuffle) until late that night, when he and Mohun encountered Mountfort in Norfolk Street, returning home. Mohun and Mountfort,

---

* Nicoll, p. 335. It seemed an unlucky season for actors. In October Sandford had mistakenly stabbed Powell with a real rather than a make-believe dagger, and the latter's life was despaired of for a time (see Luttrell, vol. II, p. 593).

apparently friends, embraced and were discussing matters quietly when Hill took offence at something or other, boxed the actor's ears, ran him through, and fled. The wound proved fatal, and within a few hours London had lost one of its best and most engaging actors.[1]

Purcell had known Mountfort not only as an actor, but as a playwright and singer as well. Mountfort had collaborated in the writing of two plays (*Distress'd Innocence* and *Henry the Second*), had played major roles in *A Fool's Preferment* (in which he took the part of Lyonel), in *The Wives' Excuse*, and perhaps a dozen others for which Purcell had supplied music. He had also sung songs for many of these plays, and had written the words for 'O how happy's he', to a tune from Purcell's music for *Dioclesian*. But possibly the best evidence in support of the claim that the composer and actor were close friends is provided by the anonymous preface to a nearly contemporary edition of *Six Plays Written by Mr. Mountfort*:

> He was buried in the vault of St. Clement Danes in the Strand, Mr. Purcell performing the Funeral Anthem; a great many gentlemen attended his obsequies...

A. S. Borgman[*] gives the following account, quoting Luttrell as his source:

> On the night of Tuesday, the thirteenth, the unfortunate actor was laid to rest in the vault at St. Clement Danes. The funeral ceremonies were said to have been attended by a thousand persons among whom were 'a great many gentlemen', who thus showed their respect 'for one whom they loved and esteemed'. Royalty was not indifferent at the passing of a player, for the funeral anthem was sung by a group of choristers from Whitehall accompanied by Henry Purcell.

(Luttrell did not plainly say that Purcell was present at the burial, and I have not found this reference in any other contemporary source.) To this melancholy account, Anthony à Wood adds a superstitious note to the effect that the great bell of St.

---

[*] *The Life and Death of William Mountfort* (Cambridge, Mass., 1935), p. 145.

Clement Danes cracked as it was ringing the death-knell for Mountfort.*

The excellence of the theatrical fare that London had enjoyed during the autumn of 1692 caused the period after the deaths of Mountfort and Leigh to seem all the more gloomy. Having been commissioned to write music for seven, perhaps even eight, plays that season, Purcell no doubt was keenly aware of the change, since the cessation of theatrical life would have had a direct bearing upon his income. For him, as well as for everyone else connected with the theatre, the double tragedy in December marked the beginning of a period of inactivity, as Motteux pointed out in the *Gentleman's Journal*:

We are like to be without new plays this month and the next; the death of Mr. Mountfort, and that of Mr. Leigh soon after him, being partly the cause of this delay. The first that is promised us is a comedy by Mr. Southern.†

Moreover, the Court went into official mourning on 2 January 1693 for the death on 24 December of the Electress of Bavaria.‡ Nahum Tate's New Year's ode, for which Blow provided music, must have seemed ironical with the incongruous optimism of the first line itself, 'The happy, happy year is born'.§ All these events deepened the general gloom, from which the theatrical world did not begin to emerge until nearing the spring of 1693.

Although not all stage productions or the revivals of these can be dated certainly, Purcell's theatrical commissions for the season probably included Shadwell's *The Libertine; or, The Libertine Destroyed*; Dryden and Lee's *Oedipus*; Mountfort and (?) Bancroft's *Henry the Second, King of England*; Southerne's *The Maid's Last Prayer*; Congreve's *The Old Bachelor*; Thomas Wright's

---

* Borgman, loc. cit. See also the *London Gazette* for 12–15 Dec. and Evelyn's entry for 4 Feb. 1692/3, with n. 2 in E. S. de Beer's edition. Luttrell's entry (vol. II, p. 641) is terse: 'Mr. Mountfort was on Tuesday night interred at St. Clement's, where were 1000 persons present; some of the choristers at Whitehall and King's organist were there, and sung an anthem.'

† Dec. 1692, p. 15; Southerne's play was *The Maid's Last Prayer* (see p. 220 below).

‡ Evelyn, 2 Jan. 1692/3.

§ McGuinness, fo. 57.

The Female Virtuosos; D'Urfey's *The Richmond Heiress*; and possibly Shadwell's *Epsom Wells*.*

The Libertine, Shadwell's tragi-comic version of the Don Juan legend, after Dorimon's *Le Festin de Pierre* — not Molière's *L'Athée foudroyé* as has been supposed — was first produced at Dorset Garden on 12 June 1675, and revived there in 1682 and again about October 1692. (Dr. Laurie† argues that the latter revival took place in 1695, but this would have meant that the March and Canzona for Queen Mary's funeral would have been introduced in a most inappropriate play while this beloved queen's memory was yet fresh in the public mind. In my opinion the traditional dating of this revival in 1692, when the text was reprinted, is the more likely.) Apart from the 'supernatural' music in Act v, Purcell provided music for an opening masque ('Nymphs and shepherds come away'), a devils' song, and a trumpet song ('To arms, heroic prince'). As for the reception the play may have had, no contemporary account is known. But from the frequency of revivals, especially after Purcell's music had been heard, we may assume that it was quite successful.‡

In the same month London theatre-goers saw Dryden and Lee's tragedy, *Oedipus*,[2] also at Dorset Garden, and again heard Purcell's music (two solo songs and two 'supernatural' choruses), probably on 13 October, for which date Luttrell records a revival.§ The plot and trimmings of the play were such as would please London audiences to begin with — hence the frequent revivals — but Purcell's contribution added the *pièce de résistance* that made irresistible to London theatre-goers that which their

> Palates relished most,
> Charm! Song! and Show!
> A murder and a Ghost.||

The play attracted enough attention to be noticed and recorded by Luttrell, who entered a note on the production for 13 October 1692.¶ The unusual success of the play might be sufficient evidence

---

* *Analytical Catalogue*, nos. 600, 583, 580, 601, 607, 596, 608, and 579 respectively.

† Fo. 214.   ‡ Laurie, folios 216–17.   § Vol. ii, p. 593.

|| Dryden and Lee, *Oedipus*, Epilogue.   ¶ Vol. ii, p. 593.

that the 1692 revival was that for which Purcell provided the music, even without Burney's straightforward, but unfortunately undocumented, statement to that effect:

He published the music to a masque sung in the tragedy of *Oedipus*, when it was revived in 1692.*

The tragedy with comic overtones, *Henry the Second*, probably represents the joint handiwork of Mountfort and Bancroft. It was first performed on 8 November, as is known from a playbill for the second night, 9 November.† Purcell wrote only the song 'In vain 'gainst Love I strove' (for Act III) for this play. The Hornpipe sometimes attributed to *Henry the Second* clearly belongs to *King Arthur*.‡ The production was a decided success, as is known from Motteux's comments:

Henry Second, King of England, a new play by the author of that called *Edward the Third* . . . hath been acted several times with applause. It is a tragedy, with a mixture of comedy . . .

We are promised a comedy by Mr. Shadwell . . . §

The piece referred to in the last line is *Epsom Wells*, which was revived in 1693, twenty-one years after its first production at Dorset Garden in 1672. The play calls for seven songs and three instrumental pieces altogether. So Purcell's one contribution (the duet 'Leave these useless arts in loving' in Act V) may have been commissioned as much for its value in lending his name to the revival as for any other reason.||

Meanwhile Mountfort had been killed and Leigh had died. What with these deaths, the stabbing of Powell, and official mourning at Court, no stage production with music by Purcell was mounted until some time in March 1693, when Southerne's comedy *The Maid's Last Prayer; or, Any Rather than Fail* was acted for the first time at Drury Lane.¶ In the January issue of the

---

* Burney, vol. II, p. 390.   † Laurie, fo. 191.
  ‡ See *Analytical Catalogue*, no. 580/Commentary.
  § *Gentleman's Journal*, Oct. 1692, p. 24. (The issue was not published until November.)
  || Laurie, fo. 199.
  ¶ Nicoll, p. 433, gives Feb. 1692/3, but I agree with Laurie, fo. 192, that early March is the more likely date.

Gentleman's Journal — Motteux by now had fallen more than two months behind schedule, as he explained in the preface — the notice that '*The Maid's Last Prayer* was acted for the third time this evening and will be acted again tomorrow' reveals both that the play was performed about mid-March, and that it was relatively successful. Anyway, it ran to at least four performances. Southerne's remark in the preface to the published version (advertised in the *London Gazette* for 9–13 March) seems to indicate that it had been performed at least once by then: 'I think it had its beauties though they *did not* appear upon the stage' (italics mine). Although Southerne wrote the comedy itself, he provided the lyrics for only 'Though you make no return to my passion', the first of the three songs that Purcell composed for the play. The poem for the second, 'No, resistance is but vain', was written by Anthony Henley, while that of the third had been variously attributed to Southerne himself and also to William Congreve, who almost certainly wrote the poem.*

Congreve's first play, *The Old Bachelor*, must also have appeared about this time, since it had reached a third printing by 23 March 1693.† In fact the first performance of this extremely successful first work must have followed immediately upon that of Southerne's play discussed above. Indeed, it may even have driven it from the boards. Purcell's contribution here consisted of a three-part overture, a full set of eight act-tunes, and two rather racy songs, 'Thus to a ripe consenting maid' and 'As Amoret and Thyrsis lay'. His splendid music no doubt contributed significantly to the success of the production.

At the Theatre Royal during the course of the next month or so was mounted the less successful production of *The Female Virtuosos*, adapted by Thomas Wright (Betterton's stage machinist) from Molière's *Les Femmes savantes*. Motteux, writing favourably but guardedly, intimates that he had seen, but not read the play (perhaps indicating that he had attended a performance some time before 22 June, when the printed play was advertised for sale in the *London Gazette*):

* *Analytical Catalogue*, no. 601/Commentary.
† Laurie, fo. 194.

We have had since May last a new comedy called *The Female Virtuosos*; something in it was borrowed from Molière's *Femmes savantes*; and as it hath wit and humour, it cannot but please in the perusal as in the presentation.

Purcell wrote only one duet for the play, setting a song text by Anne, Countess of Winchelsea, 'Love, thou art best of human joys'. The composition is not among his best.

For another play that was unsuccessful, at least initially, Purcell evidently made his best effort. His 'Dialogue between a Mad Man and Mad Woman', his catch 'Bring the bowl and cool Nantz'* and his (or D'Urfey's) song 'How vile are the sordid intrigues'† indeed may have won a good portion of the success achieved by D'Urfey's *The Richmond Heiress* upon its revival after a first unsuccessful run, being 'suffered but four days, and then kicked off for ever' as Dryden put it. But according to Gildon,‡ by altering the play D'Urfey managed to please the town in reviving the play later.

Meanwhile, Purcell must have been hard at work on another ode for Queen Mary, who had resided at Whitehall in solitary splendour after William III had departed for more battle-campaigns on the eve of Lady Day just previous.§ This ode was a setting of a text by Nahum Tate, who supplied the lyrics in celebration of Queen Mary's thirty-first birthday, 30 April 1693. Tate began the ode with a grandiose *terza rima*, which, however, he abandoned after a few terzets. On the whole it is not a bad poem, although the rhyme scheme sometimes gets in the way of sense. But it could not have provided much in the way of inspiration for Purcell. Luttrell's entry for 2 May that year leaves a description of the occasion that seems to associate the ode again with a ball:

Sunday last, being the Queen's birthday, the guns were discharged at the Tower as usual; and the next day the nobility congratulated Her Majesty thereon; and at night was a great ball at Court.

* See *Analytical Catalogue*, no. 243.
† Also sung in D'Urfey's *The Marriage-Hater Match'd* (see *Analytical Catalogue*, no. 602/2 and Commentary).
‡ Both quoted in Laurie, fo. 196.
§ Luttrell, vol. III, p. 60.

For the overture Purcell re-used the first two movements of 'Hail, bright Cecilia', transposing them to C major, possibly because he had already written the vocal part of the ode in C major, with a soprano part that could be put no higher.* His falling back on a composition that had been heard so recently in London not only testifies to his own crowded schedule about that time, but also sheds light on the complaisant attitude of his public towards 'borrowing' of musical matter. Interestingly, it also reveals that he felt quite free to deck out a work commissioned for the queen with an overture composed for another occasion.

During the first six months of 1693, very few demands on Purcell's time had been made by duties at the Chapel Royal, unless, perhaps, his compositions in *Harmonia Sacra*, book II, had been intended for performance there. Nor is there any evidence that he wrote any chamber music during this period. However, the absence of any works for these two offices cannot be taken to indicate that he had written only for the theatre.

On the contrary, a new musical outlet had appeared on the scene to challenge Berardi's tripartite classification, which categorized all music as written for church, chamber, or theatre. Indeed, for a century and a half these had provided all needed channels between musical supply and demand in Western music. But a new outlet, the public concert, already had grown to be a force to be reckoned with. Its home was London, where it had passed from the management of amateurs, such as Pepys and the Norths, into the skilled hands of established, if at times desperate, professionals, such as Banister and, much earlier, Edward Chilmead. (The latter had lost his musical livelihood long before the Restoration with the parliamentary visitation to Oxford in 1648. Thereupon he was driven to setting up a series of concerts at the Black Horse in Oxford, where he carried on for six years.)

For these, amateur music was enjoyable stuff, but apparently required nothing more in the way of concentration than could be achieved while drinks, or food, or both were being sold and consumed. Early concert life in London had had such humble bibulous origins. It is significant and revealing that the prosecution

* There are several small and insignificant changes in the Canzona.

Q

in 1658 of 'Thomas Smith at the Music-house at Blue Bell by the postern gate of London Wall' was intended to punish him for having 'one puncheon of compounded and adulterated unwholesome drink fit to have the head beaten out',* and not for having countenanced unwholesome music probably far worse than the drink, and less in conformity with Commonwealth morals, if the truth were known. Such a convivial attitude towards music sorely tried visiting virtuosos like Matteis and Baltzar, as various anecdotes reveal,† but the attitude prevailed all through the seventeenth century and into the eighteenth. (Indeed, one of the most widespread explanations of Purcell's death indicates over-conviviality.‡) Ned Ward, though writing somewhat after these times, provides the sauciest, most detailed report on such activities in his description of the Mitre in Wapping in his *London Spy*:

Remembering we had heard of a famous amphibious house of entertainment, compounded of one half tavern and t'other music-house, made us willing to dedicate half an hour to what diversion we might there meet with . . . As soon as we came to the sign of the spiritual helmet, such as the high priests used to wear when they bid defiance to the devil, we no sooner entered the house, but we heard fiddlers and hautboys, together with a humdrum organ, make such incomparable music, that had the harmonious grunting of a hog been added as a bass to a ravishing concert of caterwauling performers, in the height of their ecstasy, the unusualness of the sound could not have rendered it, to a nice ear, more engaging. Having heard of the beauty and contrivance of the public music-room, as well as other parts of the house, very highly commended, we agreed, first to take a view of that which was likely to be most remarkable. In order to which we ascended the grades, and were ushered into a most stately apartment, dedicated purely to the lovers of music, painting, dancing and t'other things too. No gilding, carving, colouring, or good contrivance was here wanting to illustrate the beauty of this most noble academy where a good genius may learn with safety to abominate vice and a bad genius as (with as much danger) to practise it. The room by its compact order and costly improvements, looks so far above the use it's now converted to, that the seats are more like pews than boxes; and the upper end, being divided by a rail, looks more like a chancel than a music-box; that I could not but imagine it was built for a fanatic meeting-house, but that they had for ever destroyed the sanctity of the place by putting an organ in it, round which hung a great many pretty

* Quoted in Robert Elkin's *The Old Concert Rooms of London*, p. 14.
† See Westrup, pp. 92–93.
‡ See p. 266 below.

whimsical pictures ... There were but a few companies in the room; the most remarkable person was a drunken commander, who plucking out a handful of money, to give the music sixpence, dropped a shilling, and was so very generous that he gave an officious drawer standing by half a crown for stooping to take it up again ...*

Banister's loss of status (and salary) at Court in 1667 undoubtedly influenced his decision to mount a regular series at Whitehall in 1672;† even though he may have been involved in the Mitre concerts mentioned by Pepys in his entries for 21 January and 18 February 1660.‡ At any rate, under his aegis concert-giving in London began to develop greater musical dignity, even though as yet unable to separate itself from its public-house origins. Here is Roger North's description of the Banister concerts:

The next essay was of the elder Banister, who had a good theatrical vein, and in composition had a lively style peculiar to himself. He procured a large room in Whitefriars, near the Temple back gate, and made a raised box for the musicians, whose modesty required curtains. The room was rounded with seats and small tables, alehouse fashion. One shilling was the price, and call for what you pleased. There was very good music, for Banister found means to procure the best hands in town, and some voices to come and perform there, and there wanted no variety of humour, for Banister himself (*inter alia*) did wonders upon a flageolet to a thro'bass, and the several masters had their solos. This continued full one winter, and more I remember not. §

There was no real concert life, however, and these concerts with their lack of order and decorum gave only gradual impetus to the growth of a public. Roger North ascribed their lack of success to their confusion:

There was a set of gentlemen at that time in town who frequently met for pure and simple private diversion. And their music was of the Baptist way, very good. They were most violinists, and often hired bass-violins (which instrument, as then used, was a very hard and harsh sounded bass, and nothing so soft and sweet as now) to attend them. At length they were spoke of about town, and made famous for their music. They came at length to use a large room in the Castle tavern for their meeting, and whether through fame or the taverner's or other folk's impertinence, divers gentlemen and ladies desired to be admitted to hear their music, [and] this grew to be so fastidious a confinement to them, that they deserted that post. And the masters observing such a penchant

* Elkin, op. cit. pp. 15–16.   † See p. 33 above.
‡ As Tilmouth points out, fo. 11.   § *Memoirs of Musick*, pp. 110–12.

after music, agreed with the taverner and held on the meeting till the crowds were too great for the place, and in the meantime the good half crowns came in fairly, which was not *cattiva musica*.

And upon this occasion and further encouragement, a place in York Buildings was built express and equipped for music, to which was made a great resort and profit to the masters, and so might have continued but for the unfortunate interfering with the plays. I observed well the music here, and although the best masters in their turns, as well solo, as concerted, shewed their gifts, yet I cannot say, whatever the music was, that the entertainment was good, because it consisted of broken incoherent parts; now a consort, then a lutinist, then a *violino solo*, then flutes, then a song, and so piece after piece, the time sliding away, while the masters blundered and swore in shifting places, and one might perceive that they performed ill out of spite to one another, whereas an entertainment ought to proceed as a drama, firework, or indeed every public delight, by judicious steps, one setting off another, and the whole in a series connected and concluding in a perfect acme, and then ceasing all at once. All which cannot be done but by an absolute dictator, who may coerce and punish the republican mob of music-masters. So this very good design failed; but ample amends hath been made since, as will be shewn.*

Then, after Matteis (and before him, Baltzar and Becker) had created a certain awareness of proper musical etiquette (although Matteis and probably others as well had had to adjust to the lack of interest of some English audiences), and after James II and William III had allowed London's musical centre of gravity to shift from the Court to the theatre and concert hall, concert life began to develop more rapidly.

Matteis's discovery 'that pistols did not walk so fast as guineas' (as North quipped, discussing the violinist's disturbing first experiences with London's noble musical audiences†) was soon shared by lesser musicians. Even as late as 1713 Mattheson could point out (in *Das neu-eröffnete Orchester*) that 'He who in the present time wants to make a profit out of his music betakes himself to England.'‡ At any rate, during the reigns of Charles II and James II, a great many foreign musicians gave concerts in London.§ For the most part these had come to England to take up appoint-

---

* *Roger North on Music* (ed. John Wilson, London, 1959), pp. 305–6.
† *Memoirs of Musick*, p. 126, also *The Musicall Grammarian*, p. 35.
‡ As quoted and translated in Tilmouth, fo. 11.
§ R. Elkin, *The Old Concert Rooms of London*, *passim*, but see especially pp. 17, 20, and 31.

ments at Court and had engaged only incidentally in public concerts. In the reign of William and Mary, however, musicians foreign and domestic began more and more to look upon London public concert-life as a most profitable area to cultivate.

Native musicians also had grasped the pecuniary advantage to be gained in these affairs, and by the last decade of the seventeenth century had themselves given considerable impetus to the growth of London concert-life. The frequent entries in the various journals and periodicals of the first six months of 1693, for instance, testify to a flourishing musical activity, even without showing how many concerts like those at York Buildings and Charles Street, at Thomas Britton's house in Clerkenwell Street, and the concerts at the Two Golden Balls, were weekly affairs. Despite North's criticisms, quoted above, these concerts were giving serious competition to the theatres and to open-air entertainments given in the gardens. Moreover, such affairs tended to pursue their own separate courses without regard for Court polity or policy. At the beginning of 1693, for instance, Margarita L'Épine, brought over from Italy by the German impresario Jakob Greber[3] in about 1692, after bridling at the English public, relented, and let it be announced in the London Gazette that:

> The Italian lady that is lately come over (that is so famous for her singing) has been reported that she will sing no more in the consort in York Buildings. This is to give notice that next Tuesday, being the 10th instant, she will sing in the consort in York Buildings, and so continue during this season.*

In addition to weekly concerts given on Tuesday nights at the Vendu and others given at York Buildings, another series had begun the year before, set for Thursday nights at 'Freeman's Yard in Cornhill, near the Royal Exchange'.† Margarita L'Épine featured prominently in both series, but whether or not she participated in the activities of yet a third rival group in Covent Garden is not known. Since her fellow-countryman Pier Francesco Tosi played there from time to time, she may have done so.‡

---

* 5–9 Jan. 1692/3.   † London Gazette, 23 Jan. 1691/2.
‡ See the London Gazette for 3 April and 26 Oct, 1692, for advertisements of Tosi's concerts.

Events such as these — signs that commercial interests were soon to take over the major share of responsibility for economic well-springs of music — did not, however, preclude musical activity at Court. For instance, Purcell himself, however much he may have been involved in the concerts at York Buildings and Charles Street, had been concerned throughout the early weeks of 1693 with revisions and additions for *The Fairy Queen*, which was again performed on 16 February for Queen Mary and the maids of honour at Dorset Garden.*

* Nicoll, p. 352.

PURCELL'S INCREASING MUSICAL ACTIVITIES IN CHURCH, CONCERT HALL, COURT, AND THEATRE

W hile King William was away in the spring of 1693, Queen Mary became involved in a financial problem inherited from both her father's and her uncle's reigns — a problem that was causing grave concern among her Court musicians. On 24 May the vocal musicians complained to the Lords of the Treasury that,

[though] the vocal and instrumental music were joined in the late reigns of King Charles and King James, with an allowance of £40 per annum each ... they were sworn in indifferently and directed to be paid to Lady Day 1690, since which the instrumental only had been paid.*

Certainly Queen Mary had gone on 'calling the tune', even though not all the pipers were paid. She ventured out early in May (probably on May morning) to be entertained on board Mr. Shore's pleasure boat against Whitehall, and to hear 'a consort of music vocal and instrumental'.† As for the complaint, apparently she skirted the issue (or, at least, remained silent while a functionary hedged), approving the minute that prolonged the problem by ordering that it 'be respited till the establishment is altered'. The import of these last words cannot at present be clarified. But it is perhaps significant that at the end of the summer there was a 'petition of Dr. Nicholas Staggins, praying the King to settle upon him the allowance of £200 per annum ...

---

* *Cal. Tr. Papers*, 24 May 1693. The entry is minuted: 'To be respited till the establishment is altered.'

† Luttrell, vol. III, p. 88.

which he received there in the time of King Charles the Second, as Master of the Music'.*

Early in June Purcell must have been putting finishing touches to the second book of *Harmonia Sacra*, for in the *Gentleman's Journal* that month Motteux announced:

A music book intituled *Harmonia Sacra* will shortly be printed for Mr. Playford. I need not say anything more to recommend it to you than that you will find in it many of Mr. Henry Purcell's admirable composures. As they charm all men, they are universally extolled, and even those who know him no otherwise than by his notes are fond of expressing their sense of his merit.

In the last sentence Motteux no doubt referred to T. Brown's dedicatory poem for *Harmonia Sacra*, which has the line, 'Thus I unknown my gratitude express'. Motteux had published the same poem, with minor differences, in the June issue of the *Gentleman's Journal*. The book was at last licensed for printing on 1 July, and advertised as ready for sale in the *London Gazette* for 6–10 July.

Apart from the relatively light task of preparing an occasional song for the *Gentleman's Journal* (the complete second volume of which was announced for publication on 13 July†), Purcell apparently spent a quiet summer. At least, extant records give no evidence of any important activity on his part. It is fairly certain, however, that he would have used any time left to him after his official duties were done in composing music for the new theatrical season, which began in the autumn. The most impressive new work, both from the musical and the theatrical points of view, was Congreve's comedy of manners, *The Double Dealer*, which Motteux referred to as follows in the November 1693 issue:

I need not say anything of Mr. Congreve's *Double Dealer* (the only new play since my last) after the character which Mr. Dryden has given of it: ...

Dryden had written to William Walsh on 12 December a letter containing the following interesting passage, which reaffirms his expression of good wishes and congratulations in the preface to Congreve's play:

* *Cal. Tr. Papers*, 17 Aug. 1693.
† Day and Murrie, no. 119.

I have remembered you to all your friends; and in particular to Congreve; who sends you his play, as a present from himself, by this conveyance; and much desires the honour of being better known to you. His *Double Dealer* is much censured by the greater part of the town: and is defended only by the best judges, who, you know, are commonly the fewest. Yet it gets ground daily, and has already been acted eight times. The women think he has exposed their bitchery too much; and the gentlemen are offended with him for the discovery of their follies and the way of their intrigues under the notion of friendship to their ladies' husbands. My verses, which you will find before it, were written before the play was acted, but I neither altered them nor do I alter my opinion of the play.*

Purcell, however, had little time to ponder over the vagaries of fortune that swept his music to fame (or oblivion) along with its vehicle, whatever its intrinsic merit. While he was composing music for Congreve, he also must have been busy with his song 'Leave these useless arts in loving' for Shadwell's *Epsom Wells*, which was revised this same autumn.

He may also have taken time to revise his contributions to *The Richmond Heiress*, which, according to Motteux, D'Urfey altered and emended for another short run about this time. In the same paragraph he referred to *Don Quixote*† as being in the offing, which meant that Purcell probably had yet another commission on hand.‡

Within this same period Purcell had also received an order from Dryden to provide a musical dialogue in his last play, *Love Triumphant*, which evidently was being rehearsed early in December, according to a letter Dryden wrote to William Walsh on the 12th:

Your critique, by your description of its bulk, will be too large for a preface to my play, which is now studying; but cannot be acted till after Christmas is over. I call it *Love Triumphant; or, Nature will prevail* . . . §

---

* *The Letters of John Dryden* (ed. Charles E. Ward), pp. 62–63. Walsh was the reputed author of *The Dialogue concerning Women, Being A Defence of the Fair Sex*, and therefore probably author of the lost play, *The Gordian Knot Unty'd* (see p. 189 above).

† *Analytical Catalogue*, no. 578.

‡ *Gentleman's Journal*, Nov. 1693, p. 374; see pp. 235–6 below.

§ *The Letters of John Dryden* (ed. C. E. Ward), p. 62.

Evelyn's entry for 11 January 1694 indicates that the play was 'shortly to be acted'. The first production probably took place, therefore, about the middle of that month. Thus between January and early June, when the second part of D'Urfey's very successful transmogrification of *Don Quixote* took place, Purcell had undertaken commissions to write music for no fewer than seven plays. For these he composed twenty-three songs and instrumental pieces.

Dryden's play unfortunately was a failure, despite Motteux's kind words:

Whatever Mr. Dryden writes spreads so soon everywhere, that I can tell you no news of his *Love Triumphant*. . . that it might not be, as he intends it, his last.*

Purcell set only the sarcastic *Epithalamium* (given to Carlos in the play, and actually written by Congreve, not Dryden), which ends the comic sub-plot. In Act v sc. i Sancho, the befooled bridegroom, listens complacently while the two children of his 'virgin' bride sing:

> How happy's the husband, whose wife has been try'd!
> Not damn'd to the bed of an ignorant bride!
> Secure of what's left, he ne'er misses the rest,
> But where there's enough, supposes a feast . . .

Purcell's setting may have included the instrumental dance by way of introduction, and the accompaniment specified by stage directions for this scene. At any rate, the Jig in *The Gordian Knot Unty'd* makes an interesting companion to the song — which, indeed, is a jig in its own right.†

Purcell's song was sung by Mrs. Ayliff, who came along with the musicians hired by Carlos, and 'Young I am and yet unskilled', the little 'Song for a Girl' (Dryden's own text, set by Eccles), was sung by 'the girl' — who may have made her first appearance on the stage in this play, the earliest production for which her name actually appeared in print. Very likely she was the 'young Gentlewoman of 12 years of age' mentioned in the *London Gazette*

---

* *Gentleman's Journal*, Jan.–Feb. 1693/4, p. 26.
† See *Analytical Catalogue*, nos. 582 and 597/5 respectively.

for 26 November that same year, in connection with the Charles
Street concerts. During the next eighteen months she sang
Purcell's songs in a great many operas and plays. Later, styled with
greater dignity as Mrs. Letitia Cross, she continued to sing in
various plays right up to the end of the century. Purcell must
have been impressed with her on this early occasion, for he soon
began to write a great many songs especially for her voice:
'Celemene, pray tell me' from *Oroonoko*; 'Dear pretty youth' from
The Tempest; 'How happy is she' (a companion-piece to 'How
happy's the husband', but in the minor) from *The Rival Sisters*;
'I attempt from love's sickness' and 'They tell me' from *The
Indian Queen*; 'Man is for the woman' from *The Mock Marriage*;
'O lead me to some peaceful gloom' from *Bonduca*; and perhaps a
few others. Although her being '12 years of age' may have
allowed a year or two by way of concert promoter's license, she
was no doubt a child prodigy, even after 1695, when she began to
be styled Mrs. Letitia Cross.

For all these plays Purcell was only one composer among
several — a sign that the demand for his songs was too great for
him to supply all the music for any but the most important
productions. The number of commissions for theatre music that
came his way at this time provides ample testimony to the accuracy
of the common observation that no producer could better
guarantee success for his play than to advertise a song by Purcell.

In the March issue of the *Gentleman's Journal* Motteux also paid
compliments to Southerne's new play, *The Fatal Marriage: or,
The Innocent Adultery*,* which was 'so kindly received' that his
gentleman correspondent was by then 'no stranger to its merit.
As the world has done it justice, and it is above my praise, I need
not expatiate on that subject.' The play's great success, also commented upon by the contributor to the 1697 edition of Langbaine,† was probably due at least in part to the excellent novel
upon which it was based, Mrs. Aphra Behn's *The History of the
Nun: or, The Fair Vow-taker*. Again Purcell's music must have
contributed measurably to its success: witness the frequency with

---

* *Analytical Catalogue*, no. 595.
† P. 135; the note was probably entered by Gildon.

which the two songs ('The danger is over' and 'I sigh'd and own'd my love') were reprinted during the course of the next few decades.

During the same month,* apparently, Fletcher's *Rule a Wife and Have a Wife* saw another of the many revivals that had established it as a Restoration favourite. At least the *Gentleman's Journal* for April 1694 printed a song with the following annotation: 'A song, the notes by Mr. Henry Purcell, the words fitted to the tune by N. Henley' — correctly identified as 'A. Henley' in the Table of Contents.

According to the single-sheet edition of the song in *Joyful Cuckoldom*, which is the only other seventeenth-century printed source for the song, and the only one to identify it with the play, Mrs. Hudson sang Purcell's composition at the revival, although no source gives the exact date of this. But that it belongs to the spring of 1694 is fairly clearly indicated by its location just before 'Strike the viol' (an excerpt from 'Come ye sons of Art', Queen Mary's birthday ode for that year) and just after 'I sigh'd and own'd my love' from *The Fatal Marriage.*†

The presence of the piece in Purcell's own little 'song autograph' (London, Gresham College MS. VI.5.6, now in the Guildhall Library) shows that Purcell not only approved of Anthony Henley's 'Mock-song', but actually participated in the revisions of the music necessary to translate the piece from the idiom of the strings to that of the harpsichord.

The exact date of the revival of Dryden's *Aureng-Zebe* is also unknown, but as Purcell's song 'I see she flies me' was first published in *Comes Amoris*, book V, that year, and since a reprint of the play was also then issued, 1694 is probably the correct date. A later print (Thomas Cross's engraved single-sheet) identifies the song with the play, in which no mention is made of any piece but the 'Soft music' called for in Act IV, Scene i, Aureng-Zebe's soliloquy. The song is also ascribed to the play in the British Museum Add. MS. 22099, fo. 69. But the dating of the song here

---

* Laurie, fo. 202.

† See also Laurie (fo. 202), who discusses other chronological evidence by association.

is surely wrong: ' "I see she flies me": Song from *Aureng-Zebe*, 1676'.

The last three plays mentioned by Motteux for the season were all based upon Cervantes's *Don Quixote*. D'Urfey's *Don Quixote* translated and altered two portions of the main story, while John Crowne's comedy, *The Married Beau*, dealt, as its sub-title indicated, with Cervantes's tale of the 'Curious Impertinent'. Purcell provided an overture, eight act-tunes and one song ('See where repenting Celia lies') for the production of the latter, which apparently was quite successful:

> We have had two new comedies since my last . . . the other called *The Married Beau, or The Curious Impertinent*, by Mr. Crown, already acted many times.*

For once Motteux's journal seems to have been nearly on time, so that his remarks might well be interpreted to mean that Crowne's play had been put on in April.

Parts I and II of D'Urfey's *Don Quixote* followed in quick succession, the production of the second being hastened by the success of the first. Evidently the second was also unexpectedly successful, as Motteux pointed out in the next issue of the *Gentleman's Journal*:

> The first part of Mr. D'Urfey's *Don Quixote* was so well received that we have had a second part of that comical history acted lately, which doubtless must be thought as entertaining as the first since in this hot season it could bring such a numerous audience.†

D'Urfey had happened onto a good thing in *Don Quixote*, and was to draw upon it yet a third time before he was finished. In the persuasiveness of their characterizations, plots, and situations, D'Urfey's *Don Quixote* plays were superior to any he had yet written (or, indeed, was to write), even though Cervantes' note of philosophical melancholy and deeper insights into the human comedy are completely absent in D'Urfey's adaptations. The success these achieved probably arose as much from their abundance of good music, of which Purcell contributed a large share, as may be seen in the following table:

* *Gentleman's Journal*, May 1694, p. 134.
† *Gentleman's Journal*, June 1694, p. 170.

The Comical History of Don Quixote. Part I. D'Urfey.   Late May 1694, D.G.

II.	Drums and Trumpets sounding (March)	—	—
II.	Dance of Knights	—	—
II.	Sing all ye muses	Purcell	CT & B (Freeman & Reading?)
II.	Young Chrysostome	J. Eccles	S
II.	Dance	(to following song?)	
II.	Sleep poor youth	J. Eccles	B (Reading?)
III.	When the world	Purcell	B (Reading?)
IV.	Let the dreadful engines	Purcell	Bowman (DP)
IV.	Dance of Slaves	—	—
IV.	'Twas early	J. Eccles	Doggett (DP)
V.	With this sacred	Purcell	Bowman (DP) & 2S
V.	Antick Dance	—	—
V.	Dance of Furies	—	—

The Comical History of Don Quixote. Part II. D'Urfey.   *c.* June 1694

I.	Musick sounds	—	—
I.	If you will love me	Anon.	S & T
I.	Entertainment of Dancing	—	—
II.	Dance of Spirits	—	—
II.	Ye nymphs	Eccles	Mrs. Ayliff (DQS)
II.	Dance of Milkmaids	—	—
III.	Damon let a friend	Pack	Mrs. Hudson (DQS)
III.	March to drum and fife	—	—
III.	Antick Dance	—	—
IV.	Since times are so bad	Purcell	Reading & Mrs. Ayliff (DQS)
IV.	Dance of Spinsters	—	—
V.	Genius of England	Purcell	Freeman & Mrs. Cibber (text) Tpt — J. Shore
V.	I burn	Eccles	Mrs. Bracegirdle (DP)
V.	Dance of 7 Champions	—	—
V.	De foolish English	Anon.	T
	Lads and Lasses	Purcell	Mrs. Hudson (TsM3)*

The large number of theatrical and occasional commissions which Purcell undertook during the last few years of his life can-

* Laurie, folios 205–7. (Abbreviations: DG=Dorset Garden; DP=Dramatis Personae; S=Soprano; CT=Counter-tenor; T=Tenor; B=Bass; DQS= *Don Quixote*, Part II; TsM3= *Thesaurus Musicus*, book 3; Tpt=Trumpet.)

not be explained entirely as a response to popular demand, however. He also needed additional income, as may be surmised from the continued omission of his name from the lists of the king's musicians receiving salaries, liveries, riding charges, and other emoluments recorded in the Lord Chamberlain's accounts. In extant documents pertaining to the affairs of musicians at Court during the reign of William and Mary, Purcell is referred to only twice throughout this whole period — once in the record of his appointments, and again when his successors are named.* It is impossible to say what exactly this signifies other than Purcell's lack of favour at Court. Similar disfavour had also forced Banister into the larger world of musical activities in the theatre.

No doubt it was to earn more money that Purcell also took pupils on the organ and spinet. At least six months before Michaelmas (25 September) 1693 he had been giving lessons to John Weldon at Eton College, as shown by the college account books:

1692–3	Allowed Mr. Walter by the College towards putting out Weldon the chorister for half a year at Michaelmas 1693	£5
1693	... Weldon for two quarters ending at Michaelmas 1693, £5 ... paid for Weldon (as part of £15. 11s. 6d.) To Mr. Purcell	£1. 10. 0
1694	Item, allowed by the College to Mr. H. Purcell with Weldon the chorister for half a year, ended at Lady Day 1694	£5. 0. 0.†

Most probably this meant that Weldon had had to travel up to Westminster or Kensington for lessons each week throughout the year. Luttrell‡ records the rather frequent comings and goings of the Court. Queen Mary remained in the vicinity of Whitehall and Kensington all this summer until William III's return. Hence Weldon could not have taken advantage of Purcell's nearness to study with him at Windsor. (He might have done had the Court gone there for the summer, as had been usual before William III's asthmatic condition had necessitated new summer quarters away from the river Thames.) Possibly Purcell visited Eton from time to

* *KM*, pp. 390–437.

† Quoted by permission of the Provost of Eton College. John Walter was the organist of the College until about 1681. (Cf. Albert Mellor, *A Record of the Music and Musicians of Eton College*, pp. 6–7.)

‡ Vol. III, pp. 302 ff., *passim*.

time, however. Weldon, just approaching his eighteenth birthday (which fell on 19 January 1694, the year he took up his appointment at New College, Oxford), probably was tutored in composition as well as in practical interpretation of music. At any rate, later he spoke proudly of himself as Purcell's pupil on the basis of these lessons.

Another of Purcell's pupils about this time was richer in means though poorer in musical talent. From at least as early as 27 July 1693 the Howards at Ashtead Manor (near Guildford, Surrey) had been entertaining hopes that their daughter, Katherine, would become proficient on the spinet, even though Purcell may not have begun giving her lessons until 1 January of the following year:

27 July	1693.	Paid Mr. Player for tuning Miss's spinet	£(0) 10. 0
8 Feb.	1693/4.	Paid Mr. Purcell for one month's teaching Miss on the harpsichord	£2. 3.6
5 March	1693/4.	Paid Mr. Purcell for one month's teaching Miss on the harpsichord	£2. 3. 6
12 Feb.	1694/5.	Paid Mr. Purcell for one month's teaching Miss 2 guineas [sic]	£2. 6.0
19 April	1695.	Paid Mr. Purcell in full	£2. 10. 0*

A final entry mentioning the name Purcell seems to refer to a period which Frances Purcell, now a widow for nearly eight years, had spent as a house guest in the Howard mansion in Ashtead, since no other reason for the following honorarium suggests itself:

13 Nov.	1703.	Given to Mrs. Purcell's maid	£(0). 5. 0

Though ambiguous, the little entry speaks eloquently for the sincerity of Frances Purcell's remarks written five years before in the dedication to *Orpheus Britannicus* in 1698, which clearly identifies Lady Katherine Howard as Purcell's former student:

To the Honourable, The Lady Howard.

Madam, Were it in the power of music to abate those strong impressions of grief which have continued upon me ever since the loss of my dear lamented husband, there are few (I believe) who are furnished with larger or better supplies of comfort from this science than he has left me in his own compositions,

* Ashtead Manor Accounts (Muniments Room, Guildford Museum), *passim*.

14b 'The Robin-Red-Breast Famous for singing every day on the Top of Queen Mary's Mausoleum Erected in Westminster Abbey, 1695.' F. Barlow, engraved by P. Tempest

14a Monument for William and Mary. Grinling Gibbons

and in the satisfaction I find that they are not more valued by me (who must own myself fond to a partiality of all that was his) than by those who are no less judges than patrons of his performances. I find, Madam, I have already said enough to justify the presumption of this application to your ladyship, who have added both these characters to the many excellent qualities, which make you the admiration of all that know you. Your ladyship's extraordinary skill in music, beyond most of either sex, and your great goodness to that dear person, whom you have sometimes been pleased to honour with the title of your master, makes it hard for me to judge whether he contributed more to the vast improvements you have made in that science, or your ladyship to the reputation he gained in the profession of it: for I have often heard him say, that as several of his best compositions were originally designed for your ladyship's entertainment, so the pains he bestowed in fitting them for your ear, were abundantly rewarded by the satisfaction he has received from your approbation, and admirable performance of them, which has best recommended both them and their author to all that have had the happiness of hearing them from your ladyship.

It would be idle to speculate on what Purcell would have taught young Katherine for such handsome fees, but his pieces in *Musick's Hand-Maid*, book II, are probably representative of the kind of music she practised. Or, if more advanced, perhaps she would have studied the pieces and instructions that Henry Playford published for Purcell's widow in *A Choice Collection of Lessons for the Harpsichord or Spinnet* (1696). These instructions may represent Purcell's own teachings, and for the beginner are well worth consulting even today, as may be seen in the following introductory paragraph:

There will nothing conduce more to a perfect attaining to play on the harpsichord or spinet than a serious application to the following rules. In order to which you must first learn the gamut or scale of music, getting the names of the notes by heart, and observing at the same time what line and space every note stands on, that you may know and distinguish them at first sight, in any of the following lessons, to which purpose I have placed a scheme of keys exactly as they are in the spinet or harpsichord, and on every key the first letter of the note directing to the names, lines, and spaces where the proper note stands.

Purcell's pedagogical method may be evaluated less conjecturally in another didactic work upon which he must have been engaged at the time, since the following year saw the publication of John Playford's twelfth edition of *An Introduction to the Skill of*

R

Music, for which Purcell revised the third book, 'A Brief Introduction to the Art of Descant: or, Composing Music in Parts'. In recasting this section (inherited from Campian, Simpson, Playford, and others) Purcell demonstrated the meticulous attention to detail that characterizes the born teacher. With exemplary brevity he disposed of the fundamentals of music, coming after half a dozen pages to the essential problems of handling dissonances. Here he displayed his attention to detail and his intuitive grasp of the necessity in teaching for gradual, but not dilatory, progress towards the achievement of understanding and skill in any discipline. In his careful approach to various techniques of counterpoint ('Of Fuge, or Pointing'), in his succinct analysis of the 'Italian manner', indeed in the whole of this 'Brief Introduction' Purcell set a model for all teachers of musical composition — a model which could be used profitably in the classroom even today.

Meanwhile, London's concert business had increased apace. Tosi's concerts, renewed on 30 October 1693, carried on every Monday night throughout the winter season. Concerts at Charles Street and York Buildings were still scheduled for Tuesdays and Thursdays respectively, all the usual concert occasions being observed as they occurred on the calendar. Purcell wrote nothing for the St. Cecilia's Day celebration in 1693, that honour falling upon Godfrey Finger, who set the eclectic verses of Theophilus Parsons's 'Cecilia, look down and see'. The music, alas, has been lost. Apparently it was of superior quality, though, for it was performed twice more that same season, as the following entries from the *London Gazette* show:

In York Buildings on Monday next will be performed the last St. Cecilia Song, beginning at the usual hour.

and

At the consort in York Buildings on Monday next the 5th instant will be performed Mr. Finger's St. Cecilia Song, intermixed with a variety of other new music at the ordinary rates.*

Henry Purcell's brother Daniel had made his début for the St. Cecilia Society when he set, for the Oxford celebrations, Thomas

* Thursday, 11 Jan. 1693/4 and Thursday, 1 Feb. 1693/4 respectively.

Yalden's 'Begin and strike th'harmonious lyre'. At least, he composed a St. Cecilia ode for Oxford that year;* but as to whether it was actually performed or not, no record is known.

The success Henry Purcell had achieved with 'Hail, bright Cecilia', first performed on 22 November 1692, was sufficient to bring about another performance of the work on 25 January 1694. The *London Gazette* advertised the event at the beginning of the week as follows:

At the consort-room in York Buildings on this present Thursday, at the usual hour, will be performed Mr. Purcell's song, composed for St. Cecilia's Day in the year 1692, together with some other compositions of his, both vocal and instrumental, for the entertainment of His Highness Prince Lewis of Baden†.

No information has come to light to make possible identification of the 'other compositions', but the *Gentleman's Journal* for January–February this year indicates that one of the songs was Purcell's 'Scotch Song', for which Motteux had written new words, 'Sawney is a bonny lad'. (No singer is mentioned.) Although the second version of 'If music be the food of Love',‡ stemming from about this time, may have been one of the songs alluded to above, no new instrumental pieces by Purcell are known, except for those designed for use in the theatre. The performance of the ode would not, in any case, have left much time for other music. It may be assumed that those who performed in November did so again on this occasion, so that Purcell, no doubt beating time from the harpsichord, would have been surrounded by the same soloists: Williams, Damascene, and Woodson (basses), Turner (tenor), Bouchier, Howell, and Pate (counter-tenors), and Mrs. Ayliff (soprano). They were no doubt accompanied by the full band of twenty-four violins, this being a royal occasion. His Majesty's 'wind music' was also called upon, presumably, for players of two flutes and bass flute, two oboes and tenor oboe (probably performed by the flautists), two trumpets and a pair of kettle-drums. For the organ parts required in the

---

* Cf. British Museum, Add. MS. 30934, fo. 58, where a performance at Stationers' Hall is indicated. See also Husk, p. 170.

† 22–25 Jan. 1693/4.　　　　　　‡ *Analytical Catalogue*, no. 379B.

great ensemble movements, Purcell could probably have had any one of several eminent performers of the day. However, since he would undoubtedly have used the same performer as for the St. Cecilia's Day celebration, the field is narrowed somewhat. (The person chosen may have been one of Purcell's colleagues at the Chapel Royal.) In addition to all these, room would also have been made for the twelve boys and the thirty-two men of the Chapel Royal.*

Purcell also had two new odes to compose for January. All the music for the New Year's Day ode for which Matthew Prior's 'Light of the World' provided the text has unfortunately been lost, unless Michael Tilmouth's very plausible guess that the trumpet sonata represents the overture to this work be correct.† However, Prior's positive reference to Purcell's setting in the past tense leaves no room for doubt that Purcell actually composed the 'Hymn to the Sun, set by Dr. Purcell and Sung before Their Majesties on New Year's Day, 1693/4'.[1] As if preparing the performance of one major ode and composing another were not enough for the New Year season, Purcell also accepted a commission to compose a work for the centenary celebration of Founders' Day (9 January 1694) at Trinity College, Dublin. The task must have occupied him throughout a good part of the winter.

The celebration was announced in the issue of the London Gazette, which also advertised a concert in London for Prince Louis of Baden at the end of January. Here, however, the event was entered as news (under Dublin) rather than as advertising in the issue for 22–25 January 1693/4:

Dublin, Jan. 9. This day was celebrated in the University of this city, the secular day of their Foundation by Queen Elizabeth, being one hundred years since their first establishment; the solemnity began in the morning about 10 of the clock, with prayers in the College Chapel ... The afternoon was taken up with speeches, verses, and music, both vocal and instrumental, in praise of their foundress and benefactors, of their majesties King William and Queen Mary under whose auspicious reign they were restored ...

* Jeremy Noble, 'Purcell and the Chapel Royal' in Henry Purcell 1659–1695: Essays on his Music (ed. I. Holst), p. 66.
† See 'The Technique and Forms of Purcell's Sonatas', Music & Letters, vol. XI, no. 2, p. 109.

John Dunton reports the same event in his nearly contemporary journal, *Some Account of my Conversation in Ireland, 1699*. Something is wrong with this conventional dating, however, for Elizabeth I had founded Trinity College on 16 March 1592. Hence Purcell's commemorative ode would have had to be written or at least commissioned for 16 March 1692, if it was indeed a centennial ode, written for the anniversary of the founding.* Since the first student had matriculated on 9 January 1594,† it is fairly obvious that this was the event chosen by the authorities for the celebration. They could not have hoped to bring the royal composer-in-ordinary to compose a 'Matriculation Ode', so a 'Founding Ode' was the title to be used. Moreover, a careful reading of the text discovers no indication that the work was intended for a centennial celebration of the founding of Trinity College undertaken on the precise date of the anniversary, although there is mention of 'Thy Muse's Second Jubilee', 'Another century commencing', and 'Bless'd Eliza's day', etc. Again, the ostensible was not the only cause for celebration. These festivities also honoured recent victories of the English army in Ireland, as is intimated by the following stanza, the seventh in the poem:

> But chiefly recommend to fame
> Maria and great William's name:
> For surely no Hibernian Muse
> Whose isle to him her freedom owes,
> Can her restorer's praise refuse
> While Boyne or Shannon flows.

Earlier in the text Tate had indicated that the celebration was intended for a date 'after war's alarms repeated and a circling age completed' — both indicating a time after 5 October 1691 when Limerick, the last of the Jacobite strongholds in Ireland, at last capitulated.‡ There followed then, according to Evelyn and other diarists, a period of uneasy peace while James II and the French

---

* S. A. O. Fitzpatrick, *Dublin, A Historical and Topographical Account of the City*, pp. 114-15.
† Loc. cit.
‡ Evelyn, 14 Oct. 1691 and n. 2.

forces seemed to threaten a new invasion from time to time. But by 9 January 1694, it was certainly clear that the war was over, and that a celebration of the first centenary of the opening of the Trinity College was in order.* Nahum Tate, a graduate of the College, was chosen to write an ode for the celebration and Purcell to provide the musical setting. The whole ceremony has been described by Samuel Fitzpatrick:

On the 8th [?] January 1693/4 the first centenary of the university was celebrated with great solemnity: *Praeces tempore meridiano solemniosis (unia cum cancione) in sacello habebuntur*. In the afternoon *Hora secunda pro meridiano Post musicum instrumentorum concentum*, a Latin panegyric in honor of Queen Elizabeth was pronounced by Peter Browne, F.T.C.D., followed by a *carmen seculare* in Latin hexameters and laudations of King James I, Charles I, Charles II, and William and Mary. King James II was, for obvious reasons, ignored, but the city of Dublin sensed a grateful recognition of the benefits conferred by her magistrates on the infant university. After a Latin debate and a *carmen seculare lyricum* recited by Anthony Dopping, son of the Bishop of Meath, Eugene Lloyd, Proctor of the University, closed the Acts *Discedentes pro sequitur perita musicorum manus*.†

Thus Purcell paved the way for Handel's musical adventures in Ireland nearly half a century later, when, as Alexander Pope put it, the 'Empress of Dullness ... drove him to the Hibernian Shore'.‡

Purcell was very active in the second half of the London concert season, which, like that of the theatre, continued into the summer, despite the sultry weather.§ Although, as the *London Gazette* had announced on 3 May, the concert on Monday, 7 May, was the last of the season at York Buildings, the concerts at the Vendu in Charles Street went on until mid-June, despite (or perhaps because of) renovations to the music-room.[2] Purcell's name is not mentioned in any of the accounts again after that advertising the

---

* Fitzpatrick, op. cit. pp. 114–15. 9 Jan. 1694, incidentally, was the date upon which Joseph Purcell, very probably the brother of Daniel and Henry, was married to Sarah Dormer, at St. James's, Duke's Place (see App. Two, XVIII, 1).

† Fitzpatrick, op. cit. pp. 118–19.

‡ *Dunciad*, IV, 348 (ed. James Sutherland; London, 1953).

§ Evelyn, however, exclaimed, 'Never more glorious and steady summer weather'. See entry in *Diary* for 8 July, also Luttrell, vol. III, p. 342.

January revival of 'Hail, bright Cecilia' for Prince Louis of Baden, but it is fairly safe to assume that his music was frequently heard thereafter, if only because of the humorous songs reproduced in the *Gentleman's Journal* and in other publications originating during these times.

The rest of the summer passed uneventfully, it seems, Purcell's time being filled with routine work, except for a few minor occurrences, such as the publication of his little song 'Celia's fond'* in the *Gentleman's Journal* for July, and the announcement in the *London Gazette* for the 5th of that same month relating to the publication of Purcell's music for *Don Quixote*, parts I and II.

A week later Purcell was called in to help draw up and to sign an agreement between the Dean and Chapter of Westminster Abbey and Bernard Smith, the order being recorded in the Chapter Minutes† as follows:

12 July 1694.
Ordered that an agreement be made by Mr. Stephen Crespian, chanter, and Mr. Purcell, organist of the Collegiate Church of Westminster, for and on behalf of the Dean and Chapter of Westminster with Mr. Bernard [Smith] organ-maker for the amending and altering and new making of the organ belonging to the said Collegiate Church in such manner as the said Stephen Crespian and Henry Purcell shall direct, and that the said Mr. Smith shall have the sum of £200 for the performance thereof, to be paid as shall be agreed.

The document itself was recorded, as follows:‡

That the same shall be viewed and approved of by Stephen Crespian, clerk chanter of the Collegiate Church of St. Peter in Westminster and Henry Purcell, gentleman organist of the said church; and what defaults shall be found by them or either of them in the composing and making of the said organ, shall be altered, amended and made good by the said Bernard Smith,

Ber. Smith

Subscribed by the said
Bernard Smith in the
presence of Steph. Crespian
          Henry Purcell
          John Nedham

* *Analytical Catalogue*, no. 364.
† 1683–1714, fo. 47*v*.   ‡ WAM 9834.

Purcell signed, not knowing that the day agreed upon for the second payment would follow his death by a week,* and unaware that he would never play upon the new organ.

* Apparently the first and second payments were made at the same time, however, for a payment of £100 to Smith is recorded in WAM 33728 (Treasurer's Account, 1695), fo. 5.

CHAPTER XVI

A TIME FOR MOURNING

In 1694–5, his last complete season, Purcell's work for the theatre reached its climax. Between November, when Edward Ravenscroft's *The Canterbury Guests** was produced, and about June or July, whenever it was that Beaumont and Fletcher's *Bonduca*† was revived early that summer, Londoners heard Purcell's music in no fewer than nine plays. In addition, he composed for *The Tempest*, *Timon of Athens*, and *The Indian Queen*.‡ All told he wrote no fewer (and perhaps more) than ninety individual pieces during the year. So much work, added to official duties at Court and at the Abbey, plus the private lessons he was then giving, must have told heavily on his strength. Although the immediate cause of his death in the midst of the following season is yet unknown, there seems scarcely room for doubt that overwork was a contributing factor.

But of all this, not a hint is to be heard in the gay little comic dialogue, 'Good neighbour, why look you awry?', Purcell's first theatre song to be heard in the new season, although he may have written it before the previous May, the month originally intended for the first performance of *The Canterbury Guests*.§ No contemporary commentary gives much indication of the reception

---

* *Analytical Catalogue*, no. 591. Laurie (fo. 208) points out that Nicoll was probably wrong in suggesting September for the date of first performance. Motteux referred to the performance as recent in the *Gentleman's Journal* for October/November. Since the issue was late, as usual, it is quite likely that the play was produced in November.

† *Analytical Catalogue*, no. 574.

‡ *Analytical Catalogue*, no. 630.

§ According to Genest, vol. II, p. 58 (and after him Nicoll, p. 426, and Laurie, fo. 208), the play must have been intended for May, since one of the characters speaks of 3 May as 'tomorrow'.

the play may have had; but Motteux's careful avoidance of any evaluative remarks* may indicate that it was not successful:

I have only just room to tell you that we have had a new comedy by Mr. Ravanscroft, 'tis call'd *The Canterbury Jests* [sic]; or, *A Bargain Broken*.

The dialogue setting, which demonstrates Purcell's prodigious skill in capturing plain-spoken invective, rises considerably above the level of the play.

William III returned at last to London on 11 November, having landed at Margate the day before, after several months' campaigning, during which the taking of Huy had been the most notable event. Evidently Purcell had ready for him an anthem, 'The way of God is an undefiled way',† on a text rendered topical by careful selection of verses from Psalm xviii (which, by the similar selection of other verses, had already been drawn upon for a Court anthem totally dissimilar in its topical import, as in its musical setting‡). The new anthem was performed to celebrate William's return. At least the anthem is reported to be dated '11th Nov. 1694' in the W. K. Gostling MS. (now untraceable), which bears also the marginal annotation 'King William then returned from Flanders'. The warlike figure depicted here contrasts oddly with the persecuted monarch depicted in 'I will love Thee, O Lord', yet both are described in the verses of Psalm xviii. Purcell's setting illustrates the martial atmosphere most convincingly.

The following Thursday, 15 November, more musical celebrations for the king's return were at last in order, his birthday ceremonies having been postponed from 4 November (the actual date) because of his absence. Luttrell§ described the event succinctly:

This day was a great ball at Whitehall, designed for the King's birthday, but put off by reason of his not being here.

Tate provided the rather mawkish text ('Spring, where are thy flow'ry treasures') and Staggins the music for the ode, which

---

* *Gentleman's Journal*, Oct.–Nov., p. 276.   † *Analytical Catalogue*, no. 57.
‡ *Analytical Catalogue*, no. N67, and see pp. 67–70 above.
§ Vol. III, p. 400.

attempted to assume the kind of military posture displayed so naturally in Purcell's anthem. Somehow it failed.

Then, just a week and a day later, on 23 November, Purcell's 'Te Deum' and 'Jubilate'* brought a new and magnificent note into the annual church service sponsored by the 'Sons of the Clergy' for the day following St. Cecilia's Day. (Husk† points out that the author and composer of the ode are unknown for this year, although a song in *Thesaurus Musicus*, book v, for the following year, 'Mr. Pickets' Song, sung at St. Cecilia's Feast by Mrs. Robart', may provide a clue to at least one composition used on that occasion.) For a church service the 'Te Deum' and 'Jubilate' must have been a new kind of composition indeed — new in its martial trumpet accompaniments, new in its unpolyphonic (though at times contrapuntal) setting of the old liturgical texts, and new, above all, in its frankly theatrical expression. But at the same time Purcell joined here a tradition, which, like Zarlino's 'Te Deum' for the Battle of Lepanto (in 1571) or Dufay's 'Supremum est mortalibus' (for the Peace of Viterbo in 1433), had tended to link outstanding occasions of Church and State with brilliant ceremonial motets, just as frankly secular in expression though performed in church. The conqueror of the Boyne and the hero of the Glorious Revolution could have had no greater or more appropriate musical tribute to the new spirit with which he had reanimated the English nation.

That William and Mary heard the 'Te Deum' and 'Jubilate' at least once, probably twice, is known from Luttrell's note for 11 December:

Sunday last [i.e. 9 December] was performed before their majesties in the Chapel Royal the same vocal and instrumental music as was performed at St. Bride's Church on St. Cecilia's Day last.‡

This raises the question as to whether the composition was performed on the 22nd or the 23rd. In the light of the foregoing announcement, I am tempted to think that Husk may have been in error in assigning it to the latter day. Since Evelyn's entry for

---

* *Analytical Catalogue*, no. 232.   † P. 34.

‡ Vol. III, p. 410. I assume that the king and queen would have heard the original performance.

that day records that 'K. William had 2 fits of an ague', it is unlikely that he would have gone anywhere on the 23rd. For that same day the ageing chronicler had entered the off-hand observation 'An extraordinary sickly time especially of the smallpox, of which divers considerable persons died.' It was indeed a bad autumn in this regard.* Smallpox had carried off 1,325 victims, as contrasted with only 257 in the same three months of 1693. Moreover, in 1694, no less than eighty-five deaths had been recorded in the Bills of Mortality for the one week of 13–20 November.

Exactly a month later it was generally feared that the scourge had reached the most considerable person in all England — the queen herself. Luttrell† reported on the 22nd that she was somewhat indisposed and that smallpox was feared, then wrote on the 25th, more hopefully or wishfully perhaps:

The Queen was taken ill on Saturday last, and 'twas feared to be the smallpox, but this morning her physicians perceived it to be the measles: she was this day prayed for in all the churches about this city: the King is so extremely concerned at it, that he has ordered a bed in Her Majesty's room at Kensington, and will not stir from her, but sees all things administered to her himself; there are no ill symptoms appear, but is in a hopeful way of recovery.

On the 27th, however, the truth was inescapable, as Luttrell admitted before going on to recount detail by grisly detail the onset of St. Anthony's fire, its attendant 'blue spots', the letting of blood and scarification of the forehead, and then, as a whole nation grieved, extreme unction, and at last death at about 1 a.m. on 28 December, the day of the Feast of the Holy Innocents.

The Privy Council had decided that her funeral rites, like those for Charles II, should be carried out privately‡ but soon realized that her subjects would not have it so. Therefore, on 1 January 1695, the members of this august body gave in to universal demands for a stately public funeral, to begin on the following Sunday (6 January) with a formal period of lying-in-state and to continue with preparations (at an estimated cost of £100,000,

---

* As E. S. de Beer points out in his footnote to Evelyn's entry for this date in the *Diary*.

† Vol. III, p. 416.   ‡ Luttrell, vol. III, p. 418.

according to Luttrell)* for the procession and final rites, at which all the peers of the realm were to be in attendance.

For some reason, affairs did not come off on schedule, probably because the Council had attempted to arrange and expedite the affair 'in committee'. At any rate, the period of lying-in-state did not begin until 21 February, when Luttrell again dutifully entered all details:

This afternoon the queen began to lie in state in the bed-chamber, all the officers of her household attending, according to their offices, under the direction of the Marquess of Winchester, her chamberlain; and the ladies of honour also attend, 4 of whom stand about the corpse, and are relieved by others every half-hour; upon her head lies the crown, and over it a fine canopy; at her feet lies the sword of state, the helmet and her arms upon a cushion, the banners and scutcheons hanging round; the state is very great, and more magnificent than can be expressed: all persons are admitted, without distinction: she is to lie so every day from 12 till 5 o'clock till she is interred.†

The general mood of the mourning populace was represented best, not by the flood of lachrymose elegies, nor in the pompous sermons which poured forth at this time, but by a sentimental though for many symbolic anecdote involving a robin which came to sing over her each day while she was lying in state (see Plates 14(a) and 14(b) for Grinling Gibbons's monument for William and Mary and 'The Robin-Red-Breast Famous for singing every day on the Top of Queen Mary's Mausoleum . . .').

Meanwhile Purcell and others had been preparing compositions both for the final rites and as general tributes. (In addition to the four pieces by Purcell actually used at the queen's funeral, and the two elegies he composed in her memory, similar musical tributes were composed by James Paisible — 'The Queen's Farewell' — and John Blow — 'No, Lesbia, no'.) Finally, on 5 March, all the elaborate preparations were at last in order for the ceremony of the queen's interment, which 'was performed with great solemnity, and all the shops throughout the city were shut . . .'. First came the three hundred old women in long, black gowns, each with a boy to carry her train.‡ What an awesome spectacle they must

---

* Vol. III, p. 421.   † Luttrell, vol. III, p. 442.

‡ Luttrell (vol. III, p. 423) also reports that each had had weekly maintenance and £5 during the prolonged period of preparation.

have formed, walking gravely before the queen's funeral car along gravelled walks between rails sheathed in black, which Christopher Wren had erected all the way from Whitehall to Westminster Abbey!* Evelyn, like everyone else who witnessed the scene, was profoundly moved:

> Was the Queen's funeral infinitely expensive, never so universal a mourning; all the Parliament men had cloaks given them, 400 poor women, all the streets hung, and the middle of the streets boarded and covered with black cloth: there was all the nobility, mayor, and aldermen, judges, etc.†

The procession moved slowly along, to the solemn harmonies of Purcell's 'March for the Queen's Funeral, sounded before her Chariot', intoned by a choir of 'flat trumpets'.[1] These dirge-like sounds were accompanied by muffled drum beats,[2] as the following entries from the Lord Chamberlain's accounts reveal:

January 1694/5.
Account for 20 yards of black baize to cover five drum cases,
at 3s. 6d. per yard   £3. 10s.
And for 8 yards ditto to cover one pair of kettle-drums at
3s. 6d. per yard   £1. 8s.
10 January 1694/5.
Warrants for the providing of mourning for the late Queen:
To the first regiment of footguards, 25 covers for drums and 6 banners for the hautboys.
To the 16 Gentlemen of the Chapel Royal.
To the sergeant-trumpet, 16 trumpeters and a kettle-drummer.
To Dr. Staggins, master of the music.‡

Furthermore, the official 'Order and Form' definitely mentions 'the Gentlemen of the Chapel and Vestry in capes and the children of the Chapel singing all the way',[3] although no record has been kept of what they may have sung while in procession. As for the March, it lent itself admirably to the occasion as a sacred instrumental *contrafactum*. Its awesome simplicity and the aura of mystic grandeur it conjures up were not created for this occasion, however, but rather for the supernatural scene in Shadwell's *The Libertine* (when it was revived in 1692), where the

---

* Luttrell, vol. III, pp. 420–1.   † *Diary.*   ‡ *KM*, p. 418.

weirdly moving harmonies supplied by the 'flat trumpets' were intended to suggest the drawing near of ghosts.* It has been argued that Purcell's music for *The Libertine* must have come after the funeral of Queen Mary, since no one would have wanted to hear a theatrical piece used for her funeral march. In my opinion, no one would have dared put the queen's Funeral March on the stage after the great public event, while few would have known that the March had once before been used in the theatre. And to those the fact would not have seemed terribly important.

The Court being still in mourning, there was no New Year's ode for 1695, nor was there any celebration of Coronation Day on 11 April. In fact the day was marked only by further obsequies officially observed with the burials in Westminster Abbey of the Marquis of Halifax and of Richard Busby,[4] Purcell's old mentor. The latter having willed him a mourning ring, it is fairly certain that Purcell attended the funeral ceremonies.

The death of the queen also had put an end to the series of birthday odes, which had brightened the last day of April every year since 1690. However, the same anniversary may not have gone unobserved in 1695, since it saw Henry Playford's publication of *Three Elegies Upon the Much Lamented Loss of Our Late Queen Mary* — the title-page appropriately edged in black — containing the works probably written to commemorate the occasion. (The elegies were entered in the Trinity Term Catalogue and advertised in the *London Gazette* for 6 May.)

The publication, a musical triptych in memory of the queen, has as its centrepiece 'The Queen's Epicedium', Purcell's setting of Mr. Herbert's translation (beginning, 'Incassum, Lesbia')† of his own 'No, Lesbia, no',[5] which John Blow set as the first of the three elegies. In depth and subtlety of expression Purcell far outdid his former teacher here. Nevertheless, a comparison of the two works provides a basis for better understanding of each. The texts are parallel, although the Latin version, being more specific in its allusions, presents the aspect rather of an original poem than a

---

* W. Barclay Squire, 'Purcell's Music for the Funeral of Mary II', *SIMG*, vol. IV, pp. 225–33.

† Probably after Catullus; see *Analytical Catalogue*, no. 383.

translation.* Here are the two, side by side under the original title-page:

THREE ELEGIES UPON THE MUCH LAMENTED LOSS OF OUR LATE MOST GRACIOUS QUEEN MARY. THE WORDS OF THE TWO FIRST BY MR. HERBERT. THE LATTER OUT OF THE OXFORD VERSE: AND SET TO MUSIC BY DR. BLOW AND MR. HENRY PURCELL. LONDON. Printed by J. Heptinstall, for Henry Playford, near the Temple-Church; or at his House over-against the Blue-Ball in Arundel-Street, 1695.

The Queen's Epicedium. By Mr. Herbert.   Latine Redditum.

No, Lesbia, no, you ask in vain,
My harp, my mind's unstrung;
When all the world's in tears, in pain:
Do you require a song?

Incassum *Lesbia*, incassum rogas.
Lyra mea, Mens est immodulata;
Terrarum Orbe lacrymarum pleno,
Dolorum: rogitas tu cantilenam?

2

See, see how ev'ry nymph and swain
Hang down their pensive heads, and weep!
No voice nor pipe is heard in all the plain;
So great their sorrows, they neglect their sheep.

En Nymphas! En Pastores! caput omne reclinat
Juncorum instar! admodum fletur;
Nec Galatea canit, nec ludit Tityrus agris:
Non curant oves, moerore perditi.

3

The Queen! the Queen of *Arcadie* is gone!
Lesbia, the loss can't be exprest;
Not by the deepest sigh, or groan,
Or throbbings of the breast.

Regina! heu! *Arcadiae* Regina
Periit! O! Damnum non exprimendum;
Non, non suspiriis, gemitibus imis,
Pectoris aut queruli singultu turbido.

4

Ah! Poor *Arcadians!* how they mourn!
O the delight, and wonder of their eyes!
She's gone! and never, never must return;
Her star is fixt, and shines beyond the skies.

Miseros *Arcadas!* O quam lugentes!
Suorum Gaudium Oculorum, Mirum
Abiit! nunquam, O nunquam reversurum!
Stella sua fixa coelum ultra lucet.

The third elegy in the collection is Purcell's setting, also in

---

* For other allusions to 'Tityrus' and 'Galatea' see also *Vota Oxoniensis pro Serenissimus Guilhelmo Rege et Maria Regina*: Oxonii: E Theatro Sheldoniano, 1689, sig. G*v*; and *Pietas Oxoniensis*, 1695, sig. P*2v*.

In the Name of God Amen I Henry
Purcell of the City of Westm Gent
being dangerously ill as to the Constitution of my Body But in good and
perfect Mind and Memory (thanks be to
God) Doe by these presents publish & declare this to be my last Will & Testament And I doe hereby give & bequeath unto
my Loving Wife ffrances Purcell
All my Estate both reall & personall
of what Nature & kind soever, to her & to
her Assignes for ever And I doe hereby
Constitute & Appoint my said Loving
Wife My sole Executrix of this my said
Will & Testament revoking all former
Will or Wills Witness my hand & Seale
this Twentyeth day of November Anno
Dni 1695 and in the seaventh Year of
the [Raigne] of King William the Third [etc]

Signed Sealed published
& declared by the sd Henry Purcell
in the presence of
Wm Eles: John Chaplin

H Purcell

16b (?)Daniel Purcell, c. 1705. Presumed to be by

16a Colonel Edward Purcell. Miniature, presumed

C minor, of 'O dive Custos Auricae domus',* a poem by Henry
Parker, of New College, Oxford. In composing the piece for
two sopranos Purcell fell back upon some of the latest Italianate
techniques for pathetic expression — the techniques of the 'trio
cantata', as they might be called, by analogy to the contemporary
Italianate trio-sonata, a form which Purcell had also championed
in England.

During the months in which these sombre occurrences trans-
pired, new decisions faced at least two members of the Purcell
family. Henry, busier than ever with an increasing backlog of
theatrical commissions, must have decided that he needed
assistance. Apparently Daniel responded to the call. At least, in
May he resigned as organist at Magdalen College, Oxford, and
moved to London.[6] Tradition has it that his move was dictated by
an urgent request from his brother for musical assistance, as if
Henry might have had a foretaste of the malady that was to prove
fatal before the year was out. Or perhaps he summoned Daniel
because he had overtaxed himself during that theatrical season
and wanted to assure himself of a helper for the next, well in
advance. It is probable that he did give Daniel professional
guidance in a remaining production or two — *Pausanias* and *The
Mock Marriage* were yet to appear on stage, possibly *Timon of
Athens* as well† — before summer's preparation for the autumn
season began.

However likely this explanation of Daniel's reasons for his
rather sudden move to London, it is probable that he acquired
the organist's position at St. Andrew's, Holborn, through the
good offices of his friend from Magdalen College, Henry Sacheverell. That Sacheverell also tried, but failed, to get a living at
St. Andrew's for yet another member of the college, the Rev.
Robert Lyddel, who was incumbent at Wytham when Edward
Purcell retired there early in the following century is also
significant. The little circle seems close indeed.‡[7]

Certainly Henry had all he could manage about 1 April 1695,

* *Analytical Catalogue*, no. 504.
† *Analytical Catalogue*, nos. 585, 605, and 632 respectively.
‡ See App. Two, III, *passim*, and V, 11-13.

when his music for *The Spanish Fryar*** probably was first performed, although he had had a period of respite since the previous
22 December,† when all acting had stopped. A performance of
D'Urfey's *Cynthia and Endymion* (with Purcell's song, 'Musing on
cares of human fate') was planned for late in 1694, but probably
this was cancelled. Indeed, the performance of December 1696
may have been its first.‡ Some time before 1 April, Purcell must
have been commissioned to provide an overture, a full complement of act-music, and a song for the revival of Aphra Behn's
Abdelazer,§ which had been first performed in 1676. Betterton's
so-called 'Patentees',|| a company which had broken away from
the Theatre Royal (effecting their escape from the rapacity of the
original patent-holder, Christopher Rich, during the period of
mourning for the queen), opened with this play, and evidently
wished to give it every chance of success by including a full
complement of music by Purcell. The revival of *Abdelazer* was an
event of some importance in the history of the London theatre,
even though the production itself did not please the first audience
in the new theatre at Lincoln's Inn Fields. At least it did not
attract a second audience, as Cibber recounts:

Forces being thus raised, and the war declared on both sides, Betterton and
his chiefs had the honour of an audience of the King, who considered them as
the only subjects whom he had not yet delivered from arbitrary power; and
graciously dismissed them, with an assurance of relief, and support —
accordingly a select number of them were empowered by his royal licence to
act in a separate theatre, for themselves. This great point being obtained, many
people of quality came into a voluntary subscription of twenty, and some of
forty, guineas apiece, for erecting a theatre within the walls of the tennis court
in Lincoln's Inn Fields. But as it required time to fit it up, it gave the patentees
more leisure to muster their forces, who notwithstanding were not able to take

* *Analytical Catalogue*, no. 610.
† Laurie, fo. 210. However, Luttrell did not record that the players were
commanded not to act until 27 Dec. (vol. III, p. 418).
‡ See *Analytical Catalogue*, no. 467; in *The Songs of D'Urfey* (p. 21), Cyrus L.
Day dates the play as early as 1685, but Nicoll (p. 160) more logically places it
in 1694, pointing out that its scheduled opening performance was cancelled
because of Queen Mary's death.
§ *Analytical Catalogue*, no. 570.
|| Actually Betterton did not hold a patent, only a licence.

the field till the Easter Monday in April following. Their first attempt was a revived play, called *Abdelazar*, or *The Moor's Revenge*, poorly written, by Mrs. Behn. The house was very full, but whether it was the play or the actors that were not approved, the next day's audience sunk to nothing.*

Purcell's next theatrical commission was to write an overture, a few tunes, and a complete masque for a revival of a very much altered *Timon of Athens*. That he did not write the F major act-tunes† has been persuasively argued by Sir Jack Westrup, who first noted that these had been garbled in the old Purcell Society edition, and misattributed as well, since they are clearly ascribed to James Paisible in a reliable, near-contemporary manuscript.‡ The preceding four tunes in D major are also suspect — a fact that seems to indicate that Purcell could not finish the commission alone, and therefore called upon the services of Paisible. It was strange that he should have turned to a foreigner — if, indeed, he was responsible — when Daniel Purcell was on hand to help him. But this is a matter that cannot be resolved on present evidence. It is at least equally probable that Paisible's tunes were written first, and Purcell's compositions added later.

More paradoxically, it seems that *Timon* had, from the beginning of its 'transmogrified' career, attracted the attention mainly of foreign composers. When Shadwell first undertook in January 1678 to season the play to suit Restoration palates, he called upon Grabu, rather than an English composer, to add music to Shakespeare's English dramatic poetry.§ Some fifteen years later Motteux turned to J. W. Franck, another foreigner, for music to the independent masque scenes, three of which Purcell was to insert into Shadwell's masque a year or two later. And finally it seems that Paisible, yet another foreigner, was brought into the affair.

The manuscript sources for these pieces do not reveal enough in

---

* *An Apology for the Life of Mr. Colley Cibber... Written by Himself*, pp. 158–9.
† *Analytical Catalogue*, no. 632/4–9.
‡ British Museum, Add. MS. 35043, fo. 66v ('Mr. Paisibls [*sic*] T. in Timon of Athens'). The pieces also appear anonymously in the set of four part-books, Add. MSS. 30839 and 39565–7. See also W. Barclay Squire, pp. 554–8 and Laurie, folios 219–23.
§ Grabu's setting of 'Hark how the songsters' was printed in full in Playford's *Choice Ayres and Songs*, book II (1679), p. 56.

the way of conclusive evidence, however, for certain ascription of all the pieces written for *Timon of Athens*. The element of doubt that remains here is paralleled by confusion about the musical performers who took part in the earliest productions for which Purcell wrote music.

One of the royal manuscripts in the British Museum,* for instance, contains an overture (differing from that regularly associated with *Timon*, with the ode 'Who can from joy refrain',† with the harpsichord transcriptions‡ and with the trumpet sonata§) and several songs. With a few of these‖ appear the names 'Jacob' and 'George', perhaps the names of boy singers. 'Jacob', not too common a name in England at that time, may have been Jacob Wood, who left the Chapel Royal with Jeremiah Clarke and Richard Henman in 1697.¶

The name 'Jacob Wood' appears seventh on the list of the Children of His Majesty's Chapel Royal, where it is followed by the name 'George Rogers'.** Of the many Georges whose surnames dot musical documents of the time,†† the latter, also listed as one of the Children of the Choir of Westminster, is the one most likely to be the George who sang in the production of *Timon of Athens* with which the manuscript in question was associated. It is unlikely, however, that this would have been the first production for which Purcell provided music, for 'The cares of lovers' (allotted to George in the royal manuscript) was printed shortly after the putative date for this performance, as sung by 'the boy' (Jemmy Bowen).

On the other hand, the two names Jacob and George, both written into the royal manuscript in a later hand than the original, may have been the names of performers who took part in an early

---

* R.M. 24.e.13.   † *Analytical Catalogue*, no. 342.

‡ *Analytical Catalogue*, no. T691.

§ *Analytical Catalogue*, no. 632/Commentary.

‖ 'Hark! how the songsters' (10b); 'Love in their little veins' (11a); and also sections 12, 17, and 18b.

¶ *KM*, p. 424.

** See pp. 125–6 above, where the lists are reproduced in full.

†† For a few examples, see Bettenham, Bingham, Carleton, Chocke, Lay, Whitcher, etc., as listed in *KM*, *Secret Services*, and *Cheque-book, passim*.

eighteenth-century revival*—perhaps that announced in the *Daily Courant* for 1 January 1707/8 which stated that a play, the *Tempest*, would be performed 'With all the original music'. To which will be added a Masque composed by the late Mr. Henry Purcell, between Cupid and Bacchus, to be performed by Mr. Leveridge, Mrs. Lindsay and others.' The possibility that the 'others' might include Jacob and George is considerably increased by the fact that Leveridge's name is also written into the royal manuscript in the same hand that entered theirs.†

William III's departure for the summer campaign in the Low Countries on 9 May‡ seems to have ended for a while musical activities at Court; at least the records are silent upon this subject for the whole of June and most of July. Then on the 24th of the latter month, Purcell's ode 'Who can from joy refrain' was performed at the celebration of the birthday of the Duke of Gloucester, of whom Princess Anne had been 'safely delivered... at Hampton Court, to the joy of the whole Court' six years before.§

The text of 'Who can from joy refrain' remains anonymous, although W. H. Cummings (who edited the work for the Purcell Society in 1891) states that it was the work of Nahum Tate, who was then Poet Laureate. Perhaps Tate did write the piece; but the awkwardness of rhythm and rhyme and the generally low quality of the poem point either to a less-experienced writer or to hasty work on his part.

Purcell too must have had to work under the pressure of haste. During late spring and summer he had had four important stage-productions for which to compose music,‖ not to mention a number of compositions to see through the press all above and beyond his regular duties. The fact that he borrowed for the ode the overture from *Timon*, the most demanding of his commissions just then, may be taken as a sign of his haste.

On 29 August according to Luttrell came an express message

---

* As Dr. Laurie suggests, fo. 222, dating the MS. as *c.* 1710.
† Tilmouth, *RMA Research Chronicle*, no. 1, p. 67.
‡ Luttrell, vol. III, p. 471.   § Luttrell, vol. I, p. 561.
‖ *Abdelazer* in April; *The Mock Marriage* in July; *Pausanias* in May; and *Timon of Athens* between April and June (dates taken from Laurie, *passim*).

from William, bringing to London happy news of the fall of the citadel and castle of Namur, against whose outworks he had been campaigning to make an assault all the summer. On the 26th the French general Boufleurs had at last capitulated, facing Louis XIV with one of the first serious defeats he had suffered since 1690, when his armies had first begun to overrun the Low Countries. For William III the victory crowned the unremitting efforts of an entire career; both as Prince of Orange and as King of England he had directed all the forces he could muster against the French monarch. Quite understandably the victory called for an official Thanksgiving on 8 September, and yet another on Sunday, the 22nd of the same month, when this and also the success of the Grand Alliance against the French at Casale were to be celebrated.*

Some of Purcell's martial tunes for performance of an anonymous adaptation of Fletcher's *Bonduca*† were well-attuned to the present temper of the English nation, whose military prowess under Marlborough was soon to lead to the pre-eminence of the army in Europe. The original play had no doubt been chosen because of its effectiveness as a vehicle for military glorification, which indeed the anonymous alterations enhanced considerably. But it was Purcell's music which really sounded the militant note and caught the spirit of the times.

In fact it is possible that the revival of *Bonduca* may have been encouraged, if not indeed commissioned by the king as part of the celebration. In the dedication George Powell speaks of unusual haste, pointing out that his 'anonymous friend' had spent only four days revising the tragedy, and that the whole production had been 'revised quite through, and likewise studied up in one fortnight'. (The presentation of such an alibi suggests that the adaptation was done by Powell himself.) Such haste may have been caused by a royal deadline such as that recorded by Evelyn in

* Luttrell, vol. III, p. 519 (Sat., 31 Aug. 1695) 'This day was published a proclamation for a public thanksgiving . . . for the success in taking the town and castle of Namur, to be observed on Sunday the 8th of September here in London . . . and on Sunday the 22nd of September in all other places.' The thanksgiving for the surrender of Casale (Piedmont) is recorded by Evelyn. (See below, p. 261.)

† *Analytical Catalogue*, no. 574.

his entry for 22 September, which announced that the following day was

> The thanksgiving day appointed for the success of the King and confederates against the French at Casale and Namur.

Furthermore, the period elapsing between Sunday, 8 September, when the capture of Namur was celebrated in church services, and the general thanksgiving was almost exactly two weeks — the time allowed for revision and rehearsal in the dedication to *Bonduca*.*

Whether or not the military cast of the more popular pieces in *Bonduca* arose from a specific commission from William III, or was merely due to the taste for martial music that had become the vogue during his reign, cannot be known. One thing is certain: two of the tunes in the play soon became inextricably associated with the successes of the British army. 'Britons, strike home' and 'To arms' were as important for England's development of world empire as Verdi's choruses, 'Va, pensiero' from *Nabucco* and 'Si ridesti il Leon' from *Ernani*, were to be for Italy's Risorgimento.

Then, in quick succession, came four more productions: Robert Gould's tragedy, *The Rival Sisters; or, The Violence of Love*;† Thomas Scott's comedy, *The Mock Marriage*;‡ Thomas Southerne's tragedy *Oroonoko*;§ and D'Urfey's *The Comical History of Don Quixote*, part III.‖ For each of these Purcell wrote only a little music, calling upon Blow, Courteville, Morgan, Akeroyde, and others to compose the bulk of the songs required.

Gould's tragedy may have been played in the summer, since the dedication mentions the absence of gentry and nobility from the town. Moreover, the play had been delayed, so Purcell could well have written his three songs for the play¶ during the previous season. At any rate, he wrote more for this play than for any others for which he composed during his last theatrical season. Although *The Rival Sisters* requires music for every act, he wrote songs only for acts II and IV, the songs and 'horn music' in acts I

---

* Luttrell, vol. III, p. 518. † *Analytical Catalogue*, no. 609.
‡ *Analytical Catalogue*, no. 605. § *Analytical Catalogue*, no. 584.
‖ *Analytical Catalogue*, no. 578. ¶ Cf. Laurie, fo. 227.

and III being lost. For Act II, Purcell set 'Celia has a thousand charms'.

The dating of another late play for which Purcell supplied three (or, perhaps, only two) songs is somewhat confused. The *London Gazette* for 14 October announced the publication of *The Mock Marriage* as an accomplished fact, and John Dennis stated very clearly in a letter dated 26 October that there had 'just been a play acted call'd the *Mock Marriage*'. Dr. Laurie, however,* reasons that Dennis was wrong, since at least three performances would have been necessary for the author to speak of the play as even a moderate success. As intimated above, there is also some confusion as to which songs Purcell actually did write. Clearly enough, 'O how you protest' (in Act II) and 'Man is for the woman made' are by Purcell. But the pedigree of the song in Act III ('Twas within a furlong of Edinboro town') lies under a cloud, being ascribed both to Purcell and Jeremiah Clarke.†

For each of his last two theatrical commissions Purcell apparently wrote only one song each, as if diminishing strength required him to conserve his energies, while competition and the need to earn his living caused him to continue being active. Whatever the reasons, Purcell was content that Paisible should compose an overture and four act-tunes for *Oroonoko*,‡ while he contributed only one piece — a setting of D'Urfey's dialogue 'Celemene, pray tell me', for which the text does not appear in the play. (However, there is little question that it belongs to *Oroonoko*, since it was published in *Deliciae Musicae*, book IV, in 1696 as part of the music for the play, along with Courteville's two songs, 'A lass there lives upon the green' and 'Bright Cynthia's power'.§ As for the music itself, there is not the slightest indication in it that Purcell's musical powers were abating.)

Then in a short while London theatre audiences heard again from D'Urfey, who obviously believed that they could never get too much of a good thing. At any rate, he fashioned yet a

* Fo. 217.

† See *Analytical Catalogue*, no. 605/Commentary, for evidence accumulated to date.

‡ Laurie, fo. 229, cited RCM MS. 1172 as the source of these.

§ Laurie, fo. 228.

third play from Cervantes's *Don Quixote*, and was both surprised and displeased that it was not successful. Caddishly, he blamed others for its shortcomings, casting aspersions particularly upon the singers, dancers, and puppeteers who evidently had not had sense enough to perform so that the audience could hear them.* (So far as is known, Purcell provided only one song for the play, that being the key song in Act v, 'From rosy bow'rs', sung by Miss Cross, who played the part of Altisidora.)

The exact month and day of the first performance of *The Indian Queen* after it had been newly composed into an opera in 1695 have not been recorded.† Laurie argues persuasively either for summer, or for November (the last month of Purcell's life), narrowing down by process of elimination the period during which the opera might have been first performed. The original production must have come after 1 April, since the members of its cast are exclusively those remaining at the Theatre Royal after Betterton and his adherents had seceded to form their own company later on at Lincoln's Inn Fields in April 1695. Since they did not act between 7 July and 9 October (except, possibly, for so special an occasion as that conjectured for *Bonduca* above), it is unlikely that any production took place during the summer. The suggestion that Betterton may have mounted *The Indian Queen* as inexpensively as possible because of financial distress brought on by the revival of *Bonduca* about this time is somewhat weakened by the last octave of the Epilogue (spoken by Montezuma), which indicates that the expenditures had been lavish, if perhaps not so impressive as for *King Arthur* and *The Fairy Queen*:

> 'Tis true, y'have marks enough, the plot, the show,
> The poet's scenes, nay, more, the painter's too;
> If all this fail, considering the cost,
> 'Tis a true voyage to the Indies lost;
> But if you smile on all, then these designs,
> Like the imperfect treasure of our minds,
> 'Twill pass for current wheresoe'er they go,
> When to your bounteous hands their stamps they owe.

* See D'Urfey's comments in the dedication, as partially reproduced by Laurie, fo. 230.

† See *Analytical Catalogue*, no. 630/Commentary.

In view of the circumstantial nature of all evidence on *The Indian Queen*, any opinions as to the date of the first performance are of necessity imprecise and conjectural. The pirating of the songs by Heptinstall, Hudgebutt, and May may have been occasioned by Purcell's final illness or death, as has been suggested. But there is not the slightest piece of evidence to support such a hypothesis, which may be unnecessarily damaging to the reputations of these gentlemen, and therefore ought to be dismissed. It is likewise possible that Daniel Purcell wrote music for the Masque in the additional act after his brother's death, as indicated in the British Museum manuscript.* But this is a posthumous manuscript (dated January 1699 on fo. 37*v*). Moreover, the statement just before the masque in Act v ('Set by Mr. Daniel Purcell, Mr. Henry Purcell being dead') cannot be offered as conclusive proof of anything for it was added in a later hand.

Nor do the comparatively small dimensions of Purcell's contributions to the opera constitute any kind of proof as to the date of the work. Apart from the Masque, which Daniel set, he apparently composed everything that was required of him. Furthermore, he was so exceedingly busy all through the last five years of his life, that the facts that he supplied only twenty-two numbers for *The Indian Queen* (as opposed to more than twice that number for *King Arthur* and *The Fairy Queen*) and that he borrowed three of these from earlier works cannot be adduced as convincing evidence that he composed this music during the last few weeks of his life. The only admissible evidence lending weight to the theory that Purcell composed this music very late in his career is to be found in the music itself. Most of the instrumental music (excepting only the pieces written earlier: the first three movements of the symphony and the dance at the beginning of Act III) and all the vocal pieces demonstrate a mature mastery suggesting extreme lateness of composition. But such 'internal evidence' can only suggest, not specify.

The dating of Purcell's musical contribution to *The Tempest* is even more conjectural, for only the song 'Dear pretty youth'†

---

* British Museum, Add. MS. 31453.
† *Analytical Catalogue*, no. 631/10.

was published in its original version before the late eighteenth century. This song appeared first in *Deliciae Musicae*, book III, released in 1696, but probably printed about November 1695, and in a single-sheet edition that same year, followed by numerous editions throughout the eighteenth century. The tune of the song 'Come unto these yellow sands' also was printed early in the eighteenth century, but with new words, 'Now comes joyful peace'.* For the rest of *The Tempest* the evidence supplied by the sources is so unsatisfactory and the internal evidence so controversial as to give rise to a dispute over the authenticity of most of Purcell's music, which dispute may well provide a musical parallel to the literary polemics that have been raging over the Restoration versions of the play for some years. Until more satisfactory evidence is found, this new disagreement is not likely to be resolved. However, two unwarranted premises, which ought to be discarded with the prejudices they tacitly introduce, now seem to underlie the dispute. There is no reason to assume because Purcell did contribute a song or two to a production of *The Tempest* mounted towards the end of 1695, that he may not have contributed other pieces on earlier occasions, of which there were a great many. Nor is it necessary that the pieces ascribed to Purcell be accepted or dismissed all at once. Each should be examined on its individual merits and judged by evidence relating to it alone. Whatever the truth may be concerning the whole of the music for the 'opera', it is unlikely that 'Dear pretty youth' was among the very last songs that Purcell wrote. Indeed the absence of any caption so indicating in the two publications of 1696 seems to indicate that it rather may have been the first of the enormous number of his songs revived and published posthumously.

As for which were the latest compositions, there is positive evidence in connection with two other songs published about this time. Shortly after having set a quaint, allegorical poem, 'Lovely Albina's come ashore', Purcell was taken ill. This was originally described as 'the last song that Mr. Henry Purcell set before he

---

* By D'Urfey in *Wit and Mirth*, vol. V (1719); cf. Laurie, fo. 138, who also mentions appearances of this version in *Music and Musica*, book II (c. 1715) and in *The Merry Musicians* (1716).

died', but afterwards printed as 'the last song the author Set before his sickness'. More probably his last song was the one mentioned above for part III of D'Urfey's *Don Quixote*. Purcell apparently wrote the music for this song ('From rosy bowers') while on his death-bed, as it is described in *Orpheus Britannicus* as 'the last song that Mr. Purcell set, it being in his sickness.' On 21 November Purcell made his Will — an uninformative document, which tells us only that he left everything to his wife, Frances.* He died the same day, upon the eve of the annual St. Cecilia's Day celebration, to which he had so often contributed.

The immediate cause of his death is not known, although Westrup's conjecture that it was tuberculosis is not unlikely. Without identifying its source, Hawkins recounted the tale that Mrs. Purcell, disapproving of her husband's habitual carousing, locked him out one cold night with the result that he caught cold and died.† Improbable at best, the story is further weakened by Evelyn's remark, entered on 3 November, that there had been very mild weather all the previous month, and no rain since the first week in October. Hawkins probably came nearer to the truth in suggesting that Purcell had rather died of a lingering than a sudden illness, perhaps consumption.

Whatever its nature, Purcell's last illness apparently continued for some time — long enough for him to have composed the two above-mentioned songs — then took a turn for the worse so suddenly that there was scarcely time to prepare his Will. At least, this seems to explain the evident haste of the clerk, who scribbled out a common testamentary form not even taking time to sharpen his quill, which obviously was blunt even before he handed it to Purcell for his signature. Other evidence that there was scarcely a moment to lose may be seen in the frequent omissions, hastily repaired, and bad planning of the space into which the text was to be fitted. (For instance, the annotation of calendar and regnal dates, along with the statement for witnesses, without which the legality of the document would have been in question, were obviously squeezed into the lower left-hand margin as an after-

* See App. Two, XIII, 7, and Plate 15.
† Vol. II, p. 748.

thought.) The odd figures 𝓏𝓈 just under Purcell's signature appear more naturally as 𝓟𝓊 when the Will is turned upside-down. (In fact the strokes are such that the inverted figures are scarcely possible.) Looked at in this way, the two letters appear to be trial strokes, made after the pen had been sharpened. (Again haste is evident, as if there had been no time for anyone to look about for a piece of scrap-paper.) Purcell also signed hurriedly, with an unsharpened quill, in a manner that contrasts sadly with his usual robust and well-formed 'round hand'. This blurred scrawl, his final signature, gives mute testimony to the swiftness with which his life's force was running out. Purcell cannot have lived long after this Will had been signed, sealed, and witnessed. He died before midnight, 21 November.

Next day the St. Cecilia Society met for the annual celebration of their Saint's Day, beginning in the morning at St. Bride's with sacred music, prayers, and service, and continuing in the afternoon with secular music in a concert at the Stationers' Hall. John Blow composed the main pieces of music for both sessions — a 'Te Deum' (like Purcell's, in D, with instrumental accompaniment) for St. Bride's, and an ode, 'Great quires of Heaven', for the Stationers' Hall.* One verse of the latter in particular must have reminded all present of the recent painful loss which they and all English musicians and music lovers had shared the night before:

> While the Musician served the Saint,
> What could she ask but Heav'n would grant?
> When pray'rs on Music's wings arise
> Heav'n, granting, does but sympathize.

Indeed, Purcell was universally mourned as 'a very great master of music', as an anonymous journalist was to style him in the *Post Boy*[8] announcement a few days later. The officials at Westminster paid him just tribute — particularly fitting perhaps in view of their past treatment of him — by unanimously voting that he be buried without expense to his heirs in the north aisle

---

* He also inherited, with Bernard Smith, Purcell's duties as 'Tuner of the regals, organs, virginals, flutes and recorders'. *Grove's* (5th ed.), article on Blow.

of the Abbey. There, while Purcell lay in state, and while the usual preparations were being made, Lady Elizabeth Howard commissioned the marble tablet* that yet commemorates him near the organ upon which he had performed for the best part of two decades:

> Plaudite, felices superi, tanto hospite; nostris
>   Praefuerat, vestris additur ille choris:
> Invida nec vobis Purcellum terra reposcat,
>   Questa decus secli deliciasque breves
> Tam cito decessisse, modos cui singula debet
>   Musa prophana suos, religiosa suos.
> Vivit, io et vivat, dum vicina organa spirant,
>   Dumque colet numeris turba canora deum.

> Immortals, welcome an illustrious guest,
> Your gain, our loss, — yet would not earth reclaim
> The many-sided Master of his Art,
> The brief delight and glory of his age:
> Great Purcell lives! his spirit haunts these aisles,
> While yet the neighbouring organ breathes its strains,
> And answering choirs worship God in song.†

The circumstances of Purcell's death and burial are better known than those for any other of the sacramental events (such as baptism, marriage, and christening of children). But even here there is not enough for anything like a full and satisfactory account of the event. Since he was apparently a member in good standing of the Anglican Church, however, the burial ceremony can be reconstructed, at least in its broader aspects, from a contemporary Book of Common Prayer.

As the procession entered the Abbey, moving to the strains of Purcell's own March and Canzona, the clergy and choir, led by Purcell's friend and neighbour Stephen Crespion, intoned the first three of the funeral sentences, 'I am the resurrection', 'I know that my redeemer liveth', and 'We brought nothing into this world'. These finished and the whole procession now in the north

---

* Westrup, p. 86.

† Transcription and translation by 'W.D.M.' in *Notes and Queries*, 5th series, vol. IV, 30 Oct. 1875), p. 359.

aisle, where the burial was to take place, they read one (or perhaps both) of two Psalms, Psalm xxxix ('I said, I will take heed to my ways' with its verses, particularly appropriate upon this occasion, 'Lord, let me know mine end' and 'Behold, Thou hast made my days as it were a span long'), and Psalm xc ('Lord, Thou hast been our refuge'). Next came the lesson (1 Corinthians xv), after which, as final preparations were made for the burial, soloists and choir began the composer's own beautiful setting of the remaining four funeral sentences, 'Man that is born', 'In the midst of life' (verse), and 'Yet, O Lord' (chorus), closing with Purcell's last version of 'Thou knowest, Lord',* which had been used for Queen Mary II's burial, also in the Abbey, just eight months before.[9] 'I heard a voice from heaven', the last of the funeral sentences, was sung after the priest had spoken again, and while earth was cast on the coffin, just before the collect that concluded the rite.

With this simple ceremony Purcell passed from the Westminster and London scenes, which he had done so much to enliven and enrich. During his last few seasons he had begun to gain general recognition as the transcendent musical genius that he was. But the great promise of new aesthetic foundations for English music and the bright hopes for its future which he had helped his fellow Englishmen to glimpse were now for ever lost. A just measure of fame did at last come to him. But it came too late to be of any real service beyond that of adding, posthumously, to the lustre of his transfiguration as the English Orpheus.

* *Analytical Catalogue*, nos. 27, 17AB, and 58C respectively.

APPENDIX ONE

NOTES

CHAPTER I

1. St. Margaret's, Westminster, Overseers' Accounts (hereafter referred to simply as Overseers' Accounts) for 1658 (E 172), 1659 (E 173), and 1661–4 (E 174–7), in the Westminster Public Library, Buckingham Palace Road.

2. I discount the putative signature of the elder Purcell in the Book of Common Prayer now in the Sion House Library. It does not look enough like his authentic signatures in Westminster Abbey documents to identify the signer with Purcell's father.

3. See Overseers' Accounts for the years 1654 to 1664 (E 168 to E 177 respectively). There is no volume for 1660, and that for 1662 (E 175) was destroyed during the Second World War. However, final proof that the 1656 performance ever took place is still wanting.

4. *KM*, pp. 59, 124, and 151 respectively. See also *Grove's* (5th ed.), which, however, assigns a probable date for Notari's death that cannot be correct. As the above entry shows, he must have died before 11 August in order that Henry Purcell, who died on that date, might succeed him. This probable date of death, 'before 28 Nov. 1664', is therefore too late by at least three months, possibly longer.

It has been suggested that only a few pre-Restoration Court musicians were again employed in the royal establishment upon Charles II's return. Actually, apart from Notari himself, the list of these who reappeared at Court in 1660–1 is rather impressive: Giles Tomkins, Dr. Charles Coleman, Henry Lawes, William Child, John Jenkins, John Hingeston, Nicholas Lanier, Henry Cooke, Christopher Gibbons, William Allaby, Ambrose Beeland, Christopher Bell, Thomas

Blagrave, George Bosgrove, Thomas Cresswell, Richard Dorney, Nicholas Duvall, William Gregory, Simon Hopper, William Howes, George Hudson, Andrea Lanier, John Mason, David Mell, Thomas Mell, Stephen Nau, George Porter, William Porter, Robert Ramsey, Anthony Roberts, John Strong, Robert Strong, John Wilson, and Edward Wormall. (*KM, passim.*)

5. Matthew Locke's 'Welcome, welcome, Royal May' (published in John Playford's *Catch that Catch Can*, London, 1667) may have served for Charles II's birthday ode, performed on 29 May 1660, and possibly for Restoration Day (23 April) as well. (For further discussion, see Rosamund McGuinness, fo. 34.)

6. He was appointed to Angelo Notari's place on St. Thomas's Day, and also was one of the chosen few to be exempted from the payment of various subsidies required by Act of Parliament. (*KM*, p. 165.)

7. Pepys's *Diary*, 26 Nov. 1663:

The plague, it seems, grows more and more at Amsterdam; and we are going upon making of all ships coming from thence and Hambrough, or any other infected places, to perform their Quarantine....

8. *Cheque-book*, p. 13: 'Mr. Henry Purcell, one of His Majesty's Gentlemen of the Chapel died the eleventh day of August, 1664, in whose place came Mr. Thomas Richardson.' See also App. Two, XII, 16, for the record of his burial in the cloisters of Westminster Abbey.

9. See accounts for 1665–9 at Westminster Public Library, Buckingham Palace Road. Information from missing volumes of the rate books will often be found in the Poor Ledger for that year. Chapter officials showed unusual dilatoriness in ratifying Elizabeth Purcell's change of residence. The legal documents were not drawn up until 31 Dec. 1669:

Ordered that a lease be made to Mrs. Purcell of a tenement in Tothill Street for 40 years under the old rent and the usual covenant.

(W.A. Chapter Minutes, 1662–85.)

T

10. A thorough search of related records produced no evidence that would explain the suspicious attitude reflected in the closing admonition.

CHAPTER II

1. WAM 61228 A (Precentor's Book, 1660–71), *passim* and 20 May 1668:

   Money warrant for £20 to Elizabeth, relict of Henry Purcell, late [one of the King's Music].

   and 8 July 1668:

   Signature by Treasury Lords of order on the hearth money for £20 to Elizabeth, relict of Henry Purcell, of the King's Music.

2. *Cal. Tr. Books*, 15 Sept. 1673. His appointment probably preceded that of one Francis Purcell, who became one of the grooms of the Privy Chamber (in-ordinary, assistant) on 8 August 1673 (see LC, 'Miscellanea', 5/53, fo. 20). Francis was a son of Thomas Purcell.

3. Admin. Act, 1695, fo. 115v. His relationship to the family is fairly certain. Since this document constitutes an official record of the

   Wardship granted to Elizabeth Purcell, widow, grandmother of Henry and Elizabeth Purcell, minors,

   his children, he seems to have been brother to Edward, Henry, Daniel, and Joseph, and son of the elder Henry Purcell. (He is not to be confused with the Charles Purcell — probably his cousin — discussed in Chapter III.)

4. The first entry in *The King's Musick* is that for 8 April 1679, which refers back to Sept. 1678. By then Daniel was at least fourteen or fifteen years of age, and was nearing the end of his choir-boy days.

5. See *Cal. S. P. Dom.* for these dates. This was not the first time Cooke had been driven to such desperate remedies, as is shown by similar entries in the *Cal. Tr. Books* for 24 Jan. 1668 and 7 Dec. 1669. See Westrup, pp. 9–16, for a discussion of

the daily activities of the choristers, and for an account of Cooke's difficult responsibilities.

6. Cummings, p. 20, states that E. Rimbault owned a manuscript copy 'in the handwriting of Pelham Humphreys'. Rosamund McGuinness, fo. 39, suggests that the ode 'See mighty Sir, the day appears' (attributed to Pelham Humfrey in the British Museum, Add. MS. 33287, fo. 69*v*) may represent the piece in question.

This is possible. However, her suggestion that the copy in question might be in Humfrey's hand would weaken the case for Purcell's authorship, since Humfrey obviously would not have claimed Purcell's rather well-advertised ode for himself. My own views on the matter at present may be summarized as follows: (*a*) the music in question would indeed be a credit to a lad of eleven; and (*b*) the copy looks to me to have been written by a hand quite similar to that of the anonymous copyist discussed by A. Hughes-Hughes ('Henry Purcell's Handwriting', *Musical Times*, Feb. 1896, p. 81), whose work shows exactly the same peculiar G-clef and end-design as those used in the copy of 'See mighty Sir' in Add. MS. 33287, a manuscript, moreover, that Hughes-Hughes discusses.

7. M. Summers, *The Playhouse of Pepys*, pp. 40, 105, and 315; and *Analytical Catalogue*, commentaries and entries in app. IV for nos. 631, 632, and S100. The two remaining Shakespearian adaptations were performed elsewhere: *King Richard II* at the Theatre Royal (Laurie, fo. 165), and *The Fairy Queen* at the Queen's Theatre (see *Analytical Catalogue*, no. 629).

8. Lafontaine's transcription seems erroneous, naming *Thomas* rather than *Henry* Cooke.

CHAPTER III

1. *KM*, p. 260 (29 Sept. 1673). 'Articles of agreement between Pelham Humfrey of Westminster, Master of the Children of His Majesty's Chapel Royal, and John Lilly of the parish of St. Andrew's, Holborn, one of His Majesty's musicians-in-ordinary':

The said John Lilly shall from time to time and at all times after the date of the agreement teach and instruct four of the said children (to be appointed by the said Humfreys) on the viol and theorbo, in place of the said Pelham Humfreys. In consideration whereof Humfreys shall pay to him the sum of £30 yearly out of such salary as shall be paid to the said Humfreys, or a proportionally greater or lesser sum according to the salary received.

2. Thomas Purcell was mentioned as the first of ten musicians 'that do service in the Chapel Royal' (he was a tenor, as we know from the entry in *KM* (p. 269) for 14 April 1674), and was also named among the musicians for 'lutes and voices, theorbos and virginals' (*KM*, pp. 121 and 122); this position may have duplicated that to which he succeeded on the death of Henry Lawes on 10 Nov. 1662. On 16 Nov. 1662 he also succeeded to Lawes's places as a member of the Private Music for lutes, viols and voices, and as a musician-in-ordinary (*KM*, p. 151). He also shared with Pelham Humfrey the place of George Hudson when the latter died in 1672 (*KM*, p. 240). His position as groom of the robes was his fifth, and the acquisition of Wilson's place brought the total to six (possibly seven, if the above-mentioned pair are not duplicates).

3. *KM*, p. 269. Grabu evidently did not live up to his part of the agreement, for more than a month later, on 27 April, the Lord Chamberlain had to sign a 'Warrant to deliver to Sir Christopher Wren, His Majesty's Surveyor-General of the works, the scenes belonging to His Majesty's Theatre at Whitehall, which were formerly delivered to Mr. Grabu for the use of the French opera in Bridges Street'. (LC, 'Miscellanea', 5/140, p. 471.)

4. 5 Jan. 1673/4. E. S. de Beer, in his edition of Evelyn's *Diary*, p. 48, suggests that the opera may have been Perrin's *Ariane*. However, Evelyn could scarcely have mistaken this for an Italian opera. Very likely the production Evelyn witnessed was a rival affair, possibly arranged for Mary of Modena, who had been persuaded (some said by Louis XIV) to take up residence in London (as the new Duchess of York) in preference to taking the veil in an Italian nunnery.

5. *Diary*. The concert took place at the house of Henry Slingsby,

Master of the Mint. Signor Francisco was probably Francesco Galli (cf. Westrup, p. 91 and n. 2).

6. The inscription on Blow's memorial at Westminster Abbey reads 'Master to the famous Mr. H. Purcell'. Already his becoming Master of the Children of the Chapel Royal in 1674 would automatically have brought Henry Purcell — whose voice had already broken — under his tutelage. (Cf. *Grove's* (5th ed.), vol. I, pp. 768–75.)

7. *Grove's* (5th ed.), vol. I, pp. 768–75. Blow gained what for all practical purposes must have been a seventh preferment later in 1674, when he married Elizabeth, daughter of Edward Bradock, then Master of the Children in Westminster Abbey, and later Clerk of the Cheque of the Chapel Royal. Add to this his annual liveries as musician-in-ordinary in the place of Giles Tomkins, and Blow becomes the master pluralist of them all. (*KM*, p. 276.)

8. Only the last of the seven settings from *Calisto* in British Museum, Add. MS. 19759 (folios 18, 18*v*) bears the ascription to 'Staggins'. However, on stylistic grounds — if indeed style can be mentioned in connection with these songs — all seven appear to be the work of one man.

9. According to an announcement in the *London Gazette* for 10 Jan. 1673/4 Banister's concerts had been resumed 'until Michaelmas next'. A later advertisement in the same journal for 24 Sept. advised of their continuance from 29 Sept. (i.e. 'Michaelmas next') onward. The concerts seem to have gone on throughout the year.

10. WAM 33709 (Treasurer's Account, 1675), fo. 5 (see App. Two, XIII, 5). However, Westrup was wrong, I think, in assuming that the £2 represented payment for an entire year. Purcell's appointment was 'in-ordinary without fee' rather than ordinary with fee. He could depend on occasional payments such as this, but not on a regular, yearly stipend.

11. See *KM*, p. 202, where it is recorded that Grabu was paid £165. 9s. 6d. for duties as a copyist from 4 Nov. 1666 to 25 March 1668. This impressive sum was paid in addition to his regular salary as Master of the King's Music.

12. See his autograph score in the Fitzwilliam Museum Library, Cambridge (MS. 88), copied in 1677 (if the deductions of the present writer and Dr. Nigel Fortune be correct). See their article, 'Purcell's autographs', in *Henry Purcell 1659–95: Essays on his Music* (ed. I. Holst), app. A. Here Purcell had copied dozens of anthems written by his English contemporaries and predecessors, including anthems by Orlando Gibbons, Tallis, Byrd, William Mundy, Thomas Tomkins, and Adrian Batten, among others, before beginning to compose regularly for Westminster Abbey and the Chapel Royal. Unquestionably the copying of these anthems and his rendering of organ parts were important to Purcell's development as a composer.

13. Fellowes was probably wrong in assuming, in his article on Christopher Gibbons for *Grove's* (5th ed.), that he was Matthew Locke's companion at Exeter. Not only was he Locke's senior by fifteen years, but he took up his appointment as organist at Winchester in 1638, the year in which Locke went first to Exeter Cathedral as a chorister.

14. MS. 88, Fitzwilliam Museum Library, Cambridge (folios 136*v*, 124*v*, and 112*v* respectively). Another work by Gibbons — a 'Gloria in G', copied anonymously into Fitzwilliam MS. 152, on p. 55 — has been described as being in Purcell's autograph. It is not.

15. To be sure, Pepys did record an occasion on which an anthem was 'tried over' — clearly a rehearsal and not merely a musical gathering (see Pepys's *Diary*, 23 Feb. 1660/1).

16. See the entry in *KM* for 22 May 1677 (p. 318); but more important, the following entry from *Cal. S. P. Dom.* for 26 Feb. 1675/6:

Pass for Nicholas Staggins, Master of the King's Music, having leave to go and remain in Italy and other foreign parts for a year, with his servants, etc., to embark for his transportation and to return.

17. For further discussion of this work see *Analytical Catalogue*, no. 472. The first line of the poem is that which suggests Purcell's authorship of the elegy (as Colles has remarked in *Voice and Verse*, p. 78): 'What hope for *us* remains now he is

gone?' (my italics). It is easy to interpret the use of the first person plural as indicating that Purcell was writing as spokesman for the younger generation of composers, all suitably impressed by Locke's virtuosity as it is described in the remainder of the poem. However, poetic licence certainly would have allowed for such usage even if some anonymous poet had written these lines. Certainly the prosodic and rhyming skill manifested would indicate that Purcell had considerable poetic talent, if indeed he did write them. It is interesting thus to find Purcell adhering to a long-standing tradition among great composers of the past, who frequently wrote laments for esteemed colleagues. For a few well-known examples, see Gombert's *Musae Jovis* in honour of Josquin; Josquin's 'Nymphes des Bois' in honour of Ockeghem; and Ockeghem's 'Mort, tu as navré' in honour of Binchois. (All these works are discussed and their sources given in Gustave Reese, *Music in the Renaissance*, New York: rev. ed. 1959.)

CHAPTER IV

1. Edward Dyer, who replaced Locke as composer-in-ordinary to the Private Music, had earlier been admitted musician-in-ordinary on 10 Sept. 1672 (*KM*, p. 247) and therefore was probably Purcell's senior by several years. Locke's successor as composer for the wind music has not been identified, but presumably the office continued. G. B. Draghi succeeded to Locke's post as organist to the queen, which must have pleased those Italian masters who, as Roger North reported (*Memoirs of Musick*, p. 95), 'did not approve of his manner of play, but must be attended by more polite hands'.

2. *KM*, p. 319. Grabu apparently gave up shortly after this exchange. On 31 March 1679, according to an entry in *Cal. S. P. Dom.*, there was issued a 'Pass to France for Lewis Grabu, late master of the King's music, native of France, with his wife and three small children'. *MGG*, vol. v, col. 617, further reports that he was unsuccessful among four com-

petitors for the place of Master of Music in the French Chapel
Royal.

3. See *Analytical Catalogue*, nos. 26, 732, 733, 363, 387, 397, 418,
and 433. The chamber works are also discussed later (see p.
76–77). As for the songs, I have as yet been unable to discover
anything more solid than stylistic evidence upon which to
reason in approaching the problem of authenticity in connection with the six ascribed to Henry Purcell in Banister's and
Low's *New Ayres and Dialogues composed for Voices and Viols*
of 1678.

4. MS. 88, Fitzwilliam Museum Library, Cambridge. For a
discussion of the inscribed date and a full list of contents, see
Nigel Fortune and Franklin B. Zimmerman, 'Purcell's
autographs', in *Henry Purcell 1659–1695: Essays on his Music*
(ed. I. Holst), p. 108.

5. WAM 33703 (Treasurer's Account, 1670), fo. 3. The account
for this year, which reads the same as for each year following,
except for the changes of scholarship holders, includes
Charles Purcell's name for the first time, along with the names
of Jacob Leisely, Thomas Neeve, and Robert Radford. Neeve
was replaced by John Antrobuspo in 1671, and Robert
Radford by one of three new scholars, John Cooper, Daniel
de Lynn, and Wildbore Ellis in 1672, there being six scholars
this year. From 1673 until 1677 other changes occurred, but
Charles Purcell stayed on.

CHAPTER V

1. But such innovations are not, as is sometimes said, to be
attributed solely to Charles II's tastes, or even to the style-
conscious borrowings from modernistic Italian and French
fashion on the part of English composers. Before the Crom-
wellian period both Byrd and Gibbons (in their respective
anthems 'Christ rising' and 'This is the record of John') had
opened the way for such developments.

2. Those of the St. Cecilia's Society, the Sons of the Clergy, and

the Yorkshire Society are probably the best known. But other groups, such as the Eton Scholars, the Hampshire, the Herefordshire, Wiltshire, and Worcestershire societies, as well as the Artillerymen and Loyal Livery Men, were quite active and are worth investigating. The following, quoted from a typical notice, was printed in the *London Gazette* for 23–26 Oct. 1682: 'The Stewards for the Annual Meeting of the Clergymen's Sons do hereby give notice that they intend to have the Sermon at St. Mary-le-Bow church . . . and from thence to Merchant Taylors' Hall to dinner.'

3. 'Anthem' was first used as a term in Charles II's Prayer Book of 1662, at the end of the third collect: 'In choirs and places where they sing here followeth the anthem. . . .' (A second was sung after the sermon.)

4. So much so that one of the most obvious identifying marks of the occasional piece is its textual source outside the Psalms (cf. the funeral sentences, the collects, and especially anthems like Purcell's 'O sing unto the Lord').

5. Also reprinted, rather inaccurately, in Cummings, p. 28, who claims that the original of the letter was in his possession. The cryptic remark at the end of the postscript is still to be clarified. Westrup explains that 'F faut' and 'E lamy' are references to very low notes in the gamut. But these are not low notes — at least they would not seem so to a bass soloist of Gostling's capabilities — but either the E and F immediately above 'middle C' or these same notes an octave lower.

6. For further information concerning this anthem, see F. B. Zimmerman, 'A Newly Discovered Anthem by Purcell', *Musical Quarterly*, July 1959, pp. 302–11.

7. According to Anthony à Wood (Bodleian, MS. Wood D 19(4), fo. 14), who also mentions his earning some money by playing on the 'Flagillet', perhaps remembering the concert he himself had reported hearing on 11 Jan. 1665/6:

Mr. Banister of London and divers of the King's musicians gave us a very good meeting at the Schools in music, where he played on a little pipe or flageolet in consort . . .

Life and Times, vol. II, p. 69.

8. Hawkins, vol. II, p. 700, erroneously calls it the first such concert series, but Robert Elkin, in *The Old Concert Rooms of London*, pp. 22 ff., sets the matter straight.

9. British Museum, Add. MS. 24889, *passim*. This manuscript consists of arrangements for strings (in parts) copied by Britton himself. The works by Purcell that it contains are transcriptions of the song 'No, no, poor suff'ring heart' from *Cleomenes*; of 'Twas within a furlong of Edinboro town' from *The Mock Marriage*; of sections from 'Behold the man' from *The Richmond Heiress*; of 'Let the soldiers rejoice' from *Dioclesian*, and of songs from *The Indian Queen* (*Analytical Catalogue*, nos. 576, 605, 608, 627, and 630 respectively). Purcell's instrumental works are represented by the 'Trumpet Tune' from *Dioclesian* (*Analytical Catalogue*, no. 627/21), and by an arrangement for strings of the little harpsichord piece 'Lilliburlero', which figured in the downfall of James II (see p. 161 below). In other words, Britton put together a potpourri of Purcell's most popular tunes.

10. *KM*, p. 337; Burney, vol. II, p. 382 n., states that Purcell had already provided music for the stage in writing an overture and act-tunes for Aphra Behn's *Abdelazer* in 1677 and the Masque in Shadwell's *Timon of Athens* in 1678. Both dates are wrong (see commentaries in *Analytical Catalogue* for nos. 570 and 632 respectively).

CHAPTER VI

1. Nicoll, p. 419, says the original production began in September, without explaining why the play should have been mounted before the opening of the season. Dr. Laurie, fo. 162, dates the first performance after the second week in October, but finds no evidence that the work might not have been performed at the end of the summer as well. Downes and Montague Summers (*The Playhouse of Pepys*) give no dates.

2. See Register of Baptisms, All Hallows the Less: 9 July 1681

'Henry son of Henry and Frances Purssell' and the Register of Burials, in the same set of records, for 18 July: 'Purssall, Henry'. No other Purcells are mentioned anywhere in extant records of the parish of All Hallows the Less, or in those of All Hallows the Great, with which it merged shortly after the Great Fire of London in 1666. At least, none of the parish registers, rate books, etc., now preserved in the Guildhall Library shows any reference to the Purcell family. Hence, it seems, Henry and Frances Purcell came into the parish especially for the event. Could this pair be any but the young composer and his bride? Possibly. But probability scarcely allows for there being two Henry Purcells who married two brides called Frances at almost precisely the same time. Moreover, the absence of any record of Henry Purcell's domestic affairs for 1680–1 makes it all the more likely that this record indeed refers to the composer.

3. i.e. Henry Purcell m. Rachel Purcell, 1653; another Henry Pursill, son of John, of Thornborough, Bucks. (see App. Three); Henry Pursell, poulterer, Norton Folgate, Middlesex (d. Buckingham), Will proved March 1689 (wife, Alice); Henry Purcell (d. *c.* 1695), son of the bursar of the Royal Navy, Charles Purcell.

4. Unfortunately, both the rate books and their duplicates for St. Margaret's, Westminster, are missing for 1681, so that it is as yet impossible to say when Purcell moved into his residence in St. Ann's Lane, where he is listed as the twenty-fourth of the ratepayers canvassed in the following year (1682).

5. However, there is evidence indicating another possible date of origin for 'Beati omnes'. In Tenbury Library, MS. 17c, there is the following annotation on p. 247, at the end of the copy of this work: 'The foregoing was undoubtedly composed by command of James the 2nd on the supposed pregnancy of the Queen, which was proclaimed in 1688.' The lateness of the annotation, the obvious confusion of this work with 'Blessed are they' (the same Psalm in English translation), the prejudice with regard to the famous pregnancy, and the earliness of the musical style of Purcell's setting — all

these factors convince me that the writer of the note had confused the two works.

6. Vaughan Williams, editor of the Purcell Society edition of this work, suggested that the occasion was Charles II's return from Newmarket on 12 Oct. 1681; since the text of the ode and Purcell's setting are concerned with an elaborate metaphor involving the river Isis (the higher reaches of the Thames), a return along the river from Windsor would seem more likely.

7. WAM 33717 (Treasurer's Account, 1681), fo. 5v. The amount paid suggests that the reference was to the large B flat major service, not to the much smaller G minor evening service. And this suggestion is strengthened by the additional reference to an anthem, which was probably the five-part work 'O God, Thou art my God'. (See F. B. Zimmerman, 'Purcell's "Service Anthem", *O God, Thou Art My God* and the B-flat Major Service', *Musical Quarterly*, Apr. 1964, p. 207.)

CHAPTER VII

1. *London Gazette*, 30 Jan.–2 Feb. 1681/2:

Whereas an indignity hath lately been offered to the picture of His Royal Highness the Duke of York, in the Guildhall of the said city, which cannot be understood otherwise than an effect of malice against his person; the Lord Mayor and Court of Aldermen of the said city, out of a just and due regard to the honour of His Royal Highness, and their deep resentment of that indolent and villainous act (to be abhorred by every good and loyal subject) and being greatly concerned, and desirous to find out the author thereof, do unanimously publish and declare that if any person or persons know of, or can discover the person who committed that fact; the said Lord Mayor and Aldermen will not only kindly receive, and acknowledge his or their discovery, as a most acceptable service to the said city, but the person or persons that shall make the said discovery, either to the Lord Mayor or the said Court, so as the person be apprehended and convicted thereof, he or they shall thereupon receive a reward of five hundred pounds. Dated this 27th day of January, in the 33 year of His Majesty's reign.

WAGSTAFFE

2. Purcell's daily journey may still be retraced, along St. Ann's Lane to Orchard Street, then through a rather narrow way leading to a small gate at the back of the Dean's Yard, and thence into a rear entrance of Westminster Abbey, which still today leads to the organ-loft, now, however, through the Muniments Room and Abbey Library.

3. WAM 33717 (Treasurer's Account, 1682), fo. 6. The copyist — probably John Needham himself — has confused the trips from Newmarket and Windsor. But his meaning is fairly clear, and can be corroborated in Luttrell.

4. In his article for *PMA* (1876–7), Cummings raises the point that Thomas may have been a close friend of Matthew Locke's, indeed so close that Thomas named his eldest son after him. For the text of the Will, see App. Two, XXII, 17.

5. *Westminster Abbey Registers*, p. 72 (also Westrup, p. 45). A younger J. B. Peters died in the parish of St. Mary-le-Bow on 26 Feb. 1710/11 (PCC 66 Leeds). But since all the daughters mentioned in his will were under eighteen at the time of his death, it may be supposed that the J. B. Peters involved in the above hypothesis was his father, who had given him the diamond ring he was then passing on to his son, Richard. Among his other children was a daughter, Frances, possibly the niece of Henry Purcell's wife.

6. Charles II had championed Pritchard ((?)1632–1705) mainly out of regard for his anti-Whig sentiments. Pritchard did not disappoint his king, but continued to persecute Whigs throughout his career (see *DNB* article on Pritchard).

7. Perhaps related to Edward Wormall, a musician who had served under James I and Charles I, but was replaced soon after the Restoration by John Harding (*KM*, p. 150). The churchwarden is probably to be identified with the Giles Borrowdell whose name appears on the covers of several of the St. Margaret's Overseers' Accounts and poor-rate books of the time.

8. As Douglas Newton has indicated, without, I am afraid, providing any proof in his book, *Catholic London*.

9. Suspicion was roused already, even though the Anabaptist

oil-merchant, Keeling, did not reveal the details of the plot until 12 April (see Bryant, pp. 334–5, for an account of the plotters' plan to establish a strong republic or else a 'doge-dom under the weak Monmouth').

10. It is not unlikely that Purcell, meticulous soul that he was, did make all the corrections in his own hand, as J. A. Fuller-Maitland suggests in his preface to the Purcell Society edition (vol. v, p. iii).

11. Tilmouth, *RMA Research Chronicle*, no. 1, p. 6. Another such advertisement for music in the Italian style was made by August Kühnel, a German composer, who advertised his works in the *London Gazette* for 23 Nov. 1684 (see p. 133).

12. Quoted in *Roger North on Music* (ed. John Wilson), p. 47. Roger North waxed enthusiastic on the subject of the sonatas, writing in an early notebook:

> Then rose up the noble Purcell, the Jenkins of his time, or more. He was a match for all sorts of designs in music. Nothing came amiss to him. He imitated the Italian sonata and (bating a little too much of the labour) outdid them. And raised up operas and music in the theatres, to a credit, even of fame as far as Italy, where Sigr Purcell was courted no less than at home.
>
> (Op. cit. p. 307.)

North also wrote very highly of the sonatas in the *Musicall Grammarian*, pp. 36–37.

13. Playford's general statement is corroborated by Maitland (vol. 1, p. 484). The latter reported, more precisely, a violent frost, which froze the Thames over and 'created a new city on ice', lasting until 5 Feb.

14. *KM*, p. 361. However, Lafontaine earlier lists one *Thomas* Hingston as the keeper and repairer of His Majesty's organs and other instruments (*KM*, p. 128).

CHAPTER VIII

1. Purcell's music for the play was dated 1685 until recently, when Dr. Laurie (folios 167–8), following a lead provided by

William Barclay Squire, demonstrated that it may have been composed in 1684, or perhaps in 1683, or even for the original production in 1677. Squire was wrong in saying that there was no place in the play where three voices could have been introduced naturally and easily.

2. E. Macrory, *Notes on the Temple Organ*, pp. 30–31. The list given in *Grove's* (4th ed.) is both defective and incomplete. Note that the cromorne and double courtall stops, which Harris challenged Smith to make within a given time later on, are not listed here. Presumably Smith did not add these permanently to his organ in taking up Harris's challenge.

3. An unspecified payment of £11. 13s. 9d. is recorded in *Cal. Tr. Books* on 13 August 'To Mr. Purcell one of the King's musicians'. The sum is for an unusual amount and therefore probably represents remuneration for some special service such as this.

CHAPTER IX

1. Sandford, *The History of the Coronation of . . . James II*, pp. 69 ff. A marginal note identifies Purcell as 'Organist of St. Margaret's, Westminster'. As Westrup has pointed out (p. 54), Bernard Smith and not Purcell held that post officially. But it does not follow with absolute certainty that Sandford made a slip in identifying Purcell with St. Margaret's. He may well have been seen performing there from time to time, as Mackenzie Walcott has suggested in *Westminster: Memorials of the City* (Westminster, 1849), p. 322. He states that Purcell and Blow both attended St. Margaret's Church and played the anthem when the Abbey choir came to sing in the afternoon service upon the great festivals of the Nativity, Easter, and Whit Sunday. To many, Purcell may have been thus identified with St. Margaret's, however unofficially.

2. *KM*, p. 379, entry for 9 Nov., which lists riding charges (paid to Staggins) for musicians for 141 days from 14 May to 1 Oct. See also Luttrell (vol. 1, p. 385), who records the return of James II and Queen Mary on the last date.

Chapter x

1. *Westminster Abbey Registers*, p. 219. He was buried on 23 Sept. in the east cloister of Westminster Abbey (according to the unofficial register), slightly more than a week after Mr. Gervase Price, sergeant-trumpeter, had been buried in the Abbey proper.

2. Purcell furnished all told twelve compositions, Blow seven and a half (he collaborated in one dialogue with Humfrey), Locke four, Humfrey three and a half, Johnson and Turner one each. Locke and Humfrey were the masters who had died to whom Playford referred in the preface.

3. Laurie, folios 175–7. It is fairly certain that he did not sing all the songs, as Westrup suggests (p. 60). For an account of the circumstances leading up to Mountfort's premature and tragic death, see pp. 216–18.

4. As quoted by E. J. van der Straeten in *The Romance of the Fiddle* (London, 1911), pp. 124–5. Signior Fede is also recorded in *KM* (pp. 384 and 388) as Master of His Majesty's Chapel Royal musicians. The lists in which his name appears are notable for the large number of foreign names they contain — including Signor Grande, Segnor Sansoni, Mr. Anatean, Seigneur Albreis, Seignr Francisco, Seignor Bernardo, *et al.* — and for the absence of any mention of Purcell, who may be represented, however, by the anonymous entry 'one organist' in the latter list.

5. *KM*, pp. 388–9. The foreign musicians named above in note 4 were listed here along with several English masters to make a total of forty-eight in the musical establishment, including Blow (also unnamed), eight Children of the Chapel Royal, two sacristans, two vergers, and one 'keeper of the tribune'.

Chapter XI

1. WAM 51117 (Coronation Papers, 1661), Colonel Chester, in *Westminster Abbey Registers*, p. 177, n. 5, records Osgood's burial in the north cloister of the Abbey on 22 Aug. 1672, and speaks of his first mention as Clerk of the Works as being an entry in the Chapter Books of 26 April 1662. The document quoted above shows that his appointment began at least one year before that date.

2. For a few instances chosen more or less at random see *KM*, p. 378 (showing that a grand sum of £2,484. 16s. 3d. owed to various musicians at Court was more than a year in arrears); p. 381 (where we find a memorandum to the effect that £220. 12s. 6d. was still due to Thomas Purcell's executrix nearly five years after his death); and p. 399 (reproducing a warrant dated 15 April 1690 to pay John Blow £30. 13s. 4d., which had been owing him since he was a musician at the Court of Charles II). In the first instance actual payments total £2,757. 5s. 11d.

Chapter XII

1. For instance, see John Evelyn's account of his daughter Mary's musical accomplishments (vol. IV, pp. 271, 421–2, 427, etc.), which he discusses in various entries in his diary. See also the account below of Purcell's having been hired to instruct Miss Katherine Howard on the harpsichord, p. 238, and John Weldon, then a student at Eton, on organ, p. 237. See also p. 139 for an account of his experience with one 'Mr. Hodg'.

2. See Purcell's partial autograph in British Museum, Royal MS. 20.h.8, fo. 125v (rev.). Lewis Maidwell was master of a school in King Street, Westminster, just a short way from the Abbey, and quite near Purcell's own residence. See F. H. W. Sheppard (ed.), *Survey of London*, vol. XXXI, p. 178.

3. See J. Max Patrick's introduction to a facsimile of Maidwell's *An Essay upon the Necessity and Excellency of Education* (1705), printed by the Augustan Reprint Society, no. 51 (Los Angeles, 1955), p. ii.

CHAPTER XIII

1. Note that Purcell appears as 'Composer' in a second list besides this, from which I quote with the permission of Lady Susi Jeans, from her article 'Seventeenth-century Musicians in the Sackville Papers', *Monthly Musical Record*, Sept.–Oct. 1958, pp. 185–6. (For the original see Kent Archives Office (Maidstone) MS. U269 D67.) The record of advances on salaries to the five oboists is to be found in *Cal. Tr. Books*, a royal warrant dormant of 17 Dec. 1690, instructing Sir Rowland Gwynne, Treasurer of the Chamber, to pay the advance to Dr. Nicholas Staggins.

CHAPTER XIV

1. For a fuller account of the affair, with maps, diagrams, etc., see Albert S. Borgman, *The Life and Death of William Mountfort*, Harvard Studies in English, vol. xv (Cambridge, Mass., 1935), pp. 123–210.

2. *Oedipus* was first performed at Dorset Garden about Nov. 1678, Dryden being called to account for having thus violated his contractual obligations to the Theatre Royal Company (Nicoll, p. 329). Being most successful then (Downes, p. 37), it was performed again in 1682, 1687, and 1692, and revised several times after Purcell's death. I concur in the views of Barclay Squire, 'Purcell's Dramatic Music' (*SIMG*, vol. v, p. 541), of Laurie (fo. 190), and of other authorities who accept Burney's choice of the 1692 revival as that for which Purcell provided music, not only because of the unusual success of the production (which Purcell's music no doubt helped to bring about), but because of certain stylistic features of the music that are characteristic of his latest style.

3. Hence known also as 'Greber's Peg' and, because of her dark complexion, as 'The Tawney Tuscan', or even, because of her very plain looks, as 'Hecate' — the last sobriquet being that

used fondly by Dr. John Pepusch after (one supposes) he had married her in 1718 (*MGG*, vol. x, col. 1026).

CHAPTER XV

1. H. B. Wright and M. K. Spear, *The Literary Works of Matthew Prior*, vol. 1, p. 125. Although Prior is in good company in awarding the doctorate 'by concensus', as it were (cf. Chamberlayne, *Angliæ Notitia*, 1694 ed.; *Flying Post*, 23 Nov. 1695; and Evelyn, 30 May 1698, to name a few), I am inclined to agree with Sir Jack Westrup, who thinks the degree was never awarded. Moreover, the ode may never have been performed. The title of the poem in the edition of 1709 contains the phrase 'intended to be sung before their majesties' as if, perhaps, difficulties had arisen to prevent performance. Such difficulties, or at least a last-minute change of plans, are mooted by Motteux, who complained that he had had very little time to write for the same occasion another New Year's ode, 'Sound, sound the trumpet, precious gifts prepare', which apparently was set by Staggins, although the music has not survived:

> You will grant, Sir, that I might begin the year with better verse than the song which was performed on New Year's Day before their majesties, but not with a better subject. I had so little time allowed me to write it, that I chiefly studied to make it lyrical.

(*Gentleman's Journal* for Jan.–Feb. 1693/4, p. 5. See also McGuinness, fo. 58).

2. It looked as if music would have to be got out of the way to make room for various merchandise, since on 24 May a 'sale of Indian goods' was advertised 'at the music room in York Buildings'. But the conflict was averted by postponement of the sale to 25 May. Concerning the concerts at the Vendu, see the *London Gazette* for 28 May and 11 June, also Tilmouth, fo. 41.

CHAPTER XVI

1. The consensus of expert opinion has it that these were trombones and slide trumpets. See W. Barclay Squire, 'Purcell's Music for the Funeral of Mary II' (*SIMG*, vol. IV, pp. 225–33), and F. W. Galpin, 'The Sackbut, its Evolution and History', *PMA*, 1906–7, p. 1. The title, incidentally, comes from the unique manuscript source of the work, Oriel College, Oxford, MS. Ua 37. See also *Analytical Catalogue*, no. 860.

2. As, indeed, Professor R. Thurston Dart of London University has shown by including drum parts in his edition of the March and Canzona (London, 1958). I follow his excellent performing edition, which includes the unscored parts for kettledrums. See also the entry in *KM*, p. 418, for Jan. 1694/5. Although contemporary prints do not show drums of any sort in company with the trumpets, the above entry in the Lord Chamberlain's accounts could scarcely mean that drums were used for anything but the queen's funeral.

3. Among them young William Croft, evidently so impressed by Purcell's setting of 'Thou knowest, Lord' that he incorporated the whole into his own burial service (published in *Musica Sacra*, 1724), acknowledging in the preface both Purcell's authorship of this setting and his dominant influence in the expressive style of the remaining movements.

4. Chester (*Westminster Abbey Registers*, p. 236) explains the apparent discrepancy between the dates given for Busby's death (on 5 April) and his burial (also 5 April) by pointing out that he was probably buried on the 11th. Barker, also, says the burial register is in error.

5. Possibly this would be George Herbert. But the presence of a semi-anonymous contemporary Mr. Herbert with some poetic inclinations leaves room for doubt. Since the poems are printed without first names and do not appear among George Herbert's complete works, it is at present impossible to say with certainty which of these men, if either, actually wrote them.

6. Several accounts in Magdalen Library (entitled 'Liber Com-

puti S. M. Magd. Coll.') provide exact information on Daniel Purcell's tour of duty at Oxford. Although accounts for 1688 and 1689 are missing, this series shows Daniel to have received his yearly stipend right up to the year 1696, when he shared the organist's salary of £80 with Benjamin Hecht. After that date Hecht alone received the salary. (See App. Two, III, 4.)

7. *A Register of the Presidents, Fellows, Demies . . . of Saint Mary Magdalen College* (ed. J. R. Bloxam), vol. II, pp. 203–4 n., gives the following account of Daniel Purcell's move:

The occasion of his coming to London was as follows: Dr. Sacheverell, Fellow of Magdalen College, 1701–1713, who had been a friend of his brother Henry, having been presented to the Living of St. Andrew, Holborn, found an organ in the church, of Harris's building, which, having never been paid for, had from the time of its erection in 1699 been shut up. The doctor upon his coming to the living, by a collection from the parishioners, raised money to pay for it, but his title to the place of organist was litigious, the right of election being in question between the rector, the vestry, and the parish at large: nevertheless, he invited Daniel Purcell to London, and he accepted it; but in February 1717 the vestry, which in that parish is a select one thought proper to elect Mr. Maurice Greene, in preference to Purcell, who submitted to stand as a candidate. In the year following, Greene was made organist of St. Paul's, and Daniel Purcell being then dead, his nephew Edward was a candidate for the place, but it was conferred on Mr. John Ishum, who died in June, 1726.

8. 26–28 Nov. 1695; see also the *Flying Post* (23–26 Nov.), *Westminster Abbey Registers*, p. 238, and Luttrell, who for this occasion wrote one of the few entries in his massive chronicle having to do directly with music:

Mr. Purcell, the great master of music, was this evening buried in the Abbey of Westminster.

9. The well-known account of Croft's borrowing the latter for his own setting of the burial service will perhaps bear repetition here. In the preface to *Musica Sacra* of 1724 he explained that:

The reason why I did not compose that verse anew (so as to render the whole service of my own composition) is obvious to every artist; in the rest of that service composed by me, I have endeavoured as near as I could, to imitate that great master and celebrated composer — whose name will for ever stand high in the rank of those who have laboured to improve the English style in his so happily adapting his compositions to English words in that elegant and judicious manner as was unknown to many of his predecessors....

APPENDIX TWO

DOCUMENTS

Note: In this appendix are reprinted extracts from contemporary documents, papers, publications, and records that concern the various members of the Purcell family. For the most part only primary sources are registered. But when what has seemed to me important data can be obtained only from secondary sources, these also have been recorded.

The first portion of this appendix is arranged alphabetically, according to the Christian names of the various members of the family. Where several Purcells share the same Christian name, the order is chronological so far as possible. Under each name the arrangement is also chronological, where such arrangement is feasible. Extant poems or other literary pieces (such as puns, in the case of Daniel Purcell) are appended to each entry, arranged alphabetically by author's name, or alphabetically by first line under 'Anonymous'.

I   CHARLES PURCELL (cousin)

1. WAM 33705 (Treasurer's Account, 1672), fo. 4.

   Annual Reddit: 'Et in Denarijs Solut ad usum Scholasticor Jacob Leisley, Johann Anthobus, Daniel de Lyne et Johni Cooper per dimd. Anni, *Carol* [*sic*] *Pursell*, et Wildebore Ellis per An°: integ Tot Stipend xxv^{li}. Et Reverendissimo Decano Thesaurar et Ludi Mag^{ro}: xx^{li} ex Dono Reverendissimi Patr. Johnis Episcopi Lincolniensis nuper Decani Westmonast in Toto hoc Anno . . . xxvi^{li}.'
   [Similar entries in 33706–10 (Rob^{to} Davies, Carolo Pursell, Wildbore Ellis, et Rogero Cooper), 33711 and 33712 (Charles Purcell is first on the list, followed by: Rogero Cooper, Wildbore Ellis, Edwardo Roberts).]

2. Testamentum Caroli Purcell. PCC: 63 Lloyd (Somerset House).

   In the name of God Amen. I, Charles Purcell, gentleman, of London in the County of Middlesex, being in good health and of sound and perfect mind and memory, praise be therefore given to Almighty God, do make and ordain this my present last Will and Testament, in manner and form following: that is to say, first and principally I commend my soul into the hands of Almighty God, hoping through the merits, death, and passion of my saviour Jesus Christ, to have full and free pardon and forgiveness of all my sins and to inherit everlasting life, and my body I commit to the earth to be decently buried, and as touching the disposition of all such temporal estate, as it hath pleased Almighty God to bestow upon me, I give and dispose thereof as followeth: First I will that all my debts be paid and discharged. *Item* I give unto my dear mother Katherine Purcell a mourning [ring, outfit?] *Item* I give unto my loving sisters Elizabeth and Katherine Purcell each a mourning ring, and my wages that is [sic] due or shall become due, my goods and what money I have I give unto my loving brother, Edward Purcell, my full and sole executor of this my present last will and testament, and I do hereby revoke, disannul, and make void all former wills and testaments by me heretofor made as witness my hand this fourth day of June in the year of our Lord One Thousand six hundred eighty two,

Charles Purcell

Signed and sealed in the presence of

M. Purcell   Eli. Purcell   Sarah Fynes*

3(a). PCC: March Admon. 1686, p. 50.

Carolus Purcell secundo die emairt [sic] Commissario Mattheo Purcell ffrati naturali et legitimo Caroli Purcell nuper de parochia Sancti Martini in Campis in Comitatu Middlesex sed in Nave rocat Le George sloope in partibus de Guyney Celibis defuncti [nentis] &c. Ad Administrandum bona, jura, et credita dicti defuncti De bene &c. Jurat Catherina Purcell matre prius renuntiante

ult' Martij 1686.

Hae Litterae Aministracionis introduct et renuntiat &c. Testamentum probat[um] mense Maij 1686.

---

* This Sarah Fynes was, very likely, the member of the Fynes family of Buckinghamshire who was buried in the Wing parish church (near Claydon House and the Verney Estates) that same summer.

3(b). PCC: March Admon. 1686 (abstract from B. Cooke, Esq.), 2 March 1685/6.

Charles Purcell late of St. Martin-in-the-Fields, Middlesex, but in the ship called *Le George* Sloope 'in partibus de Guyney', bachelor. Admon. to Matthew Purcell, brother of deceased. This admon. renounced, will was proved in May 1686.

4. Chancery Proceedings, Bridges C5/90/90. 28 Nov. 1687. Parkyny.

To the Right Honourable George Lord Jeffreys Baron of Wem. Lord High Chancellor of England.

Humbly complaining sheweth unto your Lordship your orator Edward Purcell ... of Mickleham in the County of Surrey, gentleman, brother and executor of the last Will and Testament of Captain Charles Purcell deceased. That the said Charles Purcell by commission from His M[ajesty], dated on or about the month of September in the year of our Lord one thousand six hundred and eighty and four, was appointed Captain and Commander of the good ship called the *George*, belonging unto the Royal African Company of England by which commission from his [...] Company's commission the said Captain Purcell had full authority to seize and take all ships and goods belonging unto any of his said Majesty's subjects that should be found trading to or from any parts of Africa from Sally* to Cabo de buena Esperanza. And your orator further [testifies that the said Captain] Purcell by virtue of his said commissions did take upon him the command of the said ship and within some short time after, that is to say about the month of November in the said year of our Lord one thousand six hundred and eighty and four, did sail from the port of London unto [Africa] and unto the Gold Coast of Guinea and Arda,† and other ports unknown unto the orator pursuant to his instructions given him by the said Royal

* Salli, or Salé, a seaport on the Atlantic coast of Morocco (*Encyclopedia Britannica*, 14th ed., vol. XIX, p. 871).

† Probably Ardrah, now Allada, Dahomoy, Africa (op. cit. vol. XXIV, p. 80, E 4).

Company. And your orator further shews that the said Charles Purcell did carry with him in the said ship of which he was Captain as a forf[eit] silver plate and other goods, chattels, and merchandises to the value of two or three hundred pounds and by traffic with his ready money at some of the said ports to which he arrived became lawfully possessed of and interested in diverse ounces of gold and other merchandises of great value and after [. . .] with about the month of November or thereabouts or some other time within the year of our Lord one thousand six hundred eighty and six, the said Charles Purcell, in the said ship and in his command as Captain thereof, died some time before his said voyage having made his Will is [. . .] due form published and attested and thereof made constituted and appointed your orator his sole executor and within some short time after your orator had notice of the said Charles Purcell's death your orator in due form as he is advised proved his said Will in the Prerogative Court of Canter[bury and] thereby is become intituled to all the goods and chattels, gold, silver plate, money and other things whatsoever whereof the said Charles Purcell died possessed or was interested in. But so it may please your lordship that upon the death of the said Charles Purcell all his said goods and chattels [. . .] plate money, wearing apparel, lining, and other merchandises and things did come to the hands and possession of William Bayley being mate of the said Captain Charles Purcell in the said ship or otherwise mate in the ship called *Orange Tree* who sailed in company with the said ship the *George*, unto which said ship called *Orange Tree*, some time before the death of the said Charles Purcell, all the goods and chattels of the said Purcell after his death were carried from [the *George*] the said William Bayley did possess himself of six ounces and upwards of gold and several gold rings, one large silver punch-bowl and stone fire-cup tipped and footed with silver, one fowling piece, one cane, all his wearing clothes and diverse quantities of linen, a great quantity of brandy, twelve half cases of spirits, amongst diverse other merchandises and goods unknown to your orator

which said particular goods and chattels above particularly
specified were of the value of one hundred pounds or thereabouts and the said Bayley did sell the said silver punch-bowl
unto one Mr. John Winder or some other person for sixteen
pounds or some such like other greater sum of money and did
likewise sell the said fowling piece and cane unto one John
Cabes for five pounds or some other greater sum of money,
and the said Charles Purcell's wearing apparel and linen was
sold by the said William Bayley at the mast of the said ship
called *Orange Tree* for twenty pounds or other sum of money,
all which he had and received ... And your orator further
shews that the said William Bayley having so possessed himself of the goods and chattels of the said Charles Purcell, and
sold and disposed of some of them as aforesaid, the said
Bayley, some time after came to England, and in his said
voyage and before his arrival in England died [...] after
whose decease, Anne Bayley, widow and relict of the said
William Bayley either as executrix of him the said William
Bay'ey, or by virtue of administration of his goods and
chattels to her granted, hath now possessed herself not only of
the personal estate of the said William Bayley, being of great
value, but also of diverse goods and chattels which were the
property, goods, and chattels of the said Charles Purcell
[...] and now conceals the same from your orator, well
knowing that your orator is altogether ignorant what the
same goods and chattels were or wherein they did consist or
the true values and also knowing that your orator's witnesses
who could prove the same were all seamen and under officers
of the said ships the *George* and the *Orange Tree*, and are now
either all dead or else in remote places beyond the seas, for
want of whose testimonies your orator is disabled to bring
action at Common Law for the same against the said Anne
Bayley, and only relievable in a Court of Equity by a full
discovery upon oath of the said Anne Bayley, and the more is
especially for that your orator hath been credibly informed
that since her said husband's death she has possessed herself of
her said husband's account books and papers or other books,

memorandum, or writings wherein he had made entries of diverse goods and chattels of the said Charles Purcell's, which came to his hands and possession after the said Charles Purcell's death in specie, as likewise what goods, chattels, or other things of the said Purcell's he had exposed to sale, and for what sums of money he had received upon such sale and from whom which said account books or books, papers, memorandums, or writings manifesting the same, your orator prays she, the said Anne Bayley, may also set forth upon oath and bring into this honourable court to be inspected without defacing, altering or obliteration and may produce such leaves as she has taken or torn out of any such books in order to conceal the same from your orator's knowledge. In tender consideration of all which premises, your orator prays that the said Anne Bayley may set forth whether she is not executrix or administrix of her said husband, and whether, since her husband's death, she hath not possessed herself of his personal estate, and whether she did not likewise possess herself of diverse great quantities of gold as the same came from the Indies, frequently called dust gold, to the value of two hundred pounds and upwards, amongst which was the said six ounces and upwards of your orator's said brother's, together with diverse other goods and chattels which were the said Charles Purcell's at the time of his death, and brought back in the said ships or one of them, and that she may set forth in particular what the same were and of what value, and may set forth whether several of her said husband's account books, paper memorandums and writings after his death did not come to her hands, wherein were mentioned what goods and chattels, how many ounces of gold, and how many gold rings and other matters and things therein conjoined were the proper goods and personal estates of the said Charles Purcell, and whether she hath not heard and been readily informed by some person or persons who went the said voyage in the said ships or the one of them with the said Charles Purcell and her said husband, and did return home on the said ships or the one of them, that her said husband did sell the said silver punch-bowl, gun, and cane of the said Captain Purcell, and did likewise sell some part of the linen and wearing clothes and diverse other things after his death at the mast of the said ships or the one of them for a considerable sum of money, and whether amongst her said husband's account books, etc. [...] she did not find an account thereof ... that she may give your orator satisfaction for the same, she having personal assets of her said husband's sufficient to pay all his debts and funeral expenses with great overplus [...] etc. And may your lordship grant your orator His Majesty's most gracious writ of subpoena directed to her the said Anne [Bayley] to retain etc. ....

Memb. 2. Jurat 20 Die Decembris 1687. / The answer of Anne Bayley, widow defendant, to the Bill of complaint of Edward Purcell, gentleman, Complainant.

[Anne Bayley] denies any knowledge of anything ... questions Edward Purcell's authority as executor and Charles Purcell's authority as Captain.

5. St. James's, Westminster: Overseers' Accounts.

1686: Hay Market Street: Charles Purcell   £0–12–0
1687: Hay Market Street: [no entry for Charles Purcell]
1688: Hay Market Street: Charles Purcell's house taken by Joseph Styles

Since Charles, son of Thomas, died in 1686, these records seem to refer to him, and not to the other Charles Purcell mentioned under II, below.

II CHARLES PURCELL (? brother)

See App. One, II, 3, and Genealogical Table (p. 383). For yet another, earlier Charles Purcell, see parish records of St. Andrew's, Holborn, MS. 6667/4 (Guildhall Library, London), 18 Sept. 1657: Margaret, daughter of Charles Purcell and of Margaret, his wife, [born] in Mr. Greenbold's house at Holborn Bridge (baptized 27 Sept.).

III   DANIEL PURCELL (brother)
(See Plate 16(b))

1. Bodleian, MS. Wood D 19(4), fo. 108.

Purcell, Daniel, organist of Magdalen College in Oxford, brother to Henry Purcell. [Wood originally had 'son of', but altered — not necessarily 'corrected' — the entry to read as above.]

2. Bodleian, MS. Mus.e.17, fo. 40.

Purcell (Daniel), brother to Henry, organist of Magdalen College, whence he moved to London.

3. *KM*, p. 339 (8 April 1679).

Paid £6. 12s. for summer's service as Royal Chapel choir boy at Windsor.

4. *A Register of the Presidents, Fellows, Demies ... of St. Mary Magdalen College* (ed. J. R. Bloxam).

1689 Soloist	Dr. Rogers nuper organistae	£30
	Mr. Purcell organistae	£36 13s.
1690 Soloist	Mr. Mro. Morgan Transery	
	Genty antiphonas	£8
	Mr. Harris reficienti organum	
	per compositimen	£50
	Dr. Rogers nuper organistae	£30
	Mr. Purcell organistae	£40
1691 Soloist	Clements pro 70 formulis	
	precatronem	11s.
	Mr. Harris reficients organum	£50
	Dr. Rogers nuper organistae	£30
	Mr. Purcell organistae	£30
1692 Soloist	Clements pro formantis organum	£15
	Mr. Harris reficienti organum	£51
	[Rogers and Purcell as before]	
1693	[Rogers and Purcell as before]	
1694	John Clements Bibliopolae	
	pro. form precal	6s.

                [Rogers and Purcell as before]
    1695   Mr. Harris reficienti et mun-
                  dantr. organ per comp.   £10   0s. 6d.
                Clements pro form prec   12s.
    1696 Soloist Mr. Harris refic. et mundi
                  organ. per comp.   £8
                Jacob Duke organ, villin.
                  gerenti ord. Pr. Pras   £2
                Mr. Hecht et Purcell organ   £40
    [After this date Hecht alone.]

5. *A Register of the Presidents, Fellows, Demies . . . of Saint Mary Magdalen College* (ed. J. R. Bloxam), vol. II, p. 203.

   1688. Purcell, Daniel res. 1695. Son of Henry Purcell, Gentleman of the Chapel Royal (*obiit* 1718). He was brother of Henry Purcell, and from him derived most of that little reputation which as a musician he possessed.

6. Vicar-General Marriage Licences. 8 May 1705.

   Daniel Purcell, gentleman, of St. Paul's, Covent Garden, and Elizabeth Torer of the same, spinster, aged 27, to take place at St. Paul's, Covent Garden.

   If this referred to Daniel Purcell the musician, apparently the marriage did not take place. See 7(*a*), below, where he is described as a bachelor.

7(*a*). PCC: Jan. 1717/18, fo. 10.

   Decimo Septimo die emavit Commissario Josephe Purcell fratri naturali et legitimo Danielis Purcell [nuper] paroche Sancti Andrewe Holborne London defuncti Celibis ha[b]entis &c Ad Administrandum bona jura et credita dicti defuncti De bene &c Jurat[e]

                                            Ult. Jan. 1718

7(*b*). PCC: Admon. 17 Jan. 1717/18.

   Daniel Purcell of the Parish of St. Andrew, Holborn, London, bachelor. Admon. granted to Joseph Purcell, natural and lawful brother of the deceased.

8. Bodleian, MS. Rawl. D 833.169 (referring to Daniel Purcell).

I was acquainted with him when [he was an] organist at Magdalen College: [all] allowed him the title of Punmaster General . . .

(Cf. J. R. Bloxam, op. cit., vol. II, pp. 204–5, who recounts several puns.

9. Bodleian, MS. Mus. d. 226.

(Daniel Purcell — partial autograph — from the library of James Kent, anthems and solo songs.)

AN ELEGY ON THE DEATH OF MR. DAN. PURCELL
BY L. MAN.

In softer accents or more tuneful lays
Other may mourn his death, or sing his praise
Yet none more truly can his fate bewail
But alas! will fruitless grief avail?
To paint in words the man, and faintly show
What once he was, is all we now can do.
His modest and obliging carriage gain'd
Him real friends, who always friends remain'd.
In him, two very rare perfections met,
Great skill in music, and a ready wit.
His wit, peculiar in the grace alone;
Pleas'd all who heard it, but offended none.
   In th'art of music, he perform'd so well
   That him, his brother only cou'd excell.

10. From the *Weekly Journal* of 29 June, 1717. (Burney Coll., vol. 183b.)

    A Punni-Musical Epistle to Mr. Daniel P—:
    Or, a Letter in his own Way.

.   .   .   .   .   .   Thus I
In Baralypton Blunderbuss ye.

             Ox. and Camb. Miscel. p. 189.
             Cremona, 20 Nov. 1716.

Honest Dan.

I have beaten time so often at the overture of your resting
place, without playing upon you at sight, that I perceive the
tenor of your life to be chiefly in taverns, where you will
never leave drinking a treble quantity, till your hand quavers.
If this be any slur to your reputation, and you think me a Jew
to harp upon a harsh string, I shall use no flourish or rondeau
of words, but tell you plainly, that it frets me to the guts, that
you are so hard to be found when a man is solo in an evening.
I know sometimes you take some fugues into the country air,
and I wish it prove no more than an opera pretium to you; if
it does, I must needs say you manage your purse ill. I design
to watch your ritornellos to town, and will strive to bring you
more to my bow; and knowing we shall agree to an hair, I
I desire we may wet our whistles together, and make some
recitativo's of the past crotchets of our long acquaintanc.e
Time was we could both of us have played upon the virginals;
and particularly you have been a man of note for your many
compositions upon them. I know you to be in alt, as to your
religion; and should you continue to be above Ela in your
politics, I shall never suffer myself, I assure ye, to be out of
tune with my friend on such fiddlefaddle accounts.

If the sharpest of the critics should censure this letter as flat,
they are entirely out of the key, and have not their fantasias
screwed up to the present pitch of

Dear Dan,

Yours, from the merry violin to the
german flute and the recorder,
Signior Allegro

11. British Museum, $\frac{1855 \text{ c.4}}{58}$ Broadsides, etc. 1682–1780.

JOHN JONES   [not dated.]

Whereas it has been industriously and maliciously reported,
that Mr. John Jones (now a candidate for the place of organist
to the United Parishes of Allhallows, Bread Street and St.
John the Evangelist) is a BUNGLER, etc.

This false report having already been a very great prejudice

to Mr. Jone's [*sic*] interest, in relation to his being elected
organist to the said parishes; therefore (in justice to the said
Mr. Jones) 'tis thought fit to undeceive those gentlemen who
have been thus imposed on, by such false and base insinuations,
that the said Mr. Jones is a person fitly qualified and capable of
playing on any organ, being very well recommended and
approved; as appears by a certificate of several undeniable
masters, who have given it under their own hands, and did it
before an organ was put up (or designed so to be) in the said
parish church. Any gentlemen desirous of seeing the original
of the following certificate, may do it at Steel's coffee house in
Bread Street. We, whose names are under written, do certify,
that Mr. John Jones, brought up in the Cathedral Church of
St. Paul's, is capable of playing (in any parish church in
England) on the organ.

As witness our hands.

Richard Brind, organist of St. Paul's Church.

Master of the Boys of St. Paul's and organist of St.
Bennet.

Daniel Purcell, organist of St. Dunstan's in the East and
St. Andrew's, Holborn.

Charles Young, organist of Allhallows, Barking.

Peter Horwood, organist of Christ Church.

Benjamin Short, organist of St. Sepulchre and St.
Dunstan, Stepney.

George Hayden, organist of St. Mary Magdalen, Ber-
mondsey.

Maurice Greene, organist of St. Paul's, St. Andrew's,
Holborn, and St. Dunstan's in the West.

Edward Henry Purcell, organist of St. Martin Orgar.

Gentlemen,

Your vote and interest is earnestly desired in favour of the
said Mr. Jones, who has given full assurance of a constant
attendance.

IV EDWARD PURCELL (? brother) of St. Margaret's,
    Westminster (See Plate 16(a))

1. Edward Chamberlayne, *Angliæ Notitia*, 12th ed. (1679), part
   I, p. 162.

   Mr. Edward Pursel, gentleman usher, assistant; to come in
   upon the first vacancy.

2. *Cal. Tr. Books*, 8 June 1681.

   To Mr. Purcell   £37. 10s.

3. Edward Chamberlayne, *Angliæ Notitia*, 14th ed. (1682), part
   I, p. 166.

   Mr. Edward Pursel, gentleman usher, assistant, to come in
   on first vacancy.

   N.B. In the 15th ed. (1684), Edward Purcell does not appear to have 'come
   in', since four new names appear. Perhaps he had gone off to the army by
   this time.

4. *Cal. Tr. Books*, 2 Dec. 1682.

   To Edward Purcell, gent. usher   £20

5. Charles Dalton, *English Army Lists and Commission Registers
   1661–1714* (London, 1892), vol. II, p. 27.

   The Queen Consort's Regiment of Foot, Feb. 1685. Lt.
   Edward Purcell, commissioned 20 Feb. 1685 (5 companies
   served at Sedgemore in the King's Own Regiment).

6. Ibid. vol. II, p. 135, n. 18.

   Lt. Ed. Purcell . . . Captain in the same: Nov. 1687.

7. Ibid. vol. II, p. 208. (List of Commissions for 1688, signed 1
   Dec. 1688.)

   Lt. Ed. Purcell to have Capt. Hayman Rooke's late
   captaincy as Grenadier Company in the Queen Consort's
   Regiment.

8. Ibid. vol. V, p. 126.

   The Queen's own Regiment of Marines commanded by
   Brigadier-General William Seymour . . . Major Purcell to be
   Lt. Col. *vice* Lt. Colonel Rook, preferred 1 March 1704. [n. 4:

Appointed major of Brigadier-General Seymour's Regiment of Foot, 8 June 1702. Appears to have retained his company, as his name stands as senior captain of the regiment in 1715.]

9. Charles Dalton, *George the First's Army 1714–1727* (London, 1910), vol. i, p. 140, and p. 141, n. 4.

Captain Edward Purcell. 1 May 1711. [n. 4: Appointed major of the Queen's Own Regt. 8 June 1702.] Served at Vigo and Cadiz, Regimental Lt.-Col. 1 March 1704. Appears to have sold his Lt.-Colonelcy to Kempenfelt, 1 May 1711; . . . left the regiment in May 1716.

A certain Lt.-Col. Purcell died at Kingston upon Hull on 23 October. See under v, below.

10. British Museum Add. MS. 28,888, fo. 225. (Catalogued as a letter from F. Purcell to J. Tucker, 1702, but certainly by Edward Purcell.)

May the 9th, 1702

Sir

I have above a week been laid up with the stone, or I would have waited on you myself, to desire to know if you have any directions, to draw a commission for me as major to Col. Seymore, I desire your answer by the bearer, in which you will oblige

Sir, your most humble servant,
E. Purcell

11. Westminster Public Library, Account Book, no. 1660.

A codicil or addition to the last Will and Testament of me, Edward Purcell, of the parish of St. Margaret's, Westminster, in the County of Middlesex, Esquire, which Will was duly executed by me and bears date the [. . .] day of [. . .] last past before the date hereof. I give, devise, and bequeath unto Mrs. Mary Mullins of the parish of St. Margaret's, Westminster, aforesaid widow all such plate, household goods, and furniture of what kind or quality soever books, linen and wearing apparel that I shall be possessed of at the time of my decease, and shall be in my new dwelling house in Great Dean's Yard in Westminster. In trust nevertheless to and for the use, benefit, and behoof of my niece Frances Welsted, when she shall come to the age of twenty years anything in my said Will contained to the contrary thereof notwithstanding, in witness whereof I have hereunto set my hand and seal the second day of October in the third year of the reign of our sovereign Lord George by the grace of God King of Great Britain, etc. In the year of our Lord one thousand seven hundred and sixteen.

E. Purcell

Signed, sealed, delivered, declared, and published by the said Edward Purcell, for and as a codicil or addition to his last Will and Testament in the presence of us, who have subscribed our names as witnesses thereunto in his presence. Thomas Prickard, Mary Williams, Edward Stephenson. (Probatim) Tertio die mensis decembris anno domini 1717mo emanavit commission Marie Williams solute curatrici legitime assignate France Welsted Minori Nepoti et universali legatario nominate in scedula testamentaria Edwardi Purcell nuper parochie supradicte defuncti ad administrandum bona etc. dicti defuncti cum ejus testamentaria schedula annexa in usum et beneficium et donec et quotienscumque dicta Franca Welsted Vicesimum primum aetatis sue annum compleverit de bene etc. prius iurate.

Though recorded in the Archives Room, Westminster Public Library, Buckingham Palace Road, the actual Will has been lost since being removed to safety during the Seond World War. The codicil, which apparently served also as an envelope for the original Will can be seen. But several intensive searches on the part of the author for the Will itself have failed.

12. Wytham parish registers (in portion written by 'Robertus Lydall, S.T.B. Coll. Magd. Oxon. Socius Rector' from 28 Aug. 1712 onward).

The Honourable Col. Ed. Purcell, died June the 20th and was buried in the Chancel the 23rd of the same month.

For a drawing of Wytham Manor and the parish church in the time of Edward Purcell see Knyff's drawings (engraved by Kip), and Bodleian, MSS. Top. Berks. c. 51, no. 240, and Top. Oxon. b. 3 fo. 71*v*.

13. Gravestone in the chancel, Wytham parish church, Berks.

Here lieth the body of Edward Purcell, eldest son of Mr. Purcell, Gentleman of the Royal Chapel, and brother to M:. Henry Purcell, so much renowned for his skill in music. He was gentleman usher to King Charles the 2nd, lieutenant of Colonel Trelawney's regiment of foot; in which for his many gallant actions in the wars of Ireland and Flanders he was gradually advanced to the honour of lieutenant-colonel. He assisted Sir George Rook in the taking of Gibralter, and the Prince of Hesse in the memorable defence of it. He followed that prince to Barcelona, and was at the taking of Mount-joy, where that brave prince was killed: and continued to signalize courage in the siege, and taking of that city: in the year of Our Lord 1705. He enjoyed great service, until the much lamented death of his late Mistress Queen Anne; when decayed with age, and broken with misfortunes, he retired to the house of the right honourable the Earl of Abingdon. He died June 20th 1717. Aged 61 years.

N.B. The transcript published by Hawkins in 1776 (vol. II, p. 746) departs from the original in several details. The only error that has had really mischievous results is that pertaining to Edward Purcell's age at death, which on the stone clearly reads '61' not '64'. This Edward Purcell, then, was born sometime before June 1656, not in 1653.

v   EDWARD PURCELL (? cousin) of Mickleham

For the earliest record of Edward Purcell's responsibilities as a gentleman usher daily waiter assistant, see p. 305 above.

See also under I Charles Purcell (cousin), 4, and under XXV Samuel and Temperance Wall, 1–3, 7, 8.

See also the *Gentleman's Magazine* for 23 October 1732, p. 1031, for an obituary notice of Lt.-Col. Purcel, an officer on half pay, at Kingston upon Hull. Dalton (*George the First's Army*, vol. I, p. 140) associated the name with that of Lt.-Col. Edward Purcell.

VI EDWARD PURCELL (son)

1. *Westminster Abbey Registers*, p. 74.

    Baptisms: 6 Sept. 1689.

    Edward, son of Henry and Frances Purcell.

2. St. Margaret's, Westminster, Vestry Books, no. 2419 (1724–38), p. 61.

    ### Fri. 8 July 1726

    Upon reading the humble petition of Edward Purcell, Joseph Centliure, and a letter from Mr. John Robinson, praying to be admitted organist of this parish church in the room of Mr. John Isham, ordered that the said Edward Purcell be and is hereby chosen and appointed organist of this parish in the room of the said John Isham at the salary of thirty pounds per annum during the pleasure of this vestry, he paying the blower forty shillings per annum out of the same, and that twenty-two pounds, part of the said thirty pounds, be annually paid by the clerk of this parish as hath usually been paid to former organists, and the other eight pounds by the church wardens of this parish, and that the payment of the said salary do commence from Midsummer last.

3. Court Minutes at Office of Christ's Hospital, London.

    Peter Horwood elected music master 28 Jan. 1719 (120).

    Then the Court proceeded to the election of a music master for this house in the room of Mr. John Barrett late music master deceased. The petitioners for the said place were

    Mr. Peter Horwood   Mr. John Isham
    Mr. Edward Purcell   Mr. Charles King

    All masters of music.

    After they were severally called in and their petitions read, they were severally put up for the question and reduced to two, viz. Peter Horwood and Charles King, who being again severally put up, the majority fell (and so the President declared) on Mr. Horwood who is elected accordingly and he being called in and acquainted therewith returned the Court his hearty thanks and promised faithfully to discharge his duty; and the Court referred the taking of his charge to the Committee of Almoners who are to see he take it accordingly.

4. A. W. Hughes Clark, *The Register of St. Clement, Eastcheap, and St. Martin Orgar* (Harl. Soc. Reg. 68), p. 16.

4 July, 1740.

Edward Purcell, organist, buried near the organ gallery door.

VII   EDWARD HENRY PURCELL (grandson)

1. PRO: LC 'Miscellanea', 5/70, p. 175 (July 1739).

Edward H. Purcell, late Child of the Chapel allowance of clothes. Whereas the Sub-Dean of His Majesty's Chapel in the absence of the Dean, has certified the [*sic*] Edward Henry Purcell's voice is changed who was one of the Children of the Chapel, and therefore removed from the service of the Chapel, these are as to the said Edward Henry Purcell the usual allowance of one suit of plain cloth, one hat-band, two holland shirts, two cravats, two pairs of cuffs, two handkerchiefs, two pairs of stockings, two pairs of shoes, and two pairs of gloves. And etc. given etc. this 19th day of July 1739 in the 13th year of His Majesty's reign. Grafton.

2. According to an article in the *Musical Times*, June 1931, E. H. Purcell appears in a subscription list attached to Boyce's *Twelve sonatas for 2 violins, &c* (1747), as organist of St. Clement's, Lombard Street.

3. Greater London Council Record Office. P.79/JN.1./142. Transcript of vestry minutes of St. John, Hackney.

11 Aug. 1753 (p. 198).

Agreed that the salary of the organist shall for the future be twenty pounds by the year and that for his said salary he shall attend on all Sundays in the year and on all days whereon a sermon shall be preached (fast-days excepted) and that on every Sunday throughout the year a voluntary shall be played after both the morning and evening service.

Saturday, 22 Sept. 1753 (p. 200/20).

At a vestry in order to choose an organist.

The question was put whether the vestry do now proceed to the choice of an organist of this parish and was carried in the affirmative.

The question was likewise put whether the persons who now appear as candidates for the said place be called in separately to hear the order of the last vestry read to them and was carried in the affirmative.

And the candidates were called in severally and the said order of the last vestry was read to each of them, and they were severally asked what attendance they designed to give in the said office to which they severally answered as follows, viz:

Mr. Edward Henry Purcell proposed to attend personally every other Sunday throughout the year and during the winter half year ... viz. from Michaelmas to Lady Day he will also attend personally in the afternoon of each of the four intermediate Sundays. And he promised that at these times when he shall not attend personally, he will employ such a deputy to officiate for him as shall be to the satisfaction of the gentlemen of the vestry.

Mr. David Heureux proposed to attend personally every Sunday throughout the year both morning and afternoon without employing any deputy whatsoever (sickness excepted).

Mr. William Ward proposed to attend personally every Sunday throughout the year both morning and evening and declared that he hath no other place of organist nor will apply for any other if he shall be chosen into the place of organist of this parish.

Mr. Richard Low, Mr. Thomas Archer, Mr. Moses Patence proposed 'to attend personally every Sunday, etc. without employing a deputy except in case of sickness'.

Agreed that the method of this present election be by

scratching for all at once. And that the person who hath the majority of votes shall be the person elected.

The gentlemen then proceeded to scratch for the said candidates and

Mr. Purcell, had	9 votes
Mr. L'Heureux, had	6
Mr. Ward, had	2
Mr. Low, had	0
Mr. Archer, had	1
Mr. Patence, had	0

The majority being for Mr. Edward Henry Purcell, he was declared duly elected ... at the salary settled at the last vestry, to commence from Michaelmas next on condition that he perform his proposal and promise above mentioned.

4. A. W. Hughes Clark, *The Register of St. Clement, Eastcheap, and St. Martin Orgar* (Harl. Soc. Reg. 67), p. 51.

Baptisms: 17 May 1761.

Frances, daughter of Edward Henry and Abigail Frances Purcell (born April 12th).

5. Greater London Council Record Office. P.79/JN.1./142. Transcript of vestry minutes of St. John, Hackney.

Easter Tuesday, 24 April 1764 (pp. 555–6).

Complaint having been made against Edward Henry Purcell the present organist.

Resolved that the vestry clerk do write to the said Edward Henry Purcell and acquaint him that the vestry insists on his being regular in his attendance, and that he do give in the name of his deputy to the Churchwarden, and also give notice from time to time to the Churchwarden for the time being when he shall change him, and who he shall appoint in his stead.

A note on the margin of this page reads: 'Organist, wrote to him, he promised to send the name of his deputy' signed 'R.D.' (Richard Dann) 'Vestry Clark'.

Resolved that the choice of an organist be deferred until the next vestry, and that Edward Henry Purcell the present organist do officiate until that time.

Monday, 30 April 1764 (p. 359).

The Vestry Clerk acquainted the vestry that he had wrote [*sic*] to Mr. Purcell the organist agreeable to the resolution of the last vestry, Mr. Purcell not attending this vestry.

Resolved that the choice of an organist be deferred until the next vestry, and that Mr. Purcell do officiate in the mean time.

Saturday, 3 Aug. 1765 (p. 411).

The Churchwarden declared a vacancy in the place of organist of this parish by the death of Mr. Purcell . . .

Resolved that the Churchwarden be and is hereby desired to pay to Mrs. Purcell the widow of the late organist the salary which would have been due to her late husband at Michaelmas last.

6. A. W. Hughes Clark, *The Register of St. Clement, Eastcheap, and St. Martin Orgar* (Harl. Soc. Reg. 67), p. 21.

Burials: 5 Aug. 1765.

Edward Henry Purcell, organist, buried near the organ gallery door.

VIII   ELIZABETH PURCELL (mother)

For accounts referring to disbursements in her favour for 1668, see App. One, II, I.

1. Westminster Abbey Chapter Minutes, 1662–85. (31 Dec. 1669.)

Ordered that a lease be made to Mrs. Purcell of a tenement in Tothill Street for 40 years under the old rent and usual covenant.

2. St. Margaret's, Westminster, Overseers' Accounts, 1665–6, p. 169.

Widow Pursell, Tothill Street South: Assessed four shillings, collected four shillings, arrears nil.

Similar entries in accounts up to 1682, when 'Widow Pursell's' name is not in the list, or thereafter. For the record of her lodging one Frances Crump, see p. 16 above.

3. WAM 61228A (Precentor's Book, 1660–71), folios 56v, 57v, 58, and 61.

Various payments to 'Mr. Purcell's widow' for August, September, October, and December 1664.

4. St. Margaret's, Westminster, Churchwardens' Accounts, vol. LXXX (1699–70).

Money received for burials: 22 Aug. 1699.
Elizabeth Purcell.

5. PCW: Admon. 7 Sept. 1699.

Estate administered by Katherine Purcell, wife of William Sale.

IX FRANCES PURCELL (wife)

1. Richmond Town Hall: Parish Meeting Book, 1596–1735 (St. Mary Magdalene parish church, Richmond), p. 232.

19 May 1705.
Mrs Purcell and family with Mr. Rawlins in the gallery.

2. Kathleen Courtlander, *Richmond from Kew Green to Ham Common* (London, 1953), p. 89.

Frances Purcell, widow of the composer, who acquired a house in the Royal Manor after her husband's death. She brought the deceased Henry's music manuscripts with her and made her will in the parlour of her last home.

N.B. No documentary substantiation for any of this.

3. Testamentum Nuncupativum Franciscae Purcell. PCC (Somerset House).

7 February, 1706.
Memorandum that Frances Purcell, late of Richmond in the County of Surrey, widow, deceased, did whilst she lived

and being of sound and disposing mind, memory, and understanding, and as she sat in a chair in the parlour of her
dwelling house at Richmond aforesaid, utter and declare her
last Will and Testament nuncupative in the words following
[to wit] She ordered and appointed Mr. Thomas Tovey to be
her executor until Frances Purcell her daughter should attain
the age of eighteen years, and upon her attaining to such age
her said daughter to be her executrix. And that according to
her husband's desire she had given her dear son good education, and she also did give him all the books of music in
general, the organ, the double spinnet, the single spinnet, a
silver tankard, a silver watch, two pair of gold buttons, a
hair ring, a mourning ring of Dr. Busby's, alarum clock, Mr.
Edward Purcell's picture, handsome furniture for a room and
to be maintained until provided for, and all other her estate of
houses, monies, and what she otherwise had she gave to her
said daughter Frances Purcell, which said words or words to
the same effect was uttered and spoken by the said deceased on
Thursday the seventh day of February 1705/6, being then ill
of the sickness of which she soon after died, as and for her last
Will and Testament nuncupative in the presence of us who
have subscribed our names as witnesses thereto whom she
desired to bear witness or take notice of what she said.

Ann Ecles, Ann Pendelton, Amy Howlett
Tertio die mensis Aprilis 1706 dictae Anna Eeles, Anna
Pendelton et Amata Howlett juratae fuerunt super veritate
praemisorum coram me J. Exton Surrogate presente Wal.
Hutchins. N.P.

Probatum fuit [huiusmodi] Testamentum apud London
coram venti viro Georgio Paul Legum Doctore Surrogato
[ventis] et Egregij viri Domini Richardi Raines Militis
Legum etiam Doctoris Curiae Praerogativae Cantuariensis
Magistri custodis sive commissarij legitime constituti Quarto
die mensis Julij Anno Domini Millesime Septinge[simo]
Sexto Juramento Franciscae Purcell Filiae dictae Defunctae et
Executricis in dicto Testamento nominato cui commissa fuit
Administratio omnium et singulorum bonorum jurium et

creditorum dictae Defunctae de bene et fideliter administrando eadem ad sancta Dei Evangelia Jurat. Exam. Calendar
of Grants of Probate and Administration of Commissary
Court of Dean and Chapter of Westminister.

Frances Purcell would have celebrated her eighteenth birthday on
30 May 1706 (see p. 157 above and item x below).

N.B. The Frances Peters whose birth is recorded for 5 Aug. 1669 in
Herbert Westlake's transcription of *The Registers of St. Margaret's,
Westminster* (Harl. Soc. Reg. 64, 1935), p. 90, would have been too young
in 1679–80 to have married the younger Henry Purcell.

4. *Westminster Abbey Registers*, p. 257.

Burials: 14 Feb. 1705/6.

The widow of Mr. Henry Purcell. In the middle of the
north aisle, near his monument.

x FRANCES PURCELL (daughter)

Westminster Abbey Registers, p. 74.

Baptisms: 30 May 1688.

Frances, daughter of Henry and Frances Purcell.

Recorded also at St. Margaret's, Westminster, but under 1 June, which
was probably the date of baptism.

xi FRANCIS PURCELL (cousin)

1. PRO: LC 'Miscellanea', 5/53, fo. 50v.

Francis Purcell, groom of the Privy Chamber to the King,
his warrant dormant ... We will and command you that at
the Feast of the Saints next coming you deliver unto our well-
beloved servant Francis Purcell whom we have appointed to
be one of the grooms of our Privy Chamber in ordinary ...
a livery ... to be received yearly at the Feast of All Saints.
[Warrant dormant 8 August 1673.]

2. Ibid. fo. 155 (*c.* 29 Sept. 1682).

We will and command you that immediately upon sight hereof you pay or cause to be paid unto our trusty and well-beloved servant [a livery] . . . Francis Purcell whom we have appointed to be one other groom of our robes in the place of his father, Thomas Purcell, deceased . . .

3. PRO: LC 'Miscellanea', 5/15, p. 12.

Thomas and Francis Purcell, Somerset House keepers. These are to signify unto you His Majesty's pleasure that you prepare a bill fit for His Majesty's royal signature containing a grant to pay under the Great Seal of England unto Thomas Purcell and Francis Purcell and the larger [*sic*] liver of them of the office and place of under housekeeper, Wardrobe Keeper, and Keeper of the Privy Lodgings of His Majesty's Mansion House called Denmark House, otherwise Somerset House, otherwise Strand House in the Strand in the County of Middlesex, in ordinary without fee until the death, surrender, or avoidance of Henry Brown, now living. And then to have and enjoy the said places . . . with the yearly fee of one hundred and twenty pounds payable out of the Exchequer at the 4 usual feasts . . . 1st April 1674.

4. Ibid. p. 32.

Whereas you have my warrant . . . for the place of House-keeper and Wardrobe keeper of Somerset House to Thomas and Francis Purcell after the death of Henry Browne . . . These are therefore to require you to prepare and dispatch the same notwithstanding any caveat to the contrary, as you will answer to the contrary at your peril, and this shall be your warrant . . . 30th August 1674.

5. PRO: LC 'Miscellanea', 5/86, p. 1.

Liveries and fees payable out of His Majesty's Great Wardrobe this current year, to end at Michaelmas 1675 . . .
At the Feast of All Saints:

Grooms of the Privy Chamber Assistant to the King

Richard Burns	£40	0	6
Francis Purcell	£40	0	6

Officers of the Robes to the King

Thomas Purcell, Groom   £40

6. Charles Dalton, *English Army Lists and Commission Registers 1661–1714*, vol. I, pp. 204 and 255.

King's Own Regiment of Dragoons: Cornet, Francis Purcell, Feb. 19th, 1678.

Francis Purcell, Cornet, June 11th, 1679.

7. PRO: *Cal. Tr. Books*, 26 June 1679.

£37. 15s. 0d. to Francis Purcell in full of all pay due to him as Cornet of Dragoons, under Captain Edmund Chaffin.

8. *Cal. Tr. Books*, 27 June 1679.

Cornet Francis Purcell disbanded. Order No. 769.

9. PRO: S. P. Dom. Entry Books (S.P. 44) 51, p. 313.

Whereas we have been often petitioned by the grooms assistant of our Privy Chamber concerning the disputes that have arisen about their succeeding into the places of our six grooms-in-ordinary for the determination whereof we referred the same unto you, our Chamberlain of our Household, who have certified us, that since our Restoration the grooms assistant have always succeeded to be grooms-in-ordinary upon vacancies, according to their seniority of being sworn into those places. Our will and pleasure therefore is for the settlement hereof for the future, that the present 3 grooms of our Privy Chamber assistant, by name James Davis, Francis Purcell, and St. John Mitton [or Milton] shall succeed and be admitted by you . . . into the places of the six grooms-in-ordinary upon any vacancies . . . given at our Court at Whitehall the 11th day of February 1679 [1679/80] in the 32nd year of our reign.

By His Majesty's Command. H.C.

10. PRO: Pipe Office Declared Account (E 351) 2836: 'Account of Henry Sidney, Esq. to Charles II from Annunciation, 1681–2', fo. 4*v*.

Shoes, viz. for wearing shoes, tennis shoes, galoshes, boots and buskins, and for livery boots for Gilbert Spencer, David Graham, Francis Purcell, Gervaise Price, James Gibbons, and Tobias Rustat: £122. 4. 0

11. PRO: H.O. Warrant Book 5, p. 51.

Passes for Francis Purcell and his servant James Boyce to go to Harwich for Holland and Flanders.

12. *Cal. S. P. Dom.* 30 June 1696.

Passes for Mr. Charles More, Robert Bolney, William Holforth, Richard Hunt and Francis Purcell to go from Gravesend to Portugal on the recommendation of Richard Purcell.

XII THE ELDER HENRY PURCELL (father)

For the Westminster Abbey Precentor's record of Henry Purcell's installation at the Abbey, see p. 8 above.

For Pepys's account of meeting a 'Mr. Purcell, Master of Music', see pp. 6–7 above.

1. D'Avenant, Sir William, *The Siege of Rhodes* made a representation by the art of prospective [*sic*] in scenes, and the story sung in recitative music, etc. (British Museum, 644.d.68. Pub. London, 1656; another edition, both parts, 1663).

	The Story Personated	
Solyman	(Captain Henry Cook)	
Villerious	{ Mr. Gregory Thorndel and Mr. Dubartus Hunt }	Double parted
Alphonso	{ Mr. Edward Coleman and Mr. *Roger Hill* }	Double parted
Admiral	{ Mr. *Matthew Lock* and Mr. *Peter Ryman* }	Double parted

Pirrhus	{ Mr. *John Harding* and Mr. Alphonso Marsh }	Double parted
Mustapha	{ Mr. *Thomas Blagrave* and Mr. *Henry Purcell* }	Double parted
Ianthe	{ Mrs. Coleman, Wife to Mr. *Edward Coleman* }	Double parted

The composition of Vocal Music
was performed

The { First Entry / Second Entry / Third Entry / Fourth Entry / Fifth Entry } by { Mr. *Henry Lawes* / Capt. *Henry Cook* / Capt. *Henry Cook* / Mr. *Matthew Lock* / Mr. *Henry Lawes* }

The Instrumental Music was composed by
Dr. *Charles Coleman*, and Mr. *George Hudson*.
The Instrumental Music
is performed

by { Mr. *William Webb* / Mr. *Christopher Gibbons* [sic] / Mr. *Humphrey Madge* / Mr. *Thomas Balser*, a German, / Mr. *Thomas Baites* / Mr. *John Banister* }

2. WAM 33695 (Treasurer's Account, 1661).

fo. 1*v*. Payment to Henry Purcell of £10. 0. 0. as *cantator in choro*.

fo. 2. Payment to Henry Purcell of £7. 5. 0. as Master of the Choristers.

fo. 4*v*. Paid to Mr. Pursell for the Choristers' dinner for three quarters of a year ending Michaelmas 1661, at £5 per annum: £3. 15. 0.

fo. 5. To Henry Purcell for books of services for the choristers £1. 0. 0.

Such payments recur in 1662, 1663, and 1664 more or less regularly. See his signatures for these on folios 15, 48, 48*v*, 19*v*, 50, etc.

3. St. Margaret's, Westminster, Register of Baptisms, fo. 145.
13 March 1661/2.

Katherine, the daughter of Mr. Henry Purcell, was baptized.

4. *KM*, p. 151. (14 Nov. 1662.)

... and Henry Purcell [appointed] musician-in-ordinary for lute and voice in the same place with Angelo Notari.

5. *KM*, p. 151. (15 Nov. 1662.)

Warrant to admit Angelo Notari and Henry Purcell musicians-in-ordinary for the lutes and voices, with the yearly wages of £40, to commence from St. John Baptist 1660.

6. *KM*, p. 165. (10 Dec. 1663.)

[In list of] Gentlemen of the Chapel Royal.

7. *Cal. Tr. Books*, 27 Feb. 1663/4.

Money warrant dormant for the wages and fee of £40 per annum to Henry Pursell (Pussell) for his office and place of musician-in-ordinary to the King for the lute and voice.

8. J. P. Malcolm, *Londinium Redivivum* (1802–7), vol. 1, p. 246 (from the accounts of the Treasurer of Westminster Abbey for 1664).

Cantatoribus in choro pro stipend 'et regard'. Thomas Hazard, John Harding, Christopher Chapman, Henry Purcell, Edward Braddock, William Hatton, Owen Adamson, Thomas Hughes, Richard Mabler, Thomas Shorter, Thomas Carey, and Thomas Finnell. (£8 and 40s. each.)

9. *KM*, p. 170. (20 August 1664.)

John Goodgroome appointed to the Private Music for the lutes, viol, and voices, in the place of Henry Purcell.

(See also *Cal. S. P. Dom.* 28 Nov. 1664.)

10. *Cheque-book*, p. 13.

Mr. Henry Purcell, one of His Majesty's Gentlemen of the Chapel, died the eleventh day of August 1664, in whose place came Mr. Thomas Richardson.

11. *Cheque-book*, p. 212.

Rimbault quotes the following document, of which a copy was in his possession:

These are to certify that Mr. Henry Purcell, who succeeded Segnor Angello in his place of the Private Music; that the said Mr. Henry Purcell took possession of his place in the year 1663, upon St. Thomas's Day; deceased the 11th August 1664:

<table>
<tr><td rowspan="5">There are to certify
the death of Mr.
Henry Purcell</td><td>Henry Cooke</td></tr>
<tr><td>Tho. Purcell</td></tr>
<tr><td>Alfonso Marsh</td></tr>
<tr><td>Gregory Thorndale</td></tr>
<tr><td>Edward Colman</td></tr>
</table>

12. PRO: Patent Roll C66/3009.

Charles the Second . . . to the Treasurer and Undertreasurer of our Exchequer . . . Whereas upon the humble request of Angelo Notari, one of the musicians-in-ordinary for the lute and voice, of [*sic*] his inabilities to execute that employment without an assistant, we have been graciously pleased in consideration of service done and to be done unto us, have given and granted . . . unto the said Angelo Notari and Henry Purcell, whom we have nominated his assistant, the said office and place of musician-in-ordinary to us for the lute and voice with the former annuity, wages and fee of forty pounds per annum . . . To have and enjoy the said office and place of musician to us as aforesaid during their lives and the longer liver of them . . . the first payment to commence from the Feast of St. John Baptist which was in the year of our Lord 1660 . . .

13. *Cal. Tr. Books*, 20 May 1668.

Money warrant for £46. 10. 10 to Hannah, daughter of Clement Lanier [and for various other widows, orphans, and other dependants of deceased musicians, including an account for] £20. 0. 0 to Elizabeth, relict of Henry Purcell.

14. *Westminster Abbey Registers*, p. 161.

Burials: 13. Aug. 1664.

Mr. Henry Purcell, one of the Gentlemen of the King's Chapel, and Master of the Children of this church; in the east cloister.

According to *Westminster Abbey Registers* his estate was dministered 7 Oct. 1664 by his widow; see also VIII: Elizabeth Purcell.

15. *Westminster Public Library, Westminster Account Book and Calendar*, no. 5 (1664–6), vol. v, p. 55.

Henrici Pursell: Septimo die mensis Octobris
          Adco   1664⁰

Comiss fuit Dio monis et singularit bonor Jurium et creditum Henrici Purcell misi que Sta. Margareta in Civitate Westm. defunct Elizabethae Pursell vid Relice erit Qef-do bene et fide & jurat et salvo Jure & Jurem ejtum XX^{to} iii^b.

16. WAM 61228A (Precentor's Book, 1660–71), unfoliated pages at end.

Burials: 13 Aug. 1664.

Mr Henry Purcell, one of the Gentlemen of His Majesty's Chapel Royal and master of boys of Westminster, was buried in the great cloisters near Mr. Lawes.

N.B. The signature of one 'Henry Purcell' in the front cover of the Sion Library copy of *The Faith, Doctrine, and Religion Professed and Protected in the Realm of England ... thirty-nine Articles* (London, 1661: press mark A57.3/R63(2)) may be that of Henry Purcell the elder. However, the signature is so painstakingly copied that it is difficult to identify it with the various specimens in Westminster accounts, despite such similar features as the backward 'e', the old inverse 'r' and the very similar capital 'H'.

For other documents relating to the elder Henry Purcell already quoted in the text, see pp. 6 and 10 above.

XIII THE YOUNGER HENRY PURCELL

1. Anthony à Wood, Oxford, Bodleian, MS. Wood D 19(9) (S.C. 8568–9).

Born in London — He, Dr. Child, and Dr. Blow all organists to King William and Queen Mary.

PURCELL, HENRY, originally one of the Children in the King's Chapel. Bred under Dr. Chr. Gibbons, I think, afterwards organist to King Charles 2nd, J[ames II, and] William III. Organist at St. Peter's Church at Westminster.

He and John Blow..chief authors of the second part of *Harmonia Sacra*.   [fo. 104]

His sonatas à 3 = See Dr. B. Rogers' sonatas in 4 parts. See Playford's account: catalogue 11.4.a and *bis*.   [fo. 104*v*]

[Under entry for John Blow]: Dr. Rogers tells me that John Blow was born in London, and that he, Henry Purcell, and Dr. William Child are organists to King William and Queen Mary, and . . .   [fo. 22]

He [B. Rogers] said that John Playford died 1687 . . . soon after a Pastoral Elegy was made on his death; to which musical notes were set in two parts by Mr. Henry Purcell — printed in one sheet folio. Dr. Rogers has it.   [fo. 101]

Purcell, Hen. living.   [fo. 146: Table of Contents]

2. PRO: LC 'Miscellanea', 5/86 [isolated section in middle of book, paged 1–8], pp. 1 and 3.

Ch. R: Musicians and Feasts
Great Wardrobe Anno R.R. Ch. II. 27.
Liveries and fees payable out of His Majesty's Great Wardrobe this current year to end at Michaelmas 1675.
[Selections from lists:]

		£	s.	d.
At the Feast of All Saints				
Grooms of the Privy Chamber assistant to the King {	Richard Binns	040	0	6
	Francis Purcell	040	0	6

Officers of the Robes to the King	Lancelott Thornton, Clerk	040
	Tobias Rustat, yeoman	040
	Tobias Rustat more	040
	Thomas Purcell, Groom	040
	Paul fferine, Groom	040
	James Watson, Groom	040
	Robert Rustat, Groom	040
	Thomas Bocock	040

At the Feast of St. Andrew

Erasures and names written alongside reproduced as they appear; the second set of names is in a different hand, as is 'junior' after John Bannister.

	£ s. d.
~~Lewis Grabu~~ Master of the Music,	
Dr. Staggins	16 2 6
~~Thomas Purcell~~ John Goodwyn	16 2 6
Anthony Roberts	16 2 6
~~John Hingston~~ Robert Carr	16 2 6
William Gregory	16 2 6
~~Thomas Purcell~~ Nathaniell ffrench	16 2 6
Musicians ~~Humphrey Madge~~ Jeoffrey Aleworth	16 2 6
Thomas Lanier	16 2 6
~~John Smyth~~ Francis Cryne	16 2 6
John Gamble	16 2 6
~~John Jenkins~~ John Mosse	16 2 6
~~John Lilley~~ Edmund fflower	16 2 6
*John Harding John Bowman	16 2 6
John Bannister junr	16 2 6
Edward Hooton	16 2 6
*Mathew Lock Henry Purcell	16 2 6
~~Thomas Bates~~ William Gregory	16 2 6
~~Alphonso Marsh~~ John Abell	16 2 6 etc.

3. Thomas Ford, Bodleian, MS. Mus.e.17, 'An account of Musicians & their works . . .', folios 39v and 40.

Here lies Hen. Purcell, Esq., who left this life and is gone to that blessed place where only his harmony can be excelled. obb. 21. Nov. 1695.

Purcell, Henry. Son of Hen: Purcell, Gent. of Chapel, who died Aug. 11, 1664, scholar to Dr. Blow and to Dr. Christopher Gibbons, Master of the Children and organist to Charles II and William III and organist of St. Peter's, Westminster. He died Nov. 21, 1695.

N.B. The phrase 'Master of the Children' cannot apply to Gibbons or to the younger Henry Purcell, and so must apply either to Blow, who was Master of the Children of the Chapel Royal to Charles II, or to the elder Henry Purcell, who was Master of the Choristers at Westminster Abbey.

4. PRO: LC 'Miscellanea', 5/64, fo. 83.

Clothes for a Chapel boy whose voice is changed. These are to signify unto you His Majesty's pleasure, that you provide and deliver, or cause to be delivered, unto Henry Purcell, late one of the Children of His Majesty's Chapel Royal, whose voice is changed and is gone from the Chapel, two suits of plain cloth, two hats and hat-bands, four whole shirts, four half shirts, six bands, six pair of cuffs, six handkerchiefs, four pair of stockings, four pair of shoes, and four pair of gloves. (17th Dec. 1673.)

5. WAM Treasurers' Accounts.

33709 (1675), fo. 5:
To Henry Pursel for tuning the Organ   .   .   £2. 0. 0

33710 (1676), fo. 5v:
To Henry Purcell for pricking out two books of
organ parts £5. 0. 0

33712 (1677), fo. 5:
To Henry Purcell for tuning the organs   .   .   £2. 0. 0

33713 (1678), fo. 5:
[The same entry.]

33714 (1679), fo. 4:
[For an account of Purcell's scholarship at St. Peter's College, see pp. 52–56.]

33715 (1680), fo. 2:
Organistae: Et in Denarijs Solutis Henrico
   Purcell £10. 0. 0

33716 (1681), folios 2 and 5:
[The same entry.]
To the organist in lieu of a house . . . £8. 0. 0

33717 (1682), *passim* and fo. 5:
[The same entries.]
Paid for writing Mr. Purcell's service and
   anthems £0. 30. 0

33718–20 (1683–5), *passim*:
[Similar entries.]

33721 (1687), fo. 5*v*:
Paid Mr. Purcell one quarter's rent for his house
   due Christmas 1686 . . . . . . £0. 40. 0

33722 (1688), folios 2 and 5*v*:
Et in de denar Solutis Heno Purcell . . £10. 0. 0
To Mr. Purcell the organist in lieu of a house . £8. 0. 0
Paid Mr. Purcell for making the service books . £0. 58. 6

33723 (1689), folios 2*v* and 5*v*:
Et in denar solutis Henro Purcell . . £10. 0. 0
Paid Mr. Purcell the organist in lieu of a house . £8. 0. 0

33724–8 (1690–4), *passim*:
[Similar entries.]

For an account of Purcell's judging the organ at St. Katherine Cree, London, see pp. 136–9.

6. St. Katherine Cree, Churchwarden's Accounts, 1650–91.
1686/7: List of Subscribers.

An account of the moneys given, received, and paid for the erecting an organ and building a gallery in the parish church of St. Katherine Cree. £124. £77. £80. £44. received many subscriptions of £11. £105, 5, 6, 2, 1 etc.

Payments.

Paid Mr. Bernard Smith for making the organ as contract
£250. 0. 0

Paid various sums for gallery £65 etc.

Spent on Mr. Pursell and Mr. Smith 14/-

Paid coach hire for Dr. Blowe and Mr. Pursell 5/-

For curtains and curtain rings £1. 18. 4d.

Altogether, a sum of £355. 11. 3d. was paid out.

For an account of Purcell's reimbursement of funds paid for repairing
the organs, etc. in the Chapel Royal, see p. 144 above.

7. Testamentum Henrici Purcell. PCC: 243 Irby (Somerset
House). Dec. 1695.

In the name of God Amen. I, Henry Purcell, of the City of
Westminster, gentleman, being dangerously ill as to the
constitution of my body, but in good and perfect mind and
memory (thanks be to God) do by these presents publish and
declare this to be my last Will and Testament. And I do
hereby give and bequeath unto my loving wife, Frances
Purcell, all my estate both real and personal of what nature
and kind soever, to her and to her assigns for ever. And I do
hereby constitute and appoint my said loving wife my sole
executrix of this my last Will and Testament, revoking all
former Will or Wills, witness my hand and seal this twenty-
first day of November, Annoque Domini one thousand six
hundred ninety five. And in the seventh year of the reign of
King William the Third &c. H. Purcell.

Signed, sealed, published, and declared by the said Henry Purcell
in the presence of William Eeles, John Chapelin, J. B. Peters.

Probatum fuit [huiusmodi] Testamentum apud London
coram venerabili viro Willelmo Oldys Legum Doctore
Surrogato [venerabilis] et egregij viri Domini Richardi Raines
Militis Legum etiam Doctoris Curiae Praerogativae Cantua-
rensis Magistri Custodis sive Commissarij legitime constituti
septimo die mensis Decembris Anno Domini millesimo
sexcentimo nonagesimo quinto Juramento Franciscae Purcell

Relictae dicti defuncti et Executricis in dicto Testamento nominato cui commissa fuit administracio omnium et singulorum
bonorum jurium et creditorum dicti defuncti de bone et
fideliter administrand[um] eadem ad sancta Dei Evangelia
Jurat[a]. Ex.

8. *Cal. S. P. Dom.* 6 July 1702.

Thomas Tudway.

Ever since the Reformation there have been three organists
belonging to the Chapel Royal, to attend that duty by turns.
The petitioner was bred up in that Chapel, and had a promise
in '82 from King Charles II that he should have the next place
which fell vacant. This occurred when Mr. Purcell died in
1696 [*sic*]; but his place has never been filled. Prays for it.

9. Anonymous. *Orpheus Britannicus*, book 1, 3rd ed. (London,
1721).

'ANOTHER ODE ON THE SAME OCCASION,
BY A PERSON OF QUALITY'*

Accord thy blessing to my bold design,
Thou best inspirer of harmonious grief;
Thou, who among the tuneful Nine,
In mournful melody art chief.
In music, wing'd with sighs, I soar,
A second Orpheus to deplore;
Second in time, but first in fame;
To him blind fiction gave a name.
The truthless tales, which frantic poets tell
Of Thebes, and moving stones, and journeys down to Hell,
Were only prophecies of music's force, which we
Have wonderfully seen fulfill'd in thee.
What mortal harmony cou'd do
No mortal ever knew,
Till thy transcendent genius came
Whose strength surpass'd the praises of poetic flame:
Whose raptures will for ever want a name.

* See Dryden's 'Mark how the lark', no. 17 below.

Out of thy orb a while
(Content to wander here below)
Thou did'st vouchsafe to bless our Isle,
(With high commands from heav'n for ought we know)
To try seditious jars to reconcile.
But discord in a frightful form,
With all her retinue of war,
The drum, the pulpit, and the bar,
The croaking crowds' tumultuous noise,
And ev'ry hoarse outlandish voice,
Proclaim'd so loud th'impending storm,
That frighted hence, thou didst for refuge fly,
To reassume thy station in the sky:
There heavenly carols to compose and sing,
To heaven's harmonious King.
Where rapt in transports of ecstatic song,
Amidst th'inspir'd seraphic throng,
Crown'd with celestial ever-blooming bays,
Thou sitt'st dissolv'd in *Hallelujahs*.

10. Anonymous. 'To his esteemed friend, Dr. Blow, upon pub-
    lishing his book of songs, *Amphion Anglicus*', p. iii.

    (Beginning 'Amphion's lute of old with magic art'.)

        .   .   .   .   .

        Thus has our isle been long oblig'd by Blow
        Who first with decent modesty did show
        In blooming Purcell what himself cou'd do.
        On Purcell his whole genius he bestow'd,
        And all the Master's graces in the pupil flow'd;
        But he unable long to bear the load,
        Opprest with rapture, sunk beneath the god.
        Home then the welcome deity returns,
        And Blow again with youthful transports burns.
                                Whitehall, 20 May 1700

11. Anonymous. *Harmonia Sacra*, book II, 3rd ed. (1726).

        Music and verse have been abus'd too long,
        Idly to furnish out some wanton song;

To varnish vice, to make loose folly shine,
And gild the vain delights of love, or wine:
Both heav'nly-born, but both constrain'd to fall
So far below their great original,
The erring world, not knowing how to trace
Thro' vile employments their celestial race,
Suppos'd their birth was, as their office, base.
Rescu'd by you, they have again put on
Those glorious rays with which at first they shone;
Assert their native honour; and excite,
With awful pleasure, rev'rence and delight:
Here no loud rant, no wild ungovern'd strain,
Invokes plump Bacchus, and his sordid train;
Here no fond couplet kindles am'rous fires,
No melting note gives birth to loose desires:
Each air, each line, which in this work appear,
Angels may fitly sing, and saints may hear.
Go on my friend; set sacred music free
From scandal, and move sacred poetry:
Publish'd by you, with double grace they shine,
Lovely and grave, harmonious and divine.

By an unknown hand

12. Anonymous. 'A Poem Occasioned on the Death of Mr. Henry Purcell, late Musician-in-Ordinary to His Majesty. Quocunque choros agitat mors Musica dormit.' *Bat.* [*sic.*] By a Lover of Music. (London, 1695), with a note added in a contemporary hand: '18. Decemb.' in the copy in the Yale University Library: K/Foxwell/ 26835d.

I

Ye gentle spheres
Cease now your wonted melody,
Rest and ever silent be —
Nought now remains for comfort or relief,
But a free vent to our just source of grief.
An untaught groan best language is,

For such a dismal scene as this.
Yet like our dying swans you first may tell,
In softest music to attending ears,
How the lov'd Strephon liv'd, and how lamented fell:
Tell then th'admiring world how often he,
Has ev'n charm'd you to extasie,
How oft you've envy'd at the praise he won,
Yet smil'd to see yourselves outdone.
Tell this in different notes, in such as he,
Was used to charm us here below, that make one Harmony.

II

The little birds throughout the plains,
Repeat their notes in doleful strain.
In doleful strains they all complain
As if they never were to sing again.
Sad Philomel amongst the rest
As if some story she'd relate,
Not of her own but of her master's cruel Fate.
In mournful notes her grief exprest,
In careless melancholy lays
She sung his praise.
Now all her art she tries,
Now all her strength applies,
To warble forth an elegy
Sacred to his memory.
She sings, alas her songs are all in vain,
Nothing can alter destiny,
The swain can ne'er return to life again.

III

What do I hear, what dismal groans,
What sighs, what shrieks, what melancholy moans,
Now spread themselves o'er all the pensive plains,
And tears the breasts of all the tender swains,
'Tis for Strephon dead and gone.

Mourn all ye shepherds, mourn with me your master's fate.
With me attend his funeral,
With me adorn his hearse
With never fading garland, never dying verse.
Alas! no sounds will now prevail,
To tell their melancholy tale,
Since dead he is who made their songs to live,
He their dull numbers could inspire,
With charming voice, and tuneful lyre,
He life to all but to himself could give.
No longer now the swains unto each other play,
Their arms across, their heads hung down,
Their oaten pipes, beside them thrown,
Their flocks neglected stray,
Ev'n Pan himself o'erwhelm'd with grief has thrown his pipe
    away.

IV

See Love himself all bath'd in tears,
His bow he breaks, away his dart he flings,
Then folds his arms and hangs his drooping wings,
Venus herself close mourner here appears.
No longer now she thinks herself secure,
But sighing from her throne looks down,
Her greatness cannot long endure
Since its supporter's dead and gone;
Since that the tuneful Strephon's fall'n —
Now silent lies his lyre,
No longer warms our hearts into desire,
For dead is he who could our passions move,
Who best could gentle thoughts inspire,
Who best could fan the amorous fire,
Make us at once submit and own the pow'r of love.

V

Gone is the glory of our Age,
The pride and darling of the stage

The theatre his worth well knew,
Saw how by him its greatness grew.
In him their honour, pride and glory liv'd,
For as his soul they now are fled,
And scarce can sooner be retriev'd,
For all their hopes in him are dead.
Whilst he vouchsaf'd to stay below
They were too blest long to continue so.
But oh! no more the tuneful Strephon's songs they'll hear,
No more his joyful notes will glad the wond'ring theatre.

VI

Ye sons of Phoebus, write his elegy
But let it be
Great as the subject, sad as your calamity,
Let every Muse his praise aloud proclaim,
And to the distant poles, let Echo spread his fame.
Write epitaphs that so
The world may know,
How much to him ev'n poetry did owe,
For you but say, 'tis he that makes you sing,
His Art the embryo words to perfection bring.
By us the Muse at first conceives, 'tis true,
He makes it fit to see the light, that gift to him we owe:
Naked at first, and rugged they appear,
But when by him adorn'd they be,
Assume a pomp and bravery,
Nor need they longer blush to reach a Prince's ear.

VII

How rigid are the laws of fate,
And how severe the black decree,
For nothing, nothing here is free,
But all must enter th'Adamantine gate.
The great, the good, the just, nay all must come,
To Nature's dark retiring room.
He! he! alas is gone,

Whose gentle airs did make our numbers live,
Who immortality could give,
His soul to 'ts first abode is flown,
Blasted are all our glories now,
Our laurels wither as they grow,
The Muse herself forsakes us too.
Come then, come quickly come,
Let's pay our tears for off'rings at his tomb.
Let us not strive who best deserves the bays,
He that grieves most best claims the highest praise.

VIII

Arise, ye blest inhabitants above,
From your immortal seats arise,
And on our wonder, on our love,
Gaze with astonish'd eyes;
Arise, arise, make room,
The wish'd for shade is come;
Haste, and yourselves prepare
To me [sic] the joyful chorister,
Meet him halfway with songs, such as you sing
Before the throne of the Eternal King,
With welcomes let th'aetherial palace ring,
Welcome the guardian angel says,
Full of songs and full of bays,
Welcome thou art to me,
And to these regions of serenity;
Welcome the winged choir resounds,
While with loud Fugues all the sacred place abounds
Lo now above he chants eternal lays
Above our wonder and our praise.

FINIS

13. (?)Rev. J. Bowen. *Orpheus Britannicus*, book 1, 2nd ed. (1706)
[U.C.L.A. Library 'Seminar Room' M 1616.P97.0 (on flyleaf
in contemporary hand) with 'Rev. J. Bowen' written on front
cover].

z

Great soul of music, if we right devine
Thy wondrous worth, thou of the muses nine
Art diapason, harmony divine.
Shown to the world, to teach them how to sing
Then summon'd to attend the heavenly choirs
Thy harp the seraphs with new mirth inspires
Who in thy strains hymn the eternal King.

14. Tom Brown. *Harmonia Sacra*, book II, 1st ed. (1693).

To HIS UNKNOWN FRIEND, MR. HENRY PURCELL, UPON
HIS EXCELLENT COMPOSITIONS IN THE FIRST AND
SECOND BOOKS OF *Harmonia Sacra*

Long had dark ignorance our Isle o'erspread,
Our music and our poetry lay dead:
But the dull malice of a barb'rous age,
Fell most severe on David's sacred page;
To wound his sense, and quench his heav'n-born fire,
Three dull translators lewdly did conspire.
In holy dogg'rel and low-chiming prose;
The king and poet they at once depose.
Vainly he did th'unrighteous change bemoan,
And languish'd in vile numbers not his own:
Nor stop'd his usage here ——
For what escap'd in wisdom's ancient rhymes,
Was murder'd o'er and o'er by the composer's chimes.
    What praises, Purcell, to thy skill are due;
Who hast to Judah's monarch been so true?
By thee he moves our hearts, by thee he reigns,
By thee shakes off his old inglorious chains,
And sees new honours done to his immortal strains.

Not Italy, the mother of each art,
Did e'er a juster, happier son impart.
In thy performance we with wonder find
Bassani's genius to Corelli's joyn'd.
Sweetness combin'd with majesty, prepares
To raise devotion with inspiring airs.

Thus I unknown my gratitude express,
And conscious gratitude could pay no less.
This tribute from each British Muse is due,
Our whole poetic tribe's oblig'd to you.
For where the author's scanty words have fail'd,
Your happier graces, Purcell, have prevail'd.
And surely none but you with equal ease
Could add to David, and make D'Urfey please.*

15. From the *Diverting Post*, for February 1706. (Burney Coll.,
vol. 131b.)

THE FORCE OF MUSIC: TO THE MEMORY OF THE LATE FAMOUS
HENRY PURCELL, A PINDARIC ODE

While tow'ring with seraphic wings,
    The mighty Purcell heights unknown explores,
Sublime on music's force he upward springs,
    Till to divinity he soars.
Mankind lies ravish't with his lays,
And all in vain attempts his praise;
Still while our grov'ling thoughts aspire
To reach the raptures we admire;
We but degrade the name we meant to raise.
    Boundless and free thy numbers move
    With native fury fir'd;
And with diffusive raptures rove
    By none but thy great self inspir'd,
The gods themselves, thy lays attend,
To thee their ravisht ears they bend.
A while their heav'nly rapture they decline,
And tune their own imperfect notes by thine.
Now godlike Nassaw feels thy sov'reign power,
And conquests o'er his soul, unknown before:
    Prostrate the vanquish't Hero lies,
And with each vary'd note unwillingly complies.

* Cf. Cummings, p. 83, for a version published in the *Gentleman's Journal*,
June 1693, which differs from the above in several details.

2

See, see, the mighty Purcell comes,
(Sound the trumpets beat the drums)
He leaves his triumphs in the skies
    Attempts a greater prize.
Th'angelic choir his absence mourn,
Repeat past joys and long for his return,
High in seraphic state he stands,
And with insulting force, the pliant hero bends.
His song began with Dioclesian's fame,
The trembling notes resound his mighty name.
And to the list'ning world his glorious deeds proclaim;
    Descending angels crowd around,
    And join their heav'nly lays!
The vaulted roofs improve the sound,
    And propagate his praise.
When to redeem a sinking world,
    The daring hero rose,
Around his scatter'd rage he hurl'd,
    And quell'd his numerous foes.
In vain conspiring nations join,
In vain oppose his bold design;
Himself alone subdu'd their weaker aid,
Himself alone reveng'd the injur'd maid,
And from th'insulting monarch's brow pull'd down the
    violated shade.

3

Nor earth nor sea can stop his course,
Nor Tyber's more impetuous force,
    When swelling with its weight,
Around the mighty ruin lay,
And men and arms promiscuous fill'd the way,
    And thwart his envy'd fate.
Unmov'd the dauntless hero view'd
Millions of foes and fought and swam in blood.
    Widely he dealt destruction round,

And hew'd his dreadful passage down,
And cut his mangled way and clove the purple flood.
In Virtue's just defence he rose,
And gave the troubled world repose,
At once their peace and freedom he restor'd
While grateful nations in return obey'd,
Obey'd their just, their rightful lord.
And gave him but the laurels he had won, the conquests he
      had made,
A present Dioclesian all resound;
A present Dioclesian all the vaulted roofs rebound,
The trembling strings untoucht repeat the name and swell his
      praise around,
Sooth'd with the sound the monarch rose,
To troubled nations gave a fresh repose,
And thrice he swam the Boyne and thrice he slew his foes.

4

The mighty Purcell smil'd to see
The wondrous force of harmony;
Chang'd his hand, left the lyre,
Checkt his rage and kindled softer fire.
    The mournful flute he chose
    Soft passion to infuse
    Such as parting lovers use
Such as lab'ring sighs disclose,
Such as Maria's death requires, as reaches all our woes.
    Maria's harder fate he sung,
    Maria fair and young,
In bloom of youth and beauty's pride,
Snatch'd from the trembling monarch's side,
While panting in his arms she lay,
And in soft kisses breath'd her soul away.
In vain the hero rushes to her aid,
Alas! a stronger power does invade;
With all the laurels thou hast won,
And level with the common dust, an undistinguisht shade,

The breathing notes unwillingly complain,
 And gently tell th'unwelcome news around;
Bemoaning Echo imitates in vain,
 And falters in the sound.
With down-cast eyes the monarch view'd
 All his flatt'ring hopes destroy'd,
Afresh her image he renew'd,
 Afresh his tears employ'd.
To heav'n again the tuneful conqu'ror flies,
Resumes his triumphs in the skies,
There to the blest seraphic choir
 Relates the conquest of his lays;
His wondrous skill they all admire,
And through the vocal heav'ns resound his praise.
 Th'unwelcome news Maria heard,
Much for her vanquish't lord she fear'd,
Yet knew no human force cou'd him confine,
 Nor less than harmony divine.
Much she enquires of things below,
And longs to hear her lov'd Britannia's state;
 At that the tears began to flow,
(Tears such as angels shed if they can sorrows know)
And with indulgent grief she mourn'd, th'unhappy
  Gloucester's Fate.

GRAND CHORUS

 Meanwhile th'angelic choir prepare,
To rear him trophies, and reward his care,
His brows with myrtle wreaths they bound,
(So shou'd his vast desert be crown'd)
And through the wond'ring skies aloft the conqu'ror bear.
Around his triumphs they proclaim,
 And with his conquests swell the mouth of fame.
Henceforth let Purcell and Nassau be prais'd,
Or Nassau yield the crown,
A sinking world the monarch rais'd
 He pull'd that monarch down.

16. Henry Carey, 'The Poet's Resentment', *Poems on Several Occasions* (1729).

> Ev'n heaven-born Purcell now is held in scorn,
> Purcell who did a brighter age adorn ...

17. John Dryden. *Orpheus Britannicus*, book II, 3rd ed. (1721), p. iv.

AN ODE ON THE DEATH OF MR. HENRY PURCELL
BY MR. DRYDEN

I

Mark how the lark and linnet sing,
With rival notes
They strain their warbling throats,
To welcome in the Spring.
But in the close of night,
When Philomel begins her heav'nly lay,
They cease their mutual spite,
Drink in her music with delight,
And list'ning and silent, and silent and list'ning, and list'ning
    and silent obey.

II

So ceas'd the rival crew when Purcell came,
They sung no more, or only sung his fame.
Struck dumb, they all admir'd the godlike man:
   The godlike man
Alas! too soon retir'd,
   As he too late began.
We beg not hell our Orpheus to restore;
   Had he been there,
   Their sov'reign's fear
   Had sent him back before.
The pow'r of harmony too well they knew,
He long ere this had tun'd their jarring sphere,
   And left no hell below.

III

The heavenly choir, who heard his notes from high,
Let down the scale of music from the sky:
 They handed him along
And all the way he taught, and all the way they sung.
 Ye brethren of the lyre, and tuneful voice,
 Lament his lot, but at your own rejoice.
 Now live secure and linger out your days,
 The gods are pleas'd alone with Purcell's lays,
 Nor know to mend their choice.

(This ode is set to music by Dr. Blow, and may be bound up with this collection.)

18. John Gilbert. *Orpheus Britannicus*, book 1, 3rd ed., p. v. The following lines were design'd for Mr. Purcell's monument; which being supply'd by a better hand, the author of this inscription, in veneration to the memory of that great master, prefixes it to his golden remains.

> *Memoriae Sacrum H.P.*
> En ! marmor loquax
> (Vix, heu ! prae dolore)
> Lacrymas stillatim sudat;
> Manes Purcelli sacros,
> Quisquis es, viator,
> Siste ac venerare.
> Eheu ! quam subito orbis harmonici
> Procubuit columen !
> Angliacus ille Amphion, Orpheus, Apollo,
> Deus Harmoniae Italo-Anglus,
> Certe Corellius;
> Artis musicae
> Perquam difficilis
> Facile Coryphaeus.
> Per acuta musicae victor ibat ovans.
> Et placida animam compede alligavit.
> Eheu ! quam brevi

Praecox marcescit ingenium!
Invida quippe natura juvenem,
Arte senescentem, corripuit.
At — desine tandem,
Miserantis quaerimoniae:
Non omnis moritur,
Vivunt symphoniae immortales.
Angelorum chori Purcellum stipantes,
Nectaris immemores,
Mellitiores istos bibunt aure sonos:
Et plaudentes recinunt.
Vivent, in aeternum
Aeternumque placebunt.
Abi, viator, &, si musicus, aemulare:
Sed calcibus humum leviter preme,
Ne nascentes atteras rosas.

Johannes Gilbert A. M. Coll. Christ. Cantab.

19. R.G. *Orpheus Britannicus*, book II, 3rd ed., p. i.

ON THE DEATH OF THE LATE FAMOUS MR. HENRY PURCELL,
AUTHOR OF THE FIRST AND SECOND BOOKS OF
Orpheus Britannicus

Make room ye happy natives of the sky,
Room for a soul, all love and harmony;
A soul that rose to such perfection here,
It scarce will be advanc'd by being there.
Whether (to us by transmigration given)
He once was an inhabitant of heav'n,
And form'd for music, with diviner fire
Endu'd, compos'd for the celestial choir;
Not for the vulgar race of light to hear,
But on high-days to glad th'immortal ear.
So in some leisure hour was sent away,
(Their hour is here a life, a thousand years their day)
Sent what th'aetherial music was to show,
And teach the wonders of that art below.

Whether this might not be, the muse appeals
To his composures, where such magic dwells,
As rivals heav'nly skill, and human pow'r excels.

Vile as a sign-post dauber's painting shows,
Compar'd with Titian's work, or Angelo's;
Languid and low, as modern rhyme appears,
When Virgil's matchless strain has tun'd our ears,
So seem to him the masters of our isle,
His inspiration, theirs but mortal toil:
They to the ear, he to the soul does dive,
From anger save, and from despair revive:
Not the smooth spheres in their eternal rounds,
The work of angels, warble softer sounds.

What is that heav'n of which so much we hear
(The happy region gain'd with praise and pray'r)
What but one unmolested transport, which
No notion, or idea e'er cou'd reach?
As it appears in vision, 'tis but this,
To be opprest with joy, and strive with bliss!
Confounded with the rays of ceaseless day,
We know not what we think, or see, or say!
Endless profusion! joy without decay!
So, when his harmony arrests the ear,
We lose all thought of what, or how, or where!
Like love it warms, like beauty does control,
Like hidden magic seizes on the whole,
And while we hear, the body turns to soul!

From what blest spring did he derive the art,
To soothe our cares, and thus command the heart!
Time list'ning stands to hear his artful strain,
And death does at the dying, throw his shafts in vain;
Fast to th'immortal part the mortal cleaves,
Nor, till he leave to charm, the body leaves.
Less harmony than this did raise of old
The Theban wall, and made an age of gold.

How in that mystic order cou'd he join
So different notes! make contraries combine,
And out of discord, cull such sounds divine.
How did the seeds lie quick'ning in his brain!
How were they born without a parent's pain?
He did but think, and music wou'd arise,
Dilating joy, as light o'erspreads the skies;
From an immortal source, like that it came;
But light we know, — this wonder wants a name!

What art thou? From what causes dost thou spring
O Music! thou divine mysterious thing?
Let me but know, and knowing, give me voice to sing.
Art thou the warmth in spring that Zephire breathes,
Painting the meads, and whistling thro' the leaves?
The happy season that all grief exiles,
When God is pleas'd, and the creation smiles?
Or art thou love, that mind to mind imparts,
The endless concord of agreeing hearts?
Or art thou friendship, yet a nobler flame,
That can a dearer way make souls the same?
Or art thou rather, which does all transcend,
The centre where at last the blest ascend;
The seat where Hallelujahs never end?
Corporeal eyes won't let us clearly view,
But either thou art heav'n, or heav'n is you!

And thou my Muse (how e'er the critics blame)
Pleas'd with his worth, and faithful to his fame,
Art music while y'are hallowing Purcell's name.
On other subjects you applause might miss,
But envy will itself be charm'd with this,
How oft has envy at his airs been found
T'admire, enchanted with the blissful sound?
Ah! cou'd you quite forget his early doom,
I wou'd not from the rapture call you home:
But gently from your steepy height descend,
You've prais'd the artist, and now mourn the friend!

Ah most unworthy! shou'd we leave unsung
Such wond'rous goodness in a life so young.
In spite of practice, he this truth has shown,
That harmony and vertue shou'd be one.
So true to Nature, and so just to wit,
His music was the very sense you writ.
Nor were his beauties to his art confin'd;
So justly were his soul and body join'd,
You'd think his form the product of his mind.
A conqu'ring sweetness in his visage dwelt,
His eyes wou'd warm, his wit like lightning melt,
But those no more must now be seen, and that no
          more be felt.
Pride was the sole aversion of his eye,
Himself as humble as his art was high.
Ah! let him heav'n (in life so much ador'd)
Be now as universally deplor'd!
The muses sigh'd at his approaching doom,
Amaz'd and raving, as their own were come!
Art try'd the last efforts, but cou'd not save —
But sleep, O sleep, in an unenvy'd grave!
In life and death the noblest fate you share;
Poets and princes thy companions are,
And both of 'em were thy admirers here.
There rest thy ashes — but thy nobler name
Shall soar aloft, and last as long as Fame.

Nor shall thy worth be to our isle confin'd,
But fly and leave the lagging day behind.
Rome that did once extend its arms so far,
Y'ave conquer'd in a nobler art than war:
To its proud sons but only earth was giv'n,
But thou hast triumph'd both in earth and heav'n.

And now farewell! nor fame, nor love, nor art,
Nor tears avail! — we must for ever part!
For ever! dismal accent! what alone!
But that can tell our loss, or reach our moan!

What term of sorrow preference dare contend?
What? but the tenderest dearest name of — friend!

Hail him ye angels to the Elysian shore,
The noblest freight that ever Charon bore,
Tho' Orpheus and Amphion pass'd before.
His skill as far exceeds, as had his name
Been known as long, he wou'd have done in fame.
Tho' the wide globe for tuneful souls you cull,
Hope no more such — the happy choir is full.
The sacred art can here arrive no higher,
And heaven itself no further will inspire.

20. Henry Hall. *Orpheus Britannicus*, book i, 3rd ed., p. vi.

TO THE MEMORY OF MY DEAR FRIEND
MR. HENRY PURCELL

Music, the chiefest good the gods have giv'n,
And what below still antedates our heav'n,
Just like a spirit, by a lasting spell,
Confin'd to Italy, did ages dwell.
Long there remain'd a pleas'd and welcome guest,
Lov'd best to live where best she was exprest.
By glory led, at length to France she came,
And there immortaliz'd great Lully's name;
As yet a stranger to the British shore,
Till Lock, and Blow, deep learn'd in all her lore,
And happy artful Gibbons, forc'd her o'er.
Where with young Humphries she acquainted grew,
(Our first reforming music's Richelieu)
Who dying left the goddess all to you.
There are, I own, a num'rous tuneful throng,
Composing still, though often in the wrong,
And with old air, set forth a fine new song.
These to thy juster art have no pretence,
For if they make a tune they mar the sense.
If sparkling Air the taking treble grace,

'Tis murder'd quite by the ungodly bass.
These to old Morley's maxims counter run;
In overtures rejoice, in jigs they mourn:
Whilst their too great example, mighty you,
That you might still impartial justice do,
At once to music, and the muses too;
Each syllable first weigh'd, or short, or long,
That it might too be sense, as well as song.
Where e'er thy well-known name with theirs is found,
Is as if Cowley, up with Quarles were bound.
Purcell! the pride and wonder of the age,
The glory of the temple, and the stage.
When I thy happy compositions view,
The parts so proper find, the air so new,
Your cadence just, your accent ever true;
How can I e'er enough the man admire,
Who's rais'd the British o'er the Thracian lyre!
That bard cou'd make the savage-kind obey,
But thou has't tam'd yet greater brutes than they:
Who e'er like Purcell cou'd our passions move!
Whoever sang so feelingly of love!
When Thyrsis does in dying notes complain
His hapless love and Phillis' cold disdain;
Brib'd by the magic sounds that strike the ear,
We parties turn, and blame the cruel fair;
But when you tune your lyre to martial lays,
In songs immortal, mortal hero's praise;
Each song its hearers does to hero's raise.

Hail! and for ever hail harmonious shade!
I lov'd thee living, and admire thee dead.
Apollo's harp at once our souls did strike,
We learnt together, but not learnt alike,
Though equal care our master might bestow,
Yet only Purcell e'er shall equal Blow:
For thou, by heaven for wond'rous things design'd,
Left'st thy companion lagging far behind.

Sometimes a hero in an age appears;
But scarce a Purcell in a thousand years.

H. Hall, Organist of Hereford

21. Henry Hall. *Orpheus Britannicus*, book I, 3rd ed., p. ii.

TO MR. HENRY PLAYFORD, ON HIS PUBLISHING THE SECOND
PART OF *Orpheus Britannicus*

Next to the man who so divinely sung,
Our praise, kind Playford, does to thee belong,
For what you gave us of the bards before,
Vast thanks were due, and now you merit more,
Tho' Purcell living, had our utmost praise,
And dead, almost does adoration raise,
Yet he, ev'n he, had scarce preserv'd a name,
Did not your press perpetuate his fame,
And shew'd the coming age as in a glass,
What our all-pleasing Britain's Orpheus was.
Go on my friend, nor spare no pains nor cost,
Let not the least motet of his be lost;
Whose meanest labours your collections show,
Excells our very best performance now.

Duly each day, our young composers bait us,
With most insipid songs, and sad sonata's.
Well were it, if the world would lay embargo's
On such Allegro's and such Poco Largo's:
And would enact it, there presume not any,
To tease Corelli, or burlesque Bassani;
Nor with division, and ungainly graces,
Eclipse good sense, as weighty wigs do faces.
Then honest Cross might copper cut in vain,
And half our sonnet-sellers starve again:
Thus while they print their prick'd-lampoons to live
Do you the world some piece of Purcell's give,
Such as the nicest critic must commend,
For none dare censure that which none can mend.

By this, my friend, you'll get immortal fame,
When still with Purcell we read Playford's name.
H. Hall, *Organist of Hereford*

22. Mr. Herbert. *Orpheus Britannicus*, book I, 3rd ed., p. vii.

A PINDARIC ODE ON DR. BLOW'S EXCELLENCY
IN THE ART OF MUSIC

By Mr. Herbert

Stanza I begins: 'The Liberal arts...'
Stanza II begins: 'Thus Bird, a British Worthy...'

III

Great master of the instrument divine,
Descended of inspir'd Jubal's line!
How many plants of art, set by his hand,
Have spread, and still are spreading o'er the land!
Cedars in Libanus could not thicker stand.
    One hopeful stripling soon grew very tall,
Higher than all the rest, like goodly Saul;
And, if the Muses late sorrows don't recall,
Nor we disturb a soul at rest,
T'was Purcell, Purcell — Harry the great, the blest!
His labours highly of the Muse deserve;
And she as tenderly will ever them preserve.
His fam'd Te Deum, all the world admires,
Perform'd in those renown'd Italian choirs.
The master's, which he knew to be sublime
The scholar often wished to hear
Desiring here below no longer time.
But Providence, which granted not that pray'r,
Took him away, and left us here to grieve,
And doleful sounds were heard on St. Cecilia's Eve.
Thus Orpheus fell; the hills and valleys groan,
The nymphs lament, his lyre changes tone,
Makes a most sad, most gruesome moan
When in the troubl'd river Hebras thrown.

23. P. K. *Orpheus Britannicus*, book II, 2nd ed. (London, 1702).

'To my friend, Mr. Henry Playford, on his publication of Mr. Henry Purcell's *Orpheus Britannicus*; which is now render'd complete, by the addition of this second book.'

As when the god of numbers charms the throng,
And gives melodious tunes to every song,
The voice deals inspiration and desire
To ev'ry Muse, to fill the sacred choir;
Each of the Nine, appears with her applause,
And justifies the god and music's cause;
As ev'ry tender accent gently moves,
And shews their duty, as it shews their loves;
Ev'n so must I with infant notes repair,
And wanting judgement, prove I want no care.

What great Apollo does to us deny,
He let this chosen son of his enjoy:
We poets sow the seed of Fame in vain,
T'expect a crop while we alive remain;
He puts us off till death, and then will give,
When we are not permitted to receive.

Ah! who'd be pleas'd to have these temples crown'd
Whose brains are lost, and heads are underground?
But Purcell's privilege was vastly more,
He planted all the laurels which he wore,
And heard his wide applause fly all around,
For still his fame did with his music sound.

All this to Purcell, but there's something due
To Purcell's and Apollo's friend, to you,
From injuries of time you save his lays,
And rescue him from Fate, to claim our praise.
Oh! cou'd you but the like return receive,
And have our gratitude for what you give,
Rewarded for your toil, exchange your pains,
Not only for our thanks, but for your gains,

While interloping French and Dutch oppose,
And shew themselves both your and music's foes.

But it's in vain to hope, we're all abus'd,
Fond of the riff-raff, which the world refus'd:
Each foreign fool sits wheedling in his shop,
And grinning entertains the thoughtless fop,
Whose love for trifles, makes him rove from home,
And even hug diseases brought from Rome.
Let these, my friend, a while pursue their trade,
Your province and your right alone invade,
Their feeble malice but your fame secures,
And publishes both Purcell's works, and yours.

24. Nat. Oldham. British Museum, Add. MS. 23,076. '1732.
George White. Verses at his last work and death — a print
Mezzotint of a boy playing on a fiddle, painted by Fr. Hals.'

(Col. 1)   Boy turn thy laughter into floods of tears.
           And tune the instrument to mournful airs.
           Play to the numbers of my broken verse
           Whilst I the loss of friend and art rehearse.
           A friend whom none in friendship could surpass,
           An artist worth all monuments of brass.

(Col. 2)   O Shakespeare for thy soul to raise my flame
           Thy music Purcell to resound his fame.
           But what can verse or music raise so high
           As this his last & silent harmony?
           On him nor verse nor music need be spent
           Read but George White and that's his monument.
                              Nat. Oldham arm — 1732

'Vertue Note Books', vol. III, *The Twenty-Second Volume of
the Walpole Society* (1933–4) (Oxford, 1934).

25. (?)Henry Playford. *Orpheus Britannicus*, book I, 3rd ed., p. vi.

TO THE MEMORY OF HIS MUCH LAMENTED FRIEND
MR. H. PURCELL

           Hark! what deep groans torment the air,
           Is nature sunk into despair;

Or does the trembling earth descry
A fit of falling-sickness nigh?
O my prophetic fears! he's gone!
'Twas nature's diapason'd groan.

Harmonious soul! took'st thou offence
At discords here, and fled'st from hence?
Or in thy sacred raptures hear
The music of heaven's warbling sphere?
Then mounted strait where angels sing,
And love does dance on every string.

For balms thou need'st not rob the East,
Nor strip the Phoenix spicy nest:
For, O my friend, thy charming strains
Perfume the skies with sweeter grains.
Touch but thy lyre, the stones will come,
And dance themselves into a tomb.

26. Henry Sacheverell, of Magdalen College, Oxford. *Harmonia Sacra*, book II, 3rd ed.

TO DR. JOHN BLOW AND MR. HENRY PURCELL, UPON THE FIRST AND SECOND BOOKS OF *Harmonia Sacra*

When sacred numbers and immortal lays,
Join'd to record the great Almighty's praise,
Indulgent heav'n the poet did inspire
With lofty song to fill the tuneful lyre.
Thus when of old from Egypt's fruitful land
God brought forth Moses by a mighty hand,
His joyful tongue with untaught numbers flow'd,
Th'unusual harmony its author show'd.
The sea divided as he pass'd along,
Retreating back at his triumphant song.
When David's hand upon his harp was found,
Heav'n soon repeating, listen'd to the sound.
And struggling nature chang'd her wonted course,
Unable to resist his music's sacred force.

His prince's rage this taught him to control,
And tune the discords of his troubled soul.
Not fabled Orpheus, or Amphion's verse,
Can such amazing prodigies rehearse.
We here the mystic art may learn t'unfold,
And feel the wonders which we there are told.
No cloudy passions can our breasts invade,
When sacred harmony dispels the shade.
Here sprightly numbers raise our heighten'd zeal,
And charming sounds seraphic joys reveal.
Each skilful hand and tongue at once conspire
With strings and voice to make a tuneful choir:
Whilst mighty joys the ravish'd senses wound,
And the soul labours with th'inspiring sound.
Whither aloft it tow'rs Isaiah's flight,
Wing'd by devotion to the greatest height;
Or mourning with the royal prophet lies,
And weeps Jerusalem's just miseries;
Or loves sweet Sion's beauteous joys to tell,
Where God himself chiefly delights to dwell;
Such lofty measures, notes so sweet, so strong,
Exalt the numbers and improve the song.

Dr. John Blow,
and Mr. Henry
Purcell.

Hail mighty pair! of Jubal's sacred art,
The greatest glory! ——
Not skilful Asaph understood so well,
And Heman vainly labour'd to excel.
Where e'er the Gospel's sacred page is sung
Where e'er great David's tuneful harp is strung,
Each sacred verse shall your just glories raise,
Each dancing string shall echo forth your praise.
The church as yet could never boast but two
Of all the tuneful race, from Jubal down to you.

27. John Sheffield, Duke of Buckingham: a son of the Earl of Mulgrave, born 1650 (cf. *Musical Times*, 1 Feb. 1896, no. 636, vol. 37, p. 85, article by A. Hughes-Hughes).

ODE ON THE DEATH OF PURCELL

Good angels snatched him eagerly on high:
Joyfully they flew, singing and soaring through the sky,
Teaching his new-fledg'd soul to fly,
While we, alas! lamenting lie.
   He went musing all along,
    Composing new their heavenly song.
Awhile his skilful notes loud Hallelujahs drown'd,
But soon they ceas'd their own to catch his pleasing
      sound.
   David himself improved the harmony
   David in sacred story so renown'd,
   No less for music than for poetry;
   Genius sublime in either art,
Crown'd with applause surpassing all desert
   A man just after God's own heart.
   If human cares are awful to the blest
   Already settled in eternal rest,
Needs must he wish that Purcell only might
Have liv'd to see what he vouchsaf'd to write:
   For sure the noblest thirst of fame
   With the frail body never dies
   But with the soul ascends the skies,
From whence at first it came.
'Tis no little proof we have
That part of us survives the grave,
And in our fame below still bears a share.
Why is the future else so much our care,
Ev'n in our last moments of despair,
And death despised for fame by all wise and brave?
Oh! all ye blest harmonious choir,
Who pow'r almighty only love, and only that admire
Look down with pity from your peaceful bow'r
   On this sad isle perplex'd
   And even vex'd
With anxious care of trifles, wealth and pow'r.

In our rough minds due reverence infuse,
For sweet melodious sounds and each harmonious Muse.
Music exalts man's nature, and inspires
High elevated thoughts, or gentle kind desires.

28. J. Talbot. *Orpheus Britannicus*, book I, 3rd ed., p. v.

AN ODE FOR THE CONSORT AT YORK BUILDINGS,
UPON THE DEATH OF MR. H. P.
BY J. TALBOT, FELLOW OF TRINITY COLLEGE IN CAMBRIDGE*

I

Weep, all ye Muses, weep o'er Damon's
    hearse,
And pay the grateful honours of your verse;
Each mournful strain in saddest accents dress,
His praises, and your sorrows to express.
Ye sons of art, lament your learned chief
With all the skill and harmony of grief;
To Damon's hearse your tuneful tribute
    bring,
Who taught each note to speak, and ev'ry
    Muse to sing.

II

1st Accompaniment   ⎧Hark! how the warlike trumpet groans,
Flat trumpet   ⎨The warlike trumpet sadly moans,
                      ⎩Instructed once by Damon's art

                      ⎧To warm the active soldier's heart,
Sharp trumpet   ⎨To soften danger, sweeten care,
                      ⎩And smooth the rugged toils of war,

                      ⎧Now with shrill grief, and melancholy strains
Flat trumpet   ⎨Of Damon's death, and Albion's loss com-
                      ⎩   plains.

* This ode was also published separately with the inscription 'Set by Mr. Finger', with marginal notes and instructions for repetition of the last stanza as a grand chorus.

*2nd Accompaniment
Hautbois and violins*

> The sprightly hautboys, and gay violin,
> By Damon taught to charm the list'ning ear,
>   To fill the echoing theatre,
> And with rich melody adorn each scene;
>   Forgot their native cheerfulness,
> Their wonted air and vigour to express,
> And in dead doleful sounds a tuneless grief
>   confess.

Chorus

> Weep all ye Muses, weep o'er Damon's
>   hearse,
> And pay the grateful honours of your verse.

III

*3rd Accompaniment
Flute and theorbo*

>   Mark how the melancholy flute,
> Joins in sad consort with the amorous lute,
>   Lamenting Damon's hopeless fate:
> From him they learn'd to tell the lover's care,
> With soft complaints to move the cruel fair,
> To calm her anger, and to change her hate.

*4th Accompaniment
Organ*

> The various organ taught by Damon's hand
>   A holier passion to command,
>   The roving fancy to refine,
> And fill the ravish'd soul with charms
>   divine;
> Now in loud sighs employs its tuneful
>   breath,
>   And bids each secret sound conspire
>   To mourn its darling Damon's death.
> And with consenting grief to form one
>   num'rous choir.

Chorus

> Weep all ye Muses, weep o'er Damon's
>   hearse,
> And pay the grateful honours of your verse.

IV

> Cease, cease, ye sons of art, forbear
> To aggravate your own despair:

Cease to lament your learned chief
With fruitless skill, and hopeless grief,
For sure, if mortals here below
Ought of diviner beings know,
Damon's large mind informs some active
sphere,
And circles in melodious raptures there;
Mix'd with his fellow-choristers above,
In the bright orbs of harmony and love.

Grand Chorus   Cease, cease, ye sons of Art, etc.

Printed for Francis Saunders, at the Blue Anchor in the Lower Walk of
the New Exchange. 1695. (Yale University Library: Press mark K/Foxwell/
26835d).

29. Nahum Tate. *Orpheus Britannicus*, book I, 3rd ed., pp. iv–v.

A LAMENTATION FOR THE DEATH OF MR. H. PURCELL.
SET TO MUSIC BY HIS BROTHER, MR. DANIEL PURCELL.
THE WORDS BY N. TATE, ESQ.

I

A gloomy mist o'erspreads the plains,
More gloomy grief the nymphs and swains;
The shepherd breaks his tuneful reed,
His pining flocks refuse to feed.
Silent are the lawns and glades,
The hills, the vales, the groves, the dales,
All silent as Elysian shades.
No more they sing, no more rejoice,
Echo herself has lost her voice.

II

A sighing wind, a murm'ring rill,
Our ears with doleful accents fill:
They are heard, and only they,
For sadly thus they seem to say,
The joy, the pride of Spring is dead,
The soul of harmony is fled.

Pleasure's flown from Albion's shore,
Wit and mirth's bright reign is o'er,
Strephon and music are no more!
Since Nature thus pays tribute to his urn,
How should a sad, forsaken brother mourn!

30. From R. J. S. Stevens, *Anecdotes*. MS. in Pendlebury Library, Cambridge University, fo. 18.

When Handel was blind, and attending a performance of the oratorio of 'Jephtha', Mr. Savage (my master) who sat next him, said, 'This movement, sir, reminds me of some of old Purcell's music.' 'O got te teffel' (said Handel). 'If Purcell had lived, he would have composed better music than this.'

[Related by] Mr. Savage in 1775

31. *Sixth Report of the Royal Commission on Historical Manuscripts* (London, 1877), part I, p. 395.

Eulogium — Henricus Purcell, Corellius Britannicus. (15 lines of Latin.)

Letters to Ripley Castle, to the County Record Office, York and elsewhere have as yet brought no results.

XIV ? THE THIRD HENRY PURCELL (son)

All Hallows the Less: Marriage, Burial, and Baptism Registers: College of Arms.
Baptisms: 9 July 1681.
Henry, son of Henry and Frances Pursell.
Burials: 18 July 1681.
Purssall, Henry.

XV ? THE FOURTH HENRY PURCELL (son)

Westminster Abbey Registers, p. 219.
Burials: 23 Sept. 1687.
Henry Purcell, a child: in the east cloister.
Baptized at St. Margaret's, Westminster, 9 June 1687.

XVI JOHN PURCELL (?grandfather)

Margaret M. Verney, *Memoirs of the Verney Family during the Commonwealth, 1650–1660*, vol. III (London, 1894), p. 278. (Letter to Sir Ralph Verney from Mun, housekeeper for the Verneys, 9 June 1656.)

Sir, this last week came Pursill the carpenter and his men, he only himself sat in the house, but all his men came in for their beer, and that nor seldom nor in small proportions; and by their example all the workmen do so worry me for drink, that though I many times anger them, and hourly vex myself, with denying one or other or them, yet we spend a great deal of beer — three barrels last week . . .

XVII JOHN BAPTISTA PURCELL (son)

1. *Westminster Abbey Registers*, p. 72.

Baptisms: 9 Aug. 1682.

John-Baptista, son of Mr. Henry Purcell.

2. Ibid. p. 206.

Burials: 17 Oct. 1682.

John-Baptista Purcell, a child (cloisters).

XVIII JOSEPH PURCELL (brother)

1. Marriage Licences: St. James's, Duke's Place. MS. 7894, Guildhall Library.

9 Jan. 1693/4. Joseph Purcell, Bachelor [and]
Sarah Dormer, Spinster
Frances Jackman [Witness]

2. *Christchurch, Aldersgate Street* (Greyfriars: Harl. Soc. Reg. 21), p. 110.

Baptisms: 20 Jan. 1707/8.

Ann, daughter of Joseph and Sarah Purcell (born 26th Dec. 1707).

See also under Daniel Purcell, III, 7(a) and (b).

XIX   KATHERINE PURCELL (sister)

1. *Westminster Abbey Registers*, p. 67.

   Baptisms: 13 March 1661/2.
       Katherine, daughter of Mr. Henry Purcell.
       See also XII, 3.

2. St. Mary Magdalen Registers (typescript of marriages, made by W. H. Challen, in the Guildhall Library).

   18 June 1691.
       William Sale of Seldwick in Kent and Katherine Pursall of St. Margaret's, Westminster.

   For the record of her marriage, see also p. 200 above.

XX   MARY PETERS PURCELL (daughter)

Westminster Abbey Registers, p. 76.

Baptisms: 10 Dec. 1693.
    Mary-Peters, daughter of Henry and Frances Purcell.

Not mentioned in her mother's Will; perhaps died before 1706.

XXI   MATTHEW PURCELL (cousin)

Charles Dalton, *English Army Lists and Commission Registers, 1661–1714*, vol. II, p. 161.

    Matthew Purcell, Ensign to Captain Scudamore, in Prince George of Denmark's Regiment of Foot. (Also under Colonel Sir Charles Littleton.)
July 21st, 1688.

Ibid. vol. IV, p. 17.

For the Bomb Vessels, [A list of Officers, Gunners, etc., appointed for the present train and for the Bomb and Machine Vessels in the year 1694] . . . Commissary and Paymaster: Matthew Purcell. £0. 10. 0. *per diem.*

Ibid. vol. IV, p. 200. (1 May 1698.)

Regimental Train of Artillery to be kept in time of peace. [Gentlemen of the Ordinance] Matthew Purcell.

In entry for Feb. 1698/9 his wages are listed as £40 per annum.

XXII THOMAS PURCELL (uncle)

1. British Museum, Add. MS. 5751B.
Westminster, no. 12, 22 Jan. — a pencilled note — ?1660; however, a similar warrant in PRO (LC 5/52, p. 38) is dated 22 Jan. 12 Ch. II, i.e. 1661.

Charles R/ We will and command that immediately upon sight hereof you deliver or cause to be delivered to our well-beloved servants Lancelot Thorneton, Clerk of our Wardrobes of Robes and Beads, John Duncomber, Paule Ferine, and Thomas Pursill, grooms of our robes, the several parcels hereafter mentioned for their liveries as hath been accustomed; that is to say to each of them fourteen yards of black satin for a gown, ten shillings the yard, three yards of black velvet to guard the same gown at eighteen shillings the yard, one fur of budge for the same gown price eight pounds, for furring of the same gown three shillings four pence, and for making of the same gowns six shillings eight pence. Item for eight yards of velvet for a coat at twenty shillings the yard, two dozen of silk buttons for the said coat at eight pence the dozen, two ounces of silk to it at two shillings the ounce, eight yards of cotton to line the same coat at eight pence the yard, and for making of the same coat six shillings and eight pence. Item three yards of velvet for a doublet at twenty shillings the yard, two dozen of silk buttons to it at eight pence the dozen, one ounce of silk to it, price two shillings. Three yards of fustian to line it at eight pence the yard, and for making of the same doublet three shillings and four pence. Item two yards and an half of marble cloth for a coat at twelve shillings the yard, two yards and an half of russet velvet to guard the same coat at eighteen shillings the yard, six yards of cotton to line the same coat at eight pence the yard, four ounces of silk at two shillings the ounce, two dozen of silk buttons at eight pence the dozen, and for making of the same coat six shillings eight pence. Item to each of them two yards and a half of green cloth for a summer coat etc.... during their natural lives ... Thomas Purcill and the others ... May it please your excellent Majesty: this containeth your Majesty's warrant ... amounting to £40 per annum ... signed

Will. Rumbold

2. *KM*, p. 121. (1660.)

Mentioned as the first of ten musicians 'that do service in the Chapel Royal whose salaries are payable in the Treasury of His Majesty's Chamber'.

3. PRO: *Cal. S. P. Dom.* 1665-6 (no. 63), 28 May 1666.

Whitehall: The king to the Lord Treasurer.

Henry Cook, Thomas Purcell and other gentlemen of the Chapel Royal petition, on behalf of themselves, the pages of the Chapel, and boys whose voices have changed, for payment, there being no money assigned to the Treasurer of the Chamber for those purposes. Thinks his honour concerned therein and therefore wishes full and punctual payment of all that is due to them on the next assignment of moneys to the Treasurer of the Chamber.

4(*a*). *Cal. S. P. Dom.* 16 Feb. 1662/3.

Warrant to the Master of the Great Wardrobe ... to deliver to Thos. Purcell, musician in place of Henry Lawes, materials for a camlet gown, guarded with black velvet, and

furred; for a damask jacket and velvet doublet, and to pay for
the lining and furring thereof...

4(*b*). PRO: Pipe Office Declared Account (E 351) 547.

To Thomas Purcell, another of His Majesty's said musicians
in the room and place of Henry Lawes, deceased, for his like
wages and livery, payable as before, by virtue of His Majesty's
warrant under the signet dated the 19th of November, Anno
XIIIj^{to} Regni Regis Caroli Secundi, and due to him for IIIj^{r}
years and a half ended at Midsummer 1667. £162. 11. 3.

5. *Cheque-book*, p. 85. (20 May 1671.)

It is ordered that the old books and surplices shall be to the
use of the Gentlemen of His Majesty's Chapel Royal, paying
to the Sergeant of the Vestry twelve pence for the old book,
and ten shillings apiece for their old surplices. Upon the testimony of Mr. John Harding, Gentleman for 30 years standing.
As also Mr. Thomas Purcell, Mr. Alfonso Marsh and Mr.
William Tucker, who aver they have often heard Mr.
Nightingalle to testify the same, as an ancient privilege
belonging to the said gentlemen.

6. *KM*, p. 235. (Oct. 1671.)

Petition from John Clement, Thomas Purcell, and William
Child, musicians of His Majesty's Private Music, that the
arrears due to them from His Majesty's great wardrobe for the
years 1669, 1670, and 1671, may be assigned to their fellow
musician, Humphrey Madge.

7. *KM*, 245. (2 July 1672.)

Whereas His Majesty is displeased that the violins neglect
their duty in attending in his Chapel Royal, it is ordered that
if any of the violins shall neglect to attend, either to practice
or to wait in the Chapel, whensoever they have received
notice from Mr. Purcell or Mr. Humphryes, that for such
fault they shall be suspended from their places.

8. PRO: Audit Office Declared Account A.O.1/397/90 (1672).

Paid to Thomas Pursell at xx^{li} per annum for wages, and xvj^{li} ij^s vj^d per annum for a livery — due for four years and 3 quarters ended at Mic'mas 1672. clxxj^{li} xj^s x^d ob.

9. *Cal. S. P. Dom.* 1 Sept. 1673.

Warrant for payment to W. Ashburnham of £400 a year, to be paid to Thomas Purcell for the 20 musicians who attend the service in the Chapel Royal.

10. PRO: SP 29/360, no. 128.

For his Excellency Sir Joseph Williamson, Jan. 2nd [1673/4].

Sir, I am very glad of a command from you, because I must give you an answer, which I would to your first, and all your other kind letters, but you know I cannot compliment, and I should say very many kind things to you from the kitching [*sic*] but I cannot express them, — Sir, Mr. Stefkings was joined in patten with his father and is now settled in his place. Mr. [Thomas] Purcell hath been very kind to him and would be very glad to serve you in anything, and hath desired me to present his humble service to you, so doth Mr. Rogers and very many more of your good friends, pray be pleased to present my most humble service to Sir Lionall Jenkins; [and, (erased)] Sir you know you have a most faithful friend and humble servant of William Chiffinch.

[Endorsed:] London. Feb. 6, 1673/4. R $\frac{15}{25}$ Mr. Chiffinch.

11. *Cal. S. P. Dom.* 28 Sept. 1676.

Warrant to Sir Edward Griffin and the Treasurer of the Chamber for the time being for payment yearly during pleasure by equal quarterly payments to commence from Midsummer 1673 of £46. 10s. 10d. to Thomas Purcill, one of the Gentlemen of the Chapel Royal, to be disposed of to such uses as the King shall direct.

12. Edward Chamberlayne, *Angliæ Notitia*, 12th ed. (1679), p. 171.

> In the office of the Robes, besides the Master above mentioned one Yeoman Tobias Rustat, three grooms, Thomas Purcell and two more.

13. Ibid. 14th ed. (1682), p. 178.

> Three grooms of the robes. Thomas Purcell, Gilbert Spencer, Robert Rustat.

14. British Museum, Harl. MS. 1911: Orders of a Musical Corporation, fo. 5*v*.

> 9 July 1664.
>
> Ordered that Mr. Thomas Purcell be and is hereby chosen one of the Assistants to this Corporation of Music in the room and place of Dr. Charles Coleman, deceased. Signed, Nicholas Lanier.
>
> 11 July, 1664.
>
> Ordered that all His Majesty's music do give their attendance at the chamber at Durham Yard for practice of music when the Master of the Music shall appoint them upon for feature of 5*d*. each neglect. Signed Nich. Lanier, etc.
>
> 21 Jan. 1670.
>
> Ordered that Mr. Pelham Humfrey be and is hereby chosen one of the assistants of the corporation of music in the room and place of Gregory Thorundon, deceased. These being present: Henry Cooke, Marshall, John Hingeston, George Hudson, John Lillie, wardens.
>
> Monday, 24 June 1672 (fo. 10).
>
> Whereas Henry Cooke, Esquire, being Marshal of the Corporation of Music in Westminster in the County of Middlesex hath requested the said Corporation to make choice of a fit person to succeed him in the said office of Marshal, he being by reason of sickness unable to attend the business of the said Corporation, it is therefore ordered by the

said corporation that Thomas Purcell, gentleman, be Marshal and that he the said Thomas Purcell is hereby chosen and appointed Marshal of the said Corporation accordingly. John Hingeston, Deputy Marshall, Humfrey Madge and Pelham Humfrey, wardens, Antoni Robert, George Hudson, John Strong, John Lillie, John Rogers, Alphonso Marsh, John Harding.

15. PRO: LC 'Miscellanea', 5/14, p. 80 (13 Dec. 1671).

A warrant to the Treasurer of the Chamber to pay unto Paul Ferine, Thomas Purcell and James Watson, grooms of His Majesty's robes, the sum of two and fifty pounds for their lodging out of Court fifty-two weeks, from the 20th of Aug. 1666, to the 20th of Aug. 1667, at the rate of twenty shillings by the week.

16(a). PRO: S.P. Dom. Entry Books (S.P. 44) 334, p. 208.

Our will and pleasure is that out of such our treasure as now is or hereafter shall be remaining in your hands you pay or cause to be paid yearly by quarterly payments the sum of forty six pounds ten shillings and ten pence unto our Tr. etc. [trusty and well-beloved?] Thomas Purcill one of the Gentlemen of Our Chapel to be by him disposed of and paid to such use as we shall direct without any further or other account to be by him given for the same. The first payment to commence from the Feast of St. John Baptist 1673 and to continue during our pleasure. And for etc. Whitehall, Sept. 28th, 1676. By His Majesty's command, J. W. To our etc. Sir Edward Griffin, Knight, Treasurer of our Chamber and to the Treasurer of our Chamber for the time being.

16(b). PRO: Pipe Office Declared Account (E 351) 2835: 'Account of Henry Sidney, Esq., Gentleman and Master of His Majesty's Robes . . . 1680–1681', fo. 4v.

Shoes, galoshes, boots and buskins with tennis shoes for His Majesty's use: £110. 13. 0. Seven pair of boots, viz. for Tobias Rustat, Yeoman of the Robes, Robert Rustat, Thomas Purcell etc. . . . at 35/ each pair: £12. 5. 0.

2B

17. Testamentum Thomas Purcell. PCC: 138 Cottle (Somerset House). Nov. 1682.

In the name of God Amen. I, Thomas Purcell, of the parish of St. Martin-in-the-Fields in the county of Middlesex, Esq., being of sound mind and memory do make my last Will and Testament in manner following, revoking all other Wills by me formerly made. My soul I surrender up unto Almighty God, my Creator, in the merits of Jesus Christ, my Redeemer. My body I desire may have decent burial at the discretion of my executrix. My worldly estate I do dispose in this manner, viz.: I do give and bequeath unto my dear and loving wife Mrs. Katherine Purcell the messuage and house wherein I now dwell situate in the parish of St. Martin-in-the-Fields aforesaid in a street called the Pell Mell street with all the building and appurtenances thereunto belonging for all my terms and terms of years therein now to come and unexpired. I do likewise give and devise unto my said dear wife all and every my furniture, household stuff, household goods, plate, linen, and goods whatsoever in my said house and also all sum and sums of money, debts, and other things whatsoever any ways due or owing unto me from the King's Majesty, my Royal Master, or any of his officers or any other person or persons whatsoever, and also all other my personal estate of what nature or kind soever the same may be and do recommend unto her the payment of all and every my debts which I shall owe at the time of my death. I desire my children may have five pounds a piece given them out of the arrears of my salary and pension when the same can be received. I do make my said dear wife sole executor of this my last Will and in testimony that is my last Will, I have hereunto set my hand and seal this fourth day of June, one thousand six hundred eighty one, Annoque Regni Regis Caroli secundi Tricesimo tertio. Thomas Purcell. Signed sealed and published by the said Thomas Purcell for his last Will and Testament (the same being first read unto him) in the presence of Giles Channpneys, Andrew Card.

Probatum fuit [huiusmodi] testimentum Londini[um]
coram venerabili viro Henrico Fauconberge legum Doctore
Surrogato venerabilis et egregi viri Domini Leolini Jenkins
Militis legum etiam Doctoris Curiae Praerogativae cantuariensis Magistri Custodis sive commissarij Legitime
constituti octavo die mensis Novembris Anno Domini
Millesimo Sexcentesimo Octogesimo secundo Juramento
Catherine Purcell Relictae et Executricis in dicto testamento
nominato cui commissa fuit Administratio omnium et
singulorum bonorum jurium et creditorum dicti defuncti. De
bene et fideliter Administrando eadem ad sancta Dei Evangelia
Jurat[a]. Exec.

18. PRO: Treasury Disposition Book (T 61) 2, pp. 194–5 (2 Dec.
    1682).

    Mistress Purcell, widow of Thomas Purcell [paid] £50. 0. 0.

19. Ibid. pp. 222–3.

    £100 to Mistress Purcell.

20. Ibid. pp. 260–2.

    £100 to Mistress Purcell.

21. Ibid. p. 1420.

    £10. 15. 11 to Widow Pursell in part of £302. 18. 9
    [arrears due] on [her late husband's fee of] £426. 5. 10.
    £11. 12. 8½ to same in part of £244. 6. 10½ arrears [on his
    fee of] £46. 10. 10; £11. 10. 7½ to the same in part of
    £144 10. 0 arrears on [his fee of] £46. 2. 6.

22. PRO: Treasury Money Book (T 53) 4, p. 254 (22 Aug. 1683).

    Money warrant for £100 to the executors of Thomas
    Purcell for half a year to 1678, Sept. 29th.

    A similar payment is entered for 17 April 1683.
    For a document relating to Thomas Purcell quoted in the text, see pp.
    94–95 above.

XXIII   THOMAS PURCELL (?son)

Westminster Abbey Registers, p. 216.

Burials: 3 Aug. 1686.

    Thomas Purcell, a child (cloisters).

Another Thomas Purcell is named in Sir Wasey Sterry's *The Eton College Register* (Eton, 1943, p. 273): 'Purcell, Thomas: 1672–1673, b. in London; k.s. 1672 aged 11. He may well be the Thomas Purcell recorded by Foster in *Alumnae Oxoniensis*, q.v.'

XXIV   PETERS FAMILY

1. Sir Bernard Burke, *The General Armory of England, Scotland and Wales* (London, 1684).

   Peter, Devon & Essex: Gu on a bend or. betw. 2 escallops ar. a cornish chough ppr. inter as many cinquefoils az; on a chief of the second, a rose between a fleur de lis, of the first, sceded or, barbed and leaved vest — Frest two lions heads erased, conjoined and endorsed, the dexter or, the sinister az, collared ringed and counterchanged.

   Peter (Canterland, Scotland) or, three boars' heads, couped gu.

2. J. L. Chester (ed. J. Foster), *London Marriage Licenses*, p. 1049.

   Thomas Peters, gentleman, of St. Clement Danes, 26, and Frances West, of St. Andrew, Holborn, widow, 25, at St. Mary Savoy, 17 Oct. 1627.

   [In the actual register]: 18th Oct. 1627, Thomas Petre [*sic*] and Franncis West married by licence.

3. PCC: 66 Leeds (Somerset House). Will of John Baptist Peters of St. Mary-le-Bow, gentleman, 26 Feb. 10 Anne, 1711/12.

   To his wife, remainder of an unexpired lease of the house in Jermain [*sic*] St., St. James's, Westminster, and 2 houses at Richmond, Surrey, and 1 house in Cicill Court, St. Martin's Lane, and 1 in Great Carter Lane. To his son Richard, £100 and the diamond 'which I constantly wear (which was my father's)'. To his son John Baptist, house on the corner of Duffolk Lane, in the parish of All Hallows the Great. To his son Bryan, another house in All Hallows. Bequests to other children: son Ellis, daughter Martha, daughter Elizabeth, daughter Mary, daughter Frances. [All daughters apparently under 18.] Executrix was his wife. Proved 19th March 1711/12.

XXV SAMUEL WALL AND TEMPERANCE PURCELL (*née* Wall)

1. Mickleham parish records, book I, p. 23.

26 March 1671.

Collected on a brief for the redemption of captives lately taken by Turkish pirates, the sum of £4. 2. 0.

Samuel Wall, Gentleman   £0. 5. 0
Miss Temperance Wall   £0. 1. 6

N.B. Her marriage to Edward Purcell therefore probably took place in 1671 or 1672, since she was a maiden still in 1671, and gave birth to a child in 1673.

2. Ibid. book II, p. 88.

Baptisms: 1673.

Samuel, son of Mr. Edward Persill and Temperance, wife, was baptized December 22, 1673. [Book II, p. 109 shows that he was buried a few days later, on 27 December.]

Baptisms: 1675.

Catherine Purcell, daughter of Mr. Edward Purcell and Temperance his wife was baptized July 1st, 1675.

3. Ibid. book I, p. 30.

Towards the rebuilding of the Cathedral Church of St. Paul, London, there was collected in this parish of Mickleham, Septembris 9, 1678 ... Mrs. Pursill £0. 1. 0. .... The two richest men of the Parish viz. Mr. Sam Wall, an attorney of Staple Inn; and Mr. Thomas Tooth, a Courier, contributing nothing among us.

4. Ibid. book I, p. 33.

Collected in the parish of Mickleham in the county of Surrey, October 11th, 12th, and 13th, 1680, towards the redemption of captives lately taken by Turkish pirates: Mrs. Purcell £00. 02. 06.

5. Book of Accounts kept for the Parish of Mickleham, book III, pp. 1, 4, 5, and 18.

A tax by virtue of an Act of Parliament for the raising of 688 001^{li}. 09^s 01^d by the month for 6 months payable at quarterly payments.

1689. Mr. Wall in his own compution	00	07	08
More for Mr. Wall's land	00	10	00
30 May 1689. Mr. Wall for land in his own possession for half a year	00	02	06
5 Aug. 1689. Mr. Wall for land in his own possession	00	00	08
Tho. Turner for Mr. Wall's land	0	0	4
Tho. Arnold for Mr. Wall's land	0	0	1
John Arnold for Mr. Wall's land	0	0	1
Mrs. Richards for Mr. Wall's land	0	0	3

(Same payments for other quarters to 1689, 1690.)

1 Aug. 1690. Mr. Wall for his own land	00	02	00
Thomas Turner for Mr. Wall's land	00	04	02

1 March 1691/2. Further payments.

6. Mickleham parish records, book I, p. 115.

Mr. Samuel Wall buried Aprilis 23mo, 1692.

7. PCC: Fane (Somerset House) 1692, fo. 76 (abstract from the will of Samuel Wall).

... the last will and testament of Samuel Wall of Mickleham in the county of Surrey ... I give and bequeath unto my niece [sic] Katherine Purcell all those my ten tenements in lying and being in White Lyon Court near Charterhouse Lane in the parish of St. Sepulchre's ... (and) my tenement called Juniper House with the appurtenances together with all the fields and grounds and coppin woods thereunto belonging ...

All Mickleham lands to Temperance Purcell, [daughter] ...
[mentions] £43 remaining from far greater sum taken up to
pay and discharge imprudent and extravagant debts contracted
by ... said daughter ... [hence] executrixship granted (*pro
tem.*) to Temperance Saintbarbe (niece) ... who is to satisfy
son-in-law Edward Purcell (husband [of] Temperance Purcell,
née Wall). [Executrixship to be granted to Edward and
Temperance Purcell upon discharge of above-mentioned
debts. However, such a grant does not seem to have been
recorded, but rather:] Probate April Vitesimo nono die, 1692/
Samuel Wall vitesimo nono die probatum fuit testamentum
Samuelis Wall ... de Mickleham ...

8. Abstract of Indenture drawn up between Edward and Temperance Purcell and others n behalf of daughter Katherine
Purcell, relating to ten tenements at White Lyon Court,
mentioned above.

This indenture made the nineteenth day of September Anno
Domini One thousand six hundred and ninety-eight ...
between Edward Purcell of Mickleham ... and Temperance
his wife, only daughter and heir of Samuel Wall ... deceased,
and John West ... Richard Badham, of West Smithfield,
butcher [*et al.* — followed by long description of legal history
of six of the ten tenements mentioned above] ... now this
indenture witnesseth that the said Edward Purcell and
Temperance his wife for and in consideration of twelve pence
apiece of lawful money of England to them in hand paid by
... John West ... (at the request and by the direction of
Katherine Purcell ...) have bargained, sold, assigned, and
set over ... to the said Richard Badham and Robert Browne
... (above-mentioned tenements). (Signed and sealed by
Edward, Temperance, and Katherine Purcell, witnessed by
Daniel Purcell [authentic signature of the composer, verified
by signatures in the British Museum], Edward Hobart, and
Ph. Bird.)

HENRY PURCELL'S ORIGINS:
A GENEALOGICAL PUZZLE

TO SOME who know of the delights and mysteries of Purcell's music, the intricate genealogical puzzle surrounding his life story seems neither very interesting nor important. Indeed, its solution might well await a general revival of interest in the musical legacy he left.

However important it may be, the task of sorting out various relationships in the Westminster Purcell families *is* extremely complicated. Moreover, Purcell genealogy has been sheltered from critical inquiry for several decades, since the solution seemed to have been worked out satisfactorily. It now appears, however, that the *status quo* in Purcell genealogical research may be other than satisfactory. The following account of my own recent investigations can be considered as nothing more than an interim report. But it is worth setting out in detail here, I think, if only to facilitate the discovery of further relevant information. When I may travel to England again, I hope to follow promising lines of investigation which can only be mooted here.

Most problems of tracing Purcell's family origins still remain to be solved. As is true of other aspects of his biography, scarcity of fact has left room for conjecture and confusion. First of all, no one knows exactly where he was born. The consensus of opinion, for what it is worth, has it that he was born in England (probably in London). Some go so far as to specify Westminster. Cummings even hazarded an exact address: St. Ann's Lane, Old Pye Street, Westminster. But surely this was a rash and improbable guess, for that is where Purcell lived after his marriage. Cummings's statement is questioned in the account in *Grove's* (2nd ed.), which says that after the death of the elder Henry Purcell the house in Great

Almonry South became the family home. We cannot even be sure, as a matter of established fact, that he was born in England.

One far-fetched legend, which would have it that he was born in France, has several impressive supporters. In Ernst Ludwig Gerber's *Historisch-biographisches Lexikon der Tonkünstler* (Leipzig: 1790–2) Purcell's name is entered as 'Pourcell', with 'Purcell' as an alternative spelling, and followed by the statement that he was born in France about the middle of the seventeenth century. This entry no doubt was based upon that published by another musical lexicographer, Johann Gottfrid Walther, who, in his *Musicalisches Lexicon* of 1732,* quoted Mattheson (*Critica Musica*, vol. II, p. 148) to the effect that Purcell was born in France. Mattheson himself not only said that Purcell was French by birth, but attacked an unknown opponent who could not accept his statement.

All this sounds plausible; yet any solid piece of contrary evidence would outweigh it all. One may scoff at the notion of French origin, but an unsupported scoff is not more valid than an unsupported statement. And Mattheson did have the advantage of being alive at least fourteen years before Purcell died. What is more, it is not beyond possibility that Purcell may have been born in France. His birth took place during the Commonwealth period when any number of loyal Englishmen were residing abroad. Nor is it unthinkable (though it is improbable) that his parents, or at least his mother, may have been living away from England at the time of his birth. But the notion that he was actually a native Frenchman whose immediate family was French is, I think, nonsensical.

Walther's French spelling raises another interesting point. In France the word 'pourcelle' (now obsolete, from the Latin *porcellus*) meant 'boar'. And Purcell's coat-of-arms shows three boars' heads — a Gallic device, which adds another mite, however insignificant, to the evidence that Purcell did have French connec-

---

* He also confused Henry with Daniel, as the beginning of the entry shows: 'Pourcel (Daniel) ein an. 1696 verstorbener Componist, liegt zu London in der Westmünster-Kirche mit einer zwar kurzen, aber sehr schmeichelhaften Engländischen Grobschrift, welche auf Teutsch also lautet: "Hier liegt Heinrich Purcell . . .".'

tions of later provenance than those he inherited from Hugh Porcel, the Norman ancestor who came to England with William the Conqueror.* However, these 'canting coats-of-arms' came into vogue into England in the sixteenth century. Westrup is probably right in assuming that Purcell had descended from an English family. But that he sprang from either the Shropshire, the Kilkenny, or the London branch of the family is, very likely, an erroneous conjecture, as we shall see.

There has also been a claim that Purcell was of Welsh extraction, according to the Cardiff *Western Mail* of 27 September 1930:

It may not be generally known that Purcell, the famous musician, although born in London, was a descendant of the Purcells, for many years a leading family of the then little-known town of Cardiff, and one leading old writer mentions that several of Purcell's most popular productions are only alterations or improvements of ancient Welsh melodies, among which may be reckoned his 'Joy to Great Caesar' which is very much in the Welsh style and adapted to a versification very common in the Welsh tongue.

Further inquiries have at last brought further light on this matter. Here I can do no better than to quote the letter sent to me by Mr. J. E. Thomas, F.L.A., City Librarian of Cardiff Public Libraries, whose archivist prepared the following:

The only basis for connecting the Purcell family of Cardiff with Henry Purcell, the great musician, seems to be the remarks made by Benjamin Heath Malkin in his work *The Scenery, Antiquities and Biography of South Wales* (2nd ed., London, 1807, vol. I, pp. 222–3). 'I have been told', Malkin writes 'that Wilson the painter was born in the town of Cardiff, and that he was brother to Alexander Wilson, late surveyor of the customs in that port, as well as that he was brought up by his maternal uncle, Alexander Purcell, to the trade of a goldsmith, which he quitted on going to London for the profession of a painter. The celebrated musician Purcell was claimed as an ancestor, though not in direct line, by the Purcell's of Cardiff. Henry Purcell was probably born in London; as his father and uncle were both gentlemen of the chapel at the restoration of Charles the Second when he was only two years old. But there seems reason to think from his compositions that the principality may claim the honour of connecting itself with this great master, and probably through his relations in this town. Several among the most favourite of his productions are

---

* John O'Hart, *Irish Pedigrees*, vol. II, pp. 347 ff., as quoted in Westrup, p. 3.

only alterations or improvements of ancient Welsh melodies, among which may be reckoned his Grounds. His 'Joy to Great Caesar' is very much in the Welsh style, and adapted to a versification very common in the Welsh language, but never, I believe, naturalized with the English, excepting in the loyal song written by Tom D'Urfey to the measure of that fine melody. Of his very favourite cantata, *From Rosy Bowers*, many of the parts or stanzas are on the most prevalent principles of Welsh versification, and such as both look and sound very uncouth in English poetry. From all these musical and poetical pre-dilections, which could scarcely have been the work of chance, or of accidentally meeting with a Welsh air, it is probable that he was introduced to his intimacy with this national style of melody and rhythm by family connection. There are no Purcells now remaining at Cardiff.' We have never seen any other references to the Welsh connections of Henry Purcell and his music, and with regard to the latter our own music librarian is of the opinion that Malkin had very little ground for his assertions.

There are numerous references to members of the Purcell family of Cardiff in John Hobson Matthew's *Cardiff Records* (6 vols., Cardiff, 1898–1911), a work which will be available in the British Museum and probably at some of the larger London reference libraries, e.g. Westminster. The references can easily be traced by means of the comprehensive index in volume 6. They show that the Cardiff Purcells were a substantial and well-to-do family, but they contain no information which can be used in support of Malkin's statements.

Although Benjamin Heath Malkin was headmaster of Bury St. Edmunds Grammar School and later became the first professor of history in London University, he does not seem to have been very critical of the information given to him by his friends and acquaintances in South Wales. It is interesting to note that just before treating of Cardiff and the Purcells he eulogizes Edward Williams (Iolo Morganwg), and it would be still more interesting to know whether it was Edward Williams who supplied him with information about the Purcells of Cardiff, the connection with Henry Purcell and the 'Welsh flavour' of the latter's music.

Biographies of Benjamin Heath Malkin and Edward Williams appear in the *Dictionary of Welsh Biography* (London, Honourable Society of Cymmrodorion, 1959).

18 January 1965

Apart from the fact that Purcell wrote no such song as 'Joy to Great Caesar', the lack of evidence in support of his theoretical Welsh origins bring this theory also into serious doubt.

On this same subject Sir Frederick Bridge included in his *Twelve Good Musicians* (London, 1920, pp. 121–2) an interesting extract from a letter written by his brother, Chester. The lack of a

Christian name for 'Mr. Purcell' and the absence of any supporting
evidence detract somewhat from the value of this communication, which nevertheless needs to be taken into account:

In 1661 the family had gone up to London and we find the Steward there and
recording

    Dec. 24, Paid for a quart of Purle with Mr. Purcell   .   .   .   2d.

As a rule only the names of important personages are put in the accounts. As the
Steward did not *live* in London, it looks as if Mr. Purcell was a former acquaintance from somewhere near Chirk. This place is on the borders of three counties
of which Shropshire is one, and as the Purcells probably came from Salop, their
birthplace or place of residence may have been at the Chirk end of the county.
Possibly Mr. Purcell was an old friend of the Steward's. (Chirk Castle Accounts,
kept by the steward of Sir Thomas Myddelton,)

Sir Frederick goes on to say that the elder Henry Purcell (to
whom the above quotation presumably refers) no doubt 'lived in
the place called the Almonry, where the "singing men" had
houses. These stood where the well-known Westminster
Palace Hotel now stands. And here his distinguished son was
born.'

So much for a few of many extant hypotheses. A solider,
though as yet not fully documented, case can be made for the
establishment of Buckinghamshire as the county in England of
which Purcell's father, Henry, and uncle, Thomas were native. In
Thornborough, Bucks., there flourished for a century or more
before the Restoration a numerous colony of Purcells (mainly
carpenters and artisans) who seem to be related not only to similar
colonies elsewhere in the county (particularly at Water Eaton,
near Oxford; near Bletchley, Bucks.; and at Buckingham), but
also to some of the Purcell families in London.

As the reader will have noted, the Christian names of these
Thornborough Purcells (see branches 'B' and 'C' of the family
tree in Table II) frequently correspond with the Christian names of
London Purcells. Such correspondences are particularly noticeable
in the families of Henry the elder and Thomas Purcell, traceable
in London from about 1653 onwards. The implied connection is
described in the following excerpt from a letter of the late Mr.
F. G. Gurney (of Egginton, Beds.) to Mr. A. Vere Woodman,

F.S.A., of Wing, Bucks., written on 22 February 1939 and transmitted to me on 14 February 1961:

There is hardly the slightest doubt that the great musician was a Bucks. man. His father, Henry, used for his sons the names used by the Oving* Purcells throughout. Henry Purcell, the father, was married by 1652 and was probably born between *c.* 1622 and 1631 (a statement according well with the fact that Henry Purcell of Thornborough was baptized in 1627, and Thomas Purcell in 1629/30).

All this might seem merely an interesting but wholly unsubstantiated hypothesis except for positive proof of a direct connection between the Buckinghamshire and London Purcells, in the form of an inscription on a stone in St. Katherine's chapel, at the east end of the south aisle in the parish church in Wing:

Here lies [the body of] Elizabeth, the wife of Henry Redman late of Ascot [and daughter of] Catherine and Thomas Purcell, yeoman of the robes and one of the Gentlemen of the Chapel Royal to Charles the 2nd [she died] Oct. 29 1733, Aged 73.

This inscription warrants, I believe, the recounting of a local Buckinghamshire legend, which otherwise might best be dismissed as just that and nothing more. According to this tale both Henry the elder and Thomas had been kidnapped to serve as choristers in the Chapel Royal in Westminster. There they settled in the early 1640's, founding the two families shown on branches 'D' and 'E' in Table II, and founding also the family's musical fame, which was to be brought to its highest point by the younger Henry Purcell. The phrases in the above quotation shown in square brackets have been effaced by time since Mr. Gurney transcribed them some sixty years ago; however, the remaining lines can still be read. The parish register shows that Elizabeth Redman was buried on 30 October 1733, and other records reveal that from the early sixteenth century onwards the Redmans and Purcells had lived side by side for over a hundred years in Oving. Both families disappear from the records about the beginning of the seventeenth century, but the names of the Redmans reappear

* Oving is a small village in Buckinghamshire, near Wing, which lies between Aylesbury and Leighton Buzzard.

around 1650, when they served as superior domestics in the household of the Earl of Carnarvon.

The discovery of the inscription quoted above has brought to light a numerous family of Purcells in Thornborough, headed by one John Purcell, a carpenter in the employ of the Verneys, among whose sons were Thomas and Henry Purcell, both born in just about the right years to have emerged in Westminster society as mature citizens at the Restoration, as both the musicians by these names actually did. Moreover, this discovery has also brought to light a number of interesting connections between members of the Purcell families of Westminster and several prominent Buckinghamshire families, which connections upon investigation may well shed further light on the matter. Certainly it would be too much to explain all these relationships as coincidental. Before leaving London in 1682, Charles Purcell made a Will, which was witnessed by Sarah Fynes — very probably the same young lady by that name who was buried in Wing parish church that May. A dozen years later Joseph Purcell married Sarah Dormer, as may be confirmed by an entry in the marriage register for St. James's, Duke's Place, dated 9 January 1693/4. Colonel Edward Purcell retired to the country residence of the Earl of Abingdon (Montagu Bertie) near Wytham, Berks., whose daughter, Catherine married Robert Dormer, possibly he of Dorton, also with connections in the area.* Another prominent person with strong connections in the Thornborough area was Dr. Richard Busby, a friend of young Henry Purcell's (as we know from his having bequeathed Henry a mourning ring). Finally, dwelling in Frances Purcell's neighbourhood in Richmond at the time of her death were Peregrine Bertie, Ann Eeles — a William Eeles witnessed Henry Purcell's Will — Amy Howlett, and several Dormers, all of whom had family connections in this very same area. These circumstances, it seems to me, plead for further investigation, even though the evidence they afford is circumstantial.

Whatever further investigations in Buckinghamshire records may bring to light, there is merit still in the accounts given by the earliest biographers (mainly Burney and Hawkins), who described

* Letter of A. Vere Woodman, 4 Sept. 1964.

Henry Purcell as the son of the elder Henry and the nephew of Thomas Purcell, who had adopted him upon his father's death early in August 1664. Supporting documents establish other members of the young composer's immediate family quite clearly. Elizabeth Purcell was his mother, Katherine his sister; and he had at least three brothers, two of whom may have been older than he (Edward and Joseph) and one (Daniel) who was certainly younger, despite Cummings's statement to the contrary.*

Then in 1937 Sir Jack Westrup, one of the pioneers of scientific 'musicology' in England, pointed out in his brilliant, never-to-be-surpassed life of Purcell that he may well have been the son of Thomas, like the elder Henry a Gentleman of the Chapel Royal and, moreover, a very prominent member of the famous four-and-twenty fiddlers of Charles II. Sir Jack's arguments were as discerning as they were convincing, with the result that most modern books of reference and practically all subsequent biographical accounts discuss Thomas as father. To be sure, he did write to the celebrated bass singer John Gostling in 1679 referring to young Henry as his son. But such would naturally have been his habit if, as is likely, he had been acting *in loco parentis* for fifteen years. And it may be true that Thomas had a son named Edward, just as it is *certain* that young Henry had a brother by that name. But the assumption that Thomas's son and Henry's brother were one and the same cannot continue to be accepted tacitly (as it has been for nearly three decades now, with mischievous results to Purcell genealogy). It must be either proved, disproved, or labelled hypothesis.

The two opposing genealogies are given together (pp. 382-3) for ease of reference.

At first glance the various branches of either version of this Purcell family tree present a bewildering, indeed a Shakespearian, variety of possible mistaken identities. In the younger Henry Purcell's generation alone the names Edward, Katherine, and Charles each appear twice, as if to imply that both families had soon run through a slender stock of suitable family Christian names. The confusion naturally arising from these has caused most

* In his article 'On Henry Purcell and his Family', *PMA*, 1876-7, p. 8.

TABLE I

(After Westrup, p. 307)

Showing Henry as son of Thomas

Thomas m. Katherine (d. 31 July 1682)

Henry m. Elizabeth (d. 11 Aug. 1664) (bur. 26 Aug. 1699)

Katherine m. Wm. Sale (bapt. 13 March 1662)

?

Katherine

Elizabeth (b. 1660, d. 1733, m. Henry Redman)

Charles (d. 1686)

Matthew (d. 1702)

Joseph

Daniel (d. 1717)

[N.B. Francis and Thomas omitted here]

Edward (b. 1653,[1] d. 20 June 1717)

Henry m. Frances (?)Peters (b. 1659, d. 21 Nov. 1695) (d. Feb. 1706)

See Table II

Showing Henry as son of Henry

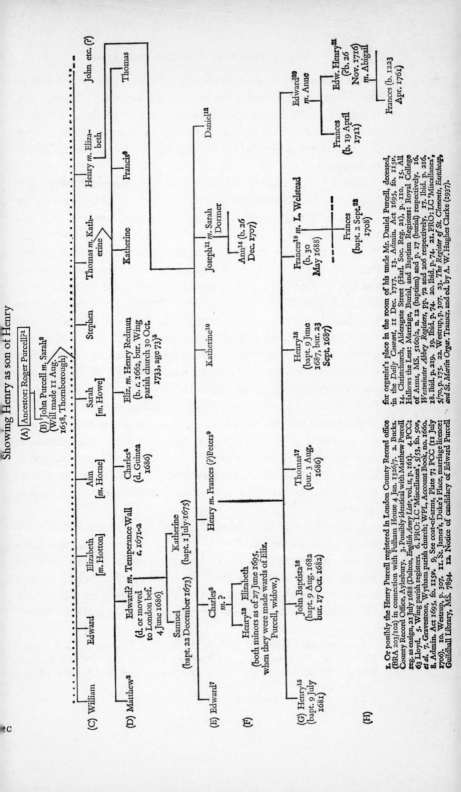

1. Or possibly the Henry Purcell registered in London County Record office (BRA 203/102) in connection with Fulham House 4 Jan. 1326/7. 2. Bucks. County Record Office, Aylesbury. 3. Possibly identical with Matthew Purcell reg. as ensign, 21 July 1688 (Dalton, *English Army List*, vol. ii, p. 161). 4. PCC: 6) Lloyd. 5. Wing parish registers. 6. PRO: I.C 'Miscellanea', 5/33, fo. 50v, d d. 7. Gravestone, Wytham parish church; WPL, Account Book, no. 1060. 8. Admin. Act 1695, fo. 115v. 9. See coat-of-arms, Plate 7; PCC (11 July 1706). 10. Westrup, p. 307. 11. St. James's, Duke's Place, marriage licence: Guildhall Library, MS. 7894. 12. Notice of candidacy of Edward Purcell for organist's place in the room of his uncle Mr. Daniel Purcell, deceased, in the *Daily Courant*, 11 Dec. 1717. 13. Admin. Act 1695, fo. 115v. 14. Christchurch, Aldersgate Street (Harl. Soc. Reg. 21), p. 110. 15. All Hallows the Less: Marriage, Burial, and Baptism Registers: Royal College of Arms, MS. 5160/2, n. 12 (baptism) and p. 17 (burial) respectively. 16. *Westminster Abbey Registers*, pp. 72 and 206 respectively. 17. Ibid. p. 216. 18. Ibid. p. 259. 19. Ibid. p. 74. 20. Ibid. p. 84. 21. PRO: I.C 'Miscellanea', 5/70. p. 175. 22. Westrup, p. 307. 23. *The Register of St. Clements, Eastcheap, and St. Martin Orgar.* Transcr. and ed. by A. W. Hughes Clarke (1937).

of the trouble. It is not enough, for instance, to prove the notion that Henry Purcell had a brother by the name of Edward; it is necessary, if he had a cousin by that name, to show which is which — not an easy demonstration, since extant records seldom furnish anything beyond the minimum of information called for in any particular kind of account.

Proving that Purcell did have a brother named Edward is a fairly simple and straightforward exercise. The brother's career can be followed in detail through various Court and military records, more or less as it is outlined in his epitaph, still to be read in its original state in the chancel at the Wytham parish church (see App. Two, IV, 13).* Other records verify the data given on the stone, which prove to be correct, or nearly so throughout. In fact, only the statement that an Edward was a gentleman usher to Charles II appears to be unverifiable. Edward Chamberlayne recorded an Edward Purcell among those employed at Court as gentleman usher in waiting, assistant, to come in at the first vacancy in the 1679 and 1682 editions of *Angliæ Notitia* (pp. 162 and 166 respectively). But in the fifteenth edition, of 1684, Edward Purcell's name is nowhere to be found, although the appearance of four new persons who held the position shows that vacancies *had* occurred in the interim. On the other hand, Chamberlayne may merely have been careless in keeping up with promotions at Court, for another account mentions Edward Purcell as gentleman usher, as does the gravestone, without the qualification 'assistant'.†

It may be that this Edward Purcell had begun his military career by this time. At any rate, in *English Army Lists and Commission Registers 1661–1714*, Dalton records for an Edward Purcell a fairly rapid rise from the lieutenancy to which he was commissioned in February 1685 to a captaincy by November 1687. On 8 June 1702 he was promoted to major, and on 1 March

---

* The erroneous transcript published by Sir John Hawkins in his *A General History of the Science and Practice of Music* (London, 1853), vol. II, p. 749, has been followed by all subsequent scholars with mischievous results, since Edward Purcell's age at death reads '61', *not* '64'.

† See App. Two, IV, 4 and 13.

1704 to the high rank of lieutenant-colonel (*vice* Lt.-Col. Rook) to Brigadier-General Seymour. Then on 1 May 1711 he sold his commission to a German officer, Kempenfeldt, but did not leave the regiment, according to official record, until May 1716, slightly more than a year before he died. (The details of the sale of the commission have not come to light, but it is difficult to imagine that within a year he would have been destitute, as some have been led to conjecture from the poetic phrases on the stone: 'decayed with age, and broken with misfortunes'.) At any rate this Edward Purcell, who can be identified in the lively miniature portrait (probably by Thomas Forster) now in the Holburne Museum at Bath (see Plate 16(*a*)), is certainly the brother of the younger Henry Purcell, and hence is also brother of Daniel and son of the elder Henry Purcell.

But what of the Edward Purcell who took part in the legal proceedings attendant upon the administration of the Will of Charles Purcell who died in 1686 off the coast of Guinea?* He is named as brother and executor of Charles's Will (drawn up on 4 June 1682), which specifies Katherine Purcell as his mother and Elizabeth and Katherine as his sisters. Moreover, in the Chancery Proceedings he is referred to as Edward Purcell of Mickleham, gentleman,† and not as Lieutenant Edward Purcell — a significant difference. The proving of the Will gave rise to a trying situation which got Edward Purcell into the Courts of Chancery.

Charles, when he died, had had in his cabin on His Majesty's sloop *Le George*, considerable bullion, brandy, and other valuable portable property. After his death one William Bayley, mate of Captain Charles Purcell, who sailed also on the companion ship, the *Orange Tree*, acquired the lot. But he also died at sea, so that these goods fell at last into the hands of his wife, Anne Bayley, who thus acquired considerable wealth and achieved widowhood all at once. The wealth she was unwilling to part with, hence Edward Purcell's taking her to court. In any event, this Edward, referred to as Mr. Edward Purcell of Mickleham, was probably very busy with this case all through the latter part of 1686 and most of 1687. Hence it is unlikely that he should be identified as

* App. Two, I, 2.   † App. Two, I, 4.

the newly fledged Lieutenant Edward Purcell, who ought to have been fully occupied discharging new responsibilities involved in various military affairs in the west of England, in Ireland, and elsewhere.

The name Mr. Edward Purcell of Mickleham provides an important lead, for it appears in the Mickleham parish records in connection with the birth in 1673 of a son, Samuel Purcell (buried that same year on 27 December), and the baptism of a daughter, Katherine Purcell, in 1675. This Edward therefore must have married his wife, Temperance (*née* Wall) at least as early as 1672, when Edward Purcell of Westminster would have been between fourteen and sixteen years old, for Temperance Wall is last mentioned as a maiden in an entry for 26 March 1671. This is not an impossible age for marriage in those days, but somewhat improbable, in view of the fact that Temperance Wall was the daughter of one of the chief citizens — at least one of the wealthiest — of Mickleham, as is known from another entry in the parish registers (see App. Two, xxv, 3). No record of the marriage itself has come to light, so that a more precise date is unobtainable at present. However, Lieutenant Edward Purcell's youth, his military preoccupation, and the fact tha he died a bachelor, neither his Will nor his epitaph making mention of relatives other than his father and famous brother, all rule against his being the husband of Temperance Wall or the father of this Katherine Purcell.

At any rate, old Samuel Wall died in 1692, leaving his Mickleham estate to one Edward Purcell and Temperance (his only daughter) and ten messuages, tenements, etc., to their child, Katherine Purcell, his only granddaughter. However, she did not come into possession of all of these. At least six were relinquished by Edward and Temperance Purcell, who were paid twelve pence apiece for their interest, according to the terms of an indenture drawn up, signed, sealed, and delivered on 19 September 1698. (Actually the Purcells may have lost out altogether here, for the names of Edward, Temperance, and Katherine are nowhere to be found in contemporary records.*)

* An 'Edward Purcell of St. Sepulchers' appears in the testamentary records now housed in Somerset House (PCC: 29 Irby), but he cannot be the same man,

At any rate, the evidence appears to establish the identity of two Edward Purcells who were in and about London during the last quarter of the seventeenth century and the first decade of the eighteenth. Proof positive may never be found, but to relate to one Edward Purcell all the records listed in Appendix Two, IV involves so many difficulties that the case is indeed improbable, if not totally impossible:

1. Edward Purcell would have had to marry at the age of fourteen or fifteen, or possibly sixteen.

2. Captain Edward Purcell would have alternatively been styled by his military rank and as Mr. Edward Purcell of Mickleham.

3. He would have taken a great deal of time off from military duties for litigation attendant upon the execution of Charles Purcell's Will.

4. Lieutenant-Colonel Edward Purcell would have died a bachelor, away from the properties in Mickleham (and elsewhere), which he and his wife Temperance had inherited in 1698, with no mention of his daughter or wife.

5. In the codicil to his Will (see pp. 306–7 above) and elsewhere, Lieutenant-Colonel Edward Purcell is mentioned as 'of the parish of St. Margaret's, Westminster', whereas the putative cousin is consistently referred to as Mr. Edward Purcell, gentleman, of Mickleham.

6. Edward Purcell would have had to be son to both Henry and Thomas Purcell at one and the same time, for an Edward Purcell is definitely referred to as both brother to the younger Henry Purcell and brother to Matthew Purcell, son of Thomas.

7. Edward Purcell would have been charged with heavy responsibilities in Charles II's Secret Service at a very tender age, hence my belief that Edward Purcell, son of Thomas, was very likely he who is mentioned in the *Calendar of Treasury*

---

having died in Feb. 1695 and left a widow named Sarah Purcell. Temperance is likewise unrecorded, or only elusively so. But Katherine's name turns up again at the bottom of Matthew Purcell's Will, which she witnessed in 1702. Her signature on this document and that made four years earlier on the indenture discussed above are precisely, unquestionably identical.

Books as receiving a warrant on 25 March 1673 for '100 marks per an.... to be for preventing uncertain charges (by bills) which he shall be put to for His Majesty's service about making ready of standing houses and progress houses in the [King's] removes and other services as Gentleman Usher *Daily Waiter Assistant*'. [Italics mine.] It is unlikely that such heavy responsibility would have been entrusted to Edward, son of Henry, then but sixteen or seventeen. However, other records of an Edward Purcell serving as gentleman usher at the Court of Charles II probably refer to the son of Henry Purcell. Thomas, incidentally, placed another son, Francis, in similar employment, as groom of the Privy Chamber, then groom of the robes to Charles II, and also as Housekeeper at Somerset House, Queen Catherine of Braganza's abode.*

If Colonel Edward was the son of Henry and Elizabeth, then the question also arises, why was he not chosen to administer his mother's estate in 1699 instead of Katherine, who is actually named as executrix?† Quite simply, Edward, then still an officer in Colonel Henry Trelawney's 4th Regiment of Foot (1692–1702), would have been very busily occupied and far from the scene, either in the Low Countries, where the regiment was on intermittent duty from 1689 until 1715, or in Ireland, where the unit was often called, or perhaps elsewhere on the continent.

Nor is it surprising to find that Daniel Purcell could not afford the time to act as his mother's executor, since he would have been busy preparing for the London theatrical season; it would therefore have been more logical for Katherine Sale (*née* Purcell) to undertake the business. Whatever the truth of the matter might be with regard to this small detail, it is in a document having to do with Daniel Purcell that we find the final, clinching evidence, which shows both Daniel and Henry the younger to have been the sons of Henry Purcell the elder. First though, to corroborate their relationship as brothers, in the *Daily Courant* for 12 December 1717, Edward Purcell (son of Henry the younger) advertised his

---

* See Genealogical Table II, under Thomas Purcell, and n. 5. See also App. Two, XI, *passim*.

† App. Two, IX, 3.

application for the post of organist 'in the room of his *uncle* [italics mine], Dr. Daniel Purcell, deceased'.

Proof that Daniel and also, therefore, Henry were sons of Henry Purcell turns up in the likeliest of all places. Daniel Purcell was organist at Magdalen College, Oxford, from 1689 to 1696 (for which latter year, having moved to London in May of 1695, he shared his pay with Benjamin Hecht). In the Magdalen College registers he is entered thus:

> 1688. Purcell, Daniel, res. 1695. Son of Henry Purcell, Gentleman of the Chapel Royal *obiit* 1718. He was brother of Henry Purcell . . .*

This leaves little room for doubt that Henry was also son of Henry, and this little room is seriously diminished by another piece of evidence brought to light recently by the researches of Rev. John A. Fitch (Vicar of Reydon) into the history of the Hingeston family. He discovered the information — and passed it on to Sir Jack Westrup, who gave it to me — that John Hingeston had in December of 1683 willed £5 to his godson 'Henry Pursall (son of Elizabeth Pursall)'.

There remain two small grains of doubt to be removed, however. Could there have been a second young Henry Purcell who was Hingeston's godson, but not to be identified as his apprentice? On legal as well as logical grounds the answer must be 'No'. Hingeston's Will was carefully drawn up, and possible confusion on this score would have been cleared up, especially where one of the Henry Purcells would have been so famous already. Then, accordingly, one might well ask why so small a gift and such scant reference to a composer already gaining national recognition. Why indeed? we inquire from our present vantage point, knowing what Henry Purcell was to become. But to Hingeston he may well have seemed a tiresome young assistant too ambitious and newfangled, and too talented for comfort. Was he not just

---

* J. R. Bloxham (ed.), *A Register of the Presidents, Fellows, Demies . . . of St. Mary Magdalen College*, vol. II, p. 203 (see also App. Two, III, 5). The fact pointed out by Westrup that Anthony à Wood first entered Daniel Purcell as 'son of Henry Purcell' later crossing out 'son' and replacing it with the word 'brother' does not indicate that he had discovered his own mistake, but only that young Henry had become famous meanwhile (see App. Two, III, 1).

then composing sonatas in the Italian vein, brashly turning his back on the sombre English instrumental polyphony which Hingeston knew and loved? Perhaps it is a wonder that Hingeston mentioned him at all. Whatever the case as concerns Hingeston *v.* Purcell, this statement definitely establishes Henry Purcell's parentage on the distaff side and, presumably, affirms that the elder Henry was his father.

The information that has led to the setting up of the second genealogical table shown above may be summarized quickly. That the famous composer's father was Henry and his uncle was Thomas seems much more tenable than the contrary theory. However, it is quite probable that all the younger members of both families referred to one another as brothers and sisters, at least after 11 August 1664, when the elder Henry died. This possibility, all the more probable in view of Thomas Purcell's reference in 1679 to Henry as his son, suggests an interesting, possibly valid, solution to the strange duplication of Christian names. That there were two Charles Purcells seems undeniably true. But given the looseness of reference suggested above, there is no reason to insist that there were really two Edwards (although the contrary case raises many difficulties none is insuperable), or two Katherines, sons and daughters of Henry and Thomas respectively. However, there were undoubtedly two Charleses.

To summarize by way of conclusion, then, it seems fairly certain that two families of Purcells moved to London, settling in or near Westminster during the Commonwealth period, and that young Henry, named after his father, was born in the shadow of Westminster Abbey, where he later was to be established as organist and England's most celebrated musical genius. After his father's death he may have moved to live with his widowed mother in South Tuttle (i.e. Tothill) Street, or he may have moved into the more fashionable area (which was to become the parish of St. Martin-in-the-Fields) where his uncle Thomas held property in Pall Mall. Even though the traditional assumption that Thomas adopted him in 1664 or 1665 cannot be proved (or disproved), it is safe to assume that he would have taken interest in the rearing of his nephew, in his schooling, and, particularly, in his musical training. After fifteen years he would have been entirely justified in referring to Henry as his son, without qualification, both by force of habit and contemporary custom.

At any rate, this mention of Henry as his son by Thomas dwindles into relative insignificance in the face of all the new solid evidence that has come to light — not to mention the fact that the source for this statement has been neither examined nor evaluated for over fifty years now.

APPENDIX FOUR

BIBLIOGRAPHY

Addleshaw, G. W. O., *The High Church Tradition: A Study in the Liturgical Thought of the Seventeenth Century*. London, 1941.

Akerman, J. Y., *Moneys received and paid for Secret Services of Charles II and James II*. London, 1851.

Andrews, H., 'Purcell and 17th-century Chamber Music', *Music Teacher*, July 1927.

Anon., *An Exact Relation of the Entertainment of His Most Sacred Majesty, William III . . . at the Hague* (translated from the Dutch). London, 1691.

— 'Dr. Purcell-Taylor's wild story', *Musical Times*, Aug. 1918.

— 'Edward Purcell', *Musical Times*, March 1905.

— 'Edward Henry Purcell', *Musical Times*, June 1931.

— 'Index to the Songs and Allusions in *The Gentleman's Journal*, 1692–4', *Musical Antiquary*, July 1911.

— 'Josiah Priest's School', *Musical Times*, Dec. 1863.

— 'Memoirs of the Life and Writings of Henry Purcell, the celebrated, with his Portrait, finely engraved from an original Painting', *Universal Magazine*, Dec. 1777.

— 'Purcell and Italian Music', *Musical Times*, April 1917.

— 'Purcell Fantazias', *PMA*, 1915.

— 'Purcell Sonatas', *PMA*, 1915.

— 'Purcell's Father', *Music & Letters*, Oct. 1955.

— 'The Music Library of Mr. T. W. Taphouse', *Musical Times*, Oct. 1904.

Antcliffe, H., 'The Naïveté of Purcell', *Chesterian*, N.S., no. 35 (1923).

Arkwright, G. E. P., 'A Note on Purcell's Music', *Music & Letters* Apr., 1921.

— 'Purcell's Church Music', *Musical Antiquary*, Jan. 1910.

— 'Purcell's Church Music: Bibliography', *Musical Antiquary*, July 1910.

Arnold, C., and Johnson, M., 'The English Fantasy Suite', *PRMA*, 1955–6.

Arnold, F. T., *The Art of Accompaniment from a Thorough-Bass*. London, 1961.

Arundell, D., 'A Masterpiece in Miniature', *Radio Times*, 27 Dec. 1947.

— *Henry Purcell*. London, 1927.

— 'Purcell and Natural Speech', *Musical Times*, June 1959.

— *The Critic at the Opera*. London, 1957.

— 'The Tragedy of Henry Purcell', *London Mercury*, 23 Jan. 1965.

Ashley, M., *England in the Seventeenth Century*. Pelican History of England, no. 6. London, 1952.

'Ashtead Manor Accounts (Thomas Howard)'. Guildford Museum Muniments, Guildford, Surrey.

Aubrey, J., *Brief Lives* (ed. A. Clark). Oxford, 1898.

'Audit Office Declared Accounts'. Extracts printed in *Musical Antiquary, passim. See* 'Lists of the King's Musicians...'

Avery, E. 'A Tentative Calendar of Daily Theatrical Performances', *Research Studies of the State College of Washington*, 1945.

Azulay, G., *Purcell*. London, 1931.

Backus, E. N., *Catalogue of Music in the Huntington Library Printed before 1801.* Huntington Library, San Marino, California, 1949.

Baines, A., *Woodwind Instruments and their History*. London, 1943.

Baker, H. B., *History of the London Stage and its Famous Players (1576–1903).* London, 1904.

★Baker, R., *A Chronicle of the Kings of England*, 6th ed. London, 1674.

Barker, E. (ed.), *The Character of England*. London, 1947.

Barker, G. F. R., *Memoir of Richard Busby* (1606–95). London, 1895.

Barrett, W. A., *English Church Composers*. London, 1882.

Bedford, A., *The Evil and Danger of Stage Plays*. London, 1706.

— *The Great Abuse of Musick*. London, 1711.

— *The Hereditary Right of the Crown of England Asserted*. London, 1713.

— *The Temple of Musick*. London, 1706.

Beeverell, J., *Les délices de la Grand' Bretagne*. Leiden, 1707.

Bell, C. F., 'English Seventeenth-Century Portrait Drawings in Oxford Collections', *Walpole Society*, vol. v (1917).

Bell, W. G., *The Great Fire of London in 1666*. London, 1920.

Bennet, J., 'Henry Purcell: An Appreciation', *Musical Times*, Nov. 1895.

Bentley, G. E., *The Jacobean and Caroline Stage*. Oxford, 1941–56.

Besant, Sir Walter, *London in the Time of the Stuarts*. London, 1903.

Beswick, D. M., 'The Problem of Tonality in Seventeenth-Century Music'. (Unpublished doctoral dissertation, University of North Carolina, 1951.)

Betterton, T., *The History of the English Stage*. London, 1741.

Bevin, E., *A Brief and Short Instruction of the Art of Musicke*. London, 1631.

Bicknell, J. C., 'Interdependance of Word and Tone in the Dramatic Music of Henry Purcell'. (Unpublished doctoral dissertation, Stanford University, 1960.)

Bidloo, G., *Komste van . . . Willem III. Koning van Groot Britanje, enz. in Holland*, 's Gravenhage, 1691.

Binyon, L., *Catalogue of Prints and Drawings in the British Museum*. London, 1902.

Birch, G. H., *London Churches of the XVIIth and XVIIIth Centuries*. London, 1896.

Blaikley, D. J., 'Notes on the Trumpet Scale', *PMA*, 1894.

Bliss, A., 'Henry Purcell', *Chesterian*, N.S., no. 17 (1921).

Blom, E. (ed.), *Grove's Dictionary of Music and Musicians*, 5th ed. London, 1954; with supplementary volume in 1961 (ed. E. Blom and D. Stevens).

Blow, J., 'Rules for Composition'. British Museum, Add. MS. 30933.

— 'Rules for playing of a Through Bass upon Organ and Harpsicon'. British Museum, Add. MS. 34072.

Bloxam, J. R. (ed.), *A Register of the Presidents, Fellows, Demies . . . of Saint Mary Magdalen College*. Oxford, 1853–85.

Bluemantle, J. P., *An Alphabetical Index of the Streets, Squares, Alleys &c of the Cities of London and Westminster*. London, 1747.

Blume, F. (ed.), *Die Musik in Geschichte und Gegenwart*. Kassel, 1949–present.

Bonavia, M., 'Purcell and the Birth of English Opera', *Everyman*, 1931.

Borgman, A. S., *Thomas Shadwell*. New York, 1928.

★Boswell, E., *The Restoration Court Stage 1660–1702*. Cambridge, Mass., 1932.

Brent Smith, A., 'Henry Purcell', *Music & Letters*, April 1937.

Bridge, J. C., 'A Great English Choir-trainer: Captain Henry Cooke', *Musical Antiquary*, Jan. 1911.

Bridge, J. F., 'Purcell and Nicola Matteis', *SIMG*, July–Sept. 1900.

— 'Purcell's Birthplace and Residences', *Musical Times*, Nov. 1895.

— 'Purcell's Editors', *Musical News*, May 1903.

— 'Purcell's Fantazias and Sonatas', *PMA*, 1915–16.

— 'The recently discovered Violin Sonata', *Musical News*, March 1903.

— *Twelve Good Musicians*. London, 1920.

Britten, B., 'Dido and Aeneas', *The Times*, 27 April 1951.

— 'On realizing the continuo in Purcell's songs', in *Henry Purcell 1659–1695: Essays on his Music* (ed. I. Holst). London, 1959.

Brockmeier, H. F., 'The Theater Music of Henry Purcell: A Study of Songs and Instrumental Numbers for English Plays from 1680 to 1695'. (Unpublished thesis, University of Southern California, 1947.)

Brown, J. D., and Stratton, S., *British Musical Biography*. Birmingham, 1897.

★Bryant, A., *King Charles II*. London, 1931.

— (ed.), *The Letters, and Speeches, and Declarations of King Charles II*. London, 1935.

Bucchi, V., 'Aci e Galatea di Haendel: Didone ed Enea di Purcell', *Scenario* (Milan), 1940.

Bucht, G., 'Purcell och den engelska Fancyn', *Musikrevy* (Stockholm), 1958.

Bucinator, 'Purcell's "Come if you dare, the Trumpet Sound" ', *Musical Antiquary*, Jan. 1911.

Bukofzer, M., 'Allegory in Baroque Music', *Journal of the Warburg and Courtauld Institutes*, vol. III, no. 1.

— *Music in the Baroque Era from Monteverdi to Bach*. New York, 1947.

Burnet, G., *A Supplement to Burnet's History of My Own Time* (ed. H. C. Foxcroft). Oxford, 1902.

— *Bishop Burnet's History of His Own Time*. London, 1753.

★Burney, C., *A General History of Music* (ed. F. Mercer). New York, 1935.

Chamberlayne, E., *Angliæ Notitia: or, The Present State of England*. London: 12th ed. (1679), 14th ed. (1682), 15th ed. (1684), 17th ed. (1692).

Chappell, W. (ed.), *Old English Popular Music* (rev. ed. H. E. Wooldridge). London, 1893.

Charles II, *An Account of the Preservation of King Charles II*. London, 1803. (A New Edition, printed by S. Gosnell for John Scott.)

Chester, J. L., *London Marriages Licenses 1521–1869*. London, 1887.

— *The Marriage, Baptismal, and Burial Registers of the Collegiate Church or Abbey of St. Peter, Westminster*. London, 1876.

Chissell, J., 'St. Cecilia: Purcell and Britten', *Monthly Musical Record*, 1943.

Cibber, C., *An Apology for the Life of Mr. Colley Cibber, Comedian*. London, 1740.

Clarke, H., 'John Blow'. (Unpublished doctoral dissertation, Harvard University, 1947.)

Clercx, S., *Le Baroque et la musique*. Brussels, 1948.

Colles, H. C., *et al*. 'Henry Purcell', in Grove's *Dictionary of Music and Musicians*, 5th ed. London, 1954.

— 'Musical London from the Restoration to Handel', *Essays and Lectures*. London, 1945.

— 'Some Musical Instruction Books of the Seventeenth Century', *PMA*, 1928–9.

— *Voice and Verse. A Study in English Song*. London, 1928.

Conley, P., 'The use of the trumpet in the music of Purcell', *Brass Quarterly* (Durham, N. H.), Fall 1959.

Cooper, G. M., 'Italian Instrumental Music of the Sixteenth Century', *PMA*, 1929–30.

— 'The Chronology of Purcell's Works', *Musical Times*, July–Dec. 1943.

Cosmo the Third, *Travels through England during the reign of King Charles II* (translated from the Italian MS. in the Laurentian Library at Florence, with a memoir of his life). 1669.

Cox, D., 'Henry Purcell, the British Orpheus', *Gramophone*, June 1959.

Crowest, F. J., 'Purcell', *Blackwell's Magazine*, 1895.

Cudworth, C. L., ' "Baptist's Vein" — French Orchestral Music and its Influence, from 1650–1750', *PRMA*, 1956–7.

— 'Some New Facts about the Trumpet Voluntary', *Musical Times*, Sept. 1953.

Cummings, W. H., 'A Brief Life of Purcell', *Musical Times*, Nov. 1895.

— 'Dido and Aeneas', *Musical Times*, June 1910.

— 'On Henry Purcell and his Family', *PMA*, 1876–7.

— 'The Mutilation of a Masterpiece', *PMA*, 1903–4.

— 'Portraits of Purcell', *Musical Times*, Nov. 1895.

— Purcell. London, 1903.

— 'Purcell and Dr. Arne', *Musical Times*, Nov. 1895.

— 'Purcell's Death', *Musical Times*, July 1889.

Dalrymple, J., *Memoirs of Great Britain and Ireland*. London, 1790.

Dart, R. T., 'Purcell's Chamber Music', *PRMA*, 1958–9.
— 'Purcell's Harpsichord Music', *Musical Times*, June 1959.
— *The Interpretation of Music*, London, 1954.
Davey, H., *History of English Music*. London, 1895.
Davidson, L. C., *Catherine of Bragança, infanta of Portugal and Queen Consort of England*. London, 1908.
Day, C. L. (ed.), *The Songs of Thomas D'Urfey*. Cambridge, Mass., 1933.
*Day, C. L., and Murrie, E. B., *English Song-books 1651–1702*. London, 1940 (for 1937).
Dawes, F., 'A Jig of Morgan's', *Musical Times*, March 1950.
Dean-Smith, M., 'English Tunes Common to Playford's Dancing Master, The Keyboard Books and Traditional Songs and Dances', *PRMA*, 1952–3.
Deane, C. V., *Dramatic Theory and the Rhymed Heroic Play*. London, 1931.
Demarquez, S., *Purcell: la vie, l'œuvre*. Paris, 1951.
Dent, E. J., 'America Discovers Purcell', *Nation*, Jan. 1924.
— *Foundations of English Opera*. London, 1951.
— 'Italian Chamber Cantatas', *Musical Antiquary*, April 1911.
— 'Italian Opera in London', *PRMA*, 1944–5.
— 'Purcell in Church', *Nation*, Aug. 1921.
— 'Purcell in the Open Air', *Nation*, July 1921.
— 'Purcell on the Stage', *Athenaeum*, Jan. 1920.
— 'Purcell's *Dido and Aeneas*', *Deutsche Kunstschau*, 1934.
— 'Purcell's *King Arthur*', *Listener*, 4 Dec. 1935.
— 'The Baroque Opera', *Musical Antiquary*, Jan. 1910.
Dezsö, L., *Purcell*. Budapest, 1959.
Dodwell, H., *Treatise concerning the Lawfulness of Instrumental Music in Holy Offices*, 2nd ed. London, 1700.
Dolmetsch, A., *The Interpretation of the Music of the XVII and XVIII Centuries*. London, 1946.
Donington, R., 'Further seventeenth- and eighteenth-century evidence bearing on the performance of Purcell's works,' in *Henry Purcell 1659–1695: Essays on his Music* (ed. I. Holst), London, 1959.
— 'Performing Purcell's music today.' Ibid.
— *The Interpretation of Early Music*. London, 1963.
*Downes, J., *Roscius Anglicanus* (ed. Rev. M. Summers). London, 1928.
Downes, R., 'An organist's view of the organ works,' in *Henry Purcell 1659–1695: Essays on his Music* (ed. I. Holst). London, 1959.
Duckles, V., 'The Curious Art of John Wilson (1595–1674): An Introduction to his Songs and Lute Music', *Journal of the American Musicological Society*, Summer 1954.
Duffett, T., *Beauties Triumph, A Masque*. London, 1676.
Duncan, E., 'The Songs of Henry Purcell', *Monthly Musical Record*, vol. xxx, no. 389 (1903).

Dunkin, P., 'Issues of *The Fairy Queen*', *Library*, vol. XXVI (1946).

Dupré, H., *Purcell*. Paris, 1927.

Dussauze, H., 'Captain Cooke and his Choirboys.' (Unpublished thesis, Paris, 1911.)

Eaglefield-Hull, A. 'A New Light on Purcell', *Musical Times*, Dec. 1927.

Ebsworth, J. W. (ed.), *The Bagford Ballads*. Hertford, 1876.

— *The Roxburghe Ballads*. Hertford, 1871–99.

Edwards, F. G., 'A Master Organ Builder: Father Smith', *Musical Times*, Aug. 1905.

— 'Three Royal Funeral Anthems', *Musical Times*, March 1901.

Egerton, J., *The Theatrical Remembrancer*. London, 1788.

Eggebrecht, H. H., 'Walthers Musikalisches Lexikon in seinen terminologischen Partien', *Acta Musicologica*, vol. XXIX: fasc. 1 (1957).

Elkin, R., *The Old Concert Rooms of London*. London, 1955.

Epstein, P., 'Gegen die Verbalhornung von Purcells Dido durch Bodansky', *Zeitschrift für Musikwissenschaft*, 1924.

Espinós, V., *El 'Quijote' en la música*. Barcelona, 1947.

— 'Las realizaciones musicales del Quijote: Enrique Purcell y su "Comical History of Don Quixote" ', *Revista de la Biblioteca*, 1933.

Evans, B. I., *Short History of English Drama*. London, 1948.

*Evelyn, J., *Diary* (ed. E. S. de Beer, 6 vols.), Oxford, 1955.

— *Memoirs of John Evelyn* (ed. W. Bray). London, 1818.

Farmer, H. G., 'Music down below', *Musical Times*, Sept. 1949.

Favre-Lingorow, S., *Der Instrumentalstil von Purcell*. Berne, 1950.

Fellowes, E. H., *English Cathedral Music*. London, 1941.

Fenney, W., 'Henry Purcell: A Short Study', *Musical Opinion*, June 1920.

Fitzpatrick, S. A. O., *Dublin, A Historical and Topographical Account of the City*. London, 1907.

Flood, W. H. Grattan, 'Irish Ancestry of Garland, Dowland, Campion and Purcell', *Music & Letters*, Jan. 1922.

— 'Purcell's "Dido and Aeneas": Who was Lady Dorothy Burke?' *Musical Times*, Nov. 1918.

— 'Quelques précisions nouvelles sur Cambert et Grabu à Londres', *Revue de Musicologie*, vol. IX (1927).

Flothius, M., 'Purcell, Stravinsky en de vooruitgang', *Mens en Melodie* (Utrecht), 1949.

Fortune, N., 'Purcell's Life and Background', *Purcell-Handel Festival* (Arts Council of Great Britain, *et al.* London, June 1959.

— and Zimmerman, F. B., 'Purcell's autographs', in *Henry Purcell 1659–1695: Essays on his Music* (ed. I. Holst). London, 1959.

Frotscher, G., *Geschichte des Orgelspiels und der Orgelkomposition*. Berlin, 1935.

Fuller-Maitland, J. A., 'A German Compliment to Purcell' (letter to the editor), *Musical Times*, Aug. 1896.
— 'Foreign Influences on Henry Purcell', *Musical Times*, Jan. 1896.
— 'Purcell's *King Arthur*', in *Studies in Music* (ed. R. Grey). New York, 1901.
— and Mann, A. H., *Catalogue of the Music in the Fitzwilliam Museum, Cambridge*. London, 1893.

Galpin, F. W., 'The Sackbut, its Evolution and History', *PMA*, 1906–7.
Garnett, R., *The Age of Dryden*. London, 1901.
Gavaldá, M. Q., *La música en las obras de Cervantes*. Barcelona, 1948.
*Genest, J., *Some Account of the English Stage . . . 1660–1830*. Bath, 1832.
Gieglung, F., *Giuseppe Torelli*. Kassel und Basel, 1949.
Gombosi, O., 'Some Musical Aspects of the English Court Masque', *Journal of the American Musicological Society*, Fall 1948.
Grace, H., 'Henry Purcell, 1659–1695', *Boletín de Programas, Radio-televisión nacional de Colombia* (Bogotá), Nov. 1959.
Granger, J., *A Biographical History of England*, 2nd ed. London, 1824.
Gray, A., 'Purcell's Dramatic Music', *PMA*, 1916–17.
Greg, W. W., *A Bibliography of the English Printed Drama to the Restoration*. London, 1939–59.
Grout, D. J., 'Seventeenth-Century Parodies of French Opera', *Musical Quarterly*, April 1941 (part I) and Oct. 1941 (part II).

Haas, R., 'Die Musik des Barocks', in *Handbuch der Musikwissenschaft*. Wildpart-Potsdam, 1928.
Halfpenny, E., 'A Seventeenth-century Oboe Consort', *Galpin Society Journal*, May 1957.
— 'Musicians at James II's Coronation', *Music & Letters*, April 1951.
— 'The Entertainment of Charles II', *Music & Letters*, Jan. 1957.
Ham, R. D., *Dryden's Dedication for the Music of the Prophetess, 1691*. (Publications of the Modern Language Association of America, Dec. 1935.)
Harding, R., 'A Thematic Catalogue of the Works of Matthew Locke.' (Unpublished, Cambridge, 1954.)
Harley, J., 'Music and Musicians in Restoration London', *Musical Quarterly*, Oct. 1954.
Harrison, P., 'A Tempest with Music', *Twentieth Century*, July 1959.
Hart, E. F., 'The Restoration Catch', *Music & Letters*, Oct. 1953.
*Hawkins, J., *A General History of the Science and Practice of Music*, new ed. vol. II. London, 1853.
Hayes, G. R., *Musical Instruments and their Music, 1500–1750*: vol. I, 'The Treatment of Instrumental Music' (Oxford, 1928); vol. II, 'The Viols and other Bowed Instruments' (Oxford, 1930).

Hodges, N., *Loimologia: or An Historical Account of the Plague in London in 1665.* London, 1720.

Holland, A. K., *Henry Purcell: The English Musical Tradition.* London, 1932.

— 'Purcell's Instrumental Music', *Listener*, 13 Nov. 1952.

Holmes, C. J., 'The Portraits of Arne and Purcell', *Burlington Magazine*, April to Sept. 1915.

Holst, G., 'Henry Purcell', in *The Heritage of Music*, vol. I. Oxford, 1927.

Holst, I., 'A note on the Nanki collection of Purcell's works', in *Henry Purcell 1659–1695; Essays on his Music* (ed. I. Holst). London, 1959.

— 'Purcell's Dances.' Ibid.

— 'Purcell's librettist, Nahum Tate.' Ibid.

Hotson, L., *The Commonwealth and Restoration Stage.* Cambridge, Mass., 1928.

Howard, M., 'An anthem by Henry Purcell', *Monthly Musical Record*, March/April 1953.

Hughes-Hughes, A., *Catalogue of Manuscript Music in the British Museum* (3 vols.). London, 1906–9.

— 'Henry Purcell's Handwriting', *Musical Times*, Feb. 1896.

— 'A Purcell Album and a Few Thoughts about it', *Monthly Musical Record*, vol. XLVIII, no. 572 (1918).

— 'Forerunners: I. Purcell and Zachau', *Monthly Musical Record*, vol. LII, no. 614 (1922).

Hume, D., *The History of England to 1688* (8 vols.). London, 1813.

Humphries, C., and Smith, W. C., *Music Publishing in the British Isles.* London, 1954.

*Husk, W. H., *An Account of the Musical Celebrations on St. Cecilia's Day.* London, 1857.

— 'Purcell', in Grove's *Dictionary of Music and Musicians*, 1st ed. London, 1883.

Just, H., 'Henry Purcell', *Musikantengilde*, vol. VII (1929).

— 'Henry Purcell zu seinem 300 Geburtstag in diesem Jahre'. *Hausmusik* (Kassel), March/April 1959.

King, A. Hyatt, 'The First "Complete Edition" of Purcell', *Monthly Musical Record*, March/April 1951.

Klenz, W., 'The Church Sonatas of Henry Purcell.' (Unpublished thesis, University of North Carolina, 1948.)

Koeltzsch, H., 'Henry Purcells Gambenfantasien', *Musica* (Kassel), Aug. 1955.

Lafontaine, H. C. de, *The King's Musick.* London, 1909.

Lam, B., 'Purcell and the Trio Sonata', *Listener*, 20 May 1954.

Lamson, R., *Henry Purcell's Dramatic Songs and the English Broadside Ballad.* (Modern Language Association of America, 1938.)

Landormy, P., 'Purcell's *Dido and Aeneas* (1689)' (translated by F. Rothwell), *Musical Opinion*, vol. II (1928).

Lang, P. H., *Music in Western Civilization*. New York, 1941.

*Langbaine, G., *The Lives and Characters of English Dramatick Poets*. London, 1699.

*Laurie, A. M., 'Purcell's Stage Works.' (Unpublished doctoral dissertation, University of Cambridge, 1962.)

Lawrence, W. J., 'Foreign Singers and Musicians at the Court of Charles II', *Musical Quarterly*, April 1923.

— 'Italian Opera in London', *Musical Antiquary*, July 1911.

— *Old Theatre Days and Ways*. London, 1935.

— ' "Rare en Tout", 1677; and James Paisible', *Musical Antiquary*, Oct. 1910.

— *The Elizabethan Playhouse and other Studies* (2 vols.). Stratford-upon-Avon, 1912–13.

— 'The French Opera in London: A Riddle of 1686', *Times Literary Supplement*, 28 March 1936.

Leach, A. F., *English Schools at the Reformation (1546–8)*. Westminster, 1896.

Lewis, A., 'A new Purcell song', *Score*, vol. IV (1951).

— 'Matthew Locke: A Dynamic Figure in English Music', *PRMA*, 1948.

— 'Purcell's Music for *The Tempest*', *Musical Times*, June 1959.

'Liber Computi S. M. Magd. Coll.' Manuscript in Magdalen College Library, Oxford.

Liess, A., 'Materialen zur römischien Musikgeschichte des Seicento: Musikerlisten des Oratorio San Marcello 1664–1725', *Acta Musicologica*, vol. XXIX, fasc. iv.

Littleton, A. H., *Purcell's Portraits*. London (n.d.).

Locke, M., *Melothesia: or Certain General Rules for Playing upon a Continued-Bass*. London, 1673.

— *The English Opera: or the Vocal Musick in Psyche*. London, 1675.

Lohr, I., 'Henry Purcell und seine Bearbeiten', *Schweizerische Musikzeitung* (Zurich), 1951.

Lucas, C., 'With Purcell in Westminster', *Musical Courier*, 27 June 1931.

Ludman, J., 'Henry Purcell: A New Look at the Great Master of English Song' *Bulletin*, 15 May 1957.

*Luttrell, N., *A Brief Historical Relation of State Affairs from September 1678 to April 1714*, vols. I–III. Oxford, 1857.

Macaulay, T., *The History of England*. London, 1870.

McCabe, W. H., 'Music and the Dance on a 17th-Century College Stage', *Musical Quarterly*, July 1938.

McCutcheon, R. P., 'Dryden's Prologue to the Prophetess', *Modern Language Notes*, vol. XXXIX (1924), p. 123.

McGuinness, R., 'Blow's Court Odes.' (Typescript article.)

*— 'English Court Odes, 1660–1820.' (Unpublished doctoral thesis, Oxford University, 1963.)

Mace, D., 'English Musical Thought in the Seventeenth Century.' (Unpublished dissertation, Columbia University, 1952.)

Mace, T., *Musick's Monument*. London, 1676.

Macrory, E., *Notes on the Temple Organ*, 3rd ed. (ed. M. M. Mackenzie), London, 1911.

Magalotti, L., *Travels of Cosmo the Third, Grand Duke of Tuscany, through England, during the reign of King Charles II (1669)*. London, 1821.

*Maitland, W., *The History of London from its Foundation to the Present Time*, 2nd ed. (2 vols.). London, 1769.

Mangeot, A., 'The Purcell Fantasias and their Influence on Modern Music', *Music & Letters*, April 1926.

Manifold, J. S., *The Music in English Drama from Shakespeare to Purcell*. London, 1956.

Marco, G. A., 'The Variety in Purcell's Word Painting', *Music Review*, Feb. 1957.

Mark, J., 'Dryden and the Beginning of Opera in England', *Music & Letters*, July 1924.

Mason, D. G. (ed.), 'Henry Purcell', in *Masters in Music*. London, 1904.

Matas, J. R., *Diccionario Biográfico de la Música*. Barcelona (n.d.).

Mattheson, J., *Grundlage einer Ehren-Pforte*. Berlin, 1910.

Maugars, A., *Response faite à un curieux sur le sentiment de la musique d'Italie*. (Escrite à Rome le premier Octobre 1639.)

Mayer, G. L., 'The Vocal Works of Henry Purcell: a Discography', *American Record Guide*, May 1959.

Meinardus, W., 'Die Technik des Basso Ostinato bei Henry Purcell.' (Unpublished dissertation, Cologne, 1950.)

Mellor, A., *A Record of the Music and Musicians of Eton College*. Windsor, 1929.

Meltzer, E., 'The Secular Songs of Henry Purcell.' (Unpublished doctoral dissertation, University of California at Los Angeles, 1957.)

Menestrier, C. F., *Des ballets anciens et modernes selon les règles du théâtre*. Paris, 1682.

— *Des représentations en musique anciennes et modernes*. Paris, 1681.

Meyer, E. H., *Die mehrstimmige Spielmusik des 17. Jahrhunderts in Nord- und Mitteleuropa*. Kassel, 1934.

— *English Chamber Music*. London, 1946.

Miller, H., 'Henry Purcell and the Ground Bass', *Music & Letters*, Oct. 1948.

*Moore, R. E., *Henry Purcell and the Restoration Theatre*. Cambridge, Mass., 1961.

— 'The Music to *Macbeth*', *Musical Quarterly*, Jan. 1960.

Motteux, P. A. (ed.), *The Gentleman's Journal, or The Monthly Miscellany* London, Jan. 1692–Nov. 1694.

Muddiman, J. G., *The King's Journalist 1659–1689*. London, 1923.

Myers, R. H., 'Henry Purcell; a tribute from France', *Chesterian*, Jan. 1952.

Nagel, W., *Geschichte der Musik in England*. Strassburg, 1894–97.

Nettl, P. 'An English Musician at the Court of Charles VI in Vienna', *Musical Quarterly*, July 1942.

Newmarch, R., 'Purcell's *Fairy Queen* at Cambridge', *Chesterian*, N.S., no. 6 (1920).

Newton, D., *Catholic London*. London (1950).

Nichols, J. B., and Sons, *London Pageants*. London, 1837.

Nicoll, A., *Restoration Drama, 1660–1700*, 4th ed. (vol. 1 of *A History of English Drama, 1660–1900*). Cambridge, 1952.

Noble, J., 'Purcell and the Chapel Royal', in *Henry Purcell 1659–1695: Essays on his Music* (ed. I. Holst). London, 1959.

Noble, R., 'The Music of Purcell', *Music in Schools*, July 1940.

North, R., 'An Essay of Musicall Ayre. Tending cheifly to shew the foundations of Melody joyned with Harmony.' British Museum, Add. MS. 32536.

— *Autobiography* (ed. A. Jessopp). London, 1887.

— *Memoirs of Musick* (ed. E. F. Rimbault). London, 1846.

— See also Wilson, J., ed. *Roger North on Music*.

— 'Some m[emoran]dums concerning Musick.' British Museum, Add. MS. 32532.

— 'Some notes upon an Essay of Musick, printed 1677, by way of comment and amendment.' British Museum, Add. MS. 32531.

— *The Lives of the Right Hon. Francis North, Baron Guildford*, rev. ed. (3 vols.). London, 1826.

— 'The Musicall Grammarian.' British Museum, Add. MS. 32533, vol. I.

— *The Musicall Grammarian* (ed. H. Andrews). London, 1925.

— 'The Theory of Sounds.' British Museum, Add. MS. 32534.

Novello, V., *Purcell's Sacred Music*. Prefatory volume. London, 1842.

O'Donoghue, F., *Catalogue of Engraved British Portraits in the British Museum*. London, 1912.

Ogilby, J., *The Entertainment of His Most Excellent Majestie Charles II, in his Passage through the City of London to his Coronation*. London, 1662.

— *The Relation of His Majestie's Entertainment passing through the City of London to his Coronation*. London, 1661.

Oldmeadow, E. J., *Great Musicians*. Philadelphia, 1908.

Parry, C. H. H., 'Purcell', *National Review*, 1895.

— *The Oxford History of Music*, vol. III, 'The Music of the Seventeenth Century', 2nd ed. Oxford, 1938.

Pears, P., 'Homage to the British Orpheus', in *Henry Purcell 1659–1695: Essays on his Music* (ed. I. Holst). London, 1959.

*Pepys, S., *Diary* (ed. H. B. Wheatley, 8 vols.). London, 1904.

— *Memoirs of Samuel Pepys* (ed. Lord Braybrooke). London, 1825.

Pereyra, M. L., 'La Musique écrite sur la Tempête d'après Shakespeare par Pelham Humfrey', *Bulletin de la Société Française de la Musicologie*, Oct. 1920.

Pincherle, M., *Vivaldi*. Paris, 1955.

Playford, J., *The English Dancing Master* (ed. M. Dean-Smith). London, 1957 (a facsimile of the edition of 1651).

[Pritchard, W.] *An Exact Account of the Trial between Sir W. Pritchard ... and Tho. Papillon, Esq. in an action upon the case 6 Nov. 1684. To which is added, the matter of fact relating to election of sheriffs ... in 1682*. London, 1689.

— *The Lord Mayor's Show: Being a description of the solemnity at the inauguration of ... Sir W. Pritchard, Kt. Lord Mayor of London ... performed on Monday, Sept XXX 1682. With several new loyal songs and catches*. London, 1682.

Prunières, H., *L'Opéra italien en France avant Lulli*. Paris, 1913.

*Pulver, J., *A Biographical Dictionary of Old English Music*. London, 1927.

— *A Dictionary of Old English Music & Musical Instruments*. London, 1923.

— 'Purcell and Dryden', *Musical Opinion*, April 1936.

— 'The English St. Cecilia Celebrations of the Seventeenth Century', *Sackbut*, July 1927.

Quervain, F. de, *Der Chorstil Henry Purcell's*. Bern und Leipzig, 1935.

Ravenzwaaij, G. van, 'Henry Purcell's Muzikale Synthese in Engelands Restauratie-period', *Miscellanea musicologica floris van der Mueren*, 1950.

— *Purcell*. Haarlem and Antwerp, 1954.

Rawlinson, H., 'Fantasia upon one note for Strings', *Strad*, Jan. 1948.

— 'Purcell's Music for String Orchestra', *Strad*, June 1959.

Rendall, E. D., 'Some Notes on Purcell's Dramatic Music, with Especial Reference to "The Fairy Queen" ', *Music & Letters*, April 1920.

— 'The Influence of Henry Purcell on Handel, traced in *Acis and Galatea*', *Musical Times*, May 1895.

Rimbault, E. F., 'An Historical Sketch of the History of Dramatick Music in England from the earliest time to the death of Purcell Anno Dom. 1695.' Introduction to *Bonduca* in *The Musical Antiquarian Society*, second year. London, 1841–2.

— 'Robert Smith', *Musical Antiquary*, April 1911.

— (ed.), *The Old Cheque-book, or Book of Remembrance, of The Chapel Royal, from 1561 to 1744*. London, 1872.

Rolland, R., 'L'Opéra anglais au XVIIe siècle', in *Lavignac: Encyclopédie de la Musique*, vol. I. Paris, 1913.

— *L'Opéra en Europe avant Lully et Scarlatti*. Paris, 1895.

Rollins, H. E. (ed.), *Pepys Ballads* (8 vols.). Cambridge, Mass., 1929–32.

Roper, E. S., 'Music at the English Chapels Royal', *PMA*, 1927–8.

Rosen, W., 'Der *Sommernachtstraum* mit Purcell-Musik', *Allgemeine Musikzeitung* (Berlin), 1937.

Rowen, R. H., *Early Chamber Music*. New York, 1949.

Runciman, J. F., *Old Scores and New Readings*. London, 1899.

— *Purcell*. London, 1909.

Rychlík, J., 'Henry Purcell', *Tempo; hudební měsíčník*. Prague, 1956.

St. Katherine Cree Church, Vestry Minutes. Guildhall Library, London, MS. 1196/1.

St. Margaret's, Westminster, Parish Church Records.

Sandford, F., *The History of the Coronation of The Most High, Most Mighty and Most Excellent Monarch, James II . . . and Queen Mary*. London, 1687.

Sargeaunt, J., *Annals of Westminster School*. London, 1898.

Schjelderup-Ebbe, D., *Purcell's Cadences*. Oslo, 1962.

Schmitz, E., *Geschichte der Weltlichen Solokantate*. Leipzig, 1955.

Scholes, P., 'Henry Purcell — A Sketch of a Busy Life', *Musical Quarterly*, July 1916.

— 'Purcell in praise of Princes', *Musical Times*, Oct. 1915.

— *The Oxford Companion to Music*, 9th ed. London, 1955.

— The Puritans and Music in England and New England. London, 1934.

Scott, H. A., 'London's Earliest Public Concerts', *Musical Quarterly*, Oct. 1936.

— 'Purcell at Chelsea', *Daily Telegraph*, 26 June 1937.

Sharp, J. W., 'The Golden Sonata', *Strad*, vol. xx, nos. 233, 234 (1909).

Shaw, H. Watkins, 'A Collection of Musical Manuscripts in the Autograph of Henry Purcell and other English Composers *c.* 1665–85', *The Library*, 5th series, June 1959.

— 'A Contemporary source of English music of the Purcellian Period', *Acta Musicologica*, vol. xxxi, fasc. 1 (1959).

— 'Blow's Use of the Ground Bass', *Musical Quarterly*, Jan. 1938.

— 'Extracts from Anthony à Wood's "Notes on the Lives of Musicians", hitherto unpublished', *Music & Letters*, April 1934.

— (ed.), *Eight concerts of Henry Purcell's Music: commemorative book of programmes, notes and texts*. (Published by Arts Council of Great Britain.) London, 1951.

— 'The British Museum Purcell-Handel Exhibition', *Musical Times*, June 1959.

Shaw, W. A., 'Three Unpublished Portraits of Henry Purcell', *Musical Times*, Sept. 1920.

Shedlock, J. S., 'Purcell', *Academy*, 1895.

Sheppard, F. H. W. (ed.), *Survey of London*. London, 1963.

Siegfried, E., 'Dido and Aeneas von Henry Purcell', *Musikalisches Wochenblatt* (Leipzig), vol. 41, nos. 17, 18, 19 (1910).

Sietz, R., *Henry Purcell: Zeit, Leben, Werk.* Leipzig, 1955.

Smart, J. S., 'The Italian Singer in Milton's Sonnets', *Musical Antiquary*, Jan. 1913.

Smith, F. M., *Purcell.* New York, 1901.

Smith, L., *Music of the Seventeenth and Eighteenth Centuries.* London, 1931.

Smith, W. C., *A Bibliography of the musical works published by John Walsh during the years 1695–1720.* London, 1948.

— *Concerning Handel, his life and works.* London, 1948.

Sorbière, S., *Relation d'un voyage en Angleterre.* Paris, 1664.

Souers, P. W., *The Matchless Orinda.* Cambridge, Mass., 1931.

Squire, J. C., 'Shakespeare Improved', *Observer*, 12 Feb. 1922.

Squire, W. B., 'An Elegy on Henry Purcell', *Zeitschrift der Internationalen Musikgesellschaft*, May 1901 (Leipzig).

— 'An Index of Tunes in the Ballad Operas', *Musical Antiquary*, Oct. 1910.

— 'An Unknown Autograph of Henry Purcell', *Musical Antiquary*, Oct. 1911.

— ' "Beauties Triumph" at Mr. Priest's School', *Musical Times*, April 1906.

— 'J. W. Franck in England', *Musical Antiquary*, July 1912.

— 'Purcell as Theorist', *Quarterly Magazine of the International Musical Society*, July–Sept. 1905.

— 'Purcell's *Dido and Aeneas*', *Musical Times*, June 1918.

*— 'Purcell's Dramatic Music', *SIMG*, vol. v, pp. 489–564. (See also *ZIMG*, Oct. 1904.)

— 'Purcell's *Fairy Queen*', *Musical Times*, Jan. 1920.

— 'Purcell's Music for the Funeral of Mary II', *SIMG*, vol. iv, pp. 225–33.

— 'The Music of Shadwell's "Tempest" ', *Musical Quarterly*, Oct. 1921, pp. 656–78.

Statham, H. D., 'Purcell's Church Music', *Musical Times*, May and June 1924.

— 'The Influence of the Elizabethan Composers on Purcell', *Musical Times*, April 1923.

Stevens, D., 'Purcell on the Gramophone', *Music & Letters*, April 1959.

— 'Purcell's Art of Fantasia', *Music & Letters*, Oct. 1952.

— *Thomas Tomkins.* London, 1957.

Stieber, H., *Henry Purcells Opernmusik 'The Fairy Queen' als festliche Begleitmusik zu Shakespeares 'Sommernachtstraum'.* Leipzig, 1936/7.

Straeten, E. J. van der, *The Romance of the Fiddle.* London, 1911.

Summers, M., *The Playhouse of Pepys.* London, 1935.

Sumner, W. L., 'The Baroque Organ', *PRMA*, 1954–5.

Svanepol, P. F., *Das dramatische Schaffen Purcells.* Vienna, 1926.

Swalin, B. F., 'Purcell's Masque in *Timon of Athens*', *Papers read by Members of the American Musicological Society*, 1946.

Talbot, J., 'Notes on Musical Instruments, c. 1695.' Christ Church, Oxford, MS. 1187.

Tanner, L. E., *Westminster School, its Buildings and their Associations*. London, 1923.

Thiele, E., 'Die Kirchenmusik Henry Purcells', *Musik und Gottesdienst* (Zurich), Sept./Oct. 1958.

Tiggers, P., '*King Arthur* van Henry Purcell', *Mens en melodie* (Utrecht), joarg. 9, no. 2 (1954).

Tilmouth, M., 'A Calendar of References to Music in Newspapers published in London and the Provinces (1660–1719)', *RMA Research Chronicle*, no. 1 (1961).

*— 'English Chamber Music 1675–1720.' (Unpublished doctoral dissertation, Cambridge University, 1960.)

— 'Henry Purcell, Assistant Lexicographer', *Musical Times*, June 1959.

— 'The Technique and Forms of Purcell's Sonatas', *Music & Letters*, April 1 959.

Towers, J., *Purcell*. Boston, 1891.

Traill, H. D., *William the Third*. London, 1888.

Trevelyan, G. M., *England under the Stuarts* (vol. v of *A History of England in Seven Volumes*, ed. Sir Charles Oman). New York, 1925.

Wailes, M., 'Four Short Fantasies by Henry Purcell', *Score & I.M.A. Magazine*, June 1957.

Walker, E., *History of Music in England*, 3rd ed. Oxford, 1952.

Walther, J. G., *Musikalisches Lexikon oder Musikalische Bibliothek*. Leipzig, 1732.

Ward, C. E. (ed.), *The Letters of John Dryden*. Duke University Press, 1962.

Warlock, P., 'Purcell's Fantasias for Strings', *Sackbut*, vol. VII (1927).

Warner, R. A., *The Fantasia in the Works of John Jenkins* (2 vols.). Unpublished doctoral dissertation. Ann Arbor, Michigan, 1951.

Welch, J., *A List of Scholars of St. Peter's College, Westminster as they Were Elected to Christ Church College, Oxford, and Trinity College, Cambridge*. London, 1788.

Wessely-Kropik, H., 'Henry Purcell als Instrumentalkomponist', *Studien zur Musikwissenschaft*, vol. XXII (1955).

— *Lelio Colista: Ein Römischer Meister vor Corelli*. Vienna, 1961.

West, J. E., *Cathedral Organists, Past and Present*, 2nd ed. London, 1921.

Westrup, J. A., 'Das Englisches in Henry Purcells Musik', *Musica* (Kassel), March 1959.

— 'Fact and Fiction about Purcell', *PMA*, 1935–6.

— 'Foreign Musicians in Stuart England', *Musical Quarterly*, Jan. 1941.

*— *Purcell* ('Master Musicians' series). London, 1965.

— 'Purcell and Dryden', *Listener*, 29 April 1943.

— 'Purcell and Handel', *Music & Letters*, April 1959.

— 'Purcell and his Operatic Style', *Listener*, 22 Aug. 1940.

— 'Purcell's Music for *Timon of Athens*', in *Festschrift Karl Gustav Fellerer*. Regensburg, 1962.

— 'Purcell's Reputation', *Musical Times*, June 1959.

White, E. W., 'Early Theatrical Performances of Purcell's Operas', *Theatre Notebook*, Winter 1958/59.

— 'New Light on *Dido and Aeneas*', in *Henry Purcell 1659–1695: Essays on his Music* (ed. I. Holst). London, 1959.

— *The Rise of English Opera*. London, 1951.

Whittaker, W. G., 'Some observations on Purcell's harmony', *Musical Times*, Oct. 1934.

Wilson, J. (ed.), *Roger North on Music*. London, 1959.

Wind, E., 'Julian the Apostate at Hampton Court', *Journal of the Warburg and Courtauld Institutes*, vol. III (1939–40).

Wood, A. à, *Athenae Oxoniensis (with Fasti)* (ed. P. Bliss). Oxford, 1813–20.

— 'Notes on English Musicians.' Bodleian Library, Oxford, MS. Wood D 19(4).

— The Life and Times of Anthony Wood . . . 1632–95 (ed. A. Clark. 5 vols.). Oxford, 1891–1900.

— *The History and Antiquities of the University of Oxford* (2 vols.). Oxford, 1796.

Wright, H. B., and Spear, M. K., *The Literary Works of Matthew Prior*. Oxford, 1955.

Young, P. M., 'Henry Purcell (1659–1695)', *Musik und Gesellschaft* (Berlin), Aug. 1959.

Zimmerman, C., *Alter Meister der Musik*. Basel-Amerbach, 1948.

Zimmerman, F. B., 'A Newly Discovered Anthem by Purcell', *Musical Quarterly*, July 1959.

— 'Handel's Purcellian Borrowings in his later Operas and Oratorios', in *Festschrift O. E. Deutsch*. Kassel, 1963.

— *Henry Purcell, 1659–1695: an Analytical Catalogue of his Music*. London, 1963.

— 'Musical Styles and Practices in Purcell's Anthems', *American Choral Review*, April 1962.

— 'Poets in Praise of Purcell', *Musical Times*, Oct. 1959.

— 'Purcell and Monteverdi', *Musical Times*, July 1958.

— 'Purcell and the Dean of Westminster — Some New Evidence', *Music & Letters*, Jan. 1962.

— 'Purcell Iconography: Missing Items', *Musical Times*, June 1960.

— 'Purcell Portraiture', *Organ and Choral Aspects* . . . . London, 1958.

— 'Purcell's Concerted Anthems: New Aesthetic Concepts', *American Choral Review*, Jan. 1963.

— 'Purcell's Family Circle Revisited and Revised', *Journal of the American Musicological Society*, Fall 1963.

— 'Purcell's Handwriting', in *Henry Purcell 1659–1695: Essays on his Music* (ed. I. Holst). London, 1959.
— 'Purcell's "Service Anthem" *O God, Thou Art My God* and the B-Flat Major Service', *Musical Quarterly*, Jan. 1964.
— 'Purcell's Polyphonic Anthems', *American Choral Review*, July 1962.
— 'Restoration Music Manuscripts at Lincoln Cathedral', *Musical Times*, Feb. 1960.
— 'Thematic Integration in Purcell's Concertato Anthems', *American Choral Review*, July 1963 (part I); Oct. 1963 (part II).
— and Cudworth, C., 'Jeremiah Clarke's "Trumpet Voluntary"', *Music & Letters*, Oct. 1960.

INDEX OF PURCELL'S MUSIC

Numbers in parentheses refer to the *Analytical Catalogue*.

SACRED VOCAL WORKS

Anthems

'Blessed are they that fear the Lord' (5), 153, 154
'Blow up the trumpet' (10), 93, 97
'Hear my prayer, O God' (14), 51
'I was glad when they said' (19), 12, 127
'I will love thee, O Lord' (N67), 68, 248
'In the midst of life' (17A,B1; 27(2)), 269
'Lord, who can tell' (26), 64
'Man that is born' (27), 269
'My heart is inditing of a good matter' (30(2a)), 127
'O God, thou art my God' (35), 282
'O sing unto the Lord' (44), 279
'The way of God is an undefiled way' (56(2)), 248
'Thou knowest, Lord' (58C), 269, 290
'Turn thou us, O good Lord' (62), 64
'Who hath believed our report' (64), 65, 84
'Yet, O Lord' (17A(2)), 269

Hymns, Psalms and Sacred Part-Songs

'Ah! few and full of sorrow' (130), 82
'Beati omnes' (131(1)), 82, 281
'In guilty night' (134(1)), 213, 214
'Jehova, quam multi sunt hostes' (135), 70
'Saul and the witch of Endor' (134), 213

Services

Service in B flat (230), 282
'Te Deum and Jubilate' (232), 249

SECULAR VOCAL WORKS

Catches

'Bring the bowl and cool Nantz' (243), 222
'Come my hearts' (246), 113
'Here's that will challenge all the fair' (253), 137
'If all be true that I do think' (255), 161
'Let us drink to the blades' (259), 201

'Miller's daughter, The' (277), 156
'My lady's coachman' (260), 156
'Now England's great council' (261), 59
'Now we are met' (262), 156
'Since the Duke is return'd' (271), 98
'Surrender of Limerick, The' (278), 201
'To all lovers of music' (282), 150
'True Englishmen drink a good health to the Mitre' (284), 157

Odes, Birthday Songs, Welcome Songs and Occasional Vocal Works
'Another century commencing' (327(3)), 243
'Arise my muse' (320), 185, 198
'Be lively then and gay' (344(5ab)), 139
'Celestial music' (322(2a)), 177
'Come ye sons of art' (323(2bc)), 234
'Fly, bold rebellion' (324(2a)), 94 n., 104
'From hardy climes' (325(2)), 104
'From these serene' (326(2a)), 116
'Great parent, hail' (327), 243
'Hail, bright Cecilia' (328(2ab)), 77, 139, 214, 215, 223, 241, 245
'Hymn to the Sun' (330), 242
'In Vain the am'rous Flute' (328(10b)), 202
'Laudate Ceciliam' (329(2)), 105, 111
'Light of the World' (330), 242
'Love's goddess sure' (331), 210
'Now does the glorious day appear' (332(2a)), 175
'Of old when heroes thought it base' (333(2)), 183
'Raise the voice' (334(2ab)), 111
'Sound the trumpet, beat the drum' (335(2a)), 146, 198
'Sound trumpet, sound' (331(13a)), 184
'Strike the viol' (323(5a)), 234
'Summer's absence unconcerned we bear, The' (327(2)), 93, 97
'Swifter Isis, swifter flow' (336(2ab)), 87
'Welcome, glorious morn' (338(2ab)), 197
'Welcome to all the pleasures' (339(2a)), 105, 110, 111, 214
'Welcome vicegerent' (340(2)), 78
'What shall be done in behalf of the man' (341(2)), 90, 91
'Who can from joy refrain' (342(2b)), 258, 259
'Why are all the muses mute' (343(1a)), 132
'Ye tuneful muses, raise your heads' (344(2)), 139
'Yorkshire Feast Song, The' (333), 183, 184, 185

Solo Songs
'Amintas to my grief' (356), 72 n.
'Celia's fond' (364), 245

'Farewell all joys, now he is gone' (368), 122
'From silent shades' (370), 100
'I resolve against cringing' (386), 72 n.
'If music be the food of love' (379), 100
'If pray'rs and tears' (380), 119
'Incassum Lesbia' (383), 254
'Leave these useless arts in loving' (389), 220, 231
'Love is now become a trade' (393), 122
'Lovely Albina's come ashore' (394), 265
'Pastoral Coronation Song, A' (437), 136
'Queen's Epicedium, The' (383), 253
'She loves and she confesses too' (413), 80, 100
'Sighs for . . . Charles II' (380), 119
'Since the pox' (471), 72 n.
'Sleep, Adam, sleep' (195), 100
'Song on a ground' (428), 100
'When first Amintas sued for kiss' (430), 150
'While Thyrsis wrapt in downy sleep' (437), 136
'Whilst Cynthia sung' (438), 136

Solo Songs with Chorus
'High on a throne of glitt'ring ore' (465), 185
'Musing on cares of human fate' (467), 256
'Scarce had the rising sun' (469), 72 n.
'What hope for us remains' (472), 46, 72, 276

Two-part Songs
'How great are the blessings of government' (494), 130
'O Dive Custos Auricae domus' (504), 255
'See where she sits' (508), 80
'Were I to choose the greatest bliss' (517), 161
'Why my Daphne' (525), 189

Three- and Four-part Songs and Larger Vocal Works
'How pleasant is this flow'ry plain' (543), 151

Dramatic Music: Incidental Music
Abdelazer (570), 256, 257, 280
'Ah, cruel, bloody fate' (606(9)), 78
'Ah me, to many deaths decreed' (586), 208
Amphitryon (572), 186, 189
'As Amoret and Thrysis lay' (607(11)), 221
'As soon as the chaos' (602(1a)), 205
Aureng-Zebe (573), 234, 235

'Behold the man' (608(1a)), 280
'Beneath the poplar's shadow' (mad-song: 590), 131
Bonduca (574), 247, 265
'Britons, strike home' (574(16b)), 261, 263
Canterbury Guests, The (591), 247
'Celemene, pray tell me' (584), 233, 262
'Celia has a thousand charms' (609(10a)), **262**
Circe (575), 76 n., 131
Cleomenes, the Spartan Hero (576), 209–10, 280
'Danger is over, The' (595(1)), 234
'Dialogue between a Mad Man and a Mad Woman' (608(1a)), 222
Distress'd Innocence (577), 189, 217
Don Quixote (578), 235–6, 261, 263, 266
  Dance of the Furies (627(4b)), 236
  Dance of the Knights (578), 236
  Dance of the Milkmaids (578/Comm.), 236
  Dance of 7 Champions (578/Comm.), 236
  Dance of Slaves (578), 236
  Dance of Spinsters (578), 236
  Dance of Spirits (578/Comm.), 236
Double Dealer, The (592), 230, 231
Double Marriage, The (593), 154, 155
English Lawyer (594), 112
Epsom Wells (579), 219, 220, 231
Fatal Marriage, The (595), 233, 234
Female Virtuosos, The (596), 219, 221, **222**
Fool's Preferment, A (571), 155, 156, 217
'From rosy bow'rs' (578(9a)), 263, 266
'Genius of England' (578(7b)), 236
'Good neighbour, why look you awry' (591), 247
Gordian Knot Unty'd, The (597), 189, 190, 231 n., **232**
'Hail to the myrtle shade' (606(8)), 59, 78
'Hail to the knight of the post' (M606(8)), 59
Henry the Second (580), 217, 218, 220
'How happy is she' (609(12)), 233
'How happy's the husband' (582), 233
'How vile are the sordid intrigues of the town' (602(2)), 205, 222
'I looked and saw within the book of fate' (598), 203
'I see she flies me' (573(16)), 234, 235
'I sigh'd and own'd my love' (594(2a)), 234
'In vain 'gainst love I strove' (580(10)), 220
Indian Emperor, The (598), 203
King Richard II (581), 100, 273
Knight of Malta, The (599), 189, 203

'Lads and lasses' (578(8)), 236
'Leave these useless arts' (579), 220
'Let the dreadful engines' (578(3a)), 236
Libertine, The (600), 218, 219, 252, 253
'Love thou art best of human joys' (596), **222**
Love Triumphant (582), 231
Maid's Last Prayer, The (601), 218, 220, 221
'Man is for the woman made' (605(3)), 233, 262
Marriage-Hater Matched, The (602), 222
Married Beau, The (603), 235
Mock Marriage, The (605), 233, 255, 261, 262, 280
'My wife has a tongue as good as e'er twanged' (594), **112**
'No, poor suff'ring heart' (576), 210, 280
'No, resistance is in vain' (601(20)), 221
'Now the fight's done' (606), 78, 97
'Nymphs and shepherds come away' (600(1b)), 219
'O how you protest' (605(1)), 262
'O lead me to some peaceful gloom' (574(17a)), **233**
Oedipus (583), 218, 219, 220, 288
Old Bachelor, The (607), 218, 221
Oroonoko (584), 233, 261, 262
Pausanias (585), 255
Regulus (586), 207
'Retired from any mortal's sight' (581), 99
Richmond Heiress, The (608), 219, 222, 231, 280
Rival Sisters, The (609), 233, 261
Rule a Wife and Have a Wife (587), 234
'Scotch Song' (605/Comm.), 241
'See where repenting Celia lies' (603(10)), **235**
'Since times are so bad' (578(6a)), 236
'Sing all ye muses' (578(1a)), 236
Sir Anthony Love (588), 189
Sir Barnaby Whigg (589), 88
Sophonisba (590), 131
Spanish Fryar, The (610), 140, 256
Theodosius (606), 59, 73, 78
'Though you make no return to my passion' (601(1)), 221
'Thus to a ripe concenting maid' (607(10)), 221
'To arms, heroic prince' (600(3b)), 219
'To arms your ensigns' (574(15b)), 261
''Twas within a furlong of Edinboro town' (605(2)), 262, 280
'When the world' (578(2)), 236
'With this sacred wand' (578(4b)), 236
Wives' Excuse, The (612), 203, 217

Opera, Semi-opera ('Ambiques'), and Masque
'Cares of lovers, The' (632(17)), 258
'Come if you dare' (628(10bc)), 198
'Come unto these yellow sands' (631(5ab)), 265
'Dear pretty youth' (631(10)), 233, 264, 265
Dido and Aeneas (626), 17, 176, 178, 179, 181, 208
Dioclesian (627), 187, 188, 189, 196, 203, 204, 212, 217
Fairy Queen, The (629), 197, 199, 205, 206, 207, 228, 263, 264, 273
'I attempt from love's sickness' (630(17h)), 233
'If so, your goodness may' (630(4h)), 202
Indian Queen, The (630), 248, 264
King Arthur (628), 7 n., 197, 198, 199, 203, 204, 209, 220, 263, 264
'Let the soldiers rejoice' (627(9b)), 212, 280
'Now comes joyful peace' (M631(5b)), 265
'O how happy's he' (627/Comm.), 217
Prophetess, The (627), 187, 188, 189, 196, 203, 204, 212
Tempest, The (631), 79, 135, 233, 247, 264, 265
'They tell us' (630(19)), 233
Timon of Athens (632), 30, 247, 255, 257, 258, 259, 280

INSTRUMENTAL MUSIC

Keyboard Works: Harpsichord
Sefauchi's farewell (656), 144

Music for Strings
Fantasias, etc. (730–752), 56, 57, 278
Sonatas of III Parts (790–801), 4, 5 n., 84, 102, 103, 284, 324
Sonatas of IV Parts (802–811), 84
Sonata in G-minor (Great chaconne) (807), 84

Wind Consort
March and Canzona (860), 252, 268, 290

DOUBTFUL ASCRIPTIONS

'Here's a health to the King' (D571/9), 97

SPURIOUS ASCRIPTIONS

'Lass there lives upon the green, A' (S50), 262

GENERAL INDEX

Abdelazer, 256, 257, 280

Abell, John, 108, 125, 131, 143, 158, 163

Abingdon, Montagu Bertie, Earl of, 308, 380

Absalom and Achitophel, 25, 68, 88, 89

Académie de Musique, 28

Academy of Music, Bridges Street, 37

Act of Attainder, 74

Adamson, Owen, 321

—— Richard, 8, 9

Akeroyde, Samuel, 150, 151, 163, 261

Albricci (Albreis), Signor, 143, 286

Aldrich, Henry, 55

Aleworth, Jeoffrey, 325

Allaby, William, 270

Allegro, Signor, 303

Allison, Charles, 125

Ambler, Mr., 9

Analeau, Mr., 143

Anatean, Mr., 286

Angello, Signor, 322

Angliæ Notitia (E. Chamberlayne), 98, 108 n., 213, 289, 305, 366, 384

Anne, Countess of Winchelsea, 222

Anne, Princess, later Queen of England, 103, 104, 146, 166, 259, 308

Anthem, term first used, 279

Antrobuspo, John (Johann Anthobus), 278, 293

Archer, Thomas, 311, 312

Argyll, Archibald Campbell, 9th Earl of, 129

Arlington, Henry Bennet, 1st Earl of, 25, 49

Arnold, John, 372

—— Thomas, 372

Arnould, Mr., 143

Arundell, Henry, 3rd B., of Wardour, 121

Ashburnham, W., 365

Ashley, Anthony Ashley Cooper, 1st B., 25. *See also* Shaftesbury

Ashmole, Elias: *Observations and Collections*, 11

Astraea Redux (1660), 6

Athée Foudroyé, L', 219

Attainder, Act of, 74

Aureng-Zebe, 235

Ayliff, Mrs. (singer), 208, 232, 241

Ayres, Francis, 211

Babington, Capt., 3

Badham, Richard, 373

Baggs, Mr., 173

Baltzar (Balser), Thomas, 15, 224, 226, 320; *Ballet et musique pour le divertissement du roy de la Grand-Bretagne*, 37

Bancroft, John: *Henry the Second*, 218, 220; *King Edward III*, 190

Banister, John, 5, 23, 33, 41, 71, 80, 90, 151, 163, 193, 223, 225, 275, 278, 279, 320; *New Ayres and Dialogues composed for Voices and Viols*, 278

—— (Bannester) John (younger), 72, 164

Banquet of Music, The, 151, 156, 161, 177, 189

Baptist, Signor Jo. (Draghi), 121, 194

Barkhurst, Mr., 203

Barkwell, Mr., 137

Baroque idiom, English, 80

Barrett, Mr. John, 309

Barton, Dr., 170

Bassani, Giovanni, 41

Bates, John, 125

Ba[i]tes, Thomas, 320, 325

Batten, Adrian, 276; 'Hear my prayer, O God', 51

'Battle of the Organs', 100

Bayley, Anne, 136, 152, 153, 297-9, 385

Bayley, William, 296, 297, 385
Beach, Mr., 138
Beaumont, Francis, 203, 247; *The Prophetess*, 187–8
Becker, Dietrich, 226
Bedford, Arthur: *The Great Abuse of Musick*, 204
Bedingfield, Edward, 118
Beeland, Ambrose, 270
'Begin and strike th'harmonious lyre' (Yalden), 241
Behn, Mrs. Aphra, 257, 280; *Abdelazer*, 256; *The History of the Nun*, 233
Belk, Dr., 67
Bell, Christopher, 270
—— Robert, 69
Benford, Aug., 125
Bentham, Samuel, 126
Berardi, Angelo, 223
Bernabei, Ercole, 144 n.
Bernardo, Seignor, 286
Bertie, Katherine (Mrs. Robert Dormer), 380
—— Montagu, Earl of Abingdon, 380
—— Peregrine, 134, 135, 380
Bettenham, George, 126
Betterton, Thomas, 112, 187, 256, 263
Bidloo, Govard, 192
Binchois, Gilles, 277
Bingham, George, 193
Binns, Richard, 324
Bird, Theophilus, 373
Blagrave, Thomas, 3, 27, 41, 108, 125, 270, 320
Blanchard, R., 55 n.
'Bloody Assizes', 93, 133
Blow, Elizabeth (Mrs. John Blow), 104, 275
—— Dr. John, 19, 39, 40, 40 n., 41, 43, 50 n., 56, 67, 73, 76, 83, 89, 90, 90 n., 96, 108, 113, 114, 116, 117, 120, 126, 127, 131, 132, 133, 138, 141, 151, 163, 183, 194, 200, 202, 205, 209, 212, 213, 215, 253, 261, 267, 275, 285, 286, 287, 324, 326, 328, 330; 'Ah heav'n! What is't I hear', 202; *Amphion Anglicus*, 202,

230; 'Arise, great monarch, arise', 89; 'Begin the song', 117, 133; 'Behold how all the stars give way', 205, 209; 'Behold, O Lord, our defender', 12, 13, 127; 'The Birth of Jove', 50 n.; Birthday ode (1692), 181; 'Christ being risen', 51; 'Club anthem', 19; 'Couch'd by the pleasant Heliconian spring', 202; 'Cry aloud', 51; 'Eurydice my fair', 156; 'The glorious day is come', 202; 'God is our hope', 51; 'God sometimes spake in visions', 127; 'Great quires of heaven', 267; 'Great sir, the joy of all our hearts', 83; 'Hail, monarch, sprung of race divine', 135; 'The happy, happy year is born', 218; 'How does the new-born infant year rejoice', 120; 'Is it a dream', 141 n.; 'My God, my soul', 51; 'My trembling song, awake, arise', 107; New Year's ode (1683), 99; 'No, Lesbia, no', 251; 'O God, wherefore art Thou', 51; 'O Lord God of my salvation', 51; 'O Lord, I have sinned', 51; 'O sing unto the Lord', 51; 'Rules for Composition', 40; 'Rules for Playing of a Through Bass upon Organ and Harpsichon', 40; 'Save me O God', 51; 'Sing we merrily', 51; 'Te Deum', 267; 'Up, shepherds, up', 83 n.; 'Welcome genial day', 215; 'Whilst he abroad does like the sun display, 215
Blue Bell (music house), 224
Blundeville, John, 19
Blunt, Charles, 202
Bocock, Thomas, 325
Bolney, Robert, 319
Bonduca, 233, 247, 260, 261, 263
Borrowdell, Giles, 100, 101, 283
Bosgrove, George, 271
Boswell Bridge, Battle of, 75
Boucher, Joseph, 194
Bouchier, Josias, 95, 125, 241
Boufleurs, Gen., 260
Bowen, Jemmy, 258

Bowman, John, 131, 163, 194
Box, Ralph, 92
Boyce, James, 319
—— William: Twelve Sonatas for 2 Violins, 310
Boyne, Battle of, 190, 213, 214, 249
Bracegirdle, Mrs. Anne, 216
Bradock, Edward, 8, 9, 125, 275, 321
Brady, Nicholas, 139
Brattle, Mr., 162
Brazong, Mr., 194
Bridgman, William, 110
'Brief Introduction to the Art of Descant', 240
Brind, Richard, 304
Britton, Thomas, 71, 72, 227, 280
Brockwell, Henry, 86, 90, 106, 131
Brown, Tom (in *Harmonia Sacra*), 230, 336; 'To His Unknown Friend Mr. Henry Purcell', 336
Browne, Peter, 244
—— Robert, 373
Buckhurst, Charles Sackville, Lord, 55
Buckingham, George Villiers, 2nd Duke of, 22, 25, 69, 89
Bull, William, 124
Burke, Lady Dorothy, 180
Burns, Richard, 318
Busby, Richard ('Sir Richard Birch-Hard'), 5, 6, 53, 55–56, 253, 290, 315, 380
Butler, Mrs. Charlotte (singer), 203
Byrd, William, 12, 57, 276, 278; 'Bow thine ear, O Lord', 51; 'Christ rising', 12, 278; 'O Lord, make Thy servant', 51; 'Prevent us, O Lord', 51

'Cabal, The' (J. B. Medina), 26 n., Plate 5
Cabes, John, 297
Cadmus et Hermione, 135 n.
Caldicut (Caldicot), Jonas, 8, 9
Calisto, 41, 275
Cambert, Robert, 28, 36, 135; *Ariane, ou le Marriage de Bacchus*, 36; *Ballet*

et musique pour le divertissement du roy de la Grand-Bretagne, 37
Campian, Thomas, 240
Canal, G. A., 130, 133
Caproli, Carlo, 144 n.
Carey, Henry: 'The Poet's Resentment', 341
Carey, Thomas, 321
Carhile, Mme., 211
Carning, William, 211
Carr, John, 90, 102, 103, 105, 112, 150, 156, 188, 196; *Vinculum Societatis*, 156
—— Richard, 136, 151
—— Robert, 143, 163, 164, 193, 202
Carteret, Charles, 203
Catherine of Braganza (consort of Charles II), 14, 22, 23, 46 and n., 48, 88, 209
Centliure, Joseph, 309
Cervantes Saavedra, Miguel de, 235, 263
Chaffin, Capt. Edmund, 318
Chamberlayne, Edward: *Angliae Notitia*, 98, 107, 108 n., 212, 289, 305, 366, 384
Chapelin, John, 328
Chapman, Christopher, 9, 321
Charole, John, 125, 126
Charles I, King of England, 8, 63, 64, 65, 89, 120, 154, 244, 283
Charles II, King of England, 1, 9, 10, 11, 14, 22–49 *passim*, 58, 60–69, 72–75, 77–99 *passim*, 104, 107–8, 112–13, 116–19, 121–23, 126–29, 136, 154, 166, 169, 170, 172, 187, 197, 198, 209, 226, 230, 244, 250, 271, 278, 279, 282, 283, 287, 319, 322, 324, 326, 329, 381, 384
Charles Street concerts, 201
Chaucer, Geoffrey, 6
Cherington, Richard, 125
Chiffinch, William, 365
Child, Dr. William, 61, 90, 108, 127, 136, 212, 270, 324, 364; 'The King shall rejoice in thy strength', 12; 'O Lord, grant the King a long life', 126; 'Sing we merrily', 51; 'Te deum', 127

Chilmead, Edward, 223
Chirk Castle, 378
Choice Ayres and Songs, 72, 73, 78, 99, 105, 257 n.
Choice Collection of Lessons for the Harpsichord or Spinnet, 239
Choice Compendium, A, 60
Christian, William, 125
Christina, Queen of Sweden, 142
Cibber, Colley, 216
Clarendon, Edward Hyde, 1st Earl of, 25
Clarke, Jeremiah, 125; "Twas within a furlong of Edinboro town', 262
Clayton, William, 163, 193
Clement, John, 364
Clifford, Thomas, 1st B., of Chudleigh, 25
Clothier, Devorax, 124
Cobb, James, 125
'Cold and Raw'(Scottish tune), 156 n., 185, 210
Coleman, Dr. Charles, 131, 163, 193, 270, 320, 366
Col[e]man, Edward, 319, 320, 322
Colista, Lelio, 144 n.
College, Stephen, 86, 87
Comes Amoris, 150, 156, 205, 234
Congreve, William, 218, 221, 231, 232; *The Double Dealer*, 230, 231; *The Old Bachelor*, 218, 221
Cooke, Capt. Henry, 5, 10 n., 13, 27–32 *passim*, 56, 60–62, 270, 272, 319, 320, 322, 363, 366; 'Let my prayer come up into Thy presence', 13; 'Te Deum', 12, 13
Cooper, John, 278, 293
—— Roger, 53, 293
Corbett, Simon, 125
Corelli, Arcangelo, 41, 149
Cornaro family, 134
Corney, Mr., 9
Cornish, Henry, 133
Cotterell, Sir Charles, 140
Courteville, R., 150, 261, 262; 'Bright Cynthia's power', 262; 'A lass there lives upon the green', 262
Cowley, Abraham, 80, 100

Cox, Joseph, 137
Crane, William, 3
Creeton, Dr., 25
Crespi[o]n (Crespian), Stephen, 36, 108, 120, 125, 169, 171, 173, 174, 245, 268
Crew, John, M.P., 6
Croft, William: *Musica Sacra*, 290, 291
Cromwell, Oliver, 5, 6
—— Richard, 5
Cross, Letitia (singer), 233, 263
—— Thomas, 234; 'Sound Fame', 196; 'Tell my why', 196
Crouch, John, 143, 163
Crowne, John, 207; *Calisto*, 41, 275; *The Married Beau*, 235; *Regulus*, 207
Crump, Frances, 16, 314
Cruse, Franciss, 193
Cryne, Francis, 325
Cuckold's-Haven, 130
Curkaw, Mr., 143

Dadi (papal nuncio), 147
Dagnall, Mr., 9
Daily Courant, 259
Damascene (Damzen), Alexander, 150, 194, 241
Danby, Thomas Osborne, 1st Earl of, 74 and n.
Dancing Master, The, 136
Dann, Richard, 312
D'Avenant, Charles, 36, 44, 131; *Circe*, 131
—— William, 3, 13, 30; *Siege of Rhodes*, 3, 13, 44, 46 n.
Davent, Henrick, 124
Davis, Mrs. Ann, 211
—— James, 318
—— Letitia, 211
—— Mrs. Lucy, 211
—— Rebecca, 211
Declaration of Indulgence, 26, 141, 157
Défense du Beau Sexe, 189, 190, 231 n.
De-lature, Alixander, 193
Deliciae Musicae, 262, 265
Delightful Companion, 137

Deliquiam, The, 85
Dennis, John, 262
Desabaye, Mr., 143
Dialogue Concerning Women, 189, 190, 231 n.
'Dite, o ciele', 156
Diverting Post, 337
'Doctrine of the Affections', 147
Dolben, Gilbert, 110
Don Quixote, 231, 235–6, 245, 263, 266
Dopping, Anthony, 244
Dormer, Ann (niece), 383
—— Catherine (*née* Bertie), 380
—— Sarah (sister-in-law), 360, 380, 383
Dorney, Richard, 271
Dorset and Middlesex, Charles Sackville, Earl of, 188
Dorset Garden Theatre, 30, 36, 78, 129, 197, 219, 220, 228, 288
Dowle, Mary, 126
Draghi, Giovanni Battista, 37, 113, 114, 121, 152, 277; 'From harmony, from heavenly harmony', 152
Drury Lane, Theatre Royal, 28, 30, 83, 189, 207, 220
Dryden, Erasmus, 90, 211
—— John, 1, 6, 25, 26, 55, 68, 69, 88, 89, 91, 101, 118, 129, 140, 152, 164, 186, 189, 198, 199, 206, 209, 230, 231, 232, 288, 341; *Absalom and Achitophel*, 25, 68, 88, 89; *Albion and Albanius*, 26, 118, 129, 135, 140, 186, 198, 199; *Amphitryon*, 185, 189; *Astraea Redux*, 6; *Aureng-Zebe*, 234; *Cleomene, the Spartan Hero*, 209; 'From harmony, from heavenly harmony', 152; *Heroic Stanzas*, 6; *The Indian Emperor*, 203; *King Arthur*, 197; *Love Triumphant*, 231; 'Ode on the Death of Mr. Henry Purcell', 341; *Oedipus*, 218, 219; *Panegyric on the Restoration*, 6; *The Spanish Fryar*, 140
Dubois, John, 92, 102
Dufay: *Supremum est mortalibus*, 249
Duffett, Thomas: *Beauties Triumph*, 178

Duncomber, John, 362
Dunton, John: *Some Account of My Conversation in Ireland* (1699), 243
D'Urfey, Thomas, 88, 129, 155, 180, 183, 184, 202, 205, 209, 210, 222, 231, 235, 261, 262, 266; 'Arise my muse', 185, 198; 'Behold how the stars give way', 209; 'Cloudy Saturnia drives her steeds', 181; *Cynthia and Endymion*, 256; *Don Quixote*, 232, 236, 261; *From Rosy Bowers*, 377; 'High on a throne of glitt'ring ore', 185; *New Poems* (1690), 185; *Pills to Purge Melancholy*, 181 n.; *The Richmond Heiress*, 219, 222; *Sir Barnaby Whigg*, 88; *Songs Compleat, Pleasant and Divertive*, 183 n., 185 n.
Duvall, Nicholas, 271
Dyer, Edward, 277

Eccles (Eeles), Ann, 315, 380
—— (Eaccles, Eagles), Henry, 193, 194
—— John: 'I burn', 236; 'Sleep poor youth', 236; ''Twas early', 236; 'Ye Nymphs', 236; 'Young Chrysostome', 236; 'Young I am', 232
—— (Eaccles, Eagles), Solomon, 132, 163, 193, 194
Edward the Third, 220
Edwards, Richard, 114
Eeles, William, 328, 380
Elizabeth I, Queen of England, 164, 206, 242, 243, 244
Elizabethan anthems, 43
Ellis, Wildbore, 278, 293
Empress of Morocco, 35
Ent, Josias, 203
Epsom Wells, 219, 220, 231
Essay upon the Necessity and Excellency of Education, An (Maidwell), 287
Evelyn, John, 5, 10, 11, 22, 24, 37, 38, 39, 41, 60, 66, 118, 120, 121, 132, 134, 141, 147, 153, 157, 160, 232, 243, 249, 252, 260, 266, 274, 287, 289
—— Mary, 121, 287

Farmer, Thomas, 5, 143, 150, 163
Fashion, Thomas, 163
Fatal Marriage, The, 233, 234
Fede, Signor, 143, 158, 286
Ferine, Paule, 325, 362, 367
Festin de Pierre, Le, 219
fforcell, Mr., 138
Finger, Godfrey, 143, 203. 240, 356
Finnell (Finall), Thomas, 9, 90, 125, 321
Fisher, Hugh, 9, 124
Fitz, Theophilus, 163, 193
Fitzharris, Edward, 86
Fitzjames, James (son of James II), later Duke of Berwick, 140
Fitzpatrick, Samuel, 244
Flatman, Thomas: '*From those serene and rapturous joys*', 116
Fletcher, John, 154, 155, 203, 247; *Bonduca*, 233, 247, 260, 261, 263; *The Double Marriage*, 154; *Rule a Wife and Have a Wife*, 234
Flower (Fflower), Edmund, 163, 193, 325
Flying Post, 289, 291
'Force of Music, The,' 337
Forcer, Francis, 110
Ford, Thomas, 325
Forster, Thomas, 385
'Founding Ode, A', 243
Francisco, Signor, 39, 286
Franck, J. W., 257
French (Ffrench), Nathaniel, 163, 325
Frost, Henry, 125
Fynes, Sarah, 380

Gabrieli, Giovanni, 66
Galli, Francesco, 275
Gamble, John, 21
Gastanaga, Marquis de, 195
Gentleman's Journal, 149, 199, 203, 205, 206, 207, 209, 218, 221, 230, 233, 234, 235, 241, 245, 289
George (sloop), 94, 116
George, Prince of Denmark, 103, 104, 111
Gibbons, Christopher, 3, 5, 9, 43, 44, 45, 61, 270, 276, 320, 324, 326

Gibbons, Edward, 44
—— Grinling, 251
—— James, 319
—— Orlando, 12, 44, 57, 276, 278; 'Almighty and everlasting God', 44, 51; 'Gloria in G', 276; 'Hosanna to the Son of David', 44, 51; 'Lift up your heads', 44, 51; 'This is the record of John', 12, 278
Gilbert, John, 342
Gildon, Charles, 222
Giles, Nathaniel, 30; 'O give thanks', 51
'Glorious Revolution', 94, 180, 182, 184, 213, 249
Godfrey, Edmund, 58
—— Mrs., 173
Gold, Melker, 74
Gombert, Nicolas: *Musae Jovis*, 277
Goodgroome, John, 125, 321
Goodwin, John, 95, 193, 202
Goodwynn, John, 143, 163
Gorges, Sir Arthur, 178
Gostling (Goslin, Gozlin), John, 17, 41, 66, 67, 108, 121, 131, 163, 194, 279, 381
Gould, Robert: *The Rival Sisters*, 261
Grabu (Grebus, Grabuche), Louis, 23, 26, 27, 36, 37, 39, 41, 42, 49, 74, 85 n., 112, 118, 129, 134, 135, 140, 186, 199, 257, 274, 275, 277; 'Hark how the songsters', 257 n.; 'Pastoral in French', 112
Graham, David, 319
Grande, Signor, 143, 286
Greber, Jakob, 227
'Greber's Peg' (L'Épine), 288
Green, Charles, 125, 150
Greene, Maurice, 291, 304
Greenville, Mr., 194
Greeting, Edward, 163
Gregory, Henry, 90
—— William, 271
Griffin, Edward, 144, 365, 367
Grossi, Giovanni Francesco (Siface), 142
Guy, Henry, 153
Gwynn, Nell, 121
Gwynne, Rowland, 288

Hall, Henry, 34 and n., 40; in *Amphion Anglicus*, 40; 'To Mr. Henry Playford on his Publishing the Second Part of Orpheus Britannicus', 349; 'To the Memory of My Dear Friend, Mr. Henry Purcell', 347
—— William, 90, 102, 163, 193
—— Mr., 143
Hall Theatre, 41
Handel, G. F., 72, 76, 117 and n., 244, 359
Harding, John, 283, 320, 321, 364, 367
—— Mr., 9
Harmonia Sacra, 141, 147, 152, 213, 223, 230, 324, 330, 336, 353
Harold, King, 160
Harris, Renatus, 100, 113, 114, 116, 141, 285
Harriss, Morgain, 125, 193
Hart, George, 125, 150
—— James, 108, 178
—— Richard, 126
—— Mr., 38
Hatton, William, 321
Hawkes, Mr., 173
Hayden, George, 304
Hazard, Henry, 9, 203
—— Thomas, 321
Head, Sir Francis, 202
Heale, Henry, 163, 164, 193
Heath, Mr., 138
'Hecate' (L'Épine), 288
Hecht, Benjamin, 291, 389
Henley, Anthony, 221; 'Mock-song', 234
Henman, Richard, 125
Heptinstall, John, 264
Herbert, George, 253, 290, 350; 'Pindaric Ode on Dr. Blow's Excellency in the Art of Music', 350
Heureaux, David, 311, 312
Heywood, Thomas, 108, 125, 131
Hickes, Capt., 3
Hill, John, 42 n.
—— Capt. Richard, 216, 217
—— Roger, 319

Hingeston, John, 1, 15, 35, 42, 43, 50, 56, 76, 86, 90, 102, 105, 106, 109, 270, 366, 367, 389, 390
Hingeston, Thomas, 284
Hingeston family, 389
Hobart, Edward, 373
Hodges, Mr., 139
—— Nathaniel, 18 and n., 287
Holder, William, 40 and n.
Holforth, William, 319
Holloway, Charles, 114
Hooper, Mr., 9
Hooten, Edward, 143, 163, 193
Hopper, Simon, 271
Horne, Mr., 383
Horwood, Peter, 304, 309
Hotton, Mr., 383
Howard, Bernard, 120
—— Lady Elizabeth, 268
—— Lady Katherine, 238, 287
—— William, Viscount Stafford, 82
Howard family, 101, 165
Howe, Mr., 383
Howell, John, 125
—— Mr., 241
Howes, William, 271
Howlett, Amy, 315, 380
Howton, Ed., 90
Hudgebut, John, 112, 264
Hudson, George, 31, 271, 274, 320, 366, 367
—— Mrs., 234
Hughes, John, 72
—— Thomas, 8, 9, 321
Humfrey, Pelham, 7, 14, 15, 19, 26, 31, 32, 34, 35, 39, 42, 47, 56, 60, 76, 80, 273, 274, 286, 364, 366, 367; 'Club Anthem', 19; 'Lift up your heads', 51; 'Like as the hart', 51; 'Lord, teach us to number', 51; 'O Lord, my God', 51; 'O praise the Lord', 51; 'See mighty Sir, the day appears', 273
Hunt, Dubartus, 319
—— Richard, 319
Husbands, Charles, 125
Hutton, William, 8, 9
Huy, 248

Hyde, Edward, 1st Earl of Clarendon, 25

Ignoramus (Ruggle), 112
Impartial Protestant Mercury, 91
Indian Emperor, The, 203
Indian Queen, The, 202, 233, 247, 263, 264, 280
Indulgence, Delcaration of, 26
Interregnum, 61, 118
'Irish Plot', 86
Isham, John, 291, 309
Italian music, introduced, 66

J. H. (1681), 60
Jackman, Frances, 360
James I, King of England, 244, 283
James, Duke of York, later James II, King of England, 11, 19, 22, 23, 26, 30, 58, 59, 68, 70 n., 74, 85, 86, 89, 91, 99, 113, 116, 123, 128, 129, 130–175 passim, 192, 197, 212, 213, 214, 226, 243, 244, 280, 281, 285, 324
James Edward, Prince ('Old Pretender'), 153, 157
Jeffreys, George (Chief Justice), later 1st B., of Wem, 93, 114, 133, 295
Jeffrys, John, 203
Jenkins, John, 56, 57, 270
—— Lionall, 365
Jennings, Thomas, 125
'Jeptha', 359
Jones, John, 303–4
Jordan, Thomas, 97
Josquin: 'Nymphes de bois', 277
Joyful Cuckoldom, 205, 234
Justiniani, Signor (Venetian Ambassador), 134

Keeling, Mr., 284
Kempenfeldt, Lt.-Col., 306, 385
Ken, Dr., Bishop of Bath and Wells, 157
Kettlewell, Mrs., 173
King, Charles, 309
—— Frank, 195
—— Robert, 150, 163, 182, 190, 193, 195

Kirkby, Christopher, 58
Knight, Mrs., 39
Knight of Malta, The, 203
Knipe, Mr., 174
Knyff, Leonard, 307
Kühnel, August, 103, 133, 134

Lake, Dr., Bishop of Chichester, 157, 173
'Lamentations for the Death of Mr. H. Purcell' (Tate), 358
Langley, Jacob, 124
—— Samuel, 53
Lanier, Andrea, 271
—— Clement, 323
—— Hannah, 323
—— Nicholas, 109, 270, 366
—— Thomas, 325
Lari, Franciss, 194
Lauderdale, John Maitland, 2nd Earl of, later 1st Duke of, 25
Law, Ann, 211
Lawes, Henry, 3, 5, 14, 16, 61, 80, 127, 270, 274, 320, 323, 363, 364; 'Come, Holy Ghost', 12; 'Zadok the priest', 12, 127
Lee, Nathaniel, 73, 78, 131
LeGrange, Claudius, 90, 143
Leigh, Anthony, 216, 218, 220
Leisely, Jacob, 278, 293
Lenthall, John, 90
Lenton, John, 163, 193
L'Épine, Margarita, 227, 288
LeRich, Francis, 163
L'Estrange, Roger, 72, 85
Leveridge, Mr. Richard, 259
Lewis, Richard, 163, 193
—— Tertullian, 124
Lilly (Lillie), John, 35, 273, 366, 367
Linacre, Thomas, 125
Lindsay, Mrs., 259
Littleton, Sir Charles, 361
—— John (also known as Tynshare), 125
Lloyd, Dr., Bishop of St. Asaph, 157
—— Eugene, 244
Locke, John, 6, 55
—— Matthew, 1, 6, 7, 21, 26 n., 35,

45, 46 and n., 48 and n., 49, 56, 61, 72, 76, 80, 165, 276, 277, 283, 286, 319, 320; 'I will hear what the Lord', 51; 'The King shall rejoice', 21; 'Lord hear thee, The', 51; 'Lord, let me know mine end', 51; 'Sing unto the Lord', 51; 'Turn thy face from my sins', 51; 'Welcome, welcome, Royal May', 271; 'When the son of man', 51

London: Great Fire (1666), 20, 21; Plague (1665), 18

London Gazette, 4, 33, 65, 79, 102, 103, 110, 133, 134, 150, 156, 178, 182, 183, 188, 195, 196, 206, 221, 227, 230, 232, 240, 241, 242, 244, 245, 253, 262, 275, 279, 282, 284, 289

London Spy, 224

Louis XIV, King of France, 26, 27, 28, 36, 73, 74, 85, 260, 274

Love Triumphant, 231, 232

Low, Charles, 170

—— Richard, 311, 312

—— Thomas: *New Ayres and Dialogues*, 278

Lowe, Edward, 90, 94, 96, 100, 102

Loyola, Ignatius, 66

Lully, 28, 36, 141, 190; *Cadmus et Hermione*, 135; *Entrée de l'Envie*, 135

Lyddell, Rev. Robert, 255

Lyne (Lynn), Daniel de, 278, 293

Mabler, Richard, 321

Macbeth, 30, 35

Maccenigo family, 134

Madge, Humphrey, 320, 364, 367

Maer, Michael, 124

Maidwell, Lewis, 178, 287

Maidwell's School, 179

Maitland, William, 60

Mariens, Francis, 132, 163

Mario, Monsieur, 131

Marlborough, John Churchill, 1st Earl of, later 1st Duke of, 191, 260

Marsh (March), Alphonso, 108, 125, 194, 320, 322, 364, 367

Mary of Modena (consort of James II), 126, 128, 129, 136, 142, 274

Mary, Princess Royal, 8

Mary II, Queen of England, 147, 170–83 *passim*, 197, 198, 206, 210, 219, 222, 228, 229, 234, 237, 269

Mason, John, 271

Massinger, Philip, 154; *Dioclesian; or, the Prophetess*, 187; *The Double Marriage*, 154

Matteis, Nicola, 38, 39, 224, 226

Mattheson, Johann, 226; *Critica Musica*, 275; *Das neu-eröffnete Orchester*, 226

Maugridge, John, 108, 124

—— Robert, 124

May, John, 264

Medina, J. B., 26 n.

Mell, David, 271

—— Thomas, 271

Milton, John, 6, 30; *Paradise Regained*, 30; *Samson Agonistes*, 30

Mitton (Milton), St. John, 318

Mohun, Charles, 4th B., of Okehampton, 216

Molière, 28, 186; *L'Athée Foudroye*, 219; *Les Femmes Savantes*, 221, 222; *Monsieur de Porceaugnac*, 190

Monk, General George, 11, 51, 129

Monmouth, James, Duke of, 22, 68, 69, 75, 77, 83, 85, 91, 100, 117, 129, 130, 132, 284

Montague, Oliver, 114

Monteverdi, Claudio, 66, 156

Moore, John, Lord Mayor of London, 92

More, Charles, 319

Morgan, Mr., 261

Morley, William, 125

Morton, Edward, 125

Moses, Mr., 137

Mosley, John, 193

Moss, John, 56

Mosse, Mr., 138

Motteux, P. A., 189, 190, 199, 202, 203, 204, 205, 207, 209, 218, 221, 230, 231, 233, 235, 247 n., 248, 257, 289; 'If Music be the Food of Love', 241; 'Scotch Song', 241

Mounset, Peter, 124

Mountfort, William, 156, 203, 216, 217, 218, 220, 286; *Distress'd Innocence*, 217; *Henry the Second*, 217, 218; 'O how happy's he', 217
Mullins, Mrs. Mary, 306
Mundy, William, 276; 'O Lord, I bow the knee', 52
Musicall Grammarian, The, 38 n., 284
Musick's Hand-Maid, 111, 177, 239
Myer, John, 90

Nau, Stephen, 271
Needham, John, 170, 172, 173, 174, 283
Neeve, Thomas, 278
Negus, Mr., 168
Newth, Clement, 124
Newton, Douglas, 164, 165, 283
—— Sir Isaac, 1, 20, 141
Neydenhanger, Mr., 143
Nicholson, Mr., 143
Nicolls, Mr., 138
Nieucomne, Thomas, 37
Nightingale, Mr., 364
Norris, William, 125
North, Dudley, 92
—— Francis, 104
—— Roger, 38 n., 41 n., 76, 104, 114, 116, 148, 223, 225, 226, 227, 277, 284
Notari, Angelo, 7, 270, 271, 321, 322

Oates, Titus, 58, 59, 60, 69, 70
Observator, 85
Ockeghem, Jean de: *Mort, tu as navré*, 277
Ogilby, John, 10, 11 n.
Oldham, Nat., 352
Ormonde, James Butler, 1st Duke of, 142
Oroonoko, 233, 262
Osgood, Adam, 166, 167, 168, 287
Oxford, 84, 85, 291

Pack, Capt. Simon: 'Damon let a friend', 236
Packer, Mr., 121
Page, Gawen, 216

Paisible (Peasable), James, 49, 50, 143, 163, 257, 262; 'The Queen's Farewell', 251
Papillon, Thomas, 92, 102
Parker, Henry: 'O Dive Custos Auricae domus', 255
Parsons, Theophilus: 'Cecilia, look down and see', 240
Pasquini, Bernardo, 144 n.
Pate, Mr., 203, 241
Patence, Moses, 311, 312
'Patentees', 256
Patrick, J. Max, 287
Pawmester, Mr., 143
Pendleton, Ann, 315
Pepusch, Dr. John, 72, 289
Pepys, Elizabeth, 6
—— Samuel, 6, 7, 10, 11, 13, 18, 19, 21, 22, 23, 25, 26, 32, 33, 45, 46, 60, 62, 66, 141, 223, 225, 271, 276
Perce, Dr., 67
Perrin, L'Abbé, 28, 36; *Ariane*, 274
Peters, Ann, 210, 211
—— Bryan, 371
—— Elizabeth, 371
—— Ellis, 371
—— Frances (Mrs. Henry Purcell), *see* Purcell
—— Frances, 283, 316
—— John (Capt.), 5
—— John Baptist, 81, 96, 283, 328, 370, 371
—— Martha, 371
—— Mary, 371
—— Richard, 370
—— Thomas, 370
—— Mrs., 371
Peters family, 101, 165, 370
Petre, Father Edward, 160
Philips, Mrs. Katherine, 140
Picket, Mr., 249
Playford, Ellen, 137
—— Henry, 136, 137, 147, 148, 150, 151, 156, 161, 177, 188, 213, 230, 253; *Harmonia Sacra*, 147; 'To the Memory of His Much Lamented Friend, Mr. Henry Purcell', 352
—— John, 72, 73, 78, 79, 80, 102, 103,

105, 137, 177, 237, 240, 284, 286, 324; *Choice Ayres and Songs*, 73; *Introduction to the Skill of Music*, 239–40

Pope, Alexander, 244

'Popish Plots', 58, 73, 92

'Popish Tory's Confession, The', 139

Porcel, Hugh, *see* Purcell

Pordage, Mr., 120, 121, 143

Porter, George, 271

Portsmouth, Louise de Keroualle, Duchess of, 69, 89, 118

Post Boy, 267

Powell, Charles, 163, 164, 193, 216 n., 220

—— George, 260

—— William, 125

Powlett, William, 114

Price (Pryce), Gervase, 108, 124, 286, 219

—— Thomas, 125

Prickard, Thomas, 307

Priest, Josiah, 178, 179, 199, 207

Prior, Matthew: 'As though Britannia's raging sea', 190; 'Light of the World', 242

Pritchard, Sir William, 93, 97, 98, 102, 283

Privy Council, 58

Prophetess, The (Dioclesian), 187, 189, 195, 196, 197, 203, 204, 207, 212, 217, 280

'Protestant Dissenters, The', 85

Protestant Mercury, 91

Protestant Tories, The, 86

Psyche, 28

Public Occurrences, 158

Purcell, Abigail, 312, 383

—— Alexander, 376

—— Ann (niece), 360, 383

—— Ann (aunt), 383

—— Anne (daughter-in-law), 313, 383

—— Charles (brother), 4 n., 16, 28, 116, 136, 152, 153, 272, 300, 381, 383, 385

—— Charles (cousin), 29, 30, 32, 52, 52 n., 53, 94, 278, 293, 294, 295,

296, 297, 298, 299, 380, 381, 382, 383

Purcell, Charles (unrelated), 299

—— Daniel (brother), 15 n., 16, 28, 32, 74, 152, 240, 255, 257, 264, 272, 291, 293, 300, 301, 302, 303, 304, 358, 360 n., 373, 375 n., 381, 382, 383, 385; 'By what I've seen', 152; 'Lamentation for the Death of Mr. Henry Purcell', 358–9; ''Twas night and all the village', 152

—— Daniel (unrelated), 301

—— Edward (brother), 3, 16, 27, 27 n., 152, 153, 272, 299, 304, 305, 307, 308, 315, 380, 381, 383, 384, 385

—— Edward (cousin), 27, 32, 87, 153, 294, 295, 371, 373, 381, 382, 383

—— Edward (son), 114, 179, 255, 291, 309, 383

—— Edward (uncle), 383

—— Edward Henry (grandson), 304, 310, 311, 312, 313, 383

—— Elizabeth (aunt), 383

—— Elizabeth (cousin), 294, 379, 382, 383

—— Elizabeth (mother), 2, 3, 16, 27, 90, 200, 271, 272, 313, 314, 323, 381, 382, 383

—— Elizabeth (niece), 383

—— Frances (daughter), 157, 315, 316, 383

—— Frances (granddaughter), 312, 383

—— Frances (great-granddaughter), 312, 383

—— Frances (wife), 53 n., 55, 67 n., 80, 81, 82, 87, 96, 112, 238, 266, 281, 309, 314, 316, 328, 359, 380, 382, 383

—— Francis (cousin), 86, 87, 272, 316, 317, 318, 319, 324, 371, 383

—— Henry, of Fulham House (?distant ancestor), 383 n.

—— Henry (father), 3, 26 n., 270, 271, 272, 319, 320, 321, 322, 323, 374, 375, 378, 379, 380, 381, 382, 383, 385

Purcell, Henry (nephew), 383
—— Henry (son), 87, 144, 146, 281, 316, 359, 383
PURCELL, HENRY: birth and birth-place, 1–4, 374, 375; childhood, 18–33; apprenticeship, 34–37, in-fluence of English composers, 44; professional debut, 48–57; concert music, 72; music for theatre, 77, 112, 187, 203, 226, 233; marriage, 80; organist of the Chapel Royal, 90; keeper of the organs, 106, 109; religion, 100–1, 164–5; Lully's influence, 135; Italian influence, 144, 208, 255; publications, 147, 151; out of favour at Court, 152, 164, 178, 237; music for opera, 187–8; visits Holland, 192; financial problems, 196–7; recognition, 204; sacred music, 213; new techniques in music, 214; collaboration with Mountford, 217; teacher, 217, 237, 239; songs pirated, 264; death and burial, 266–8; commemoration, 268, 329–59; documents relating to, 324–9; genealogy, 374, 382–3
Purcell, Hugh, 376
—— John (grandfather), 360, 380, 383
—— John (uncle), 383
—— John Baptista (son), 81, 96, 360, 383
—— Joseph (brother), 15 and n., 16, 272, 301, 360, 380, 381, 382, 383
—— Katherine (aunt), 294, 368, 369, 379, 382, 383
—— Katherine (cousin), 294, 381, 382, 383
—— Katherine (second cousin), 371, 372, 383
—— Katherine (sister), 14, 16, 28, 200, 314, 321, 361, 381, 382, 383
—— Margaret (unrelated), 299
—— Mary Peters (daughter), 361
—— Matthew (cousin), 67 n., 94, 136, 294, 295, 361, 362, 382, 383
—— Roger, 383
—— Samuel (?second cousin), 383

Purcell, Sarah (sister-in-law), 383
—— Sarah (aunt), 383
—— Stephen (uncle), 383
—— Temperance, 371, 372, 373, 386
—— Thomas (cousin), 317, 318, 383
—— Thomas (son), 137, 370, 383
—— Thomas (uncle), 2, 6, 7, 14, 15, 16, 17, 27, 29, 31, 32, 36, 42, 43, 66, 67 n., 74, 87, 94, 95, 272, 274, 287, 322, 325, 362, 363, 364, 365, 366, 367, 368, 369, 378, 379, 380, 381, 382, 383
—— William (uncle), 383
—— Mr., 378
Purcells of Oving, 379
Purcells of Westminster, 1–17

Queen's Theatre, 207, 273

Radford, Robert, 278
Ragway, Benedict, 124
Ramsey, Robert, 90, 271
Raree-Show, The, 86
Rare-en-tout, 49
Ravenscroft, Edward, 59, 112, 247; The Canterbury Guests, 247; The English Lawyer, 112; Pammelia, 59
Rawlins, Mr., 314
Read, William, 211
Reading, Mr., 143
Redding, Balthazer, 163
Redman, Elizabeth (née Purcell), 379
—— Henry, 379, 382, 383
Reggio, Signor Pietro, 38, 79, 80; 'Arise ye subterranean winds', 79
Reymes, Mr., 29
Rich, Christopher, 256
Richard II (Shakespeare), 83
Richards, Mrs., 372
Richardson, Mr., 194
—— Thomas, 125, 271, 322
—— Vaughan, 125
Robart, Mrs., 249
Roberts, Anthony, 271, 367
—— Edward, 53, 293
—— Mr., 194
Robinson, John, 309
—— Richard, 86

Roche-Guilhen, Madame de la, 49–50

Rochester, Henry Wilmot, 2nd Earl of, 22, 49

—— Laurence Hyde, 1st Earl of (2nd cr.), 121

Rogers, B., 324

—— George, 125, 258

—— H., 103

—— John, 367

—— Mrs., 365

Rook, Sir George, 308, 385

Rooke, Capt. Hayman, 305

Royal Academy of Music, 37

Royal Letany, The, 85

Ruggle, George, 112

Rumbold, Will, 363

Rupert, Prince, 99

Rustat, Robert, 325, 366, 367

—— Tobias, 319, 325, 366

Rutland, Countess of, 118, 134, 135

Rye House Plot, 94, 101, 104

Ryman, Peter, 319

Sacheverell, Dr. Henry, 255, 291, 353; 'To Dr. John Blow and Mr. Henry Purcell upon the first and second books of Harmonia Sacra', 353

Sackville, Charles, Lord Buckhurst, 55

Saintbarbe, Temperance, 373

St. Peter's College, Westminster, 2, 54

Sale, Katherine, 388

—— William (brother-in-law), 200, 361, 382

Samwell, Sir Thomas, 202

Sancroft, Archbishop, 157

Sandford, Francis, 123, 124 and n., 126 n., 127, 285

—— Samuel, 216

Sandys, George, 82

Sansoni, Signor, 143, 286

Saunderson, James, 202

Savage, Mr., 359

Savile, Henry, 49

Sawyer, Robert, 114

Sayer, John, 125

Scott, Thomas, 261

Scudamore, Capt. John, 361

Sedley, Sir Charles, 161, 210

—— Catherine, Countess of Dorchester, 139

Settle, Elkanah, 35, 207; Distress'd Innocence, 189

Sewall, Judge, 162

Seymour, Brig.-Gen. William, 305

Shadwell, Thomas, 37, 79, 80, 90, 150 and n., 175, 252, 257; Epsom Wells, 219, 231; The Libertine, 218, 219; The Tempest, 79; Timon of Athens, 280; 'Welcome, thrice welcome', 190; 'With cheerful hearts let all appear', 183

Shaftesbury, Anthony Ashley Cooper, 1st Earl of, 69, 83, 85, 86, 88, 92, 93

Shakespeare, William, 30, 35, 37, 38, 79, 83, 100, 206–7, 257

Sheffield, John, Duke of Buckingham, 354; 'Ode on the Death of Purcell', 355

Sherburne, Mr., 143

Shore, Matthew, 124

Short, Benjamin, 304

—— Daniell, 193

Shorter, Thomas, 321

—— Mr., 9

Showers (Shore), Mr., 203

Shrewsbury, Charles Talbot, Duke of, 182

Sidney, Henry, 319, 367

Siface (Giovanni Francesco Grossi), 141, 142, 143

Simpson, Christopher, 240

Skyrme, John, 124

Slingsby, Henry, 274

Smith, Bernard, 100, 113, 114, 115, 116, 138, 141, 245, 285, 328

—— Henry, 125

—— Thomas, 223

—— William, 125

Smyth, John, 325

Snow, Moses, 100, 101, 125, 138, 151, 194

Songs Set by Signior Pietro Reggio, 79

Sourdéac, Marquis de, 28

South, Robert, 6

Southerne, Thomas, 203, 209, 218, 221, 261; *The Fatal Marriage*, 233; *Maid's Last Prayer*, 218, 220; *The Wives' Excuse*, 203, 217

Spencer, Gilbert, 319, 366

Stafford, William Howard, Viscount, 82, 83

Staggins, Charles, 163

—— Nicholas, 39, 41, 42, 43, 46, 49, 73, 108, 110, 126, 128, 131, 132, 146, 163, 193, 200, 229, 248, 275, 276, 285, 288, 289, 325

Steele, Richard, 55

Steffkins, Fred., 90, 193, 365

Stephenson, Edward, 307

Stevens, Gyles, 90

Stewart, Frances (later Duchess of Richmond and Lennox), 22, 23

Stofkins, Fred., *see* Steffkins

—— Christian, 193

Strong, John, 271, 367

—— Robert, 164, 193, 271

Stuart, Frances, *see* Stewart

—— James Edward ('Old Pretender'), 153, 157

Styles, Joseph, 299

Summers, Montague, 273, 280

Sunderland, Robert Spencer, Earl of, 120

Sutton, George, 194

Swettenham, Mr., 3

Talbot, J.: 'Ode for the Consort at York Buildings Upon the Death of Henry Purcell', 356

Tallis, Thomas, 276; 'I call and cry', 52

Tanner, Robert, 100, 101, 125

Tate, Nahum, 83, 133, 180, 222, 243, 244, 259; 'The happy, happy year is born', 218; 'Lamentation for the Death of Mr. Henry Purcell', 358–9; *Richard II*, transmogrification of, 82, 100; 'Spring, where are thy flow'ry treasures', 248; 'Welcome, welcome, genial day', 181 n.

Taubman, Matt, 97

'Tawney Tuscan', (L'Épine), 288

Taylor, Charles, 125

—— Capt. Silas, 6

Tempest, The (Shakespeare), 30, 38, 79

Theatre of Music, 136, 151

Theatre Royal, 30, 36, 83, 188, 221, 256, 263, 273, 288

Thesaurus Musicus, 249

Thomlinson, Richard, 193

Thompson, Nathaniel, 150

Thorindon, Gregory, 366

Thorndel (Thorndale), Gregory, 319, 322

Thornton, Lancelot, 325, 362

Three Elegies Upon the Much Lamented Loss of Our Late Queen Mary, 253, 254

Tomkins, Giles, 270, 275

—— Thomas, 276; 'O Lord, I have loved', 52

Tomlinson, Richard, 90, 163

Tonge, Israel, 58, 60, 70

Tonson, Jacob, 206

Tooth, Thomas, 371

Torer, Elizabeth (Mrs. Daniel Purcell), 301

Tosi, Pier Francesco, 227, 240

Tovey, Thomas, 315

Townsend, James, 125

Travel, Sir Thomas, 203

Trebeck, Andrew, 125

Trelawney, Col. Henry, 308, 388

—— Sir Jonathan, Bishop of Bristol, 157

Trio-sonatas (1683), 53 n., 84, 103, 105

Tucker, William, 8, 9, 67 n., 364

—— Mrs., 173

Tudway, Thomas, 113, 329

Turner, Dr., Bishop of Ely, 157

—— Thomas, 372

—— William, 19, 38, 41, 67, 108, 125, 127, 131, 133, 150, 163, 194, 241, 285; 'Club Anthem', 19; 'Come Holy Ghost, our souls inspire' (Veni creator), 127; 'The King shall rejoice in thy strength' ('Deus in virtute'), 127; 'Tune the viol, touch the lute', 133

Twist, John, 90

Tyger, 28

Tynchare (alias Littleton), John, 20, 125, 173
—— Philip, 8, 9

Uvedal, Dr., 125

Vendu concerts, 182, 227, 244, 289
Verdi, Giuseppe: *Ernani*, 261; *Nabucco*, 261; *Si ridesti il leon*, 261; *Va, pensiero*, 261
Verney, Sir Ralph, 360
Verrio, Antonio, 70 n.
Vestment, Nathaniel, 126
Vitali, G. B., 129, 130, 133, 142; *L'Ambizione Debellata*, 130, 133; *Balli in Stile Francese*, 130

Wake, William, 46 n.
Wakeman, Sir George, 58
Walgrave, Dr., 120
Walker, John, 125
Wall, Samuel, 371, 372, 386
—— Temperance (Mrs. Edward Purcell), 371, 386
Walley, Will, 95
Walsh, William, 189, 190, 230, 231 and n.
Walters, Lucy, 77
Ward, Ned, 72, 224
—— William, 311, 312
Water Eaton, 378
Watkins, Nathaniel, 125
Watson, James, 325, 367
Webb, William, 320
Webber, Mr., 139
Weekly Journal, 302
Weldon, John, 237, 238, 287
Welstead, Frances (*née* Purcell), 307
—— Leonard, 383
West, Frances (Mrs. Thomas Peters), 370
—— John, 373
Westlake, Herbert, 316
Westminster, 2, 3, 4, 6, 16, 18, 19, 21, 48, 52, 60, 74, 81, 120
Westminster Abbey, 2, 3, 4, 7, 8, 10, 13, 16, 20, 29, 41, 42, 43, 44, 50, 52, 56, 76, 81, 88, 90, 102, 105, 107

Westmoreland, Lord, 206
Wharton, Thomas, later 1st Marquis of: 'Lilliburlero', 37, 161
White, Blaze, 126
—— E. W., 179 n.
—— George, 352
—— Dr., Bishop of Peterborough, 157
—— Mr., 137
William III, King of England, 70 n., 86, 137, 141, 160–201 *passim*, 208, 209, 213, 214, 215, 222, 226, 227, 229, 237, 242, 244, 248, 250, 259, 260, 261, 324, 326
Williams, John, Bishop of Lincoln, 2, 29, 30 and n., 53, 54
—— Mary, 307
—— William, 125
Williamson, Sir Joseph, 365
Wilson, Alexander, 376
—— John (composer), 5, 36 and n., 64, 90 and n., 271, 274
—— John (editor), 38, 271, 284
—— Mr. (painter), 376
Winchelsea, Anne Finch, Countess of, 222
Wind, E., 70 n.
Winder, John, 297
Wise, Michael, 41, 125
Wit for Money, 156
Wood, Anthony à, 2, 15, 46, 57, 87 n., 217, 279, 324
—— Jacob, 125, 258
Woodcock, Katherine (Mrs. John Milton), 6
Woodson, Leonard, 108, 194, 241
Wormall, Bartholomew, 100, 101
—— Edward, 271, 283
Wren, Christopher, 1, 55, 252, 274

Yalden, Thomas, 241
Yardeley, George, 126
Yorkshire Feast, 59
Young, Charles, 304

Zarlino: 'Te Deum', 249
Zenno, Signor (Venetian Ambassador), 134

PRINTED IN GREAT BRITAIN
BY ROBERT MACLEHOSE AND CO. LTD
THE UNIVERSITY PRESS, GLASGOW

estm. in number 16.

Yeatis fe: